SECURE

ONE WEEK LOAN

This book is due for return on or before the last date shown below.

IPPR

INSTITUTE FOR PUBLIC POLICY RESEARCH

30-32 Southampton St
London WC2E 7RA
Tel: 020 7470 6100
Fax: 020 7470 6111
postmaster@ippr.org.uk
www.ippr.org.uk
Registered charity 800065

The Institute for Public Policy Research is an independent charity whose purpose is to contribute to public understanding of social, economic and political questions through research, discussion and publication. It was established in 1988 by leading figures in the academic, business and trade-union communities to provide an alternative to the free market think tanks.

IPPR's research agenda reflects the challenges facing Britain and Europe. Current programmes cover the areas of economic and industrial policy, Europe, governmental reform, human rights, defence, social policy, the environment and media issues.

Besides its programme of research and publication, IPPR also provides a forum for political and trade union leaders, academic experts and those from business, finance, government and the media, to meet and discuss issues of common concern.

Production & design by **EMPHASIS**
ISBN 1 86030 088 X
© collection Secure Foundations, IPPR 2000
Chapter 2, Chapter 3 and Chapter 14, Crown copyright 2000

Contents

Acknowledgements
About the editors
About the contributors

Preface by Rt Hon Jack Straw MP

Introduction   1
Scott Ballintyne, Ken Pease and Vic McLaren

I: CRIME PREVENTION AND COMMUNITY SAFETY: JANUS FACES?

1. Crime prevention and community safety: 21
    Tweedledum and Tweedledee?
    Paul Wiles and Ken Pease

2. The conjunction of criminal opportunity   30
    A tool for clear, 'joined-up' thinking about
    community safety and crime reduction
    Paul Ekblom

3. Creating community justice   67
    Mike Nellis

II: WHAT WORKS? WHAT DOESN'T? HOW DO WE KNOW?
WHAT DOES IT MATTER?

4. What works and what makes what works work   91
    Julia Stafford and Les Silverlock

5. Partnership: rhetoric or reality?   102
    Sheila Stokes-White

6. The evaluation jungle   115
    Nick Tilley

7. The 'wicked' issues: displacement and sustainability   131
    Ivan Hill and Ken Pease

III: LET'S DO IT

8. Making it all happen   145
    Gloria Laycock and Barry Webb

9. **It's good to talk, but it's not good enough**   164
   Active Consultation as a Key to Safer Communities
   Scott Ballintyne and Penny Fraser

10. **From audit to strategy: a practice view**   189
    Andy Mills and Sarah Pearson

11. **Targeting resources for crime prevention**   203
    Alex Hirschfield and Kate Bowers

12. **Crime and urban layout: the need for evidence**   224
    Bill Hillier and Simon Shu

IV: BEYOND THE YEAR 2000

13. **Hot products: a new focus for crime prevention**   251
    Ron Clarke

14. **Crime reduction and the benefit of foresight**   265
    Michelle Rogerson, Paul Ekblom and Ken Pease

15. **Community safety in age of the risk society**   276
    Gordon Hughes

16. **Democratic politics and crime prevention**   296
    Jon Spencer

Acknowledgements

Many people and organisations have given of their time, energy and brainpower to the Leeds (1997) and Derby (1999) conferences which gave rise to this volume. People have contributed as authors, conference organisers, participants and sounding-boards for many of the ideas contained in the chapters. Without them this book would not have been possible. Any list of acknowledgements would be incomplete. We would therefore like to give a blanket thank you to all those who helped with the events which gave rise to the book and aided the process of realising the proceedings in print.

We would also like to thank Her Majesty's Government which agreed to waive Crown Copyright royalties in respect of those chapters provided by serving and recent civil servants. This is a practical demonstration of a commitment to open government and a willingness to seek innovative solutions.

About the editors

Scott Ballintyne is Research Associate at the Institute for Public Policy Research working on criminal justice and community safety. Recent work includes *Unsafe streets – street homelessness and crime* and *Problem-solving policing and partnership* (with Lothian and Borders Police). Current work includes *Lest we forget: Ex-Servicemen and Homelessness* and the Scottish Executive Partnership Pathfinder Programme. Previously a senior manager in local government with 20 years experience in policing and community safety.

Ken Pease is Professor of Criminology at the University of Huddersfield, having held a similar post at Manchester University. Recently Acting Head of the Home Office Policing and Reducing Crime Unit. He has published widely on crime prevention, most notably on repeat victimisation. Awarded OBE in 1996. He is currently researching the effectiveness of the Home Office Crime Reduction Programme.

Vic McLaren is Home Office Adviser to the Government Office East Midlands, having formerly been Deputy and Acting Director of the Home Office Crime Prevention College, Easingwold. Convened the Leeds and Derby conferences on which the book is based, and is active in the establishment of training standards in community safety. He was released by the Home Office to act as advisory editor in the preparation of this book.

About the contributors

Ron Clarke was formerly Director of Research and Statistics in the Home Office, became Dean of Criminal Justice at Rutgers University, New Jersey. He is influential in the development of situational crime prevention and the rational offending theoretical perspective which underpins it.

Kate Bowers recently completed a doctoral thesis on crime against businesses at the University of Liverpool. She joined the University's Urban Research and Policy Evaluation Regional Research Laboratory in 1994 as a researcher on an Economic and Social Research Council project looking at links between crime and deprivation and has been involved in the evaluation of crime prevention initiatives in the Merseyside region.

Paul Ekblom is a psychologist by training and now holds a senior post in the Home Office Research and Statistics Directorate. He evaluated the Safer Cities programme, and is now engaged in the development of a conceptual model of crime prevention. He has published widely on crime prevention.

Penny Fraser is Research and Development Manager for NACRO and has researched and published in the fields of crime prevention and community safety. She was co-author (with Ian Taylor and Karen Evans) of *A tale of two cities: global change, local feeling and everyday life in the north of England*.

Ivan Hill is a former police officer in the Royal Ulster Constabulary and has been for many years Lecturer in Social Science at the University of Sunderland.

Bill Hillier is Professor of Architecture and Urban Morphology at the University of London, Chairman of the Bartlett School of Graduate Studies and Director of the Space Syntax Laboratory at University College, London

Alex Hirschfield, after a PhD in geography, moved into local government as a policy planner and became the research co-ordinator at Liverpool University's Urban Research and Policy Evaluation Regional Research Laboratory in 1989. He became a Senior Lecturer in 1998. He is currently evaluating community safety initiatives on Merseyside and for the Home Office and directing a two-year study into the Health Impact Assessment of regeneration schemes funded by the Department of Health.

Gordon Hughes is Lecturer in Social Sciences at the Open University, after a former post at Nene College, Northampton. He recently published *Understanding crime*

prevention and has written extensively on crime prevention, social change, social policy and communitarianism.

Gloria Laycock is currently a visiting fellow at the US National Institute of Justice, and former head of the Policing and Reducing Crime Unit in the Home Office, having first joined the Prison Service as a psychologist in 1968. She has published extensively in crime prevention.

Andy Mills is Executive Officer for community safety within Leeds City Council and co-manages the new multi-agency unit which services the Leeds Community Safety Partnership. He was appointed to the Council in 1994 as its first community safety co-ordinator.

Mike Nellis is Lecturer in Criminal Justice Studies at the University of Birmingham. He has been a social worker with young offenders and is currently interested in probation training and values. He has researched and published on prison movies.

Sarah Pearson is Community Safety Manager for Kingston-upon-Hull Community Safety Partnership. Since an MPhil in town planning at the University of London in 1992, she has worked on various community safety projects for Hull City Council, NACRO, Crime Concern and York City Council.

Michelle Rogerson was formerly with the ESRC Data Archive at Essex University. She is currently part of the Applied Criminology Group at Huddersfield University, on a project funded by the Loss Prevention Council on the anticipation of crime trends and crime prevention strategies. She is also currently working on the evaluation of the Home Office's Burglary Prevention Programme.

Simon Shu is a doctoral student at University College London. He holds a Master of Architecture degree from the Catholic University of Louvain, has worked for the engineering consultancy Sinotech and has been part-time lecturer in architectural design at Feng Chia University.

Leslie Silverlock has worked with 150 community safety partnerships and 13 Safer Cities. His specialities include turning corporate and strategic ideas into plans, timetables, actions and outcomes. Before joining Crime Concern in 1994, he enjoyed careers in management, education, broadcasting, youth work and community development.

Jon Spencer is Lecturer in Criminal Justice at Manchester University and a probation officer by training. His recent publications are primarily about crime on the internet and he is a co-author with Bill Hebenton on the development of policing in Central and Eastern Europe, which he visits regularly.

Julia Stafford manages fieldwork for Crime Concern in the West of England and Wales. She takes the lead in two specialist areas: public transport and women's safety and recently managed a project, funded by the European Commission's Daphne Initiative, researching approaches to domestic violence in other European countries.

Sheila Stokes-White is Head of Strategy for the Northumbria Community Safety Partnership, a large strategic partnership covering the five metropolitan areas of Tyneside and Wearside and the County and Districts of Northumberland. She has 20 years' experience in the criminal justice field, in probation and with Crime Concern.

Nick Tilley is Professor at Nottingham Trent University, currently on secondment to the Home Office's Crime Reduction Programme. He is well known for the theoretical approach scientific realism, developed with Ray Pawson. He has published on diverse topics, from problem-oriented policing to police use of forensic science and crime against small businesses.

Barry Webb is Head of the Reducing Crime Group of the Home Office Research Development and Statistics Directorate. A psychologist by training, with a particular interest in policing and crime prevention, he has published widely and is editor of the Home Office Policing Research series.

Paul Wiles is Director of Research, Development and Statistics at the Home Office. Until July 1999 he was Professor of Criminology and former Dean of Law at the University of Sheffield, as well as being Director of its Centre for Criminological and Socio-Legal Studies. This paper was prepared during his professorship at Sheffield.

Preface
by the Rt Hon Jack Straw MP

Making people's lives safer is a matter for us all. It is too late to wait until offences have happened. This Government gives priority to preventing crime as well as responding forcefully towards those who offend against others. To achieve this, it gives priority to partnership-working, bringing together local efforts, energies and resources to prevent and reduce crime where it takes place. This is a major shift in how we tackle crime and make our communities safer. To be successful we need to widen our knowledge and understanding of partnership-working, map out the steps to effective local action and apply what we know works.

This volume is a timely contribution towards a shared understanding of community safety. The argument is presented in a way which is helpful to policy-makers, academics and practitioners. It raises as may questions as it answers but it does so within a partnership context – taking the need to work together as the starting point. This is a much needed dialogue. It shows the idea of community safety is taking deeper root and that success is possible with sustained effort.

Rt Hon Jack Straw MP

Introduction
Scott Ballintyne, Ken Pease and Vic McLaren

Tackling crime and making communities safer sits at the heart of present Government policy. It is a key benchmark against which Government success or failure will be measured. The flagship Crime and Disorder Act (1998) is seen to lay a legislative platform for local joint action and to herald a new era of partnership in crime prevention and crime reduction.

Events are moving fast – at least for an area of social policy and practice which is more accustomed to incremental rather than rapid change. The passing of the Act has moved swiftly onto the creation of local community safety partnerships, through local crime audits mandated by the legislation to the implementation of the first stages of the Government's crime reduction programme – local community safety strategies and action plans.

Government has embarked upon a national crime reduction strategy, centred upon local partnerships, funded to the tune of £400 million and has recently completed the appointment of regional Crime Directors in England and Wales. At the same time there is a flurry of training and monitoring activity which, while well intentioned, does not always come together and often reflects continuing division rather than joined-up action.

On the training front, the national Community Justice Training Organisation has launched its occupational standards for crime prevention and community safety. The police service is developing its own national training organisation. Academics and practitioners from a number of educational establishments working in the fields of community safety and crime prevention have prepared a 'Delphi Council' report setting out a model curriculum for community safety. These activities may stimulate a growing interest in community safety within the traditional schools of criminology. At the very least it is likely to increase debate and discussion around interdisciplinary work on risk management and community safety.

Evaluation and monitoring have a high profile in the push for results on community safety and crime reduction. HM Inspectorate of Constabulary are conducting a follow up to their 1997 inspection on partnership working, 'Beating Crime'. The new thematic inspection, 'Calling Time on Crime', explores crime reduction and community safety arrangements across police forces in England and Wales and is due to be completed by summer 2000. The Home Office Policing and Reducing Crime Unit is conducting research on crime and disorder partnerships, including research into consultation with difficult to reach community groups, as part of a three year programme of research activity.

Yet, two key issues consistently recur throughout the headlong rush to action. Firstly, is there a shared, common understanding of what is meant by 'community safety'? Is everyone working from similar or different scripts? Does it really matter if what is being unleashed may be a little uncertain or unfocussed so long as it is all geared towards tackling crime? Can we develop effective local partnerships if each partner has a different understanding what is meant by 'community safety'?

Secondly, how can existing better practice in crime prevention and crime reduction be introduced into the explosion of local activity arising from the legislation? Can we learn from earlier shortcomings in crime prevention and crime reduction? What lessons exist and how can these be applied to help underpin present fast-moving local action? How can local partnerships and action plans achieve sufficient calibre to give rise to sustained reductions in crime and improve community safety?

It may seem a little tardy to be posing such questions midway through the current flood of community safety activity unleashed by the legislation. But in the headlong rush into action, reflection has inevitably been in short supply. How we conceptualise community safety and put it into widespread practice within the framework of the Crime and Disorder Act (1998) may well cause ripples far beyond the usual debates over crime prevention theory and practice.

If the Act is going to be a genuine watershed in how we prevent crime, reduce it and promote community safety then we may need some shared understanding of its conceptual underpinnings, a recognition of its strengths and weaknesses, and some well-grounded reasoning for applying one local strategy over another.

This volume has its origin in two conferences, in Leeds in 1997 and in Derby in 1999. The chapters herein started life as conference papers. They grapple with the challenges of understanding community safety; exploring the connections between crime prevention, crime reduction and community safety; and teasing out what needs to be done to fulfill the spirit of the legislation. Or, they seek out what works in crime prevention and community safety, providing guidance and advice for those tasked with implementation.

They set out some signposts and highlight some conceptual and practical pitfalls in the search for a shared understanding of community safety and for quality and consistency in the minefield of local partnership activity.

The Leeds Conference was a joint venture between the Home Office Crime Prevention College and the Crime Prevention Agency. It had four objectives – to take a critical look at what works in crime prevention and community safety; to examine new trends and developments; to encourage the dissemination of good practice; and to encourage practitioners to make use of relevant research findings. Its emphasis was to revisit what is known to work in crime prevention and to match it up with the changes being brought about by the introduction of community safety partnerships. In many ways it was an early push towards evidence-led policy making and good practice.

The conference reflected the upsurge in interest and activity on crime prevention and community safety which was accompanying the new Government's

Crime and Disorder legislation. But it also highlighted the real danger that the upsurge in local activity might be diffuse, wasteful of energy and resources and difficult to sustain. Policy-makers foresaw opportunities to strengthen and broaden community safety activities across a range of partners, possibly even to generate a quantum leap in tackling crime. But, at the same time, they foresaw a lack of shared understanding and practical skills which could undermine the potential of the new policy direction.

Many more people and agencies are being asked to, and in some instances, required to become involved in community safety. Guidance has been issued on conducting local community safety audits and preparing local partnership strategies. The national training organisations which have been set up or are in the process of being set up can start to lay a broader skills base for practitioners, so long as they can come together and break down traditional inter-agency training barriers. But, initial evidence suggests that effective partnership working may require some time to take root. The Audit Commission (1998) investigation indicates fairly widespread shortcomings in the quality of local audits and a wide variation in local partnership working.

The second conference, in Derby in 1999, narrowed the focus more closely upon the search for a workable conceptual framework for community safety and its connection to the practical requirements of implementing the local community safety strategies required by the Crime and Disorder Act (1998). Co-hosted by the Institute for Public Policy Research (IPPR), the Home Office Crime Prevention College and the University of Huddersfield the conference brought together policy-makers, academics and practitioners to explore two key issues in crime prevention, crime reduction and community safety. Firstly, how does community safety fit with existing perspectives on crime prevention and crime reduction *and* secondly, what needs to be done to make sure developments arising from recent legislation learn from and apply known better practice in crime prevention and crime reduction?

The resulting chapters and answers make up this volume. **Section 1** explores three issues which are key to tackling crime and promoting community safety as envisaged by current Government policy – the connection between crime prevention and community safety; tackling criminal opportunity as a framework for reducing crime and improving community safety; and, the central importance of a workable perspective on community justice for the spirit which underpins crime and disorder legislation.

Section 1: Crime prevention and community safety – Janus faces?

In the first chapter, Paul Wiles and Ken Pease ask why a generic aim (community safety) is subsumed within an Act of Parliament dealing with only one source of danger – crime and disorder. They argue that it might be better to tackle crime and disorder within a Community Safety Act.

Adopting this broader perspective of community safety has two major benefits. It extends the recognition, which already exists in the Crime and Disorder Act (1998), that crime is only one component of the social world and that control of crime lies beyond the narrow confines of the criminal justice system (CJS). The CJS alone cannot prevent crime to the extent required to make communities safer. Secondly, it requires a joined up, decompartmentalised approach to be successful – a different way of working which cuts across agency boundaries and enables us to respond to threats to people's safety as people experience them rather than bureaucracies define them.

The authors suggest two issues are critical for the success of a wider approach to community safety and the implementation of the Crime and Disorder Act (1998). That agencies and partnerships are encouraged to integrate community safety planning into a wider hazard management perspective which should afford agencies the freedom to tackle crime across boundaries. To this end they recommend local community safety partnerships should undertake local 'risk audits'. Secondly, that performance on Section 17 of the Crime and Disorder Act (1998) is closely monitored to ensure that community safety is being fully integrated into the wider planning and delivery of local services. Section 17 encapsulates the spirit of the legislation by requiring local authorities to consider the community safety implications inherent across all services. Applied properly it is a mechanism for pursuing joined-up action to tackle crime. It may be that the spirit of Section 17 should be widened to include all Crime and Disorder partners, including national Government Departments.

In Chapter 2, Paul Ekblom develops upon his earlier work in generating a framework for community safety and crime reduction. He argues that the conjunction of criminal opportunity offers a clear tool for planning and delivering community safety and crime reduction. The conjunction of criminal opportunity is a conceptual map which allows policy-makers and practitioners to bring together four strands to tackle crime:

- how social problems are defined as crimes (a local understanding of which is seen as indispensable in identifying priorities and planning effective responses);

- how crime prevention is best seen as intervention in the causes of crime (which is crucial for diminishing the future development of crime);

- how crime reduction involves direct intervention in criminal events (to disrupt existing offending and reduce the likelihood of continuing offending);

- how crime control can be applied strategically to keep crime risks below local tolerance levels.

Ekblom is consistent in his assertion that definitions are important and that a theoretically grounded framework of approaches and how they work is necessary for the elaboration of rational crime reduction. In this he is a clear proponent of evidence-led and experience-led community safety. The contribution of this chapter can be seen at two levels : first, in its demand for rigour from all involved; second, in providing a touchstone for initiatives in understanding and elaborating what they need to think through so that they optimise their chances of success; and, if successful, of understanding how that success was achieved. This chapter is at one and the same time a framework for understanding how crime develops and for planning an effective response.

In the final chapter in this section, Mike Nellis elbows community justice into the equation. He puts forward two arguments – that as people at the start of the 21st century we need a mix of solidarity, liberty and justice if we are to live together with any degree of common security and conviviality, and that without the involvement of community justice, community safety is likely to under-achieve and will not overcome the penal regression and failure of the criminal justice system which characterises the late 20th century.

Community justice, as posited by Nellis, envisages a sustained and extensive people-centred approach to community safety and encompasses a raft of emerging alternatives to custody, including mediation, reparation and compensation programmes and family group conferencing. It is arguably a mechanism which connects three major strands of Government policy – building inclusive communities, recreating a sense of shared citizenship and concern for others, and tackling crime. As such, it is an integral part of the Crime and Disorder Act (1998) and requires local community safety partnerships to focus upon community justice as well as offending if they are to successfully prevent and reduce crime.

Nellis argues that whatever is done in the name of community safety has to result in social arrangements which we find convivial, to be inclusive rather than exclusive in its outcomes, and that we neglect the processes of community linkage which add justice into community safety at our peril.

Section 2 tackles four main questions – what works in crime prevention and community safety; how do we make partnerships work and once they are working, how do we evaluate them and make sure crime reduction is sustained and not just displaced to other areas?

Section 2: What works? What doesn't? How do we know? What does it matter?

In Chapter 4, Julia Stafford and Leslie Silverlock shift the debate away from the conceptual roots of community safety towards a pragmatic assessment of what works in community safety and crime prevention. Their approach is that of practitioners focusing upon what is known and what can be put into useful practice quickly in a rapidly developing environment. They implicitly argue in favour of evidence-led planning for community safety and identify four issues which are central to practical success – funding, standards, partnership and training.

Their elaboration of current sources of funding highlights the tension between re-applying mainstream resources towards safer communities and a continuing over-reliance upon programme and project funding. The spirit of Section 17 of the Crime and Disorder Act (1998) requires redirection of mainstream public expenditure towards community safety and crime prevention. It makes sense. Earlier spending on community safety saves greater resources in the medium and longer term. Yet, there is little evidence of an emerging shift in mainstream resources to fund community safety. Monitoring performance on Section 17 might be strengthened by monitoring of mainstream public expenditure on community safety.

The issues of standards, building partnership capacity and training go hand in hand. They are most likely to develop unevenly in a time of rapid change. Yet, they underpin the overall quality and effectiveness of the legislation and drive on community safety. Stafford and Silverlock detail ongoing developments in each area and highlight the need to devote time, energy and priority in these areas if we are not to lose momentum on community safety and experience a wide diversity in local performance.

Sheila Stokes-White, in Chapter 5, focuses upon the importance of working in partnership for the emerging changes for community safety. She argues that the legislation provides a useful platform for partnership working and that an understanding of how partnerships mature and develop is essential for a successful impact upon crime. Partnership is seen to be neither cheap nor quick; more time-consuming than single agency working; and, no substitute for single agency responsibility.

In spelling out the steps to effective partnership Stokes-White emphasises the need for top-level commitment across partners, shared goals and a willingness to invest in the partnership itself. Community safety partnership working is multi-layered, multi-faceted, multi-level and increasingly complex. This is undoubtedly the case and it reinforces the need for a shared understanding of community safety.

Nick Tilley sets out a conceptual and practical guide through the evaluation jungle surrounding community safety, crime prevention and crime reduction in Chapter 6. He presents a reasoned case for systematic evaluation and its importance for evidence-led policy-making. The premise is straightforward – if we want to move towards consistency and reliability in the deluge of activity arising from recent legislation then we need to be systematic in our evaluation of what works and what does not work. Too much effort is being diverted into re-invention. Too little time and effort is being applied to evaluation and learning from mistakes.

Tilley argues that in this time of rapid development four problems beset better practice in community safety:

- partnership consensus often breaks down over evaluation (either with disagreement on what should be evaluated or on the implications of whether a programme should be judged a success or failure);

- the social interpretation of findings is full of traps and obstacles which undermine systematic evaluation (uncomfortable or challenging findings are explained away or set aside in future planning);

- the overall quality of evaluation is poor (thereby re-inforcing arguments to set it aside);

- the challenges of designing effective evaluation of fast moving targets are often too much for programme managers.

However, none of these shortcomings is insurmountable. The author sets out a ten-step framework for evaluating community safety which can be applied to partnerships, programmes and individual projects. This chapter should be required reading for those subjecting themselves to evaluation. Understanding of the issues raised would provide at least some protection against the turmoil and falling out between partners which frequently arises from evaluation. More importantly, it would provide some much needed stability and common ground during this fast moving period for community safety.

In Chapter 7 Ivan Hill and Ken Pease use John Stewart's definition to tackle two 'wicked' issues – displacement and sustainability – which appear frequently as objections to purposive crime prevention. Wicked issues refers to those recurring problems which cut across existing boundaries, require a joint response and which organisations have difficulty in tackling. They are often used to justify inaction – the problem is too great or the outcome uncertain – or to support the status quo – agencies can do little more than they are already undertaking. As such they are real barriers to meaningful change and enemies of the spirit of Section 17 of the Crime and Disorder Act (1998) which seeks to broaden responsibility and joined-up action against crime.

Displacement contends that tackling crime in one locality often simply shifts the incidence of crime to a neighbouring area. This supports an uncritical, fatalistic perspective on crime; justifies inaction; or, at the very least, creates a side debate on managing crime at existing levels rather than reducing it. Hill and Pease argue that crime displacement is seldom if ever total and that often the opposite occurs – diffusion of benefits – whereby crime reduces beyond the edges of areas applying crime prevention programmes. More contentiously they argue that even if displacement were total, crime is so heavily concentrated upon a minority of people and areas that a more equitable distribution of crime is a defensible aim, even if there were no net reduction in crime.

Sustainability is a wicked issue for crime prevention in that it is at one and the same time a much praised goal yet the majority of incentives, particularly financial, act against it. Hill and Pease contend that there is no financial dynamic towards continued improvement in crime prevention. High crime rates attract central Government money. Retaining and expanding incoming resources to tackle crime require us to be able to point to continuing crime problems or 'hot-spots', all of which lock us into short-term planning rather than longer-term problem-solving. Existing accounting practices make it difficult, if not impossible, to re-apply a portion of an crime reduction savings in any area towards further crime reduction programmes.

In a timely contribution Hill and Pease recommend two actions – firstly, that local community safety planning should emphasise the need to tackle long-term injustices in the distribution of crime across communities rather than becoming embroiled in a displacement debate, and secondly, that national and local attention should be given to developing incentive systems which sustain rather than fragment crime prevention efforts. This chapter may help put the crime displacement bogey to rest and at the same time open up a long overdue debate on financial incentives which can reward and sustain a problem-solving rather than problem-managing approach to preventing crime.

Section 3 carries the connection between policy and practice further. The opening chapters argue the importance of having a fuller understanding of partners' community safety responsibilities and of shifting community consultation to centre-stage for effective crime reduction and a safer community. The framework having been set the rest of the chapters in this section explore issues which can inform community safety and crime reduction planning and delivery. They provide guidance on how partnerships can move from community safety audits to effective strategies; how resources could be effectively targeted using geographical information systems; and, how a different perspective on urban layout and crime might be needed to tackle breaking and entering and create safer streets.

Section 3: Let's do it

In Chapter 8 Gloria Laycock and Barry Webb bring together two conceptual tools – competence and responsibility – to help practitioners understand the dynamics of crime prevention partnership working. They apply the tools to provide sound practical advice about levering reluctant or unmotivated partners into action. The authors argue that good practice abounds in community safety and that there is no shortage of pressure on statutory agencies and others to deliver more effective and efficient services. Yet, the good ideas, if they are shared at all, are not copied, developed or evaluated.

Implementation failure is widespread and arises from a failure to connect responsibility for tackling crime with organisational competence to act. Responsibility for tackling crime is seen as being increasingly diverse, particularly in light of the Crime and Disorder Act (1998), cutting across agencies and running between services within agencies. Different partners bring different responsibilities to the community safety table. Manufacturers, for example, have a responsibility to act before the event and to harden their products before they go on sale. But, despite the drive to widen participation in community safety, there is, as yet, no reliable mapping of responsibilities. Unless this is undertaken the steps recommended in Paul Ekblom's 'conjunction of criminal opportunity' are less likely to be effective (as shown in Chapter 2).

At the same time, the authors argue that the crime prevention process is further inhibited by a lack of understanding of who is competent to act at different stages of the process. Instead, immense effort is expended towards the end of the cycle, after the criminal event, rather than more appropriately and cost-effectively up-stream.

This has national and local implications. Nationally, we require guidance and direction on crime prevention responsibilities and competencies – essentially, who is expected to act and when. It may be that Government needs to consider whether more agencies and organisations should be brought within the ambit of Section 17 of the Crime and Disorder Act (1998) and how this is best achieved. Locally, it requires community safety partnerships to map responsibilities and competencies as part of their audits and strategies. Otherwise we run the danger of developing programmes not because of bad intent but because they are inappropriately framed and require a few partners to carry responsibilities beyond their competence to act or deliver.

Scott Ballintyne and Penny Fraser, in Chapter 9, push community consultation and involvement to the centre of the community safety agenda and set out a framework which extends beyond the requirements of the Crime and Disorder Act (1998). They argue that active, involved community consultation is the essential ingredient for successful, sustained community safety. In so doing they build upon Nellis's arguments for community justice (see Chapter 3) and proffer the view that nothing short of a culture shift amongst partners which affords local communities an active role as equal partners in tackling crime will suffice if we are to go beyond short-term responses.

Community consultation and involvement is seen as more than an optional extra, rubber-stamping partnership actions agreed by organisations which may have already failed those communities which disproportionately experience crime. It is inextricably connected to the ongoing legitimacy of public services; policing by consent; and the drive to tackle social exclusion. The authors detail three main steps for practitioners:

- building strategic community involvement (including appointing community directors, setting up consultative forums and undertaking a programme of community capacity building as part of the wider community safety strategy)

- engaging in community consultation as an ongoing, quality dialogue (ensuring widespread involvement in planning and delivering projects, constantly auditing the partnership for community engagement)

● consulting and involving the community in the delivery of projects (ensuring community organisations have the opportunity and skills to actively improve safety within their own communities).

The level of community consultation and involvement in crime prevention which the authors argue to be desirable will inevitably be contentious, given we find ourselves at a stage where public agencies are tentatively learning to share information and to enjoy mutual trust. On the one hand, community consultation may confirm some community views that the Emperor's clothes, if not entirely missing, certainly need some attention with needle and thread. On the other, if pursued openly, it may galvanise partnerships and provide a pathway to sustainable crime prevention, crime reduction and safer communities.

In Chapter 10, Andy Mills and Sarah Pearson, pick up on the practicalities of moving from a community safety audit to a local strategy. They identify who might benefit from a strategy; the factors which should be borne in mind in creating one; and discuss the data collection, consultation, policy connections and expert input required to make a strategy real. It is a practice view – a guide to how to make it happen.

The authors' emphasis upon connecting community safety to other policy initiatives, for example health, education and economic regeneration, re-inforces the practical steps which need to be taken to meet the requirements of Section 17 of the Crime and Disorder Act (1998). Community safety audits need to go beyond local crime audits to assess the contribution which can be made by other existing partnerships towards tackling crime. This is a practical implication of Laycock and Webb's arguments on agency responsibilities and competencies (see Chapter 8).

In a time of rapid change and burgeoning requirements, Mills and Pearson offer practical assistance for those tasked with meeting the requirements of the legislation before partnerships and agencies have acquired new skills and knowledge on crime prevention and community safety. Their central tenet – that a community safety strategy must be seen as a living document and treated as such – is critical to successful implementation.

Alex Hirschfield and Kate Bowers address the thorny issue of prioritising different areas, individuals and properties in planning and delivering crime prevention. In Chapter 11, they argue that it is unrealistic to assume that it will ever be possible to assist everyone who could potentially benefit from crime prevention measures. This is another side to the Hill and Pease argument that the incidence of crime is disproportionately concentrated upon certain communities (usually poorer communities) and localities (as shown in Chapter 7). Not only do we require different crime prevention strategies in different areas, we also need to accept that some areas require more concentrated efforts and greater resources.

The task, according to Hirschfield and Bowers, is to develop a framework which helps partnerships and agencies gather reliable information upon which to base decisions about priorities and targets. Giving practical examples from their work on Merseyside, the authors explore the challenges of building robust information about the levels of risk from incidents of crime and disorder upon which projects can be planned and targeted. They identify a range of potential data sources for practitioners, reviewing their relative strengths and weaknesses. Geographical Information Systems (GIS) are seen as particularly well-suited for mapping crime; enabling crime information to be cross-referenced with other factors such as enumeration districts; producing populations for crime 'hotspots'; interfacing with crime pattern analysis software; and, using known crime risk factors such as housing type, deprivation and community characteristics to help provide preventive action earlier.

This chapter is particularly timely in light of the Home Office's Burglary Reduction Programme. The first round of bids invited the identification of *places* suffering high rates of burglary. The second liberates bidders from geography and encourages the identification of groups, whether defined by geography or otherwise, which suffer disproportionately from burglary. The reason for the change is that the contours to which the problem cleaves may or may not be spatial. The concentration of burglary on widely spread groups must be recognised in any targeting approach. Hirschfield and Bowers provide a useful backcloth against which to make important practical decisions.

In a similar vein, Bill Hillier and Simon Shu pursue the challenge of how we reliably identify risk and how urban layout and crime interconnect. This may prove contentious. In Chapter 12 they argue that the debate on urban layout and crime over the past two decades has been long on ideology – 'defensible space', 'territoriality', and so on – but short on evidence. Their aim is to begin to provide a new level of evidence using point of entry data and space syntax analysis of urban layout so that any relationships between crime and space across the areas are unlikely to be due to social factors.

The initial outcome of their work, reported here, is a challenge to the orthodoxy which has governed urban layout and crime prevention for two decades. The results suggest that the built-in security advantage that many have argued belongs to the cul-de-sac in fact belongs to the street with its greater potential for movement, its greater mutual visibility for higher numbers of neighbours, and greater protection from the rear. This is heresy to a generation of Police Architectural Liaison Officers.

Hillier and Shu agree that the jury remains out on the relative burglary risk in cul-de-sac or street and call for further work. But, their initial investigation highlights two key issues in the drive for evidence-led decision-making on crime prevention – the continuing importance of urban lay-out in facilitating or inhibiting crime and the difficulty in removing social factors from the crime prevention framework.

Section 4 looks to the future on three fronts – a possible model for refocusing crime prevention, an opportunity to embed crime prevention and community safety planning into technical innovation and an exploration of the wider political context within which community safety functions.

Section 4: Looking forward – community safety beyond 2000

For many Ron Clarke is the godfather of situational crime prevention. In Chapter 13 he builds upon earlier work to provide a new focus for crime prevention – hot products. He argues the need to concentrate more on the products preferred by thieves, which he terms 'hot' products, by analogy with hot spots, which are the locations preferred by those committing crime. The advantages of this new focus are threefold:

- it is a mechanism which helps shape intervention into the situational conditions giving rise to crime concentrations (potentially earlier intervention in the crime process)

- it would help businesses protect themselves from theft; assist police in advising them how to do this; and, it would help governments in persuading industry to find ways of avoiding crime waves sometimes generated by new products

- it would redress an imbalance in contemporary criminology where too much attention is still paid to the criminal rather than the circumstances of the crime

Clarke offers a new model – CRAVED – that identifies six key attributes of hot products which can be used to identify and plan crime preventive work on particular goods. The attributes which may underpin the likelihood that certain categories of goods may be more susceptible to crime are that they are generally Concealable, Removable, Available, Valuable, Enjoyable and Disposable.

He argues that the concept of hot products has much broader implications than simply preventing the theft of goods. Drug misuse is crucially dependent upon the market for stolen goods – and that market thrives upon hot products. By failing to protect their goods from theft, it could be argued that manufacturers of hot products may be indirectly helping to sustain drug misuse.

At the very least it highlights two issues raised elsewhere in this book – that practitioners require models such as Clarke's CRAVED and Ekblom's Conjunction of Criminal Opportunity to help them plan wide-reaching ways of tackling crime and that manufacturers should also be subjected to a form of Section 17 of the Crime and Disorder Act (1998) which would require them to pay attention to the crime impact of their work and products.

Michelle Rogerson, Paul Ekblom and Ken Pease pursue the challenge of integrating crime prevention thinking into all aspects of innovation. In Chapter 14 they examine the Department of Trade and Industry's Foresight Programme which aims to harness technical and social innovation within industry and commerce to promote wealth creation and quality of life in the UK. The first round of the programme has largely ignored the consequences of crime and missed a significant opportunity to integrate crime prevention into the earliest stages of technical and technological development.

They argue that the link between innovation and crime displays a recurring pattern which we cannot afford to ignore. Typically, all innovations go through three phases – design with indifference to crime consequences; reaping a crime harvest; recognising criminal consequences in retrospect resulting in the reversal of innovation or retrofitting a partial solution. Ram-raiding is a case in point.

Round Two of the Foresight Programme has sought to rectify their earlier omission. A cross-cutting crime prevention panel is working across all Round Two themes. The authors recommend three issues which would focus the work of the panel – mapping out the problem space of crime reduction (providing systematic aids for innovators); initiating an early crime consequences warning system to spot design failures and design obsolescence as early as possible in the innovation process; and, measuring the success of the panel through the extent to which it has improved capacity for preventing crime. At best, this process should shift crime prevention upstream. At worst, it should provide a repertoire of ways of thinking about future crime which will inform national and local decisions on its anticipation and prevention.

Looking to the future Gordon Hughes queries why there is an ascendant preoccupation with community safety at this historical juncture. He accepts the relative importance of mapping out what works in crime prevention but contends that it is equally important to foster a critical and reflexive culture around community safety. In Chapter 15, community safety is seen as a wicked issue in its own right not just for the challenges it raises as a public priority which cuts across traditional compartmentalised thinking but also for the theoretical, moral and political challenges it raises in a revitalised debate about how we tackle crime.

Hughes argues that the ascendant preoccupation with community safety owes much to the advent of 'risk society' with its attendant fracturing or loosening of traditional kinship and community ties and the undermining of appeals to authority and tradition to maintain wider consensus on harms and crime. Community safety takes on a broader appeal when uncertainty is the norm.

Despite these changes the future for crime control and community safety is not fixed. Hughes maps out two widely divergent possible futures:

● A dystopian future where the dangers of crime, disorder and other threatening epidemics become so great that liberties, freedoms and democratic debate are sacrificed and replaced by an all powerful single political authority (a future of gated communities and the excluded poor).

- A utopian future where the advent of new forms of local governance accompanied by increasing community involvement in tackling crime locally pull down power from central government and regenerate local identities (a future of a new 'social' local state which meets demands for security and safety).

For Hughes, the key change in crime control and community safety which opens up a route towards a more utopian future is to increase the distance between community safety and over-centralised government. The Crime and Disorder Act (1998) is a potential start down that route but, in Hughes' view, it requires a positive replacement discourse to take us beyond the present negative discourse of prevention, risk, insecurity and fear which traps us in a criminalising, law and order agenda. That positive replacement discourse would subordinate questions of crime control to those of social justice and open up new possibilities for an inclusive approach to making communities safer. The aim is to nurture debate away from the criminalisation of social policy towards the socialisation of criminal justice and crime prevention policies. The implication is for Government to take a lead in promoting a debate which values social justice above crime control and for local partnerships to seek inclusive solutions to crime, not a knee-jerk response which scapegoats or blames others in the same community.

In Chapter 16 Jon Spencer picks up on the theme that the dominant force in contemporary political discourse on crime and punishment is not democratic politics but social exclusion. Hughes' dystopian and utopian futures are crystallised by Spencer into the battleground between primary and secondary crime prevention strategies. For Spencer, primary crime prevention is increasingly focused upon technology and data analysis to such an extent that it loses sight of the very real issues which affect people's lives, those crucial elements of social process. Crime is seen to be caused by a range of other, non-social factors which take priority in crime prevention planning.

On the other hand, secondary crime prevention is people oriented, focusing upon community and changing people who are identified as potentially 'high risk' offenders and is seen as socially inclusive and democratically accountable. Spencer argues that the heart of the problem lies in how we instigate primary forms of crime prevention which are responsive to the needs of communities, victims and wider society whilst at the same time overcoming the consequences of social policies which are crime generating. Three actions are needed to reconcile this gap:

- theorising a range of crime prevention solutions which take account of community and the complex dynamic of crime;

- producing accountable and socially just frameworks to govern local community safety;

●   building community capacity to tackle crime and help communities help themselves.

But the ultimate key to overcoming socially excluding solutions to crime is power sharing between agencies and local communities. In their different ways, Hughes and Spencer provide uncannily similar futures – devolve and share power and responsibilities for community safety to communities and offer the possibility of breaking free from an agenda dominated by insecurity and fear or continue to elevate crime control over social justice and maintain an agenda dominated by social exclusion where agencies gather increasing powers in the name of crime prevention.

What next? Conclusions and implications

Many of the chapters raise as many questions as they answer. This reflects the current state of play on crime prevention, crime reduction and community safety – an arena which is searching for a common identity whilst at the same time adjusting to the demands of rapid practical changes set out in legislation. The reader should not look for uniformity of approach nor a finished template for community safety. What the reader can expect, and rightly so, are considered views on key issues facing community safety as a perspective on preventing and reducing crime *and* some practical guidance on how to go about promoting community safety in light of recent legislation.

But, some conclusions are possible. There is emerging consensus on several issues. Firstly, a shared understanding of community safety may well require a shared understanding of agencies', organisations' and communities' responsibilities and competencies towards making all communities safer. The spirit of Section 17 of the Crime and Disorder Act (1998), which requires local authorities to take crime prevention issues into consideration across every area of their work, should be mapped out more fully and widened to include central Government Departments, manufacturers, retailers and not-for-profit community organisations. This may require legislation or at least a broadening of current provisions.

It needs to work *nationally*, *regionally* and *locally*. Government should review how community safety considerations can be built into all aspects of national policy-making, service delivery and funding. Success on community safety cuts to the heart of the Government's 'Modernising Government' agenda. If we are serious about cross-cutting solutions then we need to encourage and monitor shifts in mainstream public expenditure towards community safety and identify ways in which a proportion of savings which arise from improved crime prevention and crime reduction can be reapplied to sustain the community safety cycle.

Community safety needs to be woven into the Cabinet Office Performance and Innovation Unit review of regional government. The recent appointment of Regional Crime Directors is a potentially useful step in creating a regional framework for community safety. The review of regional government is an opportunity to inject cross-cutting issues, such as community safety, into the mainstream. It should not be overlooked. At the same time, local community safety partnerships should assess local crime prevention responsibilities and competencies and find flexibility within local funding regimes to incentivise crime prevention and crime reduction.

Secondly, community safety may have to embrace social and community justice as much as crime control if it is to break out of the narrow shackles which have dominated criminal justice in the UK for several decades and effect the scale of change envisaged in many of the chapters in this volume. The effectiveness of community safety partnerships in preventing and reducing crime and, perhaps more importantly, sustaining those improvements over time requires a socially inclusive not exclusive modus operandi.

Agencies can exclude communities from active partnership in community safety or place limits upon participation. It is within their power and fits with existing patterns of compartmentalised service delivery. Likewise, partnerships can devise community safety solutions which blame, scapegoat and exclude parts of the wider communities they aim to serve. This may generate short term gains but it is difficult to see how it can be sustained without contributing further to a dystopian future.

Alternatively, partnerships can help communities help themselves, building programmes which balance crime control and crime prevention and reduce the likelihood of criminal incidents and re-offending. Neither an easy task nor a debate which is settled. The balance between crime control and crime prevention is not easy to achieve. The danger is that the dominance of crime control, however great its shortcomings, continues unquestioned into community safety partnership and impoverishes the range of programmes which emerge. Performance audits of community safety partnerships should include measures of active community involvement in planning and delivering local programmes. Strategies should be audited for a balance between crime prevention and crime control.

Thirdly, there is a broad consensus that community safety planning and implementation needs to be prioritised, targeted and evaluated. There is an emerging consensus that this needs to be undertaken with fairness in mind. Crime is not spread equitably across or between communities. The chapters in this volume provide a range of conceptual and practical tools – the conjunction of criminal opportunity, hot products (CRAVED), the route through the evaluation jungle, the guide to active community partnership, the application of geographical information systems – to help planners and practitioners develop accountable and workable local programmes. Some, for example the work on urban layout, may be more contentious than others, but they are indispensable in pulling together a broader understanding of community safety and the practicalities of making it happen.

Community safety itself needs nurturing as a critical, reflexive enterprise which challenges the traditional boundaries of social policy and crime control and asks questions of policy-makers, academics and practitioners. This volume is a starting point for a much needed debate not the end product. It is hoped that the contributions will provide a sounding board for policy-makers, practitioners and academics and will help them to reflect upon the compromises, assumptions and dilemmas which, consciously or otherwise shape their views and actions. The chapters give a flavour of the changes taking place in the field of community safety, crime prevention and crime reduction; the issues which need to be and are being addressed; and, some serious practical guidance if you are tasked with making your community safer.

I: Crime prevention and community safety: Janus faces?

1. Crime prevention and community safety: Tweedledum and Tweedledee?
Paul Wiles and Ken Pease

The Crime and Disorder Act 1998 is to be welcomed for its recognition that the levers of crime lie primarily outside the criminal justice system and that any intellectually defensible crime control effort must reflect this. The Act also advances the use of 'community safety' over 'crime prevention' as the preferred means of categorising crime control activities and the agencies needed to engender them. It is timely to stand back and see whether community safety and crime prevention are the same thing, what connotative baggage each brings with it and what pitfalls attend confusion about use of one or other phrase.

It will be concluded that community safety is the phrase to be preferred only if safety refers to the likely absence of harms (particularly serious harms) from all sources, not just from human acts classifiable as crimes. To draw the notion of community safety more narrowly, risks the emergence of double standards whereby people are protected from attack by others, while choking gently on polluted air. In what follows, crime prevention and community safety will be distinguished. While the Crime and Disorder Act draws the notion of community safety narrowly, a means will be suggested of going some way to remedying this by use of Section 17 of the Act to incorporate harm reduction, where the notion of harm extends beyond actions proscribed by criminal law. This will be no substitute in the longer term for legislation which gives equal status to crimes and other harms of equivalent impact, but may advance matters to a point where the virtues of such legislation become evident.

Crime prevention

Levels of crime are a product of our social and physical arrangements, from the ease of criminal use of manufactured products, the supply of motivated offenders who sense they have little to lose, and the ready availability of markets for stolen goods. When the robber Willie Sutton was asked why he targeted banks, he replied 'Because that's where they keep the money.'

Self-evidently, crime and disorder can be reduced by changing criminogenic objects and processes or by changing criminally inclined people. Banks can be made more secure, or Willie Sutton and his pre-criminal, would-be successors can be rendered less inclined to rob them. Proponents of people-change and object-change may disagree about the relative importance of the two strategies, but only a fool would choose one approach to the exclusion of the other. Stress on one or the other has changed enormously as criminological fashion has changed. When changing objects is in vogue, the period which must elapse, before pre-delinquent change is reflected in rates of crime, is used as a justification for that preference. That is, the lead time of effects from people-change is distressingly long. When changing people is in vogue, there is an inappropriate emphasis on the callousness involved in changing temptations and leaving those tempted to their own devices.

In spite of changing criminological fashions, people-change has been the preferred approach for most of the discipline's history. For long periods, criminology was almost exclusively concerned with theorising about the social functions of crime and, at the individual level, about the determinants of criminality. In reaction, a perspective grew in which the rationality of much offending was assumed, and the social and physical arrangements studied, in terms of the range and richness of criminal opportunities which they afforded (see Cornish and Clarke, 1986).

This perspective was supported by evidence that manipulating crime opportunities changes rates of crime (see Clarke, 1990 and 1997). The result was that, for many purposes, during the 1980s and early 1990s object-change ruled. Sometimes this manipulation was not based on adequate analysis. In the mid-1990s, some 78 per cent of the Home Office's crime prevention budget was spent on CCTV systems alone (Koch, 1996), since that means of opportunity reduction was in vogue although not well supported by evidence.

The new administration has sought to change this, and in doing so the pendulum has swung back towards people processing. The current Government has directed much more attention towards youth offending, insisted on evidence-led crime responses, and widened the notion of crime prevention to become community safety. This verbal change, first suggested in the 1991 Morgan Report, has huge implications. It was preferred by Morgan as evoking wider concerns and suggesting local accountability in tackling problems. It explicitly takes police away from centre stage. Furthermore, it requires partnerships between police and local authorities and so rescues local government from its less central role under the previous administration.

So what does community safety mean? What are the consequences of embedding it in an Act of Parliament concerned with crime, and what are the dangers of substituting the vocabulary of crime prevention with the vocabulary of community safety?

Community safety

Presumably, safety refers to the absence, or the sensed absence, of likely or serious harms, whether caused by human agency or otherwise. Whether a harm occurs through being poisoned by a murderer or through an error made by an employee of a public utility is irrelevant to its consequences for the person poisoned. Danger may be apprehended when the probability of trivial harm is high, or when the probability of serious harm is more than negligible. The sense of safety is thus reduced when the probability or seriousness of a harm is increased. In this view, the practice of community safety involves the management of risk so as to maximise public safety.

One of the problems in thinking about community safety in this sense is that our conceptions of harm tend to be compartmentalised, with each agency seeking to reduce the harms traditionally central to its function. This is no more than a reflection of bureaucratic history. The phrase 'community safety' taken alone implies the ranking of public dangers from whatever source: be it traffic, dangerous working conditions, or crime. If a car is more likely to kill you than a local psychopath, then traffic management reduces risk more than locking up the psychopath.

However, the reality of public policy is of a highly compartmentalised set of concerns. Rail services seek to reduce the probability of harms caused by crashes, insurers by subsidence, schools by bullying, social services departments by abusive relationships and so on. Persuasive evidence that any specific hazard is diminished is depressingly rare, and the role of psychological and cultural factors in evaluating risk reduction is correspondingly great (Adams, 1995).

Considering harms from any source, and trade-off of risks, is not a common approach. In this country, it is fair to say that we have a health service, but no health policy that involves the integrated consideration of food, agriculture, air and water quality together with the provision of health monitoring. Elsewhere, the decision of the Peruvian government, for example, to reduce chlorination in favour of fluoridation of the water supply in 1991 allowed cholera to flourish. As a result, 7,000 people died, 600,000 having been infected (Bate, 1998). Furthermore, the communication of hazard information is far from straightforward, with systematic psychological biases operating on the perception of hazard (see Viscusi, 1987). Even if hazard is objectively categorised across origins of hazard, the use of that information in rational decision making is far from assured (Adams, 1995).

In addition to psychological biases there are well-established public policy distinctions about types of harms, many of which are given legal expression:

- We tend to make a public/private distinction with regard to safety and are less inclined to interfere in harms occurring in the private realm. However, where the proper distinction between the private and the public realm should lie is a matter of constant public debate, so that previously private harms have been re-conceptualised as matters of public concern and therefore action – the most obvious recent examples being child abuse and domestic violence.

- We usually distinguish between harms which result from human agency and those which do not: the difference between accidents and acts of God. The distinction is important because it is assumed that whilst we can attempt to protect ourselves against acts of God we cannot, unlike accidents, prevent them. Again, the application of the distinction is constantly up for debate – for example, the history of improving car safety has increasingly involved seeing the harm caused by cars as being the result of human agency.

• We distinguish between those acts of human agency which are intentional and those which are not. Law, as the organised attempt to structure human action, is especially concerned with the link between intention and harm, most obviously in the general requirement in criminal law for *mens rea*. Here the assumption is that not only can we prevent intentional human acts but we can do so through rules, backed by sanctions.

These distinctions are important because they imply different risk management responses. We cannot prevent acts of God but we can try and protect ourselves against them. We can try and reduce accidents as a result of human activity, by engineering their probability. We can try and prevent crime and other intentional harms by altering human behaviour. Each of these risks can be seen as a public or private matter and responsibility. Although any of these types of risk might be equally injurious, we especially fear the harm resulting from intentional action, perhaps because this strikes at the very possibility of human association – society depends on the ordering created by rules.

Although such distinctions may be reasonably clear conceptually, their empirical referent is always a matter for debate. One way to categorise different social forms would be in terms of how the distinctions are referenced. Often, a precursor to taking public action against a particular risk is to re-categorise it through public debate or legal or political action, and in the process the responsibility can shift from the private to the public realm or the responsibility for managing the risk may shift between agencies. Any contemporary way of conceptualising harms and agency responsibility for risk management is therefore ephemeral, and a successful community safety strategy will have to be capable of constant change and adjustment.

In this context, thinking of community safety simply as crime prevention might appear attractive initially: its subject matter can be those harms which have, for the moment, been defined as criminal. However, this would forever separate one set of harms from others. Yet conceptual distinctions are fluid and, as will be discussed below, different harms are often empirically linked, and in ways which are not necessarily clearly understood. Thinking of community safety (being the sum of individual safety) as the minimisation of the number and seriousness of harms has many advantages over considering crime prevention alone. It also raises problems, but it has the great advantage that risks and harms can be responded to as people experience them instead of as they are publicly defined and bureaucratically allocated.

The Labour Government is keen to create joined-up government and, if that is to mean more than internal convenience and efficiency savings for government itself, then it ought to be aimed at providing joined-up service delivery. In order to deliver joined-up services, public agencies must first dissolve their differences, at least at the strategic planning stage. So far, central government has attempted to achieve this by requiring joint planning bodies and multi-agency delivery structures in many areas, of which those required by the Crime and Disorder Act are merely one example.

At local level there is concern that such bodies are multiplying beyond control. This can be avoided through thinking about problems and conducting strategic planning at a level beyond that created by Whitehall-led legislation. In other words, helping Whitehall create the joined-up government it seems to find difficult within itself. But, how far can the requirements of the Crime and Disorder Act be used to create this broader, joined-up thinking?

Starting from here

Community safety was located in the Morgan Report within a crime context: its full title being *Safer communities: the local delivery of crime prevention through the partnership approach*. Furthermore, the report stated that it 'could encourage greater participation from all sections of the community in the fight against crime.'

Community safety, as legislated, is simply presented as re-badged crime prevention, not as a broader way of ranking and dealing with the dangers facing people. It is an irony that while crime prevention is conceptually a subset of technique for achieving community safety, it is legislated as though the opposite were true. Thus *community safety* is found within the *Crime and Disorder* Act when it would be common sense for *crime and disorder* issues to be found within a *community safety* act.

Recent local authority community safety programmes initially emphasised the simplest forms of target hardening and then shifted to some types of offender reduction programmes. Far from liberating crime prevention into a wider framework, these recent developments have served to ghettoise community safety as narrowly-focused crime prevention of one sort or another. This is evident from the exclusion of trading standards and environmental health functions from local partnership committees, despite the fact that they deal with important aspects of risk management, (much of the risk being crime-generated, suggesting that even the modest conceptual shift needed to incorporate them is beyond the scope of those engaged).

Whatever the advantages of the notion of community safety as an overarching purpose, incorporating crimes alongside other harms, we must acknowledge that community safety is now employed as a synonym of crime prevention, with fluffy overtones added. Does this matter?

One question whose answer may prove illuminating is why *community* safety is invoked rather than *individual* safety? The feeling is that the choice is not a reasoned one, but that the word community invokes fluffiness and a feeling of all being in this together – which in terms of crime risks we emphatically are not. If the choice of phrase had been deliberate, it would necessarily have been sinister. Community safety departs from the sum of individual safeties only if hazards are distributed unevenly. If each person's safety contributes equally to the summed safety of an entire community, community safety and individual safety are indistinguishable. If community safety is something other than the sum of individual safeties, it can be attained only by sacrificing the safety of some for the safety of others. Some areas pay the crime dues for a town and the remainder have crime levels held at a point associated with citizen feelings of safety. Adams (1995) shows how the typical measures of policy effectiveness discounts the interests of some citizens relative to others. Invoking community safety rather than the sum of individual safeties threatens to do the same.

The Morgan Report has a subtext of community activism and partnership. Its implicit notion of community safety is expansive, in that its implied perfect world is one in which safety is not achieved in retreat from the dangers outside one's door, but in co-operating to allow everyone to feel safe outside. However, by limiting its concern to crime and disorder, it excludes harms resulting from the way in which goods and services are presented. In one sense, it conveniently diverts the sense of danger from authorities and the market to one's erring fellow citizens. Narrowing community safety to the control of crime has all the functions of blaming fellow citizens rather than the social arrangements to which conflict theorists have repeatedly drawn attention.

All those involved in providing public services know that crime risks are closely related to other risks. Communities that suffer from crime are also quite likely to suffer from poor housing, deprivation, exclusion, poor educational achievement, pollution and so on. Furthermore, we have good reasons for believing that these risks are connected. It is a criminological commonplace that a wide range of social and physical variables contribute to crime risk, and that they do so both alone and in interaction (see for example Tseloni *et al*, 1998). These variables include affluence, region, area type, parity, household composition, land use and physical attributes of a home, car or person. They should not necessarily be thought of as directly causal. The attempt to establish causal relationships of this kind are both technically difficult and criminologically naïve, because of complex vicious and virtual spirals in area atmosphere. Other social variables may both drive and be driven by rates of crime, or be independent manifestations of other variables. So, concentration of single parent households *may* be associated with crime:

●   because crime changes population composition, with the more desperate moving to less desirable areas

●   because the lifestyle of single parents changes natural surveillance and other area attributes which increase crime

- because both single parent households and crime may be attributes of an area's economic decline, which drives both.

In the face of such complexity, the only sensible policy option involves remaining alert to non-crime indices. Thus, in principle, decisions about any of the social and physical characteristics of an area which have associations with crime should be considered under the terms of S17 of the Crime and Disorder Act. We should not be precious about the direction of causal relationships, because we cannot always be certain of this.

Connections between crime and other variables are dynamic over time. The 'broken windows' approach has at its centre a dynamic wherein community indifference feeds the impulse to prey and the wish to move away. In principle, community safety is not restricted to crime. Indeed, the work of George Kelling and others (see Kelling and Coles, 1996 and Skogan 1990) shows that signs of disorder, of a society which is 'out of control', are what fuel citizen concern and may lead a community to spiral into high rates of crime victimisation and/or socio-economic decline. Concretised as the 'broken windows' hypothesis, it suggests that broken windows that remain unrepaired are signs that no one cares about the building, and predation can begin.

Addressing such disorder has become fashionable and is claimed to have been a major factor in the dramatic reduction in crime in New York during the 1990s (Bratton, 1998). The badging of the 1998 Act as Crime *and Disorder* reflects the fact that noise, troublesome neighbours, and the ubiquitous 'youths causing annoyance' calls for the police service, are central to a sense of safety. Over three decades, housing policy in Sheffield has been shown to have this kind of dynamic relationship with crime (see Bottoms and Wiles, 1998). Tackling each risk in isolation, with crime as the focal risk, is therefore likely to be less successful than an integrated response.

Of equal importance, a community's experience of risk and harm is a totality and is not neatly broken down to fit the remit of different service providers. Only by making all public service providers responsible for an integrated service can a community make them effectively accountable.

For better or worse, we now have an Act in which other factors are subsumed under the crime control purpose. Is there any means by which the Act can be implemented in ways which are more inclusive of risk type? One possibility is S17 of the Act, which requires all local authorities to consider crime and disorder reduction while exercising all their duties. If taken seriously, this leads towards a general risk orientation. It includes decisions about street lighting, school design, housing allocations and just about everything else. The potential benefit of using S17 in this way is that it allows problems associated with crime to be addressed legitimately.

There are severe limits to this advantage, however. We may well be clutching at the only straw available. First, not all harms are statistically associated with crime and disorder. There are harms which may not be associated with crime and disorder problems which deserve serious consideration and which would not be incorporated in the S17 approach. Second, there may be a tendency to use links to crime and disorder as a spurious justification for addressing social ills. For instance, the relationship between rates of unemployment and rates of crime are far less compelling than is popularly imagined. One can too readily see job creation programmes (for example) put in place because of their illusory links to rates of crime.

In other words, S17 allows a host of socially desirable initiatives to be put in place for reasons which are not intellectually defensible. If S17 is used in the way envisaged, there should be some safeguards in that implementation must always be explicitly linked to, and justified by, presumed mechanisms whereby crime and disorder reductions might occur. For example, street lighting improvements could be justified by reference to a small area with a high rate of disorder, of which a non-trivial proportion occurs during the hours of darkness, and where there is citizen dissatisfaction with current lighting. Such detailed specification of the problem suggests how implementation could be made optimal, as well as providing some defensible links between mode of change and crime and disorder outcomes.

But really...

While S17 might be a stopgap of sorts, in the middle and long term the benefits of the notion of community safety over crime prevention will only be realised by an integrated consideration of diverse harms. What, then, should happen?

First, the major public authorities, at district level, should be required to carry out an overall *risk audit* of their area on a geographical basis, at least down to ward (preferably enumeration district) level. This audit should include *all risks*. The same agencies should be given a collective responsibility to produce an integrated, strategic plan for *risk management* in their areas which should be locked into a standard management structure to ensure proper evaluation and accountability.

The planning infrastructure for this will need encouragement. Government could:

- *require* an information strategy for each area

- *speed up* the spread of Geographic Information Systems to map risk properly

- *insist* that such new technologies are not locked up in head office but given to community level service managers and providers to ensure the most direct means of responsiveness and, to ensure accountability, be shared with citizens

- *encourage* the horizontal integration of information systems

- *stop* undermining such integration by insisting on inflexible vertical integration

- *solve* Data Protection Act problems either legislatively or technically to ensure a pan-risk analysis.

If this does not happen, the local reduction of crime problems will be seen as offender problems, where youth services offer programmes in the hope of mid-term improvements, while Trading Standards Officers cannot afford to investigate or prosecute those ripping off the public; where analyses of the times and places where people die and are injured, remain unsophisticated because the attention is on the harming person rather than the harming circumstance; where local service providers compete rather than share real understanding of the nature and distribution of the dangers to which the public stands liable; and where school lessons in moral responsibility in using weapons, for example, coexists with the absence of adequate overseeing of shops selling hunting knives.

References

Adams J (1995) *Risk* London: UCL Press

Bate R (1998) 'Fear and precaution: a lethal mix' *RSA Journal* 4

Bottoms AE and Wiles P (1998) 'Environmental criminology' *The Oxford Handbook of Criminology* 2nd ed. Oxford: Clarendon Press

Bratton W (1998) *Turnaround* New York: Random House

Clarke RV (1992) *Situational crime prevention: successful case studies* New York: Harrow and Heston

Clarke RV (1997) *Situational crime prevention: successful case studies* 2nd ed. New York: Harrow and Heston

Cornish DB and Clarke RV (1986) *The reasoning criminal: rational choice perspectives on offending* New York: Springer-Verlag

Kelling GL and Coles CM (1996) *Fixing broken windows* New York: Free Press

Koch B (1996) *National crime prevention policy in England and Wales 1979-1995* D.Phil thesis, Cambridge University

Morgan Report (1991) *Safer communities: the local delivery of crime prevention through the partnership approach* London: Home Office

Tseloni A, Osborn DR, Trickett A and Pease K (1998) *The lifestyle and socio-economic environment of households experiencing high property crime rates in England and Wales* Unpublished paper, School of Economics, Manchester University

Viscusi WK (1987) *Learning about risk: consumer and worker responses to hazard information* Cambridge, Ma.: Harvard University Press

2. The conjunction of criminal opportunity©
A tool for clear, 'joined-up' thinking about community safety and crime reduction
Paul Ekblom

Recent developments promise to give considerable impetus to community safety and crime reduction (CSCR) in England and Wales. The Crime and Disorder Act 1998, accompanied by substantial official guidance, places local, partnership effort in this field on a statutory basis. The Audit Commission's recent report on community safety suggests how Best Value may be achieved by the partnerships, and a £250 million, three-year national Crime Reduction Programme has been launched. This will develop knowledge of what is cost effective across the entire range from early intervention among children at risk of offending, to design against crime and to sentencing and treatment of convicted offenders. The strategy aims particularly at ensuring that knowledge gained is incorporated into mainstream policy and practice.

A consensus is emerging from these developments and elsewhere that cost effective and appropriate practical action in CSCR must be evidence- as well as experience-based. However, this evidence – of what works and what is cost effective – is both inadequate and insufficient. It is inadequate because there is still a severe lack of reliable evaluation results for thorough coverage of the field. It is insufficient because the effectiveness of an intervention usually depends on the particular social and physical context in which it is implemented. The context, moreover, includes any other interventions that may together be part of a package (such as lighting and CCTV and enhanced police patrols). Evidence and experience must, therefore, be more than a pile of disconnected (and sometimes inconsistent) observations and results. It must be organised through clear principles, reflecting an understanding of the causes of crime and how to plausibly intervene in those causes in specific contexts. This covers that majority of cases where knowledge of 'what works' is currently missing, or its applicability to particular circumstances is unknown.

Ideally, the principles themselves should derive from clear and tested (or at least plausible) theories. However, available criminological theories have limitations in their turn. Theories are notorious for covering only part of the field of 'things to be explained'; they overlap, compete for explanation and may be untested or already actually proven wrong. Despite recent attempts at integration, the theoretical basis for deriving practical principles to support good quality CSCR remains very patchy, but practitioners facing particular crime or safety problems cannot wait for theory or research to be 'finished'. Despite major gaps in theory, they must intervene when circumstances demand.

Whilst shortcomings of evidence and theory are widely acknowledged, the lack of a good conceptual framework for CSCR is rarely discussed. Practitioners are significantly hindered by shaky concepts and loose, conflicting and inconsistent terms. This could destabilise the whole edifice and prevent the practice of CSCR reaching its full potential as a professional discipline, equivalent, for example, to health sciences. (Interestingly, a similar approach is being pursued within the community development context.) In the absence of such foundations, much of the effort and enthusiasm currently being put into CSCR could be wasted in action that is of poor quality or inappropriately matched to the crime problem targeted. There is a serious need for such a framework covering the entire field of activity, developed in a practical context, drawing together 'what works' knowledge, strategic policy, practical principles and theory into a set of high-level concepts. The aim is to support local Crime and Disorder Partnership action and that of the Crime Reduction Programme.

The framework suggested here stemmed from my involvement in the Safer Cities Programme and other crime prevention activity, and drew on a range of earlier schemata in the field. Based on this, definitions were developed further and agreed by a national steering group with a remit to work towards arrangements and a curriculum, for education and training in CSCR. Its membership included senior representatives of the former Home Office Crime Prevention Agency and Crime Prevention College, the police, probation service, former local government associations, Crime Concern, NACRO, academics and others. A related group subsequently convened to produce guidance material on training for the Crime and Disorder Act 1998. The framework was developed in that context and appeared, in abbreviated form, on the guidance website (*www.homeoffice.gov.uk/cdact/cstrng5.htm*).

Muddling through – not good enough

Society's ways of attempting to reduce crime and promote community safety are many and varied – from imprisonment of robbers to motor schemes for joyriders; from better locks to puppet shows with a moral; from family support to fines and from police patrolling to publicity campaigns urging self-protection. Policy makers, practitioners and academics within each domain of crime control have their own traditional language and concepts, which differ in significant ways. Some focus on criminal events in the community while others focus on the convicted offender. There is a serious cultural divide between those in practice, policy and research who pursue the situational approach versus those who favour offender-oriented action (often known as criminality prevention). The formal (CJS) is built around concepts of free will and criminal responsibility, which sit uneasily alongside more scientific notions of causality. Retribution, in particular, focuses on events past, while crime prevention looks to the future.

There are understandable reasons why these distinct conceptual domains have become established – including pursuit of specialist expertise, development of occupational cultures, and constitutional separation of the judiciary from the executive branches of government. But when we seek, as now, to bring together the entire CSCR field in the furtherance of local and national strategy and to foster its development as a professional discipline, we find at the heart of crime reduction and community safety a veritable Tower of Babel. All too often crime prevention is contrasted with detection, repression, punishment or deterrence (they overlap); or with criminality prevention (a subset of crime prevention when defined, as below, as reducing the risk and seriousness of criminal events). The terms crime prevention, crime reduction, crime control and community safety are used much less to denote clearly different ideas than to bestow nuances or flavours, to indicate allegiance to particular schools or traditions, or even to follow fashion.

There is also much confusion from labels focusing on different facets of the whole field of action:

- *what is done* (crime prevention through environmental design, for example)

- *who does it* (perhaps police-based prevention)

- on *which targets* (reducing property crime, for example)

- against *which offenders* (perhaps juvenile crime prevention)

- at *which class of risk* (primary, secondary or tertiary prevention)

- in *what context* (community crime prevention, for example).

These, or similar headings, are often seen juxtaposed in lists of activities or responsibilities. Arguably, the central facet should be *what is done* – the methods and causal mechanisms of CSCR interventions – although each of the other facets needs to be on view in appropriate circumstances.

With experience, most practitioners and policy makers know what they mean in this situation and can make intelligent guesses about what their professional partners mean. Nevertheless, serious consequences result from conceptual confusion when combined with gaps in the coverage afforded by theory and evaluation:

- *Partnership*-based working groups, whose diverse members are unable to communicate efficiently, to share understanding and to articulate proposals, are hindered from progressing beyond the talking-shop level and superficial consensus about what needs to be done. Tried and *un*tested popular approaches to CSCR are often proposed. Any expert authority that professionals develop has difficulty making itself heard.

- *Strategic thinking* across local and national CSCR is inhibited and remains compartmentalised and method- rather than problem-oriented. No one strategic decision-making body in central or local government has complete awareness of the range of policy levers at its disposal. In particular the newer approaches to CSCR (such as situational prevention) tend to remain strategically (and hence operationally) isolated from conventional law enforcement and penal systems.

- *Failure to focus on how, precisely, CSCR measures are intended to work* (the causal mechanisms, or more broadly-speaking principles, through which interventions have their impact). This leads to weak implementation, weak quality assurance and uncertain integrity of programmes in the first instance, and limited scope for evaluation in the second (if a scheme is not well-specified it is difficult to evaluate and may not be worth evaluating anyway). This in turn limits replication, through failure to accumulate specific 'what works' knowledge for best practice. When CSCR actions themselves fail, constructive lessons are lost if it proves impossible to describe exactly what had been intended to be implemented, and how. Further problems arise for evaluation particularly at the strategic, policy level. There may be a lack of clarity about the precise goals (reduction of crime in absolute terms, or relative to expected growth, for example); and there may even be lack of agreement over the terms and concepts used in evaluation itself.

- *Obstacles to closer coupling between practice and theory mean failure of practice to test and refine theory*, and failure of theory to inform practice.

- *It is hard to define and compare cost effectiveness* of different CSCR interventions when outputs and outcomes are depicted in different ways in different fields.

- *Education and training lack a coherent basis* to develop a curriculum and core competencies.

- *Collaboration and exchange of 'what works' information is inhibited* (especially development of efficient computerised databases). In the international context, in particular, no lexicon will help if the underlying concepts themselves are loosely defined.

If we remain content with conceptually just muddling through, we increase the risk of wasting both national and local effort and squandering opportunity to reduce crime and improve community safety on a grand scale. The attempt here to develop a framework comprises both terminology and a conceptual map. These cover definitions and descriptions of crime prevention, reduction and control, and community safety, as distinguishably different perspectives of what is mostly the same territory and underlying activities. It also explores how these relate to the crime-reducing function of the CJS.

It has been argued in some circles that attempts, such as this, to introduce greater rationality into what is, admittedly, an intensely political, fashion-driven and gesture-prone field are pointless. However, one can equally argue that it is precisely because of the lack of conceptual clarity, hard evidence and good theory that CSCR is currently prone to these features.

The utility of the framework

The framework should be judged on its utility in providing tools for thought in policy, practice, theory and research.

At the policy level, such tools should help think about prisons, probation, community penalties, situational or offender-oriented prevention and crime-reduction implications of wider social policy in equivalent terms no longer isolated by terminological and cultural domains – what they do, how they work, what problems they are most suited to tackle, how they should be compared and contrasted.

At the practice level, the tools should help practitioners think about how to draw on *all* the available methods of CSCR to tackle specific local and national crime problems. This should apply whether these are provided by national programmes for implementation of policy, by statutory law enforcement, judicial and penal bodies, local partnership plans, private security services or by the everyday acts of ordinary people for informal self-protection and social control.

The tools should facilitate systematic envisaging and choosing of soundly specified and evidence-based options for intervention to match the crime problem and its context, whilst aiding communication between diverse stakeholders. (Here, the aim is to move considerably beyond the 'practical, but limited' frameworks such as the problem analysis triangle (features of the victim, features of the location, features of the offender). These have value as an elementary teaching and thinking aid in the short term but, if seen as the last word, constrain the development of more sophisticated and ambitious approaches.)

There is a need to foster the operational integration of diverse approaches – for example tackling a severe local car theft problem by resident surveillance, fitting of vehicle security devices, improving security in car parks, police patrolling, crackdown on illegal activity by car breakers, targeting of high-rate offenders and schemes to address offender motivation. It is currently rare for such 'combined operations' to be pursued, although some notable efforts have been made in the field of repeat victimisation.

The tools should also help practitioners and their managers identify key aspects of their monitoring and quality assurance action. More broadly speaking, they should contribute to the development of a professional discipline of CSCR. This should help reconcile two desirable aspects of practice, which up to now have often been sought at each other's expense: local autonomy in addressing local problems, and national standards of quality.

At the theory, research and evaluation level, the tools for thought should act as a two-way conduit between theory and practice. They should also help identify where theories overlap or conflict, and where gaps exist. The framework should do this by providing a common language to describe the elements of the various theories of crime and map out the elementary processes which the theories cover, or collectively fail to cover. It should help evaluators plan what to look for in advance of implementation, and afterwards help them systematically uncover the reasons for its success or failure. This applies whether the evaluators are working in a local context of Best Value, and the Audit Commission's (1999) concept of a learning culture, or within a national context of 'what works'.

In support of all these tasks, it is essential that the terms defined in the framework below have a logical relationship with one another. This implies that inevitably, there will be times when it is necessary to unpack the meaning of particular concepts in some detail. However, this is not pedantic but practical. Relying on connotations and traditional (mis)understandings will simply perpetuate the problems.

It is also worth stating what the framework does *not* do. It makes absolutely no assumptions about the (cost) effectiveness of any method of achieving community safety or crime control. In mapping all the methods of CSCR it largely only covers their *intended* functions. (Not all are effective, of course, in particular contexts. Some may be generically ineffective – as *Reducing offending*, the recent Home Office review made clear. They may even at times exacerbate crime or feelings of insecurity.)

While such deliberate agnosticism on (cost) effectiveness may seem odd given the cost-effectiveness orientation of the national Crime Reduction Programme and the Best Value equivalent in local partnership CSCR, our state of knowledge of 'what works' is currently so limited that it would be presumptuous to rule out any approach completely. 'What is thinkable' should be a far wider set of CSCR activities than 'what is currently known to be cost effective'. Constructing the framework is therefore an entirely separate exercise from evaluating the activities which are described by it.

The framework favours no particular theory of the causes of crime. Instead, it aims to provide a means of expressing any such theory in common terms, and of making diverse theories, covering adjacent parts of the map, join up. Nor does it promote, say, situational prevention at the expense of offender-oriented prevention. Rather, it tries to bring these approaches together.

A framework: the conjunction of criminal opportunity

Describing a framework which does justice to something so rich and multifaceted as CSCR, and aims to meet the utility criteria set out above, cannot be done in one move. It must be built up in layers, starting with a brief look at how social problems are defined as crimes, and a comparison of the alternative perspectives on CSCR:

community safety, prevention, reduction and control of crime all cover more or less the same activities, but adopt different perspectives on criminal event or careers, and time frame – past, present and future orientation.

Crime prevention is then defined as intervention in the causes of criminal events and the generic situational and offender-oriented causes are mapped out as the 'conjunction of criminal opportunity'.

Turning to the interventions in each of these causes, crime prevention is covered in two main ways:

- in particular – a review of the generic interventions at the disposal of prevention and

- in general:
  i)   the core elements of action – intervention, implementation, and insertion;
  ii) doing prevention at different procedural levels – operational practice and policy, capacity-building and gearing up against crime.

Crime reduction is then considered and defined more broadly than prevention. It covers 'present-tense' intervention directly in criminal events and the halting of their further consequences, as well as 'future-tense' intervention in their causes. There is special consideration of how crime reduction (and by implication, prevention) relates to the formal process of the Criminal Justice System, and to the wider work of the CJS agencies.

Finally, a somewhat different strategic perspective is considered – crime control. This focuses on the concept of keeping crime risks below tolerance thresholds, defined with reference to the consequences of criminal events on individuals and community.

Defining social problems as crimes

Every problem faced by society requires an appropriate blend of generic solutions: care, control, conflict resolution and collaboration. Defining problem behaviour as a crime not only places it firmly in the realm of formal control (alongside infringements that require regulation), but immediately presupposes how it should be controlled, and by whom. (This can happen as much at practice level as at policy level – an incident of disorder reported to the police may get an enforcement response; the same incident reported to the local social work department may receive a welfare response.)

This has sometimes closed minds to the wider range of solutions now envisaged under the heading of crime reduction and community safety. Partnership approaches can be seen as an attempt to overcome some of the disadvantages of rigid division of labour in handling these cross-cutting problems whilst preserving the advantages. A wider review of solutions to social problems should not rule out the possibility, for some offences, of decriminalisation (the behaviour is no longer defined as an offence), or offence abolition (the offending behaviour is no longer possible – for example, replacing vehicle excise duty with increased fuel tax so that driving untaxed can no longer happen). Of course, the opposite strategy – criminalisation of previously legal actions – is also an important policy option, both nationally, and locally through bye-laws.

Alternative perspectives

The criminal event/crime risk focus has to be reconciled with the criminal career focus of criminal justice disposals and with certain kinds of crime prevention or reduction – particularly criminality prevention. Of these two perspectives, event/risk takes priority in the present framework – because it fits best with crime as a problem in the community, best draws together a unified picture of causes and thus gives greatest scope for considering alternative cures and comparing their effectiveness and cost effectiveness. However, the framework does aim to encompass careers.

Crime prevention, which is forward-looking, has to be linked in a logical way to the somewhat different concepts of crime reduction and control. Prevention and reduction must also be linked to the retrospective aspects of criminal justice and victim support systems. This connection follows from both the scope of the national Crime Reduction Programme, the general nature of the local community safety partnerships and specific criminal justice provisions that form much of the Crime and Disorder Act.

Crime prevention and reduction are often implemented in the service of the wider goal of community safety. This is a rather elusive concept and it may be premature to define it too closely. However, community safety is perhaps best seen as an aspect of quality of life: people, individually and collectively, are protected as far as possible from hazards or threats resulting from the criminal or anti-social behaviour of others, and are equipped or helped to cope with those they do experience. It should enable them to pursue, and obtain, fullest benefits from their social and economic lives without fear or hindrance from crime and disorder. Further discussion of community safety along these lines may be found at *www.homeoffice.gov.uk/cdact/cstrng5.htm*.

Underlying much of the confusion between terms and perspectives are the questions of time frame, and the particular criminal event in focus. Reaction to *past* crimes prevents *future* crimes – victims shut the stable door before the next horse bolts and offenders are deterred through anticipation of future punishment. Intervention in *present*, ongoing, crimes similarly prevents future offending. Likewise, if a crime preventer – perhaps a security guard in a store – is attacked in the course of one crime, shop theft, then they become the target of a *fresh* crime: assault. Therefore, subsidiary crimes may be committed during preparation for the principal offence (as with stealing the getaway car for a robbery) or afterwards (such as intimidation of witnesses).

Related to these issues is the confusion which frequently slips in over the status of a particular CSCR action. The terms crime prevention and crime reduction can both be taken to refer either to aspiration (we aim to prevent/reduce crime by 20 per cent); to activity (we are introducing these crime prevention/reduction measures); to attributable achievement (our scheme has worked – we have successfully prevented/reduced crime); and even to accident (the compulsory motorcycle crash-helmet law has serendipitously prevented/reduced a significant amount of motorcycle theft).

Crime and crime prevention

Crime prevention focuses on the future. It is about reducing the risk of occurrence and potential seriousness of crime and disorder events by intervening in their causes. These causes are many and complex, and can be quite remote – such as a child's early upbringing, socio-economic influences generating deprivation and inequality, or even the market price for car spares. However, the remoter influences all have to act through chains of cause and effect, which ultimately channel through a common set of immediate precursors combining to generate the criminal or disorderly event.

In a 'universal story' of the criminal event, an offender encounters, seeks out or engineers a crime situation comprising a suitable target, in a favourable environment and in the absence of capable preventers (or guardians). This can be called the conjunction of criminal opportunity. Before we can discuss crime prevention itself we must first expand the view of this conjunction, to get a clear picture of what we seek to prevent (Figure 2.1).

The conjunction of criminal opportunity – a map of the immediate precursors of crime

For a crime to occur the following elements must be in place.

The potential offender, whether an individual, an informal group or a corporate body, must be ready, willing (or, depending on the law, merely negligent), able and equipped for crime:

- Having a predisposition for crime (criminality – longer-term, personality-based influences involving excitation or the absence of inhibition, such as aggression, antisocial attitudes, lack of conscience, criminal self-image, habits or 'standing decisions to offend' such as drug addiction).

- Lacking the resources to avoid crime (such as social skills and ability to gain a legitimate living).

- Being currently ready to offend (shorter-term influences relating to current life circumstances and recent events such as motivation by boredom, shortage of

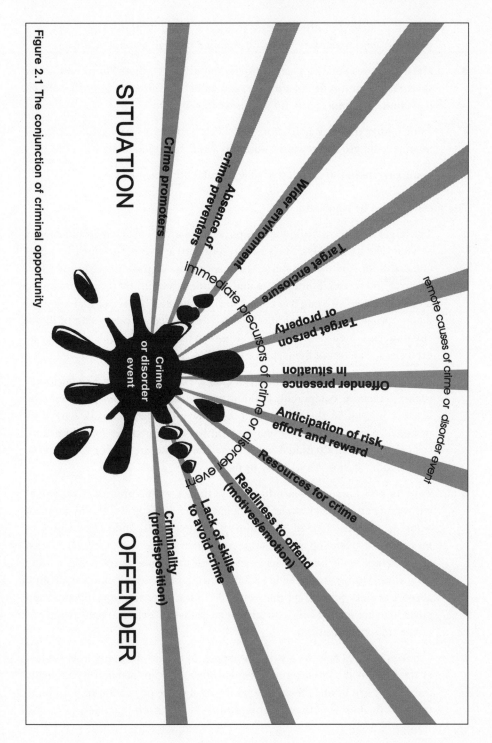

Figure 2.1 The conjunction of criminal opportunity

money or need for drugs; being in a conflicting relationship; being in a particular emotional state; being disinhibited through alcohol or drugs).

- Having the resources for crime (for example, physical, technical and social skills, inside knowledge of attractive and vulnerable targets, criminal contacts, and crime facilitators such as tools or weapons).

- Anticipating that risk and effort and likely feelings of guilt and shame are minimal enough, and reward sufficiently large, to decide to act.

- Being present in the situation or able to influence it remotely.

The situation must be conducive:

- The target of crime may be human, physical property, data, environmental or service-related. Targets must be present, attractive or provocative, and vulnerable (in the passive sense – susceptible to damage or injury, forgery, removal and so on). Some crimes and disorderly events, by their definition in law, do not involve a target at all, but merely comprise behaviour that is judged inappropriate (disorder, nuisance), or self-destructive; or possession of illegal substances which can harm the possessor or others, such as drugs or explosives. The rest of the picture still applies.

- The target may be sited within a vulnerable and perhaps attractive enclosure such as a fenced compound, building or safe. In some cases these may be layered one within the other. Enclosures have (by definition) demarked or protected perimeters, official entry or exit sites (or interfaces for transaction, such as a computer terminal or cash machine), and an interior that may be protected by alarms, surveillance or patrols.

- Targets and enclosures are located within a wider physical and social environment which may attract or generate crime. Logistically, the environment helps the offender (access, concealment, escape), and hinders preventers. It may motivate offending, particularly through setting the scene for conflict (such as thin party walls between flats, giving rise to disputes over noise; narrow gangways causing unavoidable jostling; uncertain ownership and use of land; absence of rules governing behaviour). Or it may otherwise bring offender and target together (particularly through routine activities such as at railway stations or entertainment districts).

- Crime preventers must be absent, incapable, or at least not credible as a threat at the time of the crime or afterwards. Preventers are active, or potentially active: they can be anyone with either a formal crime prevention responsibility (police, probation officers, community safety staff, concierges – and increasingly, active computer software, for example in detecting and responding to fraudulent transaction patterns); or an informal responsibility (residents, parents, teachers, employees in general, even passers-by simply *being* there, or exercising legally-sanctioned powers such as citizen's arrest or reasonable force in defence).

- In advance of the criminal event, preventers can reduce its likelihood by shaping the situation (by locking doors, for example) or by influencing the offender (perhaps, by applying social pressure not to steal). They can intervene during the event (defending themselves or protecting their own property, or that of others) or react after it. The preventers' *potential* to intervene and react can influence the current crime event through the offender's anticipation ('Will the victim or passers-by overpower me? Will I be identified to the police?'). Preventers can also influence the next event by the action taken (as victims securing their house against repeat burglary, or reporting an assault to the police in the hope of initiating detection, criminal proceedings and punishment).

- Crime promoters may be present or exert influence in other ways. In contrast to preventers, promoters have a role in increasing the likelihood of a criminal event through careless or provocative behaviour, encouragement and highlighting an offender's reputation (including labelling as a criminal), or through more practical contributions such as criminal service providers supplying weapons or buying stolen goods.

Note that the situation need not be a physical one but could be remote, such as an interface with a computer network hosting a benefit system or other vulnerable and attractive target. Offenders can make obscene telephone calls or hack a computer via the Internet. Preventers may be linked to the situation by CCTV. Promoters may have 'wound the offender up' some time before the crime is committed. Note also that victims of crime play remarkably diverse roles: owner of the target of property crime, target of crime against the person, legal complainant, crime preventer and (in the case of carelessness or provocation) crime promoter. In the rest of this chapter, victim means human target or owner of target property – the rest comes under the active preventer or promoter roles. In a street fight, which combatant is later assigned the role of victim or offender may depend on the turn of events and subsequent judgements as to who used unreasonable force or who provoked whom.

Criminal events (and their prevention) are so complex and dynamic because of the interactions between these immediate precursors – the active roles of offender, preventer and promoter each perceiving, anticipating and dealing with the others and with the target, enclosure and environment. The conjunction itself is brought together through social, economic and psychological processes ranging from the structure of society and the market, to channelling by transport and the rest of the built environment, and to the victims' and offenders' current circumstances, routine activities and lifestyle. Remote causes in particular rarely operate through just a single, analytical ray of Figure 2.1.

From the offender's perspective, the aim is to exploit or otherwise cope with the situation, using available resources to maximise material, psychological or social reward from the crime whilst minimising effort, guilt and the risk of detection, punishment and shame. This process ranges from the rational, sophisticated and organised planning and completion of a range of preparatory and consummatory scenes (seeking out target bank, stealing getaway car, executing robbery, escaping and disposing of the proceeds), to the opportunist scanning for a house with an open window, or to an impulsive violent retaliation for an insult in a bar.

The concept of opportunity has usually been associated with purely situational crime prevention, but an open window three floors up is only an opportunity for an offender who is agile and courageous. It is worth bearing in mind, therefore, that opportunities are made as much by offenders' resources for creating or exploiting a situation as by the situation itself. (Hence reference to the conjunction of opportunity.) The outcome of one crime event will of course influence the offender's inclination to commit more, whether through a temporary decision to rest until the police crackdown is over, or a more permanent 'standing' decision to desist because on average, the rewards are significantly outstripped by the effort and risk.

Theories of crime cover the gamut of the structures and processes alluded to above. However remote and subtle the causes they envision, it should without exception be possible to re-express them in terms of how they generate or influence the various immediate precursors of the criminal event, or how they help bring the precursors together to produce the conjunction of criminal opportunity. The conjunction of criminal opportunity itself is only a theory in a minimalist sense – indeed, it is more of a truism, a detailed description of what makes up a criminal event. But it is, in effect, where all substantive theories of crime have to converge or project; the point of the map at which gaps, conflicts and overlaps can be identified.

Disrupting the conjunction: the methods of crime prevention

From the preventer's perspective the aim is to intervene to disrupt the conjunction of criminal opportunity, either by changing the situational or offender-related precursors in advance of the criminal event, or by preventing them coming together. This is illustrated in Figure 2.2.

There are two ways of looking at crime prevention, both necessary for clear understanding, practical competence and good research and evaluation. We begin with the particular, reviewing the range of interventions and the methods that bring them

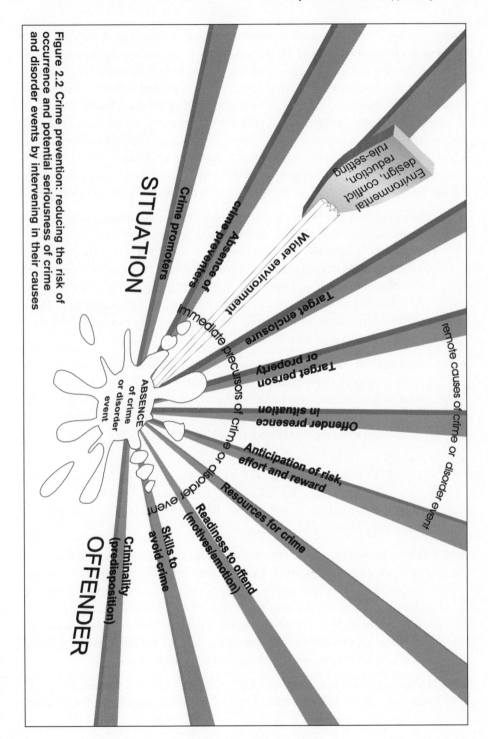

Figure 2.2 Crime prevention: reducing the risk of occurrence and potential seriousness of crime and disorder events by intervening in their causes

about; and move on to the general, covering the core elements of preventive action common to all interventions, and the levels at which the actionit can be conducted. The general is a rather less exciting topic than the particular, but neglecting it, whether in the practice of running a scheme, or in setting up the local and national infrastructure to support preventive action on the ground, risks much misdirected effort.

Returning to the conjunction of criminal opportunity, we can map on to the immediate causal precursors, the corresponding types of crime prevention interventions that disrupt or divert them at some point upstream (Figure 2.3). Each intervention is achieved by various methods – examples of which are listed below.

On the *offender-oriented* side, six types of intervention can be distinguished:

- Early or remedial intervention (alternatively criminality prevention or tackling the roots of criminality). This includes influencing the potential to offend by intervening in early life (through families, schools and peers) to change the trajectories of development and the 'programming in' by family and subculture of motivations, values and emotions. It also includes remedial post-conviction interventions such as control of sexuality or reduction of persistent theft. Many of these interventions act by establishing inhibitory processes in the offender – such as conscience, or a more general curbing of impulsivity.

- Supplying offenders with resources to avoid offending, principally through cognitive or social skills enhancement. This is a more positive set of approaches aimed at helping offenders obtain desired ends by legitimate means (such as the ability to obtain a job through improved competence at reading and writing), and teaching them how to avoid or manage conflict.

- Changing current life circumstances of individuals (such as debt, poor entertainment facilities, membership of offending peer groups, or reputation for aggression). These may be influencing their current state of motivation, emotion or decisions to offend, or be bringing them into conflicting relationships or into contact with promoters.

- Restricting resources for crime that offenders can bring to bear on the crime target or use to deal with crime preventers and logistically difficult environments. (This may include anything from control of firearms, to clearing bottles and bricks from downtown streets before the weekend, limiting use of colour photocopiers, crackdowns on fences of stolen goods, denial of passwords or decryption software, regulating the purchase of night vision goggles, or keeping inside knowledge secure or traceable).

- Deterrence and discouragement – influencing the offender's decision to commit crime by increasing the perceived risk of arrest and punishment or informal

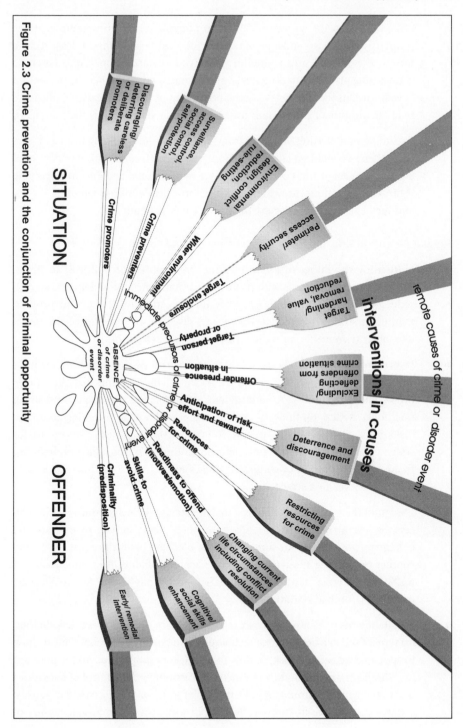

Figure 2.3 Crime prevention and the conjunction of criminal opportunity

censure; increasing perceived effort to commit crime (for example, using property marking to render stolen goods unsaleable or so they at least require hours to repaint), and reducing perceived reward from crime (such as confiscating profits from drug dealing). It is immaterial whether the perception is valid or illusory. There is also the possibility of disabling excuses offenders may offer to others and to their own conscience ('shoplifting is theft' notices).

• Excluding or deflecting offenders from crime situation – ranging from stopping more than two children entering a shop together or incapacitation of convicted criminals through imprisonment, curfew or electronic tagging, to supplying legitimate attractions elsewhere which divert offenders from tempting targets and may constructively occupy their time (such as youth clubs).

On the *situational* side, the focus of preventive methods is on:

• Hardening the target of crime (making banknotes more difficult to forge, supplying security guards with protective armour, encrypting data and so on); reducing its value (through property identification or changes to product marketing strategy) or concealment and disguise, or removal of the target altogether (removable car radios, cashless public telephones).

• Improving perimeter, access or interior security of the target enclosure – respectively fencing-in storage yards, locking windows and installing posts before shop fronts to stop ram-raiders; strengthening doors and improving their locks, setting up firewalls against computer hackers, screening computer disks for viruses, screening people for weapons on entry to airports or for stolen goods on exit from shops; detecting intruders inside a factory, in-house fraud or the operation of computer viruses missed when the infected disk or internet file was first screened.

• Design of the wider environment – making residential neighbourhoods or city centres less attractive logistically as a place for criminals to operate, by enhancing possibilities for surveillance, or blocking paths of retreat. Reducing conflict by tackling motivating aspects such as colliding flows of pedestrian traffic, or uncertain territorial boundaries; or by rule-setting (as in libraries, camp-sites, football stadia).

• Facilitating the presence, motivation and capability of crime preventers: in their exercise of self-defence (combat techniques, avoidance of personal danger, how to spot a particular con-trick, or how to alert fellow shopkeepers to the presence of a shoplifting gang); in their perimeter, access or interior control of enclosures and in the wider environment of formal or informal surveillance (police patrols, security guards, Neighbourhood Watch); in social control (informal censure of young people's misbehaviour, getting peer members, family or other 'intimate handlers' to dissuade or divert the offender from crime).

- Aids for preventers, including spyholes in doors for access control, CCTV and street lighting for wider environments, or tamper-evident seals on food jars. The effectiveness and motivation of a preventer may also be boosted by clearly marked territorial boundaries, as with Defensible Space, or by simple warnings such as 'beware – people are passing off forged banknotes in this area'. Formal preventers, such as police officers, may have special legal powers and duties to intervene.

- Discouraging, deterring or alerting deliberate, reckless or inadvertent crime promoters (disruption of markets for stolen goods, police crackdowns on fences, publicity campaigns of the practical 'lock it or lose it' type or the moral 'don't ask someone to drink and drive', training in social skills for ticket inspectors on trains in order to reduce assaults, and so on).

Figure 2.3, and the above description, are of course much simplified. Even quite a narrow crime prevention method may intervene through several disruptions simultaneously: target hardening may both physically block a crime and discourage the offender from attempting it; surveillance may supply crime preventers who can then intervene during the approach to the target and can also deter in anticipation). An intervention often has parallel or 'interlocking' effects on the situational and offender sides simultaneously. Thus, improving perimeter security may make it easier for crime preventers to exclude offenders from the crime situation.

The disruption achieved may not always be the disruption intended; the knowledge of the mere act of installing a preventive scheme in an area may be enough to deter offenders, whether or not the scheme's intervention worked as planned. What appears at first glance to be a single method may, when seen in close-up, comprise a mix of interventions; a 'motor' club for convicted joyriders, for example, may involve remedial changes to criminal attitudes, supplying skills for holding down a legitimate job and finding constructive ways of occupying time. Sometimes many methods are combined in more or less holistic packages that address a number of causes together.

Some uncertainty is always attached to whether the intervention will succeed in preventing the criminal event. The intervention may not be intense enough to do so, or other influences may switch the causal stream back to its original channel. Hence, it is sensible to talk of interventions causing reductions in risk of criminal events rather than inevitably knocking those events out. This also helps bridge the gap between the single-event perspective used here for purposes of clarity, and the fact that in the real world prevention acts probabilistically against classes of events (such as 'all possible criminal events which may occur against parked cars in this car park', or broader or narrower variations).

The point of intervention may be causally remote from specific criminal events (community-level action to influence children's upbringing, or adjusting production and marketing processes for computer memory chips), or it may be immediate (occupying specific young people's leisure time more constructively to prevent vandalism, rehabilitating specific offenders post-conviction, or installing screens in buses to prevent assaults on drivers).

Remote interventions may have the strategic benefit of influencing a wider class of criminal events, but may also have the disadvantage of greater uncertainty, there being 'many a slip 'twixt cup and lip'. Immediate interventions reduce the risk of a much narrower class of event – as with much situational prevention – but offer the prospect of a much more intense and targeted treatment. However, the promise of greater impact may not always be realised. Such intensity can bring with it the possibility of displacement, recidivism of offending and offender replacement (arrest Mr Big and Mr Not-so-big takes his place). With remoter interventions, however, the causes which eventually lead people to offend may not have been conclusively established. The only indications of where to intervene may be so-called risk factors – positive correlates of offending such as poor parental discipline – and protective factors or negative correlates, such as good social bonding with teachers.

Crime prevention in general

Making interventions happen requires the familiar concept of implementation and the new concept of 'insertion'. These additional core elements of crime prevention action are identified below. The view is then widened to distinguish between different types of procedural levels of action within which the core elements are conducted or supported. These are operational practice and policy (concerned with the here and now of crime problems), capacity-building and gearing up against crime.

Core elements of crime prevention action – intervention, implementation and insertion

Intervention (fully discussed in the previous section) remains the most important, defining element of crime prevention action, but as practitioners will attest, a typical preventive scheme, such as a local burglary reduction project, involves far more. Crime prevention interventions themselves have to be implemented – set up and perhaps maintained (such as an alarm or CCTV system).

Implementation focuses on the relevant actions on the ground that lead to the intervention and the processes that lead to the actions. Implementation has methods of its own such as 'how to select appropriate locks', 'how to do a crime prevention site survey', or 'how to conduct a course of treatment for convicted repeat burglars'. Some interventions, particularly in the criminal justice context, are implemented as routine, heavily embedded in other organisational procedures, rather than as distinct, one-off schemes. Examples are police patrolling, treatment of offenders in prison, or supervision of probation clients. Even here, though, the introduction of problem-oriented approaches mean that routines are not what they used to be.; and within some routines, cases – such as offenders receiving treatment – have distinct boundaries.

The professional preventer may intervene directly in the chain of cause and effect leading to the criminal event, by installing an alarm system or working to reduce a youth's aggression, for example. More often, the professional's role is to act at a distance – to motivate, inform and assist other, often informal, preventers (such as place managers or 'intimate handlers' of potential young offenders, including families and teachers) in implementing and/or maintaining the intervention. Acting at a distance is not in itself an intervention, as defined above, and could be termed insertion. Methods of insertion typically involve setting up local working groups, running publicity campaigns, of the 'lock it or lose it' kind, or supplying information packs. This requires an understanding of the perspective, and resources of the front-line preventers themselves, and of the incentives that can acceptably and effectively be manipulated to get them to act, or indeed to change from promoters to preventers.

Thus insertion by professional preventers is intended to lead to implementation of interventions by others. These then disrupt the conjunction, reduce the risk of crime occurring and hopefully succeed in preventing some classes of criminal (or disorder) events, at least reducing the seriousness of those that do happen. This absence of criminal events may have consequences such as knock-on improvements in individual or collective quality of life (a core aspect of community safety), regeneration and wealth creation. This sequence is illustrated in Figure 2.4, a universal story of a crime prevention scheme.

The methods employed in inserting, implementing and intervening act on or through a diverse set of entities in the real world, ranging from the individual offender or target, to features of society as a whole. These entities can be described in terms of a range of social levels:

● the individual – individual target, environment or offender;

● family and intimates;

● the peer group;

● institutions – schools, work organisations;

● the media;

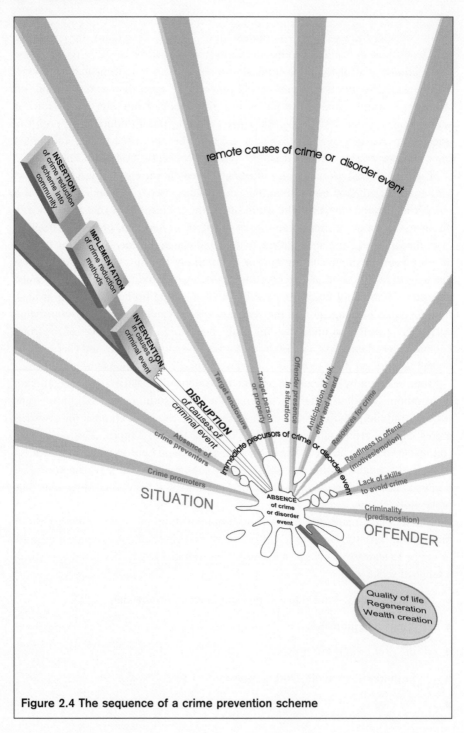

Figure 2.4 The sequence of a crime prevention scheme

- the area of residence, leisure or work;

- the community, involving some kind of common interest, with multiple role relationships and networks;

- the societal level, involving processes operating within society as a whole, such as employment, manufacturing, distribution and transport;

- and, inevitably, the global level.

Interventions in the causes of criminal events at one of these levels may lead to reductions in risk, and ultimately in the frequency of criminal events, at other levels (for example, intervention in the criminal subculture of a local community may reduce the offending of its individual members). Likewise, wider benefits may occur at still other levels, for example, a reduction in individual risk may improve collective quality of life.

A public-health distinction widely-used in crime prevention further structures the choice of an intervention's subject:

- primary – focusing on the general population of potential offenders, or of potential crime situations or on the human and material targets of crime;

- secondary – focusing on people at particular risk of offending, on targets at risk of victimisation or on places at risk of setting the scene for victimisation;

- tertiary – focusing on those *already* convicted or victimised, or on targets and scenes of existing crime (linking to the concepts of repeat victimisation, repeat offending, and hot-spots).

Up to now, these distinctions have mainly been made at the individual social level, as in the illustrations above. But there is no reason why they could not be applied to any social level – for example 'the general population of institutions', 'areas at risk', or 'communities with a manifest criminal subculture'.

Doing crime prevention – procedural levels

The classic CSCR activity is the territorial scheme. Here, action implemented usually has a clear outcome objective in terms of reducing specific types of crime in specific places. Other common types of activity involve preventing crimes which might be committed in the future by specific offenders in the course of their criminal career. However diverse, these activities function at what can be called the operational level. This involves deploying currently available capacity to address particular crime or criminal problems, which may occur in specific places or may be committed by specific individuals, in the here and now.

A great deal of CSCR action, however, functions at one remove from the here and now. In many cases the formally planned and implemented actions and outputs of a scheme stop at insertion, and the intention is that the preventers out in the community take over the relay baton to bring the scheme to implementation, intervention, disruption and outcome. At one extreme, such CSCR actions have quite specific courses to run, and funds and other resources are handed over to the preventers, with the usual strings attached. At the other extreme, the actions may comprise little more than raising awareness, or making self-help material, such as property-marking kits or packs for 'what to do if you suspect your child is on drugs', generally available to the public to act on as they choose. In all cases, it is not the intervention itself being supplied, but the capacity for implementing interventions – the capacity-building level of action. A parallel level to capacity building, of particular importance to insertion, is that of motivation – including creating and manipulating incentives to encourage preventers and discourage crime promoters.

Needed capacities may not always exist ready-made. A third level, even more removed from operations, covers identifying the requirement for new capacities and developing them. This can be called gearing up against crime. We now look more closely at the operational, capacity-building and gearing-up levels in turn.

The operational levels – practice and policy

Most of the discussion so far on crime prevention, both in particular and in general, has centred on the operational level, but plenty more remains to be said about it. In identifying how crime prevention is best effected, experience suggests that a cookbook approach – rigidly applying preventive methods drawn from a limited repertoire – is inadequate. The ability to apply theoretically sound first principles in designing an intervention is vital.

Sometimes, however, what is special and worth emulating about a CSCR scheme is less the intervention itself – which may be familiar, and of purely local relevance – than the intelligent process by which it was arrived at and put into place. More generally, experience has shown that insertion and implementation deliver the most effective interventions for the crime problem in question, and the most cost-effective outcomes, when embedded in a wider procedure. This procedure has become known simply as the preventive process, a term which has close affiliations with problem-oriented policing. At the local level it involves several stages:

- Homing in on specific crime and disorder problems identified and targeted through a strategic audit and target-setting process, by collecting and analysing more detailed local information .

- Local setting of objectives and quantitative CSCR targets for reducing crime or keeping it below specified levels.

- Devising preventive action closely tailored to the specific circumstances, with interventions based on evidence of effectiveness and application of theoretically sound principles.

- Inserting and implementing the selected intervention on the selected crime problem at the appropriate social levels.

- Managing the progress of the action through
  i)   internal monitoring of insertion and implementation,
  ii) external monitoring of performance against CSCR targets and
  iii) local evaluation of impact and cost effectiveness for accountability and Best Value purposes.

- Evaluating the conduct of the preventive process itself, and the attributable impact of the outputs on outcomes, both for immediate management purposes and in support of the more strategic procedural levels (capacity building and gearing up, described below).

Routine interventions such as police patrolling or probation supervision will have an equivalent set of processes – more similar if a problem-oriented approach is adopted. A related approach to the local preventive process is involved when identifying and dealing with crime problems best solved at the national or international level. Typically this embraces interventions involving design of cars and other 'hot products', and design of services and procedures vulnerable to crimes such as fraud.

Many aspects of the local preventive process have already been discussed, especially inserting and implementing the intervention. Although the intention is not to go exhaustively through the rest, it is worth covering other aspects that can benefit from the clarity offered by the conjunction of criminal opportunity framework.

From an objective-setting perspective, selecting which crime problems to tackle may not always be easy to articulate. Likewise, when practitioners are planning their preventive action, and trying to learn from prior experience, information retrieval from a 'what works' database will be inefficient unless there is some uniformity of nomenclature. To aid these activities, the scope of a scheme can be defined in terms of any of the immediate precursors of the criminal event. For example, reducing crime against particular targets, in particular environments, committed by specific types of offenders, using particular MOs and other resources for offending. The dimensions of primary/secondary/tertiary, and social level can also be used.

Experience has shown that in many cases, the more specific the focus, the more likely interventions are to succeed. However, inclusiveness may work better in other cases, particularly where causes of crime are wide-ranging (for example, the local offenders are all adaptable generalists, there is a pervasive criminal subculture, or socio-economic causes influence criminal predisposition in a broad way). Paradoxically, such inclusiveness, particularly when combined with holistic interventions and intervening in remoter causes, requires an even greater clarity and professionalism, to understand which causes of crime are involved, and what the broad package of interventions are aiming to achieve, by which causal mechanisms. Without this, holistic action is at particular risk of degenerating into superficial and ineffectual efforts with drifting objectives.

From managerial and evaluative perspectives, human or material resources can be fed in by professional preventers and others at any stage during insertion, implementation and intervention. The products of these stages are activities (such as confronting offending behaviour through role-play) and outputs (such as the number of young offenders exposed to a confrontation experience of a certain recognised standard). It is these which deliver the intervention. The disruptions caused by the interventions amount to impacts on risk of criminal events (for example, as measured by the number of offenders graduating from the course who pass some test criterion of acknowledging their wrongdoing), which may be construed as an intermediate outcome. The ultimate crime prevention outcome is the set of 'non-events' themselves. The last may confer direct cost savings to the victim, community and state, and their consequences may give wider benefits in terms of improved quality of life, economic regeneration and wealth creation.

From the managerial perspective, outputs, outcomes and wider benefits can be viewed as the objectives, of various kinds, aspired to by those who fund, manage or implement the scheme. From the evaluative perspective they are the attributable effects actually achieved by that scheme. Figure 2.5 shows these additional concepts mapped on to the previous diagram.

A number of feedback loops are built into the preventive process – some short and elementary to guide immediate tactical action, others longer and wider in scope to inform strategy. Internal monitoring of insertion and implementation involves ensuring that the various objectives set for activities and outputs are being met or are on course – including quality assurance of the actions undertaken – and taking action to correct those which are not. External monitoring of performance involves ensuring that crime reduction targets are being met, (such as 'a 30 per cent fall in vehicle crime'). A full-blown local evaluation with attribution of cause and effect, (such as 'vehicle crime fell by 40 per cent and of this, 25 per cent can be attributed to the scheme'), may be conducted to ensure accountability and foster the achievement of Best Value by informing decisions to continue, modify, expand or replicate the scheme elsewhere within the partnership. Such local evaluations need not be particularly sophisticated, unlike those done for gearing-up purposes – building up the strategic knowledge base of 'what works'.

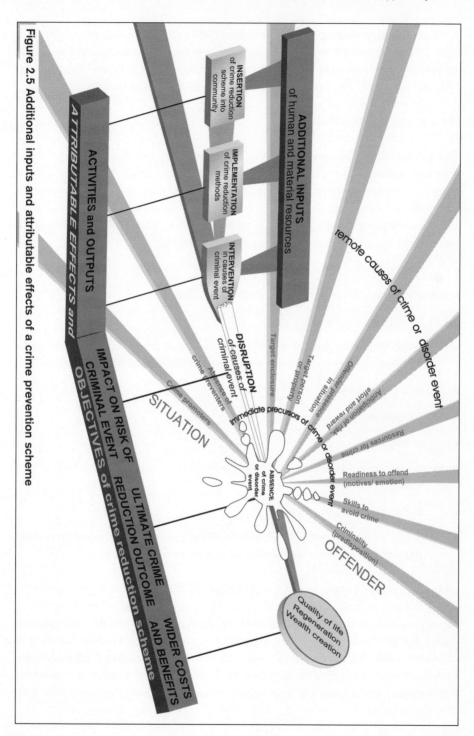

Figure 2.5 Additional inputs and attributable effects of a crime prevention scheme

What has been covered so far is best described as day-to-day operational practice. Such action is now likely to be formally encompassed within a wider strategic community safety process set out in the Guidance on Audits for the Crime and Disorder Act 1998. This could be called the operational policy level.

The capacity-building level

This involves action to deploy currently available resources to give particular crime preventers the capacity to reduce crime as and when they need it. Such action may be instigated in response to feedback from internal monitoring or external monitoring and evaluation of operational schemes. The crime preventers who receive the capacity may either be professionals, or those in the wider society whom the professionals are encouraging to act. The resources in question may include:

- realisation that crime can be prevented;

- information on crime risks, and offenders' MOs;

- awareness of types of solution;

- policy expertise – how to handle policy issues of acceptability, such as trade-offs between privacy and prevention, or equity in distributing CSCR resources;

- technical know-how;

- equipment;

- money;

- other infrastructure such as setting up community organisation, or ring-around warning networks;

- leadership skills;

- access to incentives to influence 'subsidiary' preventers and disincentives for promoters, and know-how for applying it in acceptable ways.

Obviously, some of these – particularly in the top half of the list – are specific to CSCR. They can best be described under the umbrella-term of competencies – education and training for a professional discipline of CSCR – and the underpinning knowledge that supports the competence. Others are fairly general in nature, merely requiring sufficient priority and funds. Establishing community organisations (community development of residents' associations, for example) can be activity which is particularly challenging and prolonged. It may be motivated by wider concerns than CSCR alone.

At its widest, CSCR links to empowerment of citizens and institutions to reduce crime and disorder through informal social control and self-protective behaviour. It also connects with conflict resolution and depends on broader social and economic policy and practice – for example the reduction of some sources of criminal motivation in the short term, and criminal predisposition in the longer term, by tackling social exclusion. It follows that the competencies and knowledge of the profession as a whole – covering both principles of prevention and how to apply them in these very different contexts – need to be extremely wide-ranging. But the central defining features of professional practice in this area must be: competence in how to carry out, or supervise, the various stages of the preventive process; a thorough underpinning knowledge of

- the causes of criminal and disorderly events, risk and protective factors

- the offender's perspective on crime opportunities – risk of punishment, effort and reward

- evidence-based interventions, and how these work in particular contexts;

- and of course, like any other profession, a conceptual framework to knit all the competencies and knowledge together into a functional whole.

Gearing up against crime: catching up and keeping up with changing opportunities and adaptive offenders

The gearing-up level involves action to identify, and remedy, qualitative gaps in society's armoury of capacities. These are resources which cannot simply be made available by disseminating existing knowledge, or distributing and paying for existing materials from stock; they first need to be designed and developed. The gaps in capacity relate to crime problems which may be current, emergent or anticipated.

Again, gearing up may be instigated in response to feedback from internal or external monitoring or evaluation of operational schemes. This will happen less often than excursions into capacity-building, which in turn are likely to occur less often than operational policy and practice adjustments. Gearing up covers all the capacities discussed above – except these are to be developed, rather than supplied *ex stock*. In the case of incentives for preventers and disincentives for promoters, gearing up will include creating fresh rewards and sanctions where existing ones are inadequate. These might take the form of a law to criminalise a new harmful activity, support the collection of evidence or boost police powers; or softer approaches (Pease, 1998) such as naming and shaming, or citations of good citizenship to individuals or companies.

Current crime problems – strategic evaluation

There is plenty of work still to be done to fill current gaps in the capacity we can bestow on practitioners and less formally involved preventers. The list of competencies and underpinning knowledge for crime prevention as a professional discipline, discussed above, remains largely a shopping list. The accumulated body of knowledge on 'what works', how best to implement it, in what context, and at what cost effectiveness in particular is extremely patchy (and indeed it is the aim of the national Crime Reduction Programme to begin to remedy this systematically). Crime prevention education and training needs further raw material of knowledge and competence to impart if it is to play its part in supporting initiatives like the Crime Reduction Programme and the new local Crime Reduction Partnerships.

We have already seen how evaluation of impact and process can be conducted, as part of the preventive process, as a managerial means of ensuring accountability and Best Value. The other purpose of evaluation is to contribute to the collective body of 'what works' knowledge. At this level, such strategic evaluations are part of the gearing-up process.

Outcome evaluation of operational-level CSCR action is the process of reliably attributing changes in outcome measures (in particular crime rates) to the outputs and interventions of particular CSCR schemes. Where the interventions are remote from the criminal events they are ultimately intended to reduce, it may be necessary in the short-term to substitute impact on some reliable indicators of risks of future offending. These could include immediate disruptions, such as a change in attitude, or changes further downstream such as improvements in school attendance and performance. Where action centres on criminal careers, it may be desirable, but difficult, to link impact on these risks with reductions in local area crime rates, to place comparisons between different crime reduction approaches on an equal footing. Assessment of cost effectiveness quantitatively links the inputs to the outcomes; and cost-benefit analysis, in turn, links cost effectiveness to the immediate savings from reduced crime and wider benefits such as improvements in quality of life.

Process evaluation of individual schemes or scheme-based programmes centres on insertion, implementation and intervention but assesses the entire preventive process – how it was conducted, what problems and issues were encountered and how they were coped with. In the strategic, gearing-up context, both outcome and process evaluators should aim to learn as much as possible from failures as well as successes – it is wasteful to reinvent the wheel, but even more so to reinvent the flat tyre. The concept normally cited at this point is Rosenbaum's distinction between theory failure (the fundamental idea was flawed, or inappropriate for the context), implementation failure (idea sound, but implementation weak) and measurement failure (idea sound and well-implemented, but evaluation was insufficiently sensitive to register the impact). The framework of insertion, implementation, intervention and wider preventive process presented here can in fact offer a far more detailed, generic checklist for what went wrong – like the accident investigator's mental toolkit.

Emergent and anticipated crime problems

However we improve our ability to evaluate and apply preventive methods to current crime problems, crime prevention cannot expect criminals to wait for it to catch up; and past patterns of offending are not always a sure guide to the future. Offenders will often adapt and find ways round existing preventive practices. And as Chapter 14 describes, new crime problems are constantly emerging as a result of social, economic, financial and technical changes in society.

These changes can affect any of the immediate precursors of the criminal event, supplying new tools for offenders (such as cordless drills) or new crime targets (such as mobile phones). Action at the gearing-up level is needed to set up systems to spot emergent crimes as soon as possible, and to go further, by fostering the anticipation of crime problems when products, environments and procedures are still at the design stage. This involves:

- Trying to predict offenders' likely countermoves, including the various kinds of displacement, to current interventions.

- Keeping alert to the obsolescence of existing crime prevention methods as adaptive offenders find ways round them, perhaps through exploiting new tools; planning and maintaining existing methods to keep them effective.

- Tracking new emerging crime problems and new potential offenders – the latter through audits of risk and protective factors (affecting individuals, particular jobs that expose employees to temptation, or whole neighbourhoods).

- Scanning further ahead to identify unfolding trends (such as demographic growth in an area's youth population), new causes and new patterns of crime.

- Conducting crime impact assessments – which can play a role similar to environmental impact assessments – in such fields as planning (what are the likely crime consequences of siting a particular housing estate next to a particular industrial estate?), proposed changes to local policies on employment or housing allocation, or the design of buildings and the surrounding environment. Competence in crime impact assessment not only prepares local or national partners for the future, but also helps foster alertness to crime and disorder issues throughout their organisations.

Setting up systems and supplying motivation to make this work requires an infrastructure of its own. Crime impact assessment and scanning for new causes of crime and possibilities for prevention will obviously be a rather hit and miss process, but can be made more systematic, if impending changes are sought under each of the immediate precursors of criminal events. What new potential targets or sources of motivation or resources for offending are on the horizon? What is going to empower or inhibit, supply or remove crime preventers from a particular kind of situation?

CSCR action can generally be characterised as being at one or other of the four procedural levels just described. However, action primarily designed to contribute at one level will usually have the scope for acting at others. Operational actions, besides (hopefully) delivering reductions in crime, will usually have the additional benefit of capacity-building – in terms for example of training up practitioners, or installing crime pattern analysis software – which continues to yield dividends after the formal scheme has finished. If the scheme was evaluated adequately, the cumulative body of 'what works' knowledge may have grown – a case of gearing up.

Acquiring the ability to conduct the preventive process is a key aspect of capacity-building; developing new techniques to apply in the process (such as smart, pattern-seeking geographical information systems for crime pattern analysis) is also gearing up. Some initiatives deliberately set out to systematically build up evidence-based knowledge whilst simultaneously tackling particular crime problems on the ground. Prime examples of this are the Crime Reduction Programme's strategic development projects on domestic burglary.

To be fully reflexive, of course, ways need to be defined for evaluating these in their turn. This is a challenge that faces the Crime Reduction Programme.

Crime reduction

Crime reduction is, from a policy perspective, about diminishing the volume and consequences of crime. Whether the policy is implemented within the national Crime Reduction Programme, or by local CSCR partnerships, a key concern is how to make the best use of the resources currently available. For this, it is necessary to examine cost effectiveness, in this context, the amount of crime reduction that can be achieved by a particular activity, for a given resource input (usually expressed as money). The policy perspective is also concerned with addressing the totality of the picture – for example, taking account of: net benefits after allowing for displacement or diffusion of benefit; competition for limited resources between different crime reduction priorities and unintended side effects of specific CSCR activities on other crimes or wider quality of life. How such a totality might be balanced is considered under crime control, below.

From the practical perspective of criminal events and specific crime reduction activities, the definition above translates into reducing the number of criminal and disorderly events and the severity of their consequences. The current framework is deliberately agnostic about the cost effectiveness of the activities it describes – although the feedback loops discussed under crime prevention do of course reflect policy makers' and practitioners' *own* use of cost-effectiveness information in guiding their tactical adjustments and strategic decisions. Although unintended consequences of the individual crime reduction activities – such as geographical displacement, crime switch and rise in fear – are considered, the strategic overview is a policy matter.

Logically, crime prevention is a means to achieving crime reduction. The reduction of risk of future, potential crime and disorder events is intended to lead to the reduction in observable numbers of actual events over a particular period of time. There can thus be no act of crime prevention which is not also crime reduction. (Note the observation above that both prevention and reduction can be seen as aspiration, action, attributable achievement and accident.)

What about the converse? Which acts of crime reduction can we contemplate, which do not act via prevention? Prevention, as defined here, acts by intervening in the causes of future criminal events. The only logical alternatives to this are i) intervening directly in criminal events as they unfold, and ii) stopping past events becoming progressively more serious. So from the event/risk perspective, acts of crime reduction tackle crime both directly, and via its causes and immediate consequences. Reduction thus comprises:

● The future orientation of prevention, whether directed towards reducing the risk of individual criminal events (perhaps intercepting a specific racial attack planned for the weekend) or decreasing more general crime risks (the high risk of burglary in a neighbourhood, or making offending by particular individuals less likely).

● The present orientation of disrupting and frustrating specific crimes as they happen (through police action to halt a fight or a citizen's action to repulse a pickpocket) and limiting progressive harm after a crime has happened (halting further misuse of a stolen credit card, for example).

In practice there will be very few crime reduction actions that do not have a preventive aspect. All that is needed for this to be invoked is for an offender to anticipate the present and retrospective actions and their consequences, and take avoiding action – hopefully by not committing the contemplated crime.

An alternative focus on ongoing processes and conditions rather than individual events would place more crime reduction activities in the present. This would emphasise intervening in:

● chronic or repeating crime problems such as domestic violence, racial harassment or other repeat victimisation;

- planned or organised crime involving preparatory acts which themselves may be additional criminal events, such as theft of a getaway car, or a systematic series of offences such as continual fraud;

- the convicted offender's criminal career to reduce the rate and severity of offending.

Nonetheless, when seen from the event level, the interventions will mostly be preventive in nature, reducing future risk. Whatever the case, with a few minor adjustments and shifts of emphasis, the conjunction of criminal opportunity framework can apply equally to interventions seen from a crime reduction perspective.

Crime reduction and the criminal justice system

The CJS focuses its procedures on dealing with past wrongs in dealing equitably with those coming before the courts and maintaining public confidence by imposing punishment commensurate with the offence. Justice is in a dimension of its own and, in formal terms, has no direct utilitarian purpose – it is an end in itself. But the justice process and the punishment it delivers inescapably have a crime reductive (and preventive) potential, if not always a measurable effect. This applies in equal terms to the CJS taken as a whole, and to its component agencies and processes.

In dispensing fair and satisfying justice, the judicial and penal process reduces the motivation for the proliferation of crime through vigilantism and revenge and reinforces the moral order that underlies self-control and informal social controls. Reaction also has the aim of reducing present and future crime through arrest, incapacitation and deterrence (law enforcement – 'repression' in European circles), and rehabilitation. Incapacitation within the CJS (imprisonment, driving bans or electronic tagging) aims to exclude convicted offenders from crime situations. Deterrence, as delivered by the CJS – the anticipation and fear of being caught by the police and judicially punished – seeks to influence convicted offenders' decisions to commit the next crime and through example, potential offenders' decisions to commit any crime.

From a public health perspective, specific deterrence falls under tertiary reduction, general deterrence under primary and secondary. In theory, at least, deterrence reinforces much of situational prevention which relies on heightening perceived risk of apprehension. More broadly speaking, however, current research evidence suggests that increased use of the CJS as a crime reduction tool is unlikely to be cost effective.

Judicial crime reduction can be defined as, that which reduces the number of crime and disorder events and the severity of their consequences. This is done by intervening in their causes or by intervening directly in the events themselves, through the very existence of the CJS and through its formal processes in prosecuting, trying, sentencing and punishing individual offenders.

For constitutional reasons, judicial crime reduction is tightly circumscribed, and therefore generally difficult to link explicitly with partnership activities. However, application of specific civil and criminal legal powers may form part of a wider local crime reduction strategy, together with the basic legal authority of the police to intervene in present and future crimes and react to past ones. Indeed, legal remedies of this kind feature in the Crime and Disorder Act 1998. Other statutes confer preventive powers enabling the police and courts to intervene by imposing bans on driving, requiring offenders' attendance at classes to reduce alcoholism, debarment from being a company director or possession of certain tools or weapons. Conflict containment and resolution in particular extends beyond the purely judicial to include civil law, informal mediation, restitution or restorative justice and even the town planning process. All of these have the potential to significantly reduce violence and criminal damage between neighbours, for example, or between landlords and tenants.

The rest of crime reduction, acting outside the formal process of the CJS, can be called extra-judicial. This is implemented by a range of agencies, partnerships and private companies and individuals. However, there is an intermediate area, within extra-judicial crime reduction, which is important to distinguish. The various agencies involved in the CJS also implement a range of activities which are intended to exercise powers to prevent impending criminal events, to deflect groups at risk of committing crime or to rehabilitate existing offenders. These operate, for example, by altering the predisposition or motivation to offend or by supplying skills and the social and economic opportunities to avoid offending. Cognitive and social skills enhancement, for example, may be done in prison. Supervision in the community, through the probation service, may set the scene for efforts to resolve problems in offenders' life circumstances (such as unemployment) which may be motivating them to commit crime. And the police, of course, patrol the streets, frustrate offenders' preparations for crime, intervene in ongoing crimes, administer formal cautions and advise on prevention.

As a result of their significant impact on individual liberty and privacy, these activities are subject to stringent procedural checks and balances and are often formally linked to the penal process. Together they might be called 'para-judicial' crime reduction, defined as crime reduction which acts through the agencies of the CJS. This may be formally linked to the criminal process but is not strictly part of it. Figure 2.6 illustrates the relationship between judicial, parajudicial and the rest of crime reduction/prevention.

Crime control

Crime reduction and prevention aim simply to reduce the frequency and seriousness of criminal events, on the reasonable assumption that they are already intolerably high. But it is possible to set reduction in a particular strategic framework which may

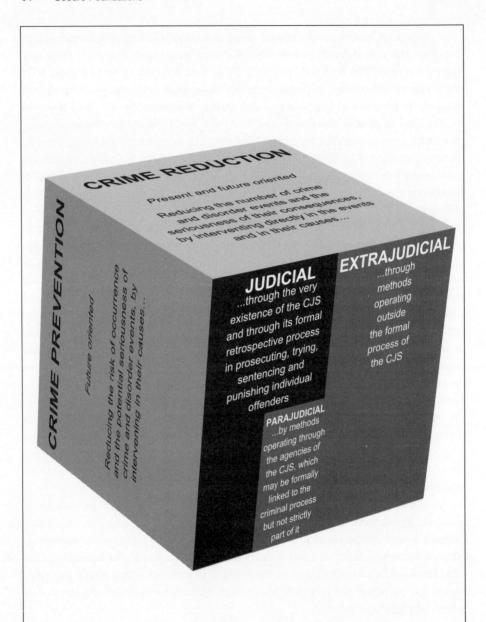

Figure 2.6 Defining crime reduction and crime prevention

help to prioritise the use of finite crime reduction resources with particular reference to the severity of consequences of crime and disorder. (Severity is thus seen from a real-world perspective rather than a purely legal one expressed as a punishment tariff.) The term 'crime control' captures this strategic viewpoint, which can also be set in the wider frame of community safety.

The bottom line of crime control simply involves halting rapid or accelerating growth in crime risk. Such growth may happen with a specific crime problem (such as a spate of convenience store robberies in a city), or on a wider front. It may be a qualitative deterioration as well as quantitative, and may feed back on itself, with increasing seriousness and organisation of offending, intimidation, and possible corruption of agents of the CJS. Ultimately, as has happened in some countries, it can lead to partial collapse of the state's power and legitimacy.

The more everyday aim of crime control involves (it is suggested) holding the risk of criminal events and related misbehaviour below a tolerable level. This level is determined, primarily, by considering the harmful consequences of the particular criminal events in question for individuals and the community. These consequences include fear, harm to person or property or restrictions on economic and social behaviour, and generation of further crime problems. (With serious crimes and disorder problems, those which severely affect vulnerable people, or those minor ones which, left unchecked, may lead to wider trouble or inter-ethnic tension, it may be appropriate to strive to hold their level down as low as possible.)

Other considerations relate to the availability of cost-effective methods to reduce the relevant crime problems, competing priorities for funds and other resources. Also relevant are side effects of attempts to control crime, such as exacerbation of other kinds of offending (as with the prohibition experience of the US), or adverse effects on other social policy areas or quality of life (as with privacy).

A tolerance threshold for a given type of crime nationally, or in a given locality, or for particular groups of victims, could thus be an important consideration in setting community safety targets. In practice, however, it may have to remain more a way of thinking than centre on explicit crime risk figures, given the difficulty of achieving consensus over priorities (a problem faced in equivalent areas such as health service rationing). With disorder-type offending particularly, where the impact of crime has a significant subjective element, it may even be difficult to establish consensus over what constitutes serious misbehaviour – what is acceptable in the city centre may be very different from what is acceptable in rural villages. Crime control also has a particular overlap with community safety, as defined here, given a common focus on consequences of crime and the strategic target-setting approach to crime levels.

Two processes that are particularly relevant in a crime control context are displacement of offending and replacement of offenders. The former involves existing offenders reacting to crime reduction initiatives by changing the time, place, method or type of crime target. The latter involves new offenders moving in to fill the niche vacated by those who have been arrested or reformed (such as drug dealers). Although displacement, particularly, has now been shown to be partial at the very worst, little is known about offender replacement. In both cases, the rate of displacement or replacement, balanced against the rate of implementation of new and effective crime reductive action will dynamically determine the crime level.

Conclusion

This chapter has sought to show how good practice and policy in crime prevention, reduction and community safety depend on theory, education, training, briefing, quality assurance, research and evaluation being brought to a focus through a clear conceptual framework. The conjunction of criminal opportunity framework began with the crime or disorder event, and built on to it successive layers covering the causes of the event, interventioning in the causes to disrupt their conjunction, implementation, insertion in the community, the operational context of the preventive process and the support and development of these at the capacity-building and gearing-up levels. Finally, the distinctive features of crime reduction and crime control were then added. The layers resemble the structure of an onion – and like an onion, probably brought tears to the eyes of the reader!

References

Audit Commission (1999) *Safety in Numbers: Promoting Community Safety* London: Audit Commission

Ekblom P (1996) 'Towards a discipline of crime prevention: A systematic approach to its nature, range and concepts' *Preventing Crime and Disorder: Targeting Strategies and Responsibilities* Bennett T (ed) Cambridge: Institute of Criminology

Ekblom P (1997) 'Gearing up against crime: A dynamic framework to help designers keep up with the adaptive criminal in a changing world' *International Journal of Risk, Security and Crime Prevention* 214

Goldblatt P and Lewis C (eds) (1998) *Reducing Offending: An Assessment of Research Evidence on Ways of Dealing with Offending Behaviour* Home Office Research Study 187 London: HMSO

Tilley N (1994) *After Kirkholt – Theory, Method and Results of Replication Evaluations* Crime Prevention Unit Paper 47 London: Home Office

Wikström P-O, Clarke R and McCord J (eds) (1995) *Integrating Crime Prevention Strategies: Propensity and Opportunity* Stockholm: Swedish National Council for Crime Prevention

3. Creating community justice
Mike Nellis

> We need justice, we need liberty, and we need as much solidarity as can be
> reconciled with justice and liberty. But we also need, as much as anything
> else, language adequate to the times we live in. We need to see how we live
> now and we can only see with words and images which leave us no escape
> into nostalgia for some other time and place. (Ignatieff 1986)

The term 'community justice' is beginning to enter the vocabulary of those who work
with offenders and victims, although no one is sure what it means. A Community
Justice National Training Organisation has recently been established, for example,
with a remit to develop training for probation officers and community safety
personnel. Some of the new, specialised qualifications for probation officers involve
degrees in community justice. Using this term, and drawing on Ignatieff's observation
above, this chapter aims to offer policy-makers and practitioners concerned with
community safety, together with their equivalents in the alternatives to custody field,
a common framework for conceptualising their work. It is by no means a blueprint,
merely an attempt to start an argument about probable, preferable and possible
futures.

Some years ago, in a harsh, insightful study of crime and conflict in the inner city,
Dave Robins (1992) decried the peddlers of unrealisable utopias; 'tarnished visions'
he called them, and pleaded instead for something more practical: 'real grounds for
hope'. What he envisaged was a sustained and extensive people-centred approach to
community regeneration.

> This means putting less faith in prisons, which have little effect on crime,
> and more faith in health, education, training and child care, which may
> have an effect, and ensuring firm but fair policing [...ensuring that]
> neighbourhoods are safe places for everyone to live in.

All of this sounds rather utopian, for Robins describes things long called for, but
rarely achieved. The term utopian realism, originated by Giddens (1991), might have
helped him. It involves the envisioning of alternative futures, embedded in the world
as it is but sensitive also to its latent possibilities, ideas 'whose very propagation
might help them to be realised.'

As conceived of here, community justice is an expression of utopian realism. It is
not, at least initially, intended to conjure up something which does not already exist.
Grounded in the actual work of a number of established agencies – notably those

concerned either with supervising offenders in the community or increasing community safety – it aims to heighten the affinity between them, and increase their common focus. It is not an exercise in gratuitous rebranding, for as Ignatieff avers 'we can only see with words and images', and we need to choose words carefully if, on the cusp of the 21st century, we are to salvage our humanitarian commitments from the jaded vocabularies into which they have dwindled. Notably, these are the overly technicist discourse of 'crime prevention', and the morally shallow discourse of 'social work'.

A suppressed tradition

The term 'community justice' is not new, having been deployed periodically in analyses of informal or popular justice. This covers justice outside the state, usually abroad, with which most criminologists, if not policymakers, are familiar. Henry (1978) used the term as a catch-all for workplace tribunals – community courts of the kind used in Soviet Russia and China to administer punishment by public disgrace. He felt that the inclusion of such mechanisms would be beneficial in western societies, whose statutory criminal justice agencies, even then, were sensing their remoteness from civil society, and finding it increasingly difficult to cope with the pressure of ostensibly trivial cases. More recently, Pavlich (1996) has spoken of community justice in his account of locally-based mediation programmes in British Columbia.

Using the now more popular term 'restorative justice', two social theologians, Zehr (1990) and Consedine (1993) have sought to recover a rich, but suppressed, tradition of community justice. Under the auspices of state-based justice, they argue, we have lost sight of a time when crime was understood more as an interpersonal harm than as a violation of an abstract legal rule. Such harms created obligations and liabilities which had to be put right by the parties concerned, their representatives and allies, and with the state only minimally involved. Not all past expressions of community justice are reasonable by late 20th century standards, (blood feuds, for example) but Zehr and Consedine argue convincingly that modern forms of those based on negotiation, restitution and reconciliation could usefully be redeveloped.

Zehr and Consedine, among others, see state-administered systems of justice as unduly bureaucratic, (obsessed with rules and legal procedures), overly punitive, (especially when underpinned by retributive philosophies) and overly individualised in their response to offenders, (commonly neglecting the needs and interests of crime victims). Although it is somewhat exaggerated, this critique has gained ground in the last ten years because it has become clearer that contemporary state-based criminal justice systems can make no grand claims to superior effectiveness. Crime levels at the end of the millennium remain a major source of social anxiety, (not just in England and Wales), generating public demands for increased government action, including tougher sentences.

Partly to avoid nostalgia, as Ignatieff rightly recommends, the concept of community justice developed here does not preclude the involvement of state agencies. The starting point of the argument is otherwise the same as Zehr and Consedine's; namely, the failures of contemporary criminal justice policy and, in particular, the alarming over-reliance on imprisonment.

Crime at the millennium

Sir Leon Radzinowicz (1991) has characterised the late 20th century as a time of 'penal regression', a time of retreat from what were once considered civilised ideals in criminal justice, whose hallmark was at least a notional commitment to the reintegration of reformed offenders into mainstream society. Ethical and empirical critiques of rehabilitation, heightened class divisions, victimisation surveys, specific moral panics, the collapse of social democratic and egalitarian ideals, the empowerment of women and a rising threshold of tolerance to violence, have all contributed to this. On the public agenda, crime has moved from being a threat at the margins of society (to be mopped up by professionals) to an ever-present risk which potentially affects us all. Patterns of crime control are, if not shifting completely away from the processing of individual offenders (with a view to either punishing, deterring or reforming them), then at least towards encircling this approach with strategies for the more collective management of a dangerous underclass.

Radzinowicz sees these developments in the crime control sphere as incipient authoritarianism, and as harbingers of an authoritarian state. It is perhaps paradoxical, therefore, that they have mostly been welcomed across the political spectrum: not only traditional law and order interests whose support one might have expected, but also ostensibly progressive voices. These might include campaigns against rape, domestic violence and child sexual abuse, anti-racial violence movements, some crime victim's movements more generally, and some environmental protection movements. They have seen in criminalisation – and its usual corollary, punishment (often imprisonment) – a solution to experiences of victimisation and oppression and a means of creating safer and fairer societies. Dissenting voices, such as those of Cohen (1992) and Snider (1998), have been few and far between.

Much of what was once thought of as good (caring) practice in work with offenders now seems to go against the grain of the times. Momentum has been lost from the loosely constituted humanitarian movements which leavened our responses to crime and our attitudes to punishment throughout this past century. This loss has been seen by many commentators – left, right and postmodern – as a timely return to a realism and common sense. From an alternative, more ethically nuanced standpoint, however, it might also be seen as a serious withdrawal of compassion, a calculated repudiation of the concern, hope and practical understanding that once animated the 'social work' tradition. The shift is partly signalled in the way that the Probation Service has been pressed by government to shift away from its traditional 'ethic of care' towards more overtly punitive objectives, and latterly towards being an agency of public protection. It is apparent too in the even greater ease with which penal reform organisations can be stigmatised as mere do-gooders, and the difficulty they now have in setting agendas of their own, as opposed to simply responding to the agenda set by government.

The shift can be read into the expansion of zero-tolerance policing (or its more subtle cognates), and in the marked ascendancy of situational over social means of crime prevention – especially the ubiquitous scanning of public space by CCTV. While the intellectual focus on prevention per se is undoubtedly welcome, initiatives to date have been overwhelmingly, if not exclusively, technicist and short-term. Government policy neglects, and sometimes seeks to suppress from consciousness, the deeper political, economic and cultural milieus in which violence germinates. Amongst these are de-industrialisation, poverty, the collapse of welfare safety nets, media images, consumerism and, not least, the forms of masculinity that have been so productive of harmful behaviour (Snider, 1998). Crime is conceived of as something to be dealt with in isolation from these, although it is only sometimes possible to do this.

The rising star of crime prevention (even when broadened and reframed as community safety) reflects cracked confidence in formal criminal justice agencies. Compared to the institutions and networks of civil society, these agencies have only a limited, late-in-the-day impact on patterns of crime. In itself, the rising star does not portend better times. The slightly contracting role of direct state provision in crime control, and the correspondingly expanded role being played by 'responsibilised' individuals and an array of commercial and voluntary organisations (in partnership), does not mean that contemporary strategies are any less a form of social defence in an increasingly divided and fearful society. The agenda remains a state-dominated one, actively supported in many instances by powerful sectional interests within civil society, who can lock, light and zone themselves out of harm's way. Areas blighted by de-industrialisation are the least likely to have the dense network of civic associations that meaningful 'community care' presupposes, or local leaders with the requisite weight or connections (Campbell, 1993). In any case, without commercial investment in 'human capital' in such areas – the provision of regular work and serious prospects – hope dies and nihilism sets in.

Under the New Labour Government it has become marginally easier than under its Conservative predecessor to acknowledge links between crime and issues of disadvantage and citizenship. Far more attention, though, has been paid to implementing the first half of its famous slogan, 'tough on crime and tough on the causes of crime', than to the second. There has been a conscious emphasis on social inclusion, but several commentators openly doubt whether welfare-to-work schemes which merely get crime-prone young people on to the lower rungs of an increasingly lengthening ladder of social inequality constitute real grounds for hope in Dave Robins' sense. The lowering of expectations that inter-generational poverty produces, the disengagement from politics, the psychic damage and the expressive and instrumental attractions of crime as a lifestyle, all militate against simple attempts to engineer inclusiveness (see Davies, 1997 and Danziger, 1997). Jock Young (1998) rightly says that 'crime occurs when citizenship is thwarted', all the more so when citizenship has ceased to be something potentially available, distant but denied, and becomes something not even imagined or desired. The causes of much crime lie in injustice, but the brutalising effects of crime – the poor preying on the poor, the ruthlessness of the state response – only compound it. In suggesting how we might move forward, Young's choice of words is singularly auspicious:

> The solution lies not in the resurrection of past stabilities, based on nostalgia and a world that will never return, but on a new citizenship, a reflexive modernity that will tackle the problems of justice and community, of reward and individualism, which lie at the heart of liberal democracy. (Young, 1998)

'Community' is important

Far too many words have been wasted by academics (criminologists included) on debunking the idea of 'community' – claims for example, that it is nostalgic and nebulous or, on a different tack, intrinsically oppressive. The term has acquired many meanings but in everyday speech locality and shared interests (vicinity and affinity) are by far the most common referents, and both continue to influence people's sense of belonging and identity. Many late-modern people sustain complex ties outside a given local domain. This does not mean that those within it are unimportant (though they can become so, and disembedding, or rootlessness, is an acknowledged feature of late modern life). Local spatial relations and a sense of place remain significant influences on individuals, perhaps more so on the disadvantaged than on affluent, mobile elites. Both analytically and politically, locality still serves as 'a context for a distinct social order'; it is only at local level that many social institutions and social practices, including crime itself, manifest themselves as 'a tangible process of activity' (Hobbs, 1998).

Understanding community as locality does not imply that communities have 'firm boundaries, fixed membership and rigid patterns of inclusion and exclusion' (Hobbs 1998). The experience of community-as-place is, depending on where boundaries are drawn, structured by class, status and power, by gender and generation, by race, and by dint of being defined rough or respectable. The kinds of communities (inner cities, peripheral estates) and symbolic locations that generate disquiet about crime are often brutal and desolate places, ravaged by multiple social problems from which crime as a specific behaviour is hard to disentangle. Their populations may be heterogeneous, territory and traditions contested and solidarity minimal, but precisely because their residents are bound together by conflict and mistrust it is not inappropriate to call them communities, albeit forlorn ones.

If the term 'community' did not exist, it may have had to be invented, to specify, albeit loosely and elastically, the geographical and social terrain between the domestic and national spheres. Terms like 'local social system', 'social network' and 'locality' have their academic uses, but have never caught on as vernacular alternatives. In a criminological context we should also note that the term 'intermediate sanctions' (Morris and Tonry, 1990), which deliberately disconnected non-custodial (community) penalties from the symbolism of locality, in order to make the formal gradations of punishment more transparent, failed to catch the imagination of British policy-makers or practitioners. That in itself does not prove by default the analytical or descriptive worth of the term 'community', but it suggests an absence of anything better, and a belief that it is at least serviceable.

What settles the matter, for this chapter's purposes, is the obvious fact that local administrative structures and policies can have a major bearing on the pattern of relationships that emerges in any given community. The range and depth of people's social networks may not be determined significantly by patterns of local governance but their quality of life (or lack of it) is undoubtedly affected by the resources, service delivery structures and efficiency levels created and achieved within particular administrative units. Whether run locally or nationally, public services need to be near-to-hand if they are to be meaningful to users and potential users. Local community action has often been designed to garner resources for localities, and although it is currently unfashionable to emphasise it, there is a tradition in British politics which has long held that the maximum devolution of power to local level is a democratic imperative. Ruing the years of Conservative rule, and the damage done to local government, David Donnison has recently reaffirmed the tradition's importance:

> If we are to recreate a sense of shared citizenship and concern for our fellows, if we are to rebuild the credibility of public service and the professions responsible for it, if we are to help people who have been out of work for a long time to find a way back into the economy, if we are able to help people in the precarious middle third of our social structure to feel a responsibility for those in the excluded lower third, that will mainly have to be achieved at urban and neighbourhood levels. (Donnison 1997).

Future responses to crime must take account of this insight, as, to a degree, the Crime and Disorder Act 1998, with its highly localised audits and strategies, has already begun to do. Many useful lessons have been learned from the centrally sponsored local initiatives that took place under the Conservatives in the community safety field (Safer Cities and City Challenge, for example). Within the New Labour Government, however, a dirigiste, centralising tendency (not least in relation to the Probation Service) runs firmly counter to them (Marquand, 1998). New Labour in general, and the Crime and Disorder Act in particular was undoubtedly influenced by the mid-1990s debate on communitarianism, but – perhaps because it failed abjectly to capture other citadels of progressive opinion, that feared it would increase punitiveness – the lessons New Labour drew were highly selective. It is important for the further development of the idea of community justice that we salvage a little more from communitarianism, before it is consigned prematurely to the scrapyard of failed (or untried) social policies.

Communitarianism – succour for punishment?

Communitarianism was introduced to Britain in 1995, largely by the think-tank Demos, through the work of its main American populariser, Amitai Etzioni (1995 and 1997). Even weightier North American intellectuals lie behind it, and not all who articulate the perspective (in the criminal justice arena), or kindred ideas, actually call themselves by this name (Braithwaite and Pettit, 1990, Burnside and Baker, 1995; see also Margalit, 1997). Demos's strategy certainly influenced New Labour, although the party's communitarian sensibilities had already been roused by Tony Blair's political and religious commitments, and in respect of crime, at local council level, by left realism.

Despite Demos's radical reputation, communitarianism in general, and Etzioni's work in particular, has been seen as an expression of moral conservativism, seeking, against the individualistic grain of late modernity, to restore traditional forms of authority in family, neighbourhood, workplace and courtroom, based on an idealised image of small-town America. Some communitarians are moral conservatives whose transcendent notion of community does requires the suppression of individualism. Others, however, distinguish between the legitimate pursuit of individual fulfilment, which respects and needs civic ties, and selfish egoism, which does not. These more liberal communitarians recognise, with Giddens (1998), that 'we have to make our lives in a more active way than was true of previous generations' and that one consequence of this is that 'we have to look for new means of producing ... solidarity' amongst ourselves.

Questions about solidarity are central to communitarianism. Its guiding ideas are human interdependence and the common good; its watchwords are co-operation, reciprocity, fellowship and, in some versions, friendship. Within this matrix, the maturing, responsible individual is expected to become an active participant in the collective, democratic creation of the good society. Pace the moral conservatives, the good society is defiantly pluralistic – diverse, cosmopolitan, argumentative, always unfinished – and mutual tolerance is a very necessary feature of it (Ignatieff, 1986 and Tam, 1998).

Communitarianism's emphasis on co-operation, reciprocity and the common good gives it a certain *prima facie* applicability to debates about anti-social behaviour, at least if prevention-by-inclusion and the reintegration of reformed offenders are to be taken seriously. Nonetheless, the responses to crime which even the more moderate and reflective communitarians have emphasised are those of which the British liberal-left (especially in its 'social work' manifestation) have often been sceptical. Etzioni, for example, emphasises neighbourhood watch (and other kinds of watch), child curfews, community service as a penalty, and, worryingly, public shaming (car stickers proclaiming that the driver has a drunkenness conviction, body-placards declaring that the wearer is a thief, and so on). Zehr (1990) and Braithwaite (1989) discriminate more carefully between shame and humiliation, and favour interventions which, wherever possible, bring offenders face-to-face with victims.

Braithwaite's theory of reintegrative shaming and the related, more elaborate, theory of civic republican justice (Braithwaite and Pettit, 1990:54) contribute considerably to an understanding of community justice. Braithwaite argues that even complex modern societies best maintain order through a complementary mix of formal and informal means. That is, a range of statutory, voluntary and communal bodies acting at local level, with families, schools and neighbourhoods at one end and prisons and probation at the other. 'Most social control is [already] communitarian control, rather than state control' he writes, 'and most day-today successes are achieved by dialogic regulation, with state regulation stepping in to mop up the failures.' (Braithwaite (1998.)

The prevention and punishment of drink driving, domestic violence, white-collar crime and most types of juvenile crime, for example – which therefore means a large proportion of all crime – is best thought of in the context of carefully graded enforcement pyramids. These rely on everyday social processes to dampen and contain anti-social and criminal behaviour; if it escalates despite them they can be augmented as required by a range of informal and formal interventions of varying intensity, up to and including incapacitative criminal law. Although for current purposes it extends too far in both directions, encompassing both the domestic and the custodial, the idea of the enforcement pyramid is still a useful, if crude, conceptual bridge between the spheres of community safety and alternatives to custody.

Braithwaite's work is useful in other ways too. The primacy which he gives to the moralising role of civil society does not mean that state agencies are unimportant.

They play a vital role not least in resourcing, supporting, and regulating, civil institutions, lest their interventions degenerate – as they can – into mere vengeance and cycles of retaliatory violence (vigilantism). The state is crucial to the orchestration of policing and prosecution, and central to the punishing of those who don't respond to informal intervention or low-level civil sanctions. For a variety of reasons (psychological, cultural and political) there will still be many such people. Prevention is certainly the communitarian ideal, but while people are free – as, in a democracy they should be – punishment, at least of a certain type, remains indispensable to the maintenance of the social order.

There are ideas here on which the Probation Service in England could usefully dwell. In addition to Braithwaite, other communitarian thinkers (Lacey, 1988, Cragg, 1992 and Duff, 1995) have recently developed cogent intellectual defences of punishment – the principle, rather than all its actually existing forms. These could enable the Service to sustain the best of itself while finally jettisoning the obsolete language of social work values. These defences have largely developed as critical responses to the retributivist 'back to justice' movement which emerged in the late 1970s, (with which the Service, even after 1991, never properly reconciled itself). Seemingly, this led, sometimes against the expectations and wishes of its exponents, to large increases in the use of imprisonment. Communitarians openly accept punishment as the inevitable concomitant of law enforcement, censure as a mostly legitimate response to wrongdoing, and denunciation in the name of both the immediate victim and the common good as morally appropriate. In insisting however, that punishment-in-practice should encourage contrition, and either allow for, or actively assist reintegration into mainstream society, communitarians incorporate, in modified form, all the primary concerns of rehabilitationists.

The communitarians' bias towards informal, denunciatory, educational and above all reintegrative solutions makes it hard to characterise them en masse as law and order conservatives. Some are, but even Etzioni, whose acceptance of humiliating penalties does admittedly leave him on dangerous ground, is at one with Elliot Currie (1998). This is apparent in his hostility to present levels of imprisonment, in seeing prison as an essentially violent environment, quite possibly a way of making offenders more dangerous, and certainly as expensive (all the more so if treatment programmes are not even provided). Both concede that some imprisonment is necessary either to mark up the seriousness of the crime committed, or to detain the incorrigible, but both also believe that its high level of use in America is a tragic sign of social breakdown, not to be emulated anywhere else.

Communitarian animus towards the inappropriate use of imprisonment is part of a wider hostility to encroaching state authoritarianism, and provides a framework in which Leon Radzinowicz's concerns, mentioned earlier, might be addressed. This critique of authoritarianism is all of a piece with communitarianism's critique of possessive individualism. The argument is that if strong, inclusive communities fail to restrain the predatory egoism which fuels so much criminal activity, the harsher features of the enforcement pyramid will inevitably be called into play. 'Unless civil and moral order is shored up' Etzioni writes (1995) 'more and more people will call for strong-armed leadership.' Braithwaite warns similarly that:

> if citizens' persons and property cannot be secured by moralising against criminals, then political demands for the repressive state will prevail. To the extent that moralising social control collapses, a vacuum is created that will attract the most brutal, repressive and intrusive of police states. (Braithwaite, 1989.)

Enough has surely now been said to show that communitarianism has possibilities as well as pitfalls, and – in the spirit of community justice – some important messages for those involved in both community safety and the provision of alternatives to custody. The more coherent versions of communitarianism are a serious attempt to balance the demands of solidarity and liberty in the conditions of the late 20th century. Its end result is nonetheless a more tough-minded stance towards offenders than liberal-left social workers have traditionally subscribed to, and that may yet be a sticking point. Communitarianism does accept the legitimacy of punishment, but gives no succour either to extreme forms or excessive use of it, promoting instead the painstaking, piecemeal construction of inclusive communities, with inbuilt disincentives to crime, and the moral re-education and social reintegration of recognised offenders. At its heart is a distinctive perspective on justice, the elaboration of which might help sensitise the more technocratically inclined community safety professionals to the moral dimensions of their work, and also soften whatever remains of Probation Service resistance to these useful ideas.

Justice and community

Justice is one of several universal human values identified by communitarians (Tam, 1998), although historically its concrete forms have been notoriously diverse (Burnside,1994). Even John Macmurray (1961), a communitarian *avant le lettre*, saw justice as largely a matter of custom and belief, whose substance shifted over time. 'Justice' he wrote, 'seems to be the *sine qua non* of morality, the very essence of righteousness', but there is no absolute yardstick by which it can be measured: thus 'if all parties to a bargain are satisfied with their bargain then the arrangement is fair to them all.' This obviously begs the question of whether people know their own interests well enough to judge whether they should be satisfied, but the core point is well made – justice is a process of reconciling interests. Its content or quality depends on values and norms other than, sometimes higher than, justice itself, but without a commitment to justice the very possibility of sustaining co-operation between people is quickly imperilled.

In western democracies, steeped in the liberal tradition, questions of justice arise in three separate but related contexts – the control of power, the distribution of the means of well-being (distributive justice) and the response to harm (remedial justice), including crime, (all at local, national and international levels). Complex laws and rules, inevitably imperfect because of the corrupting political process in which they are forged, have evolved in respect of all three contexts. A liberal conception of rights has dominated the debate, and the benefits of this rights-perspective to the humanitarian cause cannot be denied. Communitarians still see significant weaknesses, however. Liberalism tends in theory, if not always in practice, a) to assume the autonomy of abstract individuals regardless of the real social context which shapes their actions; b) automatically to privilege the protection of individual rights against the state, and c) to underplay the issue of responsibility for the common good.

Communitarian conceptions of justice modify these propositions. They emphasise the groundedness of individuals in particular social circumstances; mutual interdependence – no interest is automatically right; and responsibilities towards a common good, at least as much as rights. In this respect, as Zehr's work (1990) in particular testifies, communitarians draw on a strand of the Judaeo-Christian tradition in which the moral quality nowadays isolated as justice, and interpreted narrowly as fairness or impartiality, was semantically entwined with conceptions of love and respect, peace and community.

This conceptual matrix, condensed in the word shalom, (meaning wholeness, the dynamic peace of the community), and the sensibility which results from it, arguably yields a richer understanding of justice than modern western legalism seems, on its own, to allow (Curle, 1981, Williams and Collier, 1984 and Townsend, 1994). It is a conception of 'justice' founded less on the protection of individual rights and more on the overriding moral importance of healing rifts in community. That is, it creates inclusive communities as far as possible – more akin to what we might nowadays understand as dispute-settlement or peacemaking than to the kind of justice we associate with criminal (if not civil) courts. This did not preclude the imposition of agreed penalties by established authorities – redress, penances, losses – or sanctions for failure to accept or abide by them, but it put a primary emphasis on reconciliation, insisting that there could be no sustained peace, no harmonious social order without this kind of justice.

Is this conception relevant in the 21st century? While it may have slipped to the margins of Western jurisprudence, an essentially communitarian view of justice has continued to inform the actions of many church-based 'justice and peace' workers worldwide (Kammer, 1995), especially in poorer communities, living under authoritarian regimes. It has to a degree been rediscovered intellectually by 'peacemaking criminologists' (Pepinsky and Quinney, 1991), and is finding some practical expression in family group and community conferencing initiatives (Braithwaite and Daly, 1994). The late John Pendelton (1985), a chief probation officer, was ahead of his time in believing that this perspective might inform the future vision of the Probation Service Regrettably, since his death, no one has really taken it up (though see Lacey and Ward, 1995).

There are, however, faint signs of interest. David Donnison does not quite make the justice/peace connection, but it is significant that in a recent book *Policies for a Just Society*, he includes a chapter on safety, emphasising throughout the democratic necessity of local, community-based initiatives. Some of the examples he gives of initiatives set up in the name of community safety involved doing justice, settling a dispute in a fair manner, in a way akin to communitarian prescriptions. An example of this was the Crosstalk project, which aimed to foster dialogue between older residents of an estate and young people who plagued their lives. Compensation strategies in criminal justice, and most mediation and reparation projects can be seen in the same peacemaking light, though they are not themselves panaceas, and a certain level of order and security is needed before they can work.

Potentially, the pursuit of community safety is a step towards community justice, safety being, as Donnison says, integral to a sense of a just society. But safety initiatives alone do not guarantee justice, and unless they are animated by moral, and not just technical, considerations, even they can lead to excesses of either inclusive or exclusive control. Local CCTV schemes may well have increased safety and security, but whether the asymmetry of watchers and watched, and the institutionalisation of suspicion and mistrust which this entails contributes much to justice or peace is more debatable. Recent legal-administrative attempts to improve community safety – the child curfew, anti-social behaviour and parenting orders in the Crime and Disorder Act 1998, for example – also pose awkward questions, constructing 'the problem' in too narrow a way:

> The 'problem families', 'noisy neighbours' and 'delinquent youth' are residents and citizens as well, invoking both rights and statutory responsibilities from those who govern them locally. In this sense then, the responsibility for community safety which local authorities now wish to take upon themselves, will also be a responsibility of governance and of justice. (Hope, 1997)

This arguably tilts towards a more liberal understanding of justice and fails to appreciate the valuable elements of communitarian justice in the Act's provisions. It risks, as liberalism has often done, minimising crime victims' experiences, downplaying the immediate demands of remedial justice in favour of the longer term requirements of distributive justice, whereas both need attention if true justice is to be done. This, as Hope rightly recognises, requires something more than narrow legal initiatives. It certainly requires, as almost all community safety issues do, sustained attention to educational and employment opportunities, access to health and welfare services and challenges to power structures (whether complacent or hostile) in order to restore faith in decent political institutions and to increase citizen participation.

These are not enough in themselves, not least because they are medium- or long-term strategies. The clear and present dangers – the people responsible for fear and violence – need to be confronted and controlled (and if all else fails excluded, their immediate needs subordinated for the good of others, to be dealt with later). For no matter how much their behaviour is rooted in disadvantage, predatory or uncivil behaviour towards others, especially weaker others, compounds rather than alleviates it. Justice, remember, assists us with the control of power, the distribution of resources for well-being, and the construction of responses to harm. It therefore cannot but underpin and unify our responses to crime – which can be an abuse of power just as surely as the failure of the authorities to act effectively against crime can be a form of harm.

Community justice as a social movement

It is one thing, however, to identify an abstract unifying principle. It is quite another to create a common enterprise at ground level. Can a range of existing developments in the alternative to custody and community safety fields be brought together within a single communitarian framework? In practice, in a rather haphazard fashion, a degree of melding has been going on for some time, especially in youth justice, and it is one of the more progressive intentions of the Crime and Disorder Act 1998 to facilitate an approximation to it at least. Conceptually, however, they are still perceived as separate worlds. Ending that separation is a key task for the early years of the new century.

The groundwork has already been done. Ken Pease (1995) suggested several years ago that the split was 'fundamentally misguided'. His starting point then was the need to reduce the use of imprisonment, a need which is arguably even more pressing now. He suggested that the prevailing image of alternatives to custody (as the rungs immediately below custody on the penal ladder) could be stretched until it extended 'as far back in the offending/sanctioning process as possible. Just as it makes more sense to consider the avoidance of heart disease in terms of childhood diet and exercise than in major surgery', he wrote 'so it makes more sense to consider alternatives to custody in terms of crime prevention than [as] last ditch penal interventions.'

Although this stretches the concept of alternatives to custody a little far and ignores some very reasonable anxieties about early intervention and net widening, the gist of the argument is right. If imprisonment is to be reduced, the provision of alternatives to custody and the development of community safety initiatives needs to be seen as an integrated sphere of action (though by no means the responsibility of a single unified agency). This sphere would encompass not only existing alternatives, but also

> the least demanding sanction available upon conviction; the least demanding sanction available without recourse to a court; the least demanding mediated agreement between offender and victim; [and] the avoidance of circumstances which lead to the commission of an offence. (Pease 1995).

Although Pease does not say so, the affinity he seeks to forge between two hitherto separate spheres would be considerably strengthened by a term which gives them a common ethos. The term community justice would serve this purpose, and is apt for a number of things which are happening even now.

It could be more apt still in the future. Important though it is to link the existing spheres of alternatives to custody and community safety, it would be a mistake simply to venerate their present forms, as if nothing needed to change. There would, in any case, be little point in promoting new terminology if it did no more than rebrand the status quo. So, the concept of community justice as envisaged here is intended to open up further possibilities, in a way that other terms and ideas do not. Over time and under the rubric of community justice, new practices might develop which will further tilt the centre of gravity away from imprisonment and purely penal response to offenders, towards the creation of inclusive communities, freer of crime than at present.

Prime among these are initiatives in restorative justice – victim-offender mediation, reparation and compensation programmes – which Zehr (1990) himself saw as integral to community justice. These could be used on a much greater scale than has been attempted hitherto, and there is a movement pressing for this which already provides momentum for community justice more generally (Restorative Justice Consortium, 1999). 'Restorative' may not be the best, or a lasting, term for this kind of work (because of its retrogressive connotations), but as it has only recently been taken up by government and carries many good ideas in its train, this is not the time to change or abandon it.

Beyond restorative justice are the concerns of the abolitionists to redefine crime, wherever possible, as a conflict or tort (van Swaaningen, 1997). This might involve limiting criminalisation as a strategy, reducing but certainly not eradicating the specialist professional management of crime, displacing the formal agencies of the criminal justice system and fostering – as communitarians propose – more dispersed systems of regulation and redress. It might involve abolishing, if not the very principle of punishment, then the vast majority of custodial institutions (for all but the dangerous few, especially for women) (Christie, 1981 and Carlen, 1990). At present, too few practitioners have been exposed (through education and training) to the potential of these ideas, or encouraged to test their practicability. It is surely not obvious – or honest – that practitioners should be denied the chance to consider ways of avoiding the socially polarised, prison-centred, surveillance-heavy futures that abolitionists and others have warned us of, and to judge whether present polices are equal to the challenge.

Any emergent community justice movement – indeed any form of utopian realism – will inevitably exhibit creative tensions between pragmatists and idealists. Pragmatists who can face the worst and manage the intractable are essential, but the movement as a whole would be incomplete without maverick personalities in and around it, stimulating new thoughts, trying new ideas, pressing in new directions. The unexpected take-up of John Braithwaite's work neatly exemplifies the way in which the idealist-to-pragmatist transition can be made, but mavericks need not always be academics. They may be social entrepreneurs (community activists) like Dick Atkinson (1994), who orchestrated efforts to end prostitution and kerb-crawling in Balsall Heath, Birmingham. While the Balsall Heath experience also showed how easily sensible community action against crime can slip towards vigilantism, Atkinson remains an important exemplar of communitarianism in practice.

Penal reform groups also have a part to play in a community justice movement. As penal reformers have recognised, the reduced use of prison requires 'activating and empowering a much wider spectrum of practitioners' (Rutherford, 1991) than those concerned with prison alone, or even with formal alternatives to it such as probation. Vivian Stern's (1998) conception of a penal reform movement seems to emphasise coalitions of professionals and volunteers concerned only with offenders, and to underplay the role of community activists like Atkinson. However, if community justice is to become a reality there needs to be sufficient numbers of people in all localities, willing – she hopes – to make it a source of pride for a community to gradually shift its resources out of imprisonment and into violence prevention; to help disturbed families; provide more educational opportunities; support the children (who without such help become the next generation of prisoners); create new alternatives where members of the public are involved and who can use the skills present in so many people for mediating and resolving conflicts (Stern, 1998)

As conceived by Ian Taylor (1997), the existing crime prevention movement has not as yet encompassed alternatives to prison, but he rightly acknowledges that there are already tensions between its several disparate elements. Enlarged into a community justice movement, the additional mix of sectors and agencies will inevitably struggle, at least initially, to discern common ground, although as this chapter is committed to showing, it does exist. Some tensions are likely to be permanent; there will probably always be different perspectives on community justice, for example, between the Probation Service and youth justice services on the one hand, and the voluntary and community sector – 'the third sector' – on the other. The statutory sector will probably provide the administrative framework, and set the tone, but it may well be 'the third sector' that becomes the pace setter for new thinking in community justice, as Tam (1998) envisages it being for communitarianism more generally.

Certainly, voluntary organisations of both the service-providing and the campaigning kind have had more influence on the administration of criminal justice, locally and nationally, than is often recognised. This was true even before the 1990s vogue for partnership, which has sometimes turned such organisations into little more than on-the-cheap agents of the state. They are prominent in the substance abuse field, in work with mentally disordered offenders, in work with children and young people, in the provision of accommodation and employment opportunities and in victim support work. They touch the lives of many individual offenders and, via their boards of trustees and patrons, play a significant part in both public education and lobbying government. The sector has no consistent politics – there are groups within it with opposing goals and objectives – but its very diversity helps to define democracy and to channel the myriad forms of civic concern. It is understandable that innovative responses to crime should have periodically emerged from this milieu, and highly desirable that it should continue, linked to broader ideas about community regeneration.

How might community justice acquire consciousness of itself as a movement? Many agencies will need to talk it up. Conferences and publications will be important, but perhaps the churches could have an important catalysing role here. For some of these at least, the communitarian concept of justice is already congenial, in ways that it is not (yet) in statutory agencies (see Catholic Bishops Conference, 1997 and Nellis, 1998). In addition, faith communities are arguably less constrained than secular organisations to affirm, against the grain of public and media opinion if necessary, the importance of care and compassion in work with offenders, (albeit not at the expense of victims) and to keep alive the humanitarian impulses which all too often shrivel under the managerialist gaze in the statutory and voluntary sectors. In practical terms, the Anglican and Catholic churches, the Salvation Army, and an array of Black churches, already have a significant presence among the poorest of the population, sometimes working alongside other agencies, sometimes alone. Last, but by no means least, the churches' inter-faith networks could usefully contribute to the creation of a genuinely multicultural conception of community justice.

Conclusions

The belief expressed here in the conceptual importance of community justice has been guided and constrained throughout by Michael Ignatieff's view, expressed at the head of this chapter, that as people at the start of the 21st century we need a mix of solidarity, liberty and justice. That is, if we are to live together with any degree of security and conviviality. We have a moral obligation to pursue and sustain these things in both our professional and personal lives. While perfect justice may well be unattainable, the determined striving for it is a good in itself. The ideal may be beyond our reach, but as Margalit (1996) argues, it is the hallmark of a decent society to work towards it.

What if we do not work towards community justice? At best, we will settle for a lesser quality of life – less decency – than we might with reasonable effort achieve. At worst, we will drift into the authoritarianism that Etzioni, Braithwaite, Stern and Radzinowicz all fear. The latter is more likely if it is not actively worked against. Michael Howard's incumbency of the Home Office showed how easily government can shift gear; in the absence of cultural and political impediments there was no way of stopping the rise in imprisonment which Howard wanted and which the sentencers who took their cues from him facilitated. Nothing has in fact changed under New Labour except the rhetoric (and, perhaps, the goodwill): we still lack reliable mechanisms for preventing a drift into higher levels of incarceration, although we certainly have the rudiments of them in the structures with which this chapter has been concerned. But within them all, the will to assert justice, exerted locally, is all-important.

If this only constitutes a preliminary case for taking community justice seriously, it might still be claimed that Ignatieff's larger challenge about adequacy, has not been met, as a result of falling into nostalgia. That is, that the language and possible practices of community justice are simply not adequate to the challenges posed by any of the futures that we are likely to face. Against this is the argument that it is familiar terms like social work and probation (the earlier carriers of humanitarian concern in the crime and punishment field), and crime prevention (a narrowly focused term suited to rather more orderly times) that are losing their semantic force and properly belong in the 'nostalgia paradigm' (Hobbs, 1998). The mind-sets associated with them offer limited guidance on the way ahead, not least because they neither evoke even-handed concern for offenders and victims, nor the inter-relationship of preventive and reactive approaches.

The words community and justice may not in themselves be new. Juxtaposed, and invested with the right kinds of meaning, however, they could invigorate a number of emerging responses to crime, and equip us, better than any existing vocabularies, to navigate the transition to a new century with our humanitarian commitments intact. Much depends on whether we want a just and decent society, and whether we have the will and capacity to resist those who do not. There is more at stake here than how we punish and prevent crime, and if we fail to create community justice the rather harsh penal landscape that will be the likely result will, in fact, be the least of our worries.

References

Atkinson D (1994) *The Common Sense of Community*, London: Demos

Braithwaite J (1989) *Crime, Shame and Reintegration*, Cambridge: Cambridge University Press

Braithwaite J and Daly K (1994) 'Masculinities, Violence and Communitarian Control', in Newburn T and Stanko E (eds) *Just Boys Doing Business: Men, Masculinities and Crime*, London: Routledge

Braithwaite J and Pettit P (1990) *Not Just Deserts: A Republican Theory of Justice*, Oxford: Clarendon Press

Burnside J (1994) 'Tension and Tradition in the Pursuit of Justice', in Burnside J and Baker N (eds) *Relational Justice: Repairing the Breach*, Winchester: Waterside Press

Burnside J and Baker N (eds) (1994) Relational Justice: Repairing the Breach, Winchester: Waterside Press

Campbell B (1993) *Goliath: Britain's Dangerous Places*, London: Methuen

Carlen P (1990) *Alternatives to Women's Imprisonment*, Milton Keynes: Open University Press

Christie N (1981) *Limits to Pain*, London: Martin Robertson

Catholic Bishops Conference of England and Wales (1997) *The Common Good and the Catholic Church's Social Teaching*, London: Catholic Bishop's Conference of England and Wales

Cohen S (1988) 'The Object of Criminology: Reflections on the New Criminology', in Cohen S (ed) *Against Criminology*, London: Transaction Publishers

Cragg W (1992) *The Practice of Punishment: Towards a Theory of Restorative Justice*, London: Routledge

Consedine J (1995) *Restorative Justice: Healing the Effects of Crime*, Lyttleton, New Zealand: Ploughshares Publications

Curle A (1981) *True Justice*, London: Quaker Home Service

Currie E (1998) 'Crime and the Market Society: Lessons from the United States', in Walton P and Young J (eds) *The New Criminology Revisited*, Basingstoke: Macmillan

Danziger N (1997) *Danziger's Britain: A Journey to the Edge*, London: Flamingo

Davies N (1998) *Dark Heart: The Shocking Truth about Britain*, London: Chatto and Windus

Donnison D (1998) *Policies for a Just Society*, Basingstoke: Macmillan

Duff A (1996) 'Penal Communications: Recent Work in the Philosophy of Punishment', in Tonry M (ed) *Crime and Justice 20*, Chicago: University of Chicago

Etzioni A (1995) *The Spirit of Community: Rights, Responsibilities and the Communitarian Agenda*, London: Fontana

Etzioni A (1997) *The New Golden Rule: Community and Morality in Democratic Society*, London: Profile Books

Giddens A (1990) *The Consequences of Modernity*, Cambridge: Polity Press

Giddens A (1998) *The Third Way: The Renewal of Social Democracy*, Cambridge: Polity Press

Henry S (1978) *The Hidden Economy: Context and Control of Borderline Crime*, London: Martin Robertson

Hobbs D (1998) 'Going Down the Glocal: The Local Context of Organised Crime', *Howard Journal* 37

Hope T (1998) 'Community Safety, Crime and Disorder', in Marlow A and Pitts J (eds) *Planning Safer Communities*, Lyme Regis: Russell House Publishing

Ignatieff M (1984) *The Needs of Strangers*, London: Chatto and Windus

Kammer F (1995) *Salted with Fire: Spirituality for the Faith/Justice Journey*, New York: Paulist Press

Lacey N (1988) *State Punishment: Political Principles and Community Values*, London: Routledge

Lacey M and Ward D (1995) (eds) *Probation: Working for Justice*, London: Whiting and Birch

Loader I (1998) 'Criminology and the Public Sphere: Arguments for Utopian Realism' in Walton P and Young J (eds) *The New Criminology Revisited*, Basingstoke: MacMillan

MacMurray J (1961) *Persons in Relation*, London: Faber and Faber

Margalit A (1997) *The Decent Society*, London: Harvard University Press

Marquand D (1998) 'Can Labour Kick the Winning Habit?', *New Statesman*, 23 October

Morris N and Tonry M (1990) *Between Prison and Probation Intermediate Punishments in a Rational Sentencing System*, Oxford: Oxford University Press

Nellis M (1998) 'The Sense of Community Justice', *The Friends Quarterly*, July

Pavlich G C (1996) *Justice Fragmented Mediating Community Disputes under Postmodern Conditions*, London: Routledge

Pease K (1995) *The Future of Imprisonment and its Alternatives*, Paper presented at the Fifth Conference on Crime Policy, Strasbourg, November, 1995, Strasbourg:

Council of Europe

Pendleton J (1995) 'More Justice, Less Law', in Ward D and Lacey M (eds) *Probation: Working for Justice*, London: Whiting and Birch

Pepinsky H and Quinney R (eds) (1991) *Criminology as Peacemaking*, Bloomington: Indiana University Press

Radzinowicz L (1991) 'Penal Regressions', *Cambridge Law Journal*, 50

Robins D (1992) *Tarnished Visions: Crime and Community and the Inner City*, Oxford: Oxford University Press

Rutherford A (1991) 'Penal Reform and Penal Realities', in Whitfield D (ed) *The State of the Prisons – 200 years on*, London: Routledge

Snider L (1998) 'Towards Safer Societies: Punishment, Masculinities and Violence Against Women', *British Journal of Criminology*, 38

Stern V (1998) *A Sin Against the Future Imprisonment in the World*, Harmondsworth: Penguin

Tam H (1998) *Communitarianism: A New Agenda for Politics and Citizenship*, Basingstoke: MacMillan

Taylor I (1997) 'Crime, Anxiety and Locality Responding to "the condition of England" at the end of the century', *Theoretical Criminology*, 1

Townsend C (1994) 'Believing in Justice', in Burnside J and Baker N (eds) *Relational Justice: Repairing the Breach*, Winchester: Waterside Press

van Swaaningen R (1997) *Critical Criminology: Visions from Europe*, London: Sage

Williams R and Collier M (1984) *Beginning Now: Peacemaking Theology*, London: Dunamis

Young J (1998) 'Writing on the Cusp of Change: A New Criminology for an Age of Late Modernity', in Walton P and Young J (eds) *The New Criminology Revisited*, Basingstoke: MacMillan

Zehr H (1990) *Changing Lenses: A New Focus for Crime and Justice*, Waterloo, Ontario: Herald Press

II: What works? What doesn't? How do we know? What does it matter?

4. What works and what makes what works work?
Julia Stafford and Leslie Silverlock

Since 1 April 1999, when the dust began to settle on the newly produced crime and disorder strategies, community safety practitioners have been faced with the next challenge: implementation. The audit process was over, raising as many questions as it has answered and leaving everyone relieved, many exhausted, and more than a few resolved to do better next time. But there is no time to sit back and enjoy the satisfaction of achievement, or even to lament the shortcomings of the gaps in the audit. The production of a strategy is only the first step. Though a crucial step, a strategy does not prevent crime, it is only a tool to help focus energy and resources. If it is to mean anything, strategy needs to be translated into action.

Do we know what to do and how to do it? Do we know what works, and if we do, does 'we' include the 'we' who are actually out there, in the police, the youth services, the housing department, the schools? If we know what works, do we know why it works, the conditions necessary to make it work, the processes by which it works? Do we have access to the resources – financial and human – to make it happen? Do we have the authority necessary to stop those involved in doing what will not work, and mobilise and motivate them to do what evidence suggests will make a difference?

This chapter reviews what is currently available to the practitioner to inform action. It considers whether this information is getting through to those responsible for implementation, identifies some of the obstacles which face the practitioner and suggests ways in which these might be overcome.

Do we know what works?

It is now thirteen years since the first Home Office Crime Prevention Unit (CPU) paper – or 'brownie' was published. The intervening years have seen the production of a further 90 or so, covering a range of subjects including crime problems such as shop theft, domestic violence, fraud, and racial harassment. The brownies became 'pinkies' (and larger) mid-series, and were re-badged as the Crime Detection and Prevention series. The CPU became the Police Research Group (PRG), and more recently, the Policing and Reducing Crime Group (PRC). The only difference to the publications was that the cover ink no longer stained your fingers. This series perhaps offered the most accessible fund of experience for crime prevention in England and Wales.

In 1993, the Home Office published *A Practical Guide to Crime Prevention for Local Partnerships*. Directed at crime prevention practitioners and partnerships, this presented a model process as well as a pointer towards what kind of action might be taken to prevent crime.

Most of the more recent attempts to direct the practitioner towards effective crime prevention measures are referenced elsewhere in this volume. In addition, the list should include the work of Utting (1996), the International Centre for the Prevention of Crime (1997) and Hough and Tilley (1998).

From these publications we can begin to build a picture of what has been tried, and what has worked. The brownies are a useful source of reference for the practitioner to dip into as the issue arises. While all present an informed analysis of the crime problem and issues raised by preventive action, they vary in the extent to which they can be used to provide a guide towards what works. It is not clear to the reader – nor was it perhaps to the authors – for whom these publications are written. If they are intended for the practitioner, many fall short by being too academic in flavour, presenting an interesting background to and context for, rather than a guide to, action. That said, some (such as numbers 25 and 49, dealing with the role of victim support in a crime prevention project and domestic violence respectively) put forward the lessons learned from research studies and raise the issues for future development. Some (such as number 36, dealing with racial attacks in East London) go as far as suggesting an intervention strategy.

The work of Larry Sherman and his colleagues (1997, 1998 – see previous chapter) sets out some general points and presents the results of evaluating specific crime prevention measures. Amongst the general points it concludes that:

- crime prevention programmes should be targeted in high crime locations

- in such locations it is necessary to intervene in many domains simultaneously (the family, school, labour market, community, criminal justice system)

- neighbourhood-based programmes are more likely to be effective if they include both situational and social crime prevention.

Sherman distinguishes between what works from what is promising. He differentiates between those evaluations which have included a fully randomised control trial of the intervention, and those which are only able to demonstrate a correlation between the intervention and reduced crime. He concludes that we need to undertake more rigorous testing of promising approaches before we can be confident about replicating them more widely. Sherman also identifies approaches that don't work, or at least have not been demonstrated to work through effective evaluation.

While Sherman provides pointers, his findings are of limited use to the practitioner. As Tilley points out in Chapter 6, what works has only been shown to do so in certain circumstances, and so has little interest for those who want to replicate. Moreover, it does not provide enough information on 'how', and so fails to equip the practitioner for action. As for what doesn't work, it is not always clear to the reader whether the fault lies in the measure itself, in the way it has been implemented, or in the evaluation lacking sufficient rigour.

The ICPC (1997) publication is not and does not profess to be an academic document based on rigorous evaluation. It presents, in the form of a series of short case studies (one page each) a hundred examples of practical initiatives to prevent crime. The case studies are categorised under the headings of types of prevention (for example, designing the physical environment and social control, supporting young people and families, enhancing responsibility, city action plans and partnerships). Each case study sets out the problem (or challenge) being addressed, a description of the initiative, its impact (in terms of percentage reduction in crime), partners, further lessons, and selected sources. While it could not claim to pass Sherman's test of promoting only what has been rigorously evaluated, it does provide some useful, practical information upon which to base action.

Goldblatt and Lewis (1998) provide a useful assessment of the comparative effectiveness and cost effectiveness of different methods of reducing crime. They present, in each chapter, a description and analysis of approaches to reducing offending. Like Sherman, they draw some general conclusions as well as identifying specific measures that have been demonstrated to work. Amongst their general conclusions are the following:

- the need to target interventions at those children and families most at risk,

- the need to combine this targeting with increased social control and cohesion in communities that are vulnerable

- the need to target situational measures on hot spots

- the need to combine long-term measures that prevent criminality with situational measures to reduce crime more immediately.

So, material exists to inform the practitioner about what works, and to sound a note of caution about what is as yet unproven, but it does not constitute a template for action. Increasingly, research findings are available on the Internet, and the Home Office and National Institute of Justice (NIJ) sites provide particularly rich pickings.

On the whole we should be safe in assuming that the Home Office publications reach the field, or get at least as far as the community safety specialists, thus making research findings – both from this country and abroad – readily available. The extent to which these are in a form that can be easily understood and used is variable. More problematic, however, is reaching those other specialists who are working on community safety issues across the range of agencies, not all of whom are plugged into the Home Office networks. The importance of adopting a *package* of measures targeting crime reduction, and of involving as partners the people nearest to the problem – residents, businesses, schools, young people – is only recently beginning to be understood amongst practitioners.

What does make what works work?

This chapter owes its title and its existence to Jon Bright, former Director of Fieldwork at Crime Concern, currently on secondment to the Government's Social Exclusion Unit (SEU). His paper to the Crime Prevention Agency's 'What Works' conference in September 1997 asked whether crime prevention practitioners were applying what works systematically. Bright identified some indicators that would suggest that we were. These included crime prevention being a feature of national and local governance, serious public investment, consistent monitoring of quality, a system for informing practitioners and a professional group of practitioners with accredited training such as to maintain a level of expertise. He referred to the need for real political support at national level, and the need for a whole of government strategy.

In September 1997, the Home Office had just published its consultation document *Getting to Grips with Crime – A Framework for Local Action* and the future looked promising. Things have moved on apace since then, the Crime and Disorder Act 1998 bringing with it statutory responsibility for the development of local crime and disorder plans. After fifteen years of voluntarism, with local partnerships doing – or not doing – what they thought was needed, there is now an imperative to produce a strategy with performance targets, and a clear expectation that it will be delivered upon.

The vision of a whole of government strategy has been reflected in the term 'joined-up thinking' that is now so well used, and was illustrated in the SEU's (1998) report. This strategy sets out roles for the various government departments to achieve its overall objectives.

Funding

The Government was careful to make it clear at the outset that there was little new money. The Home Office Guidance on Statutory Crime and Disorder Partnerships (1998) refers to assessing how resources are currently devoted to crime reduction, the 'scope for reallocating efforts', and 'opportunities for contributions from partners'. This did not augur well for 'serious public investment'.

However, subsequent Home Office announcements under the umbrella of the National Crime Reduction Programme have promised over £400 million including : £250 million over three years for research and development; an additional £3 million for external research, and extra funds worth £2 million for drugs research. As to implementation, the Home Office has already announced a budget of: £217 million over three years for a drugs strategy with a focus on young people and drug related crime; £50 million over three years to reduce domestic burglary, and £32 million for targeted policing, focusing particularly upon crime hotspots, repeat victims and offenders. Future funding (at the time of writing) is expected for: domestic violence; truancy, school exclusions and bullying; restorative justice; fine enforcement; more informal sentencing, and prison and probation programmes covering literacy, cognitive skills and violent offenders.

Standards

In relation to the monitoring of quality, the Audit Commission has been given the task of auditing the crime and disorder audits and strategies, ensuring that minimum standards are reached and identifying improvements attainable in the next cycle. The Government has placed a firm emphasis on delivery and performance targets, and these too will need to be monitored to ensure that the fine words are turned into effective action.

Practitioners are undoubtedly becoming better informed, but to describe this process as systematic might still be an overstatement. The fact that 10,000 copies of Goldblatt and Lewis' (1998) work have been distributed and that a further 3,000 copies have been printed from the Internet, suggests an unprecedented appetite in the field for this kind of information. There is now a need to provide information in a form that is useful, and to establish networks for dissemination to all those who need it. The time has come for a regular publication which provides abstracts from recent research and evaluation studies and information about funding competitions and other serious crime prevention issues.

In relation to the existence of a professional group of practitioners, Jon Bright referred in his speech almost two years ago to crime prevention being a low status profession, staff being transferred into posts without training, and variable levels of knowledge and expertise amongst practitioners. In this respect the Crime and Disorder Act, at least in the short term, may have aggravated the problem. While the status of crime prevention has been raised by the Act and its statutory duty to prepare local community safety strategies, in reality this has meant that many individuals in the local authority or police have been deployed to work in an area which is not – nor would they claim it to be – their field of expertise. While many of them are doubtless talented and resourceful individuals who, faced with the challenge to sink or swim, will not only keep their heads above water but will soon achieve a degree of proficiency, others will doubtless struggle and some will fail.

The longer-term future looks more promising. It is evident from the job advertisements that appeared during 1998 that a number of local authorities are taking their statutory duty seriously, and rating the work involved highly enough to create a position or small team dedicated to the task. The senior level at which some are pitched indicates a recognition of the complexity of the work, and the need for the individual to command the respect of senior staff from a range of professional backgrounds.

Learning to deliver: the role of training and coaching

One path towards raising both the status of the profession and the standard of performance may be through developing accredited training and qualifications for practitioners. This would be the usual pattern for an emerging professional cadre.

A National Training Organisation (NTO) has been established for community justice to develop quality standards, competencies, learning resources and certification. The NTO's title is an amalgamation of community safety and criminal justice. There are estimated to be 67,000 practitioners in this catchment group. It will be a test for the community safety part of the equation to gain as much attention as the pre-existing and much larger criminal justice services.

There is now a large demand for training and capacity building at all levels in community safety. This thirst encompasses content knowledge (such as youth crime, women's safety, vehicle crime, drugs, neighbourhood crime, domestic violence, safer travel), as well as process skills for audit, strategic planning, effective partnership working, monitoring and evaluation. There is an acknowledged need to know what works best and to take action as quickly as possible.

Until now resources have tended to be spent on conferencing in community safety, with too little emphasis on transferring knowledge and developing skills through action learning. Among the exceptions are: the Safe Neighbourhood Unit distance learning certificates at the University of the West of England; the National Tenants Resource Centre's residents' courses, and Crime Concern's modular programme of in-house seminars for partnerships of police, education, housing, health, probation, youth, and local authority officers. Easingwold and Bramshill Colleges provide training for the police, some with their local authority partners; and there are a number of other occasional providers, including criminology departments of universities.

Other than the co-coaching which networks of practitioners organise for themselves, little action learning, of the sort typified by 'Planning for Real' exercises, has been in evidence. Multi-agency partnerships spend the bulk of their time together meeting and planning, rather than reviewing, reflecting, updating and upskilling. These probably need to be regular agenda items in future, rather than once-a-year events. Evaluation of training and its impact on practice has been even more scarce.

The dynamics of inter-agency working and the emotional intelligence required are beginning to spread beyond the pioneers, due in part to the accelerated activity brought on by the Act and the ensuing guidance. It is not yet a mature enough environment to match the expectations being put upon its practitioners. Working with schools, health, police and housing services, for example, at both the executive and the delivery level requires complex technical knowledge, information processing and organisational and interpersonal skills. An understanding of how networks, authority, hierarchy, cultures, loyalties, commitment, expectations, confidentiality and accountability operate in the context of a partnership, has to be learnt alongside matters such as resources, budgets, workloads, regulations, protocols, data, media, community involvement, target setting and monitoring. Evidence from other fields suggests that partnerships may be able to increase their productivity if they take this learning together, on the job.

Other issues to bring out during this kind of training will include differences in organisational cultures, operating principles, and access to resources, networks and information. High performance teams in other 'industries' are also characterised by quality leadership, constructive disagreement, valuing difference, and their ability to reward and celebrate.

Partnerships: help or hindrance?

Multi-agency working has for some time been seen as the cornerstone of effective community safety, a view endorsed by the Morgan Report in 1991 and given statutory recognition in the Crime and Disorder Act. When Morgan reported, there were 80 community safety partnerships; now there are more than 400, many developed by local partners without legislation, before the Act became law. It is clear that hard-pressed local partners believe inter-agency co-operation is a necessity.

Partnership working makes sense in the context of community safety. An effective community safety strategy involves the commitment and active participation of a range of agencies and departments, including those responsible for housing, youth services, education, social services, health services, working with offenders and the police. A partnership approach can enable a package of measures to be developed, creating a dosage that is capable of making an impact.

The new legal requirement for mainstreaming (S17) means that individual agencies and departments will need to consider how they can incorporate prevention within their core services. For the housing department this might involve security audits and improvements to properties at risk of burglary, management through caretakers and concierges, reducing opportunities for crime through environmental design, or offering voids as family centres. For the Youth Service this might mean outreach youth work, targeting resources in high-crime neighbourhoods, even discarding ambitions of social education for all young people in favour of working with those most at risk. For people in schools and local education authorities it might involve action to reduce truancy and exclusion, helping those excluded return to mainstream education or training, establishing family literacy schemes and lifelong learning programmes. For this to happen effectively and consistently within all the other targets they are required to hit, there will need to be incentives for each of the agencies expected to deliver.

Working in a partnership should help each agency to understand its potential role in preventing crime and reducing criminality. Partnership working can offer a perspective that enables individual agencies to develop their distinctive contributions. It is therefore important for partnerships to highlight and maintain the essential differences which brought them together, while at the same time building corporate and cohesive working practices. Developing the partnership is arguably as important as the audit process in laying the foundations for implementation.

The arguments for partnerships are well established and accepted. However, experience tells us that not all partnerships work effectively or achieve their potential. Some fail by becoming a talking shop, a forum for sharing information and opinion that only endorses decisions that have already been made elsewhere. Others fail by allowing the agenda and priorities of those with most power to direct action, without regard to what the available data tells them is the real problem, or to what research tells them is the appropriate solution. Liddle and Gelsthorpe's (1994a and b) research showed us that much time is spent on reporting and recording backwards and forwards between various committees, while crucial decisions are made between meetings of the partnership, by its most powerful members.

One of the biggest problems facing crime prevention practitioners is that they do not start with a 'green field'. The partnership comes together around them, to assist them in their work, but it comprises people who are already out there, wrestling with the issues, and believing in what they are doing. Members of the partnership will often have their own idea about what the main local crimes are, and what should be done about them. These views may be based more upon their own experience and interests than on the evidence. Each has his or her own theory about the problem and how it can successfully be addressed, not necessarily welcoming other views. They have their own subject expertise, be it education, policing, youth work, electronic surveillance, and their own experience of what appears to work. They may already be doing it that way, in which case the challenge will be to demonstrate that another way would be more effective. Or, they may see this as an opportunity to develop a new initiative, in which case the challenge will be to ensure that the new initiative is the one most likely to work.

Developing an effective partnership: what works?

The literature on partnerships is, on the whole, historical, descriptive or rather academic. While it provides an interesting background and raises some interesting issues, it falls short of providing practitioners and their partners with practical guidance.

Gordon Hughes (1998) presents a history of the development of multi-agency working and a review of the literature about it. This provides the practitioner with an interesting contextual analysis, but with little about what works.

Sutton (1996) presents a detailed description and analysis of the Home Office Safer Cities initiative, with some reference to the impact of differing partnership styles. Once again, while providing an illuminating context, the book neither professes to be, nor is, a manual for partnership development in the future.

Gilling (1997) explores some of the problems of multi-agency work and while his analysis will ring true for practitioners and does offer an understanding of why the problem arises, he does not steer towards a solution.

The closest we come to a guide is found in Liddle and Gelsthorpe (1994a and b), Crawford and Jones (1995) and in the Audit Commission (1998).

Liddle and Gelsthorpe (1994a and b) examine the organisation of crime prevention, raising the implication of different approaches. They go on to look at how partnerships work in practice, and address such issues as the composition of steering groups, the effectiveness of meetings, approaches to decision-making, and factors affecting the durability of a partnership. While their stated aim is merely to investigate and assess, they are prepared to point the reader to what works. Their work could provide the basis for practical guidance.

Similarly, Crawford and Jones tackle some of the real and knotty problems of making partnerships work. Their starting point is the earlier work of Harry Blagg and his colleagues (1988), which they subject to what they describe as 'a sympathetic critique'. In doing so they address such issues as power difference and its potential for creativity; confronting and managing conflict, and ways in which using informal settings to make decisions can hinder progress. They raise problems that will be familiar to the practitioner, offering some valuable insights and pointers towards effective working. Again, while not providing a manual for what works, their work could well be drawn upon in the production of such a handbook.

As the audit, strategy, targets, and action plan unfold, leading them to adopt a mixture of measures, improve internal and external communications, and involve the community, partnerships will need to make explicit what is in it for each member. In what way are they going to be stakeholders in the desired outcomes? Some agenda time needs to be set aside regularly to review explicitly those issues which might otherwise be taken for granted in single-agency working. This will be necessary to avoid losing commitment, particularly of those partners not at the heart of the activity, for whom community safety is likely to be only a peripheral issue.

Finally, the partnership needs to address the thorny issue of bridging the gap to the local community. How are its members going to become stakeholders from the outset and not be surprised by the partnership's decisions? The community too needs to raise its sights beyond a desire for more Bobbies on the beat and faster response times and chasing young people off to another area of town. Crime Concern's (1998 and 1999) publications begin to point the way as practical guides.

References

Audit Commission (1998) *A Fruitful Partnership: Effective Partnership Working* London: Audit Commission.

Blagg H, Pearson G, Sampson A, Smith D and Stubbs P (1988) 'Inter-agency Coordination: Rhetoric and Reality' in T Hope and M Shaw (eds) *Communities and Crime Reduction* London: HMSO

Crawford A and Jones M (1995) 'Inter-Agency Co-operation and Community-Based Crime Prevention' *British Journal of Criminology* 35

Crime Concern/DETR (1999) *A Perfect Match: the voluntary sector and community safety* Swindon: Crime Concern

Crime Concern/Housing Corporation (1998) *Safe as Houses* Swindon: Crime Concern

Gilling D (1997) *Crime Prevention* London: UCL Press

Goldblatt, P and Lewis, C (eds) (1998) *Reducing Offending: An Assessment of the Research Evidence on Ways of Dealing with Offending Behaviour*, Home Office Research Study 187, London: HMSO

Home Office (1993) *A Practical Guide to Crime Prevention for Local Partnerships* London: Home Office

Home Office (1997) *Getting to Grips with Crime – A Framework for Local Action* London: Home Office

Home Office (1998) *Guidance on Statutory Crime and Disorder Partnerships* London: Home Office

Hough M and Tilley N (1998) *Getting the Grease to the Squeak: Research Lessons for Crime Prevention* Crime Detection and Prevention Paper 85, London: Home Office

Hughes G (1998) *Understanding Crime Prevention: Social Control, Risk and Late Modernity* Buckingham: Open University Press

International Centre for the Prevention of Crime (1997) *Worldwide Best Practice in Crime Prevention* Montreal: ICPC

Liddle M and Gelsthorpe M (1994a) *Inter-Agency Crime Prevention: Organising Local Delivery* Crime Prevention Paper 52, London: Home Office

Liddle M and Gelsthorpe L (1994b) *Crime prevention and inter-agency cooperation* Crime Prevention Paper 53, London: Home Office

Morgan Report (1991) *Safer Communities: The Local Delivery of Crime Prevention through the Partnership Approach* London: Home Office

Sherman L, Gottfredson D, MacKenzie D, Eck J, Reuter P, and Bushway S (1997) *Preventing Crime: What Works, What Doesn't, What's Promising: A Report to the United States Congress*, available at internet address: www.ncjrs.org/works/index.htm

Sherman L, Gottfredson D, MacKenzie D, Eck J, Reuter P, and Bushway S (1998) *Preventing Crime: What Works, What Doesn't, What's Promising*, National Institute of Justice: Research in Brief, Office of Justice Programs, US Department of Justice

Social Exclusion Unit (1998) *Bringing Britain Together: a National Strategy for Neighbourhood Renewal* London: The Stationery Office

Sutton M (1996) *Implementing Crime Prevention Schemes in a Multi-Agency Setting: Aspects of Process in the Safer Cities Programme* Home Office Research Study 160, London: HMSO

Utting D (1996) *Reducing criminality among young people: a sample of relevant programmes in the UK* Home Office Research Study 161, London: HMSO

5. Partnership – rhetoric or reality?
Sheila Stokes-White

This chapter will contribute a perspective on partnership in the context of community safety and regeneration, exploring some of its main characteristics, strengths and weaknesses. Major themes concern the paradox at the heart of all partnership – that of rhetoric and reality: is it simply political and policy rhetoric or is it political reality manifested through meaningful policy? By considering the evolving stages of the development process of partnership the key themes are further examined.

Concentrating on strategic outcomes rather than individual projects, this chapter will look at partnership at all levels (local, regional, strategic, national and European) to demonstrate that, whilst both rhetoric and reality are involved, there are essential characteristics which are common to all working partnerships. An understanding of these can facilitate successful outcomes.

The chapter first grapples with the concept of partnership in general and examines partnership in the fields of regeneration and community safety. Strengths and weaknesses, contentious issues and tensions between stakeholders are considered. The chapter goes on to describe the process of partnership suggesting factors to consider at the outset including some words of caution and some of hope.

Moving on to key themes, the justification for partnership will be covered assessing the possible direct benefits, added value and potential strategic outcomes. The possibility of a European dimension and its effect on partnership will be explored together with funding regimes, resources and the key importance of evaluation. It will also cover the wisdom of allowing for unexpected developments

Finally, the issues will be summarised, the core aspects of successful partnerships will be considered and the opening question re-examined – is partnership rhetoric or reality?

An introduction to the concept of partnership

What does partnership mean?

Partnership is a word of the Nineties, but what do people understand by it? Are the same principles or ideas at work whichever kind of partnership one is describing? Clearly the word has become overused, yet it is still a necessary prerequisite of all the latest strategic developments or major legislation. For example, the Crime and Disorder Act 1998 proposes the partnership approach to, amongst other things, reducing crime and tackling youth crime and improving youth justice. This latter poses some difficult problems for emerging youth offending teams where the staff will be drawn from a variety of professional backgrounds and organisational cultures, yet will work jointly to a team manager. At the same time, there has recently been a proliferation of strategic initiatives that advocate the partnership approach such as Health and Education Action Zones.

A simple explanation of partnership may be two or more people who join together to undertake a business, a venture, an initiative or an action. This, however, does not cover the issues of power and control and goes no way towards explaining the extremely complex, delicate and dynamic nature of the sort of professional partnerships with which most of us are dealing. Compounded by information overload and very short timescales, the struggle in these partnerships is with the human, the messy, the intractable and sometimes the apparently impossible.

Partnership is not necessarily susceptible to rational organisation, to focus, clarity and structure. It does not exist within a scientific or structured discipline though it may need to use some of that expertise. The concept may often seem ephemeral and unrealisable, existing only in the wishes and dreams of its proponents. One of the problems is that we all think we know about partnerships. After all, we are all partners in our lives, our relationships, our sporting and recreational activities, our businesses and legal affairs and we are partners in our professional lives both as individuals, one with another, and as representatives of organisations whose interests and well-being we are charged with.

There is no professional or academic body of knowledge that exists to guide and help us with the partnership process. For many of us, the experience upon which we draw in order to make partnerships work in our professional lives is accessed from other parts of our lives where, in our families, our relationships and our networks, we are practising our partnership skills all the time. At work, whether we know it or not, we draw on this emotional experience as well as our professional expertise in order to forge new partnerships and make them work. You cannot simply learn about partnership from a book or a course or a model. You can learn some basic principles usually distilled from the hard won experience of others, but the vital factor to be added to any partnership equation is yourself

Does partnership then always imply an implicit core – equality, common aims, shared vision, agreements, cultural understanding and so on, or can it exist without any preconditions? It does seem that, whilst both rhetoric and reality are involved, there are essential characteristics common to all working partnerships. An understanding of these can facilitate successful outcomes. Partnership is of course a two way process, with advantages and gains to set against losses and responsibilities. The management gurus of the 1980s – Tom Peters (Peters, 1987 and Peters and Waterman, 1982), Rosabeth Moss Kanter, (1989) and Charles Handy (1989) gave us new ways of looking at the working environment. Meetings and committees could be seen as a good way of ensuring that nothing was actually achieved. For today, the paradox is that the pivotal requirement for meeting, sharing and committee agreement lies at the heart of partnership. Somehow, we have to find a new way of working which combines effective meeting with positive agreement and real outcomes.

Partnership in the fields of regeneration and community safety

It is worth remembering that twenty years ago, policy was characterised by single-agency responses. Responsibility was carried by local authorities or allocated to individual organisations within a particular locality and funded by grants. Policy now requires multi-agency responses, drawing together public, private and voluntary sector interests to develop formal partnerships and deliver integrated programmes to promote regeneration. Embedded within these structures lies much of existing community safety activity.

Partnership has grown into a central pillar of government policy for the last decade, with an emphasis on joint planning, joint working and consultation in almost all policy areas. This emphasis can be traced to a range of factors – the growing number of different agencies involved in delivering services at local level, the attractions of synergy, the pooling of expertise and resources, the realisation that problems have multiple causes and require an integrated approach if they are to be resolved, and the fact that communities and other partners must have involvement and consultation.

Individual partners report that partnerships encouraged them to think more broadly and extend their knowledge particularly of the cultures of other organisations. They also revealed considerable ambivalence, as partnerships can become exclusive, elitist and self interested and there can be tensions between accountability to the public and the interests of different partners. There are tensions between leadership and participation. Partnership can, and often does, slow down decision making and requires leaders of organisations to meet with other leaders to reach a consensus.

Tensions between stakeholders

Partnerships established to regenerate environments and improve the safety of the environment typically have multiple stakeholders, all of whose interests have to be taken into account. As a result, there can be considerable cultural difference within such partnerships and a delicate balance of interest and motivation. The balance can easily be disrupted with damaging consequences. Many of these partnerships also have networks of provision operating in complex inter-agency environments. Smaller organisations may rely on larger ones for assistance and, together, they may all work to provide a network of linked services, which would not otherwise be possible.

The terms partnership and network are often used in imprecise ways or are seen as interchangeable (McCabe *et al*, 1997). One of the most important differences between them is the formal relationship between organisations involved in a partnership, manifested by the establishment of a board or company. Networks, on the other hand, rely on relationships which have indistinct boundaries and fluid memberships and which operate on the basis of shared interests. Networks and partnerships coexist and networks are often formalised into partnership bodies. What is clear, is that managing the complexities of these relationships on a day-to-day basis is very complex and demanding and there is little guidance by way of reference information.

Strengths and weaknesses

In networks rather than partnerships, there is typically a wide spread of activity with a flat structure giving managers a very broad span and with staff taking on a wide range of tasks. Roles may appear unclear or ambiguous, which can reflect in low staffing levels, or funding structures requiring core functions to be spread among project-funded staff. It may also reflect the complexity of relationships between unpaid management committees and paid staff.

There is wide variation in practice according to origins and dominant constituencies. Staff recruited from other backgrounds, such as the private sector, typically comment on the lack of systems and clear responsibilities. There can also be a reliance on trust and a reluctance to address issues of authority. Alternatively, there are many examples of centralised organisations, structured along hierarchical lines, dominated by a charismatic individual adopting a decentralised model but with strategy, budget and standards firmly dictated from the centre.

One of the strengths often attributed to partnerships that are specifically created to tackle issues across a range of organisations and structures, is innovation. This is felt to be the result of having the opportunity of adopting a new and creative approach to intractable problems. Whilst this may be the case, it is more often true that such partnerships import tried and tested ideas and initiatives, which may be new to that locality, but are not new in concept.

Other contentious issues

Whilst not wishing to explore issues of funding in any detail, it is worth observing that, particularly with newly created partnerships, there is rarely spare capacity to absorb additional core costs. Core and management tasks are frequently under-resourced What seems to have been happening is that organisations are simultaneously managing growth and constraint (Taylor, 1997) – either under-funded or having one-off pots of money thrown at the partnership with little thought for focused outcomes. This has created two major problems for partnerships in this field: funding is patched together from many sources and vast amounts of time and energy are required to secure and retain it. This issue arises later in the chapter.

The partnership process described

Clarity is a vital component of partnership development as is the formation of an appropriate structure, depending on whether the partnership has been created to govern, manage or consult. There is a lot of room for confusion in partnerships. This can be over roles and responsibilities, agreed tasks, levels of commitment and over what the scope of the remit is.

The rules of engagement should be addressed. Partnerships can consist of different types of structure – disparate organisations working together, organisations working to a given agenda but retaining an individual perspective or organisations pooling resources to achieve a common goal. The style of the partnership, as to how the work is managed, developed, promoted and recorded, is an important early issue. Where there is a clear and simple structure, some partners can feel left out of the real decision making, which may seem to be made other than through formal channels.

Factors to consider

The development of a partnership follows a process. It can be helpful to understand this process before beginning. Most partnerships go through life-cycle stages. These are well documented already and include such stages as initiation, development, consolidation, maturity, review and evaluation, exit strategy and/or rebirth. These stages are mirrored by behaviours and characteristics displayed by the partner organisations and their representatives. The first characteristic is excitement and interest and this tends to increase as the partners begin to realise the partnership potential and become enthused by it. This is followed by communication and exploration as each partner seeks to learn more about other organisations and experiments with the possibilities and boundaries. A loose agreement of aim and objectives may be struck at this stage and there is considerable commitment to working together.

The first piece of collaborative practice, small or large, marks the next stage and real difficulties can emerge as the partnership struggles through the implementation process. These include difficulties over control of resources and, in the case of funding, its distribution. Power, control, ownership and authority pace also have to be addressed before the partnership can move to the next stage. On issues such as these, the early promising foundations of the partnership may founder. For the organisations involved, the issue 'is not so much that they are different...but that the degree of difference is rarely recognised' (Wilson, 1995 in Taylor, 1997).

The next stage is disagreement and conflict. Exploration of the boundaries and existing agreements may be revisited. If a breakdown in communication occurs at this stage, it helps if a complete split can be avoided and a compromise, if only temporary, reached. This enables a return to the drawing board, bringing people back to the table for the further discussions. These precede the next stage, which is more informed debate leading to conciliation; an acceptance of difference and an agreement about future action to safeguard the achievement of the aims.

The final stage of resolution and acceptance can result in a sense that the partnership has reached a sufficient stage of maturity to withstand future conflict. The signs are that flourishing and healthy partnerships continue to work on these issues, to learn lessons raised by earlier disagreement, and to resolve difficulties that may give rise to future conflict. Long-lasting partnerships seem able to create a continuous cycle of learning for themselves, so that differences between the organisations are used positively to develop the partnership.

As the partnership moves into the final stage of resolution and acceptance, it is helpful if there is an external source of funding which can generate immediate joint work towards a key objective. This process of engagement can act as a catalyst to weld the partnership together. A further characteristic that seems to mark out successful partnership is that a real sense of identity also emerges from this process. This identity acts as a continuing form of both internal and external validation.

Some words of caution

Partnership is not cheap or quick. It is more time consuming than single-agency work. It is also not a substitute for single-agency responsibility. In addition, tensions exist between: fragmentation and integration; competition and co-operation, and centralisation and localisation. Further complexity is added by terminology. A new language is growing up around partnership with words such as sustainability, capacity-building, succession strategies and added value. There is not necessarily a common understanding of these terms.

The Crime and Disorder Act 1998 now places statutory responsibility jointly and firmly with police services and local authorities. Whilst other partners will join the table, it will be in a different capacity. The new partnerships will have partners involved at different levels or for multi-task purposes. There will be those who are there by statute, those who wish to co-operate on a voluntary basis and those who wish to collaborate on a voluntary basis. One way of handling this, recently recommended by central government, is to arrange meetings which are multi-purpose to save time and resources, and that with careful agenda planning, members can leave and join as relevant matters arise. Whilst partnership is still enshrined in the delivery mechanism it has shifted its emphasis again.

Clearly the professional and cultural backgrounds of the partnership organisations involved are a crucial issue to consider when trying to create and develop a working partnership. It is important to balance the needs of different partners and to move at a pace that allows everyone to participate. The police service and local authorities do work at different paces, and in very different ways. This issue can manifest itself as a range of difficulties and will differ depending upon the level of coterminosity between the police service and the local authority/authorities. Other partners' perception of the police service can be that they want to control and drive everything, whilst the police service itself can feel a very single-agency responsibility for issues which clearly involve the reduction and management of crime.

Where a regional dimension can be used for strategic direction, acting as an umbrella for a number of local authorities usually within one police authority area, some of these tensions can be managed in a more diffuse, less localised way.

Northumbria has been fortunate to have had this regional dimension. Partnership was developed as a result of the police service acknowledging that tackling crime as a single agency was unlikely to result in the successful crime reduction needed to reassure the public and increase public confidence. They sought the co-operation of other organisations. As crime levels were extremely high and escalating there was self-evidently a problem to solve. It was therefore not too difficult to reach some early agreement with core partners who were themselves struggling with the consequences of high crime levels. What the police service and the resultant strategic partnership were able to draw on was the legacy of co-operation and good will which existed in the region following many years of informal multi-agency work. A further significant factor was that the benefits of such a partnership approach to all potential partners could be readily identified. These included a reduction in the crime rate, a reduction in fear of crime and an improvement in inward investment. Even when the partnership was extended to a larger number of organisations (making 25 in all, including six local authorities) it was still possible to retain these common goals.

In other parts of the country which had similar structures and problems, this strategic approach, which some partners would clearly find useful, has been more difficult to create. This does seem to be due to attitude rather than concrete inhibiting factors. It may be that the perceived problems need to reach a level which is impossible to ignore before attitudinal issues can be overcome.

The lessons in Northumbria included the avoidance of short-term funding crises, a standing forum with top-level commitment which helped to avoid demarcation and dissension, and the identification of key strategic issues as priorities which provided a broad framework for activity.

The major factor here is often the issue as to who is actually leading. Many emerging or potential partnerships struggle to decide whether or not all partners have equal rights and responsibilities and, if not, how to accommodate the different contributions that can be made. The mechanisms used for organisational matters are material to the issue of control and significantly affect perceptions about the partnership. These are often the key differences between charitable partnerships with private sector members, but with trustees who have clearly delineated responsibilities, and public sector partnerships which may have some private and voluntary sector memberships but which, for reasons of expediency, have few clearly identified rules.

A significant word of caution is about funding. Funding can be readily identified by most partnerships as the first thing necessary for progress. However, successful funding bids bring their own issues as to division of the spoils and this needs to be addressed at an early stage.

Contextual factors also impinge on partnerships. The Crime and Disorder Act 1998 is only one piece of legislation amongst many which are making demands on those involved. The legislation concerning drugs 'Tackling drugs to build a better Britain' makes recommendations which will require strategic alignments between crime and disorder and drugs action team strategies. These will need to be located within a context where other partnerships in the environment are in the process of either initiation or decline. Central, regional and local government structures are also undergoing major review, so that the overall context is one of fluidity and uncertainty.

It is perhaps important to reflect that for existing and currently developing partnerships, many individuals will have seen and handled these changes within their own professional lifetime. Some of the problems encountered by partnerships may be exacerbated by varying professional experience. Those who were used to a single-agency approach may feel that partnership poses a considerable risk to their own organisation. Could it, like the Eurosceptic view of the EU, require them to modify their aims and activities as a result of pressure from an unconstitutional and loosely structured outside body? What happens if one agency cannot meet its partnership commitments, or fails to deliver against agreed funding targets?

Partner agencies may, or may not, have a shared understanding of the goals or even purpose of the partnership. The commitment of individuals and organisations to partnerships may change over time and this can and, indeed is, likely to be affected by developments outside the control of the organisations themselves. Again, healthy partnerships have taken account of this in their contingency planning. Partnerships are, after all, drawing together people with differing histories, priorities and cultures. They may have been established very quickly to meet the criteria for a new funding initiative.

Some words of hope

In some partnerships, these problems have been partly overcome by an overwhelming political commitment, an opportunistic vision coupled with determination, commitment from the top in the partner organisations, and a concentration on strategic focus whilst addressing issues of pace, balance and control.

Issues like ownership and authority could be tackled at an early stage to avoid future difficulty. Local authorities need to be convinced that sharing power will enhance their capacity to do the job rather than undermine it. Multi-agency initiatives and single-agency responsibility towards achieving them, need to be articulated and agreed. It can often be assumed that if approval is given at a board meeting then someone else will carry it out.

The justification for partnership

There are advantages to partnership, working beyond the political drive towards it. Closer examination shows that there are benefits beyond the simplistic ones of meeting funding criteria or statutory requirements. Indeed, partnerships created from the determination and will of the partner organisations, and which meet funding criteria or statutory requirements, are more susceptible to long-term success than those formed with a single aim in mind.

Direct benefits and added value

The first and most important benefit of a well-motivated partnership is the provision of better services to the community with an integrated agreement about common aims. Partnerships can also work positively to facilitate ownership by local communities themselves.

The second benefit is the avoidance of short-term funding crises. This has been, historically, the biggest single problem for partnerships developed to tackle community safety. Short-term funding regimes, such as Safer Cities, could never hope to achieve the long-term strategies needed to deal with the intractable problems created by rising levels of unemployment due to industrial decline, high levels of social deprivation and increasing levels of crime. The case is nowhere more poignantly made than in the recent (1998) report from the Cabinet Office's Social Exclusion Unit.

A further benefit is the avoidance of demarcation and dissension if partnerships wish to work together and not bid for resources in competition with each other. In turn, this allows the possibility to create economies of scale across local communities. Partnerships also open up the possibility of disseminating good practice in a way which single-agency action could not.

Potential strategic outcomes

In order to facilitate ownership by all partner organisations, it is important to encourage diversity and accept differences of culture and style. Partnerships can allow for a wider scope and a more strategic focus to work. There are also spin-offs to other aspects of people's lives, when partnerships are sufficiently mature to tackle key themes affecting a whole region. For example, safer transport, repeat victimisation and domestic violence, which can be laid on top of existing local activity.

Partnership can be seen as a response to the inefficiencies caused by lack of co-ordination. When resources are tight, better co-ordination is a sensible way of making finite budgets spread further. Also, the mismatch of administrative boundaries for those organisations involved in criminal justice, health, and local authorities, the voluntary and the private sector has to be overcome. The report *Beating Crime* (HMIC, 1998) comments that much of the total effort invested by partners was rendered ineffective by a lack of co-operation and direction.

The European dimension and its effect on partnership

The development of a European dimension, either to pursue transnational links to prepare a European funding bid or to simply share experience, can greatly enhance the local commitment to, and understanding of, partnership. Individual partners, in articulating their own role in the partnership to European colleagues, can come to see and value it more clearly for themselves. Furthermore, in a setting where global issues of concern could be discussed, such as youth crime and disorder and drug misuse, differences of culture, approach, treatment and prevention can be shared dispassionately. The different national approach of member nations is striking and it is possible to understand more clearly how both national and regional structural issues are a vital clue to solutions and choices.

The contention here, is that partnership across the EU, and even internationally at an appropriate level, should be nurtured in addition to the regional and local partnerships closer to home. It is only when partnership is truly seen as a philosophical issue – a way of living and working – that the potential of working partnerships can be exploited to the full.

Further words on funding regimes and resources

It cannot be over-emphasised that issues of funding and resources must be planned for in the long term and addressed vigorously and sensibly at the outset. However, they must also be kept in their place or they will consume all available time. The danger is for the partnership to become locked in a round of fund raising activity with little or no time for project appraisal or evaluation. Knee jerk responses to new regimes create a cycle of boom and bust, which has been so vividly described by the Chancellor, Gordon Brown, in another context.

In Northumbria, the approach has been to secure the core resources from mainstream sources on a permanent basis and to use funding regimes for delivery of projects and programmes. Very little of this funding is used for administration and management. This can put pressure on core staff in the appraisal, monitoring and evaluation processes. Other national and regional partnerships have used a substantive regime such as the single regeneration budget to deliver a seven-year programme with in-built management and administration. One objective during the lifetime of the programme is to have both core costs and the most successful initiatives absorbed into the mainstream work of partners. A further approach is the creation of a charity which could allow greater potential for involvement with, and possibly sponsorship by, the private sector.

It is helpful for the partners to have opportunities to reflect and review progress and consider whether or not they are on course to meet their main aims. Partnerships that have gone for a mix and match approach to funding, and have mainstream resources, seem to weather the funding pitfalls better than those which are wholly dependent on one regime.

Evaluation

The lack of evaluation has been the downfall of many a successful scheme or partnership. Whilst evaluation can sound like a tedious process, it must be seen as a central part of any community safety work. Without a continuous process of assessment, monitoring and evaluation, none of us can know what works. As an emerging profession, community safety practitioners should not be satisfied to continue assuming that activity equals productivity. A great deal of existing community safety activity was undertaken in a spirit of hope and optimism. The belief that doing things in local communities, which were self-evidently environmental improvements or community initiatives, would, without any criteria or means of assessing the links, reduce crime and improve community safety. Clearly we have developed beyond this to a stage where we would all welcome more rigorous methods to assess outcomes.

Evidence is vital to convince funding bodies, to satisfy the public, who have only the media to rely on otherwise, and to begin laying down a body of knowledge in the field of community safety which, can stand comparison with any scientific discipline. In another ten years we do not want to hear another prime minister tell us that 'Prison Works'. Perhaps the most important part of evaluation is to begin before the beginning.

Unexpected developments

These include the decline in the financial markets of the world and the impact on national economies. This is already having a major effect on the UK economy, the impact on the North East of England being of serious concern. Those factors which exacerbate the problems that many strategic partnerships are being set up to alleviate, will be affected. There is also the proliferation of new legislation and the growth of nationally driven strategic partnerships and the amount of organisational and cultural change across all professional and voluntary sectors.

Perhaps the best change of all is the growing body of partnerships who have a genuine desire to find new ways to deal with intractable problems and who have access to information about the realities of life for communities across Britain not previously available. Accounts such as that so vividly chronicled by Ian Taylor, Penny Fraser and Karen Evans (1996) in *A Tale of Two Cities*, describing the real experiences of people in the cities of Manchester and Sheffield, paint a realistic and compelling picture of the tasks facing today's partnerships.

Summary of issues

Partnership, whilst the subject of considerable rhetoric, is also for many of us a reality. It is our everyday work. We make few single decisions. We meet in small and large groups to consult, discuss, collaborate, disagree, refine and amend. We have no choice about engaging with the process, as we know that the single-agency approach has been tried and that whilst there remains an appropriate place for it, more can be done together. Furthermore, there is a refreshing side to some of our newer partnerships in that they are now multi-agency, multi faceted, multi layered and multi level. All our work is dense and complex needing professionals skilled in leading a multi-tasked flexible working life.

As the work of the partnership increases, so the density and complexity increase. Expansion of the membership creates yet more change. This can be exciting, endlessly fascinating, varied, tangled, infuriating and a sometimes tortuous way of doing things. The reward is better services and better quality of life for our communities – the ones in which we all live and work.

The core aspects of successful partnerships include agreements about balance, equality and common goals. They tend towards a concept of sharing not competing. They are characterised by top-level and political commitment, strong will, determination, and an ability to focus on long-term outcomes. Partnerships which have gone for a mix and match approach to funding and have mainstream resources seem to have more robust survival skills.

In addition, partnerships encourage diversity and accept differences of culture and style in order to facilitate ownership and involvement by all partner organisations, accepting a common view that partnerships can allow for a wider scope, and a more strategic focus to work. Perhaps the most important aspect of a successful partnership is that it has been created from the determination and will of the partner organisations themselves *and* has been created to tackle issues which they have identified and to which they are highly committed.

References

Handy C (1989) *The Age of Unreason* London: Hutchinson.

Kanter R M (1989) *When Giants Learn to Dance* London: Unwin

Taylor I, Evans K and Fraser P (1998) *Tale of Two Cities* London: Routledge

Peters T (1987) *Thriving On Chaos* New York: Harper & Row

Peters T and Waterman R H Jr. (1982) *In Search of Excellence: Lessons from America's Best Run Companies* New York: Harper & Row

Hough M and Tilley N (1998) *Getting the Grease to the Squeak: Research Lessons for Crime Prevention* Crime Detection and Prevention Series 85, London: Home Office

HMIC (1998) *Thematic Inspection: Beating Crime* London: Home Office

McCabe A, Lowndes V and Skelcher C (1997) *Partnerships and Networks – an Evaluation and Development Manual* York: Joseph Rowntree Foundation

NACRO (1997) *Hanging around the Bus Stop* London: NACRO

Perri 6, Jupp B, Perry H and Lasky K (1997) *The Substance of Youth* York: Joseph Rowntree Foundation

Social Exclusion Unit (1998) *Bringing Britain Together: a National Strategy for Neighbourhood Renewal* London: The Stationery Office

Taylor M (1997) *The Best of Both Worlds – the Voluntary Sector and Local Government* York: Joseph Rowntree Foundation

6. The evaluation jungle
Nick Tilley

The case for systematic evaluation seems watertight. The current rhetoric on evidence-led policy looks like common sense. Who could argue with it? We all have an interest in preventing crime effectively. We would all like real reductions in the risk of becoming crime victims. Taxpayers are concerned that levies on them should lead to real social benefits. The Treasury wants to be assured that public expenditure is cost effective. Home Office officials want to provide informed advice to their political masters. Responsible ministers want to be able to claim credit for genuine achievements. Those with professional responsibilities for crime prevention (in whatever capacity) are ordinarily committed to their work and to having a real impact. None of us in the crime prevention trade wants to spend time, money or effort achieving little or nothing.

Even those who are, for whatever reason, antipathetic to any particular measure to reduce crime – because it involves intrusive surveillance, the creation of a fortress society, the labelling or exclusion of certain groups marked out for treatment/separation, a reduction in the assumption of culpability of offenders, or the bestowal of privilege on delinquents – submit to the evaluation rhetoric. Critics want hard data on the effects of crime prevention measures, even if they want to include in the agenda unintended as well as intended effects.

The shortage of proper evaluations in crime reduction is often remarked. Nevertheless, there has been and continues to be a great deal of crime-prevention and community safety related evaluation of one kind or another. We have inspectorates for the police, probation and prison services. They collect and publish a host of performance indicators, including those touching on crime prevention. We have the Audit Commission looking at community safety work, and developing further performance indicators. We have had Safer Cities Phases 1 and 2, with innumerable efforts at evaluating individual initiatives. There were over 3,500 schemes in Safer Cities Phase 1, all of which were supposed to be evaluated. In addition there were overall evaluations of Safer Cities and efforts to look thematically at suites of Phase 1 schemes. CCTV challenge has led to the installation of many CCTV systems, whose effectiveness has to be evaluated as a condition of the grant. The Home Office itself has funded externally or has directly conducted quite a large number of evaluation studies. The Crime and Disorder Act 1998 makes evaluation a requirement of the crime prevention partnerships it has put on a statutory footing.

The interest in evaluation is not confined by any means to the UK. In 1997, a very extensive review of the findings of crime prevention evaluations was published on the Internet. It had been mandated and funded by the US Congress and conducted by an impressive team at the University of Maryland (Sherman et al, 1997). This review takes a particular view on the attributes of an adequate evaluation, scores studies accordingly, and summarises findings in terms of the strength of the studies conducted. It highlights many continuing areas of uncertainty.

The rhetorical power of evaluation is substantial. Hard (or hard-looking) evidence can be very effective in eliciting resources. The crime reduction programme set in train following the Government's 1998 Comprehensive Spending Review is a notable recent example. To some degree building on the Maryland work, the Home Office collected together findings from quite a wide range of evaluations deemed to satisfy minimum standards of technical adequacy to show what had been found to be sufficiently promising to proceed with (Goldblatt and Lewis, 1998). The crime reduction programme agreed on the basis of this review will itself include a very substantial evaluation component, to add to the evidence base for future crime reduction efforts.

In many areas of public life, for example, health, education, and development as well as criminal justice, the evaluation industry has grown substantially over the past couple of decades. We now have a UK Evaluation Society, devoted to improving the quality, appropriate use, and ethical standards of evaluation studies across all sectors, through informed and open discussion. The increase in evaluation is global. Over the past few years, for example, American, Australasian, Canadian, European, French, German, Italian, Kenyan, and Swiss evaluation societies have emerged, and there is now serious discussion of a World Federation. The arrival and dissemination of the new public management has spawned myriad performance indicators and aspirations to evidence-based policy decisions and resource allocation.

The editors of this volume asked me to write about the 'evaluation jungle'. The title suggests that, notwithstanding the strength of and enthusiasm for what is a veritable international industry, there are dangers, pitfalls and difficulties, and risks of becoming lost in the thickets. Help for fellow travellers can come in three ways. First, through knowledge of each other with a warning that some of those who look as if they are there to help can turn out to be predators. Second, by highlighting some of the traps, obstacles, and poisonous snakes that we all need to confront. Third, through pointers about ways of getting through the jungle, and how we should comport ourselves to reduce risks to ourselves and to those who follow.

This advice is framed in the language of *crime* prevention and *crime* reduction. These are construed as a subset of community safety, which potentially covers a wider range of hazards. Though some of the points made in the chapter relate specifically to problems in evaluating programmes aiming to prevent or reduce crime, most of the argument is also applicable to policies or practices directed at reducing the risk of other harms.

Smiles, tigers and crocodiles

Whilst the many stakeholders in crime reduction evaluation studies may say they want them to be conducted, and whilst all are apt to begin with a commitment to telling it as it is, to providing opportunities for learning from mistakes, and to avoiding the need to reinvent the wheel, unhappily the consensus is apt to break down. All too often it ends in tears. Frequently, especially where an independent evaluator comes out with negative findings, there are mutual recriminations, ill-feelings, accusations of betrayal or (at best) unfairness, and claims that the evaluator has not properly grasped what the programme is about.

There is, moreover, a strong success imperative amongst all bar the evaluator. Obviously the intended beneficiaries want the scheme to be successful, though they will not necessarily have a strong investment in publicly defining the scheme as a success. Architects of schemes clearly believe that what they propose will bring about crime reductions, and will want vindication. Those agreeing to the resources for a scheme, provide them in the conviction that what is planned will produce its intended benefits. Unless practitioners are committed to the work they are doing there is little prospect of real benefits following – they are, thus, typically convinced that it is effective. Ministers, responsible for programmes and policies within which individual schemes are run, are keen to capitalise on achievements. They are on the lookout for good news. To this end officials often comb programmes for success stories, especially for ministerial speeches. At the start of schemes, everyone is optimistic. This explains the shared enthusiasm for objective independent evaluation, which will enjoy external credibility.

The evaluator's sober assessment can easily appear threatening in these circumstances. The evaluator can be shocked that the erstwhile co-operative commissioners of the evaluation, the scheme practitioners, and the policy makers can turn quite nasty. There is often negotiation over the text: an effort to soften this passage, change the nuance of that, to highlight this point and to reduce another to a footnote. What is eventually said publicly can be shaped as much by the distribution of power as by the empirical findings from the studies that have been conducted.

The following examples must, for obvious reasons, remain anonymous. The reader in this case has to trust the author. The examples go back over the past fifteen years.

A major police service had committed itself to a high profile community crime prevention strategy. It commissioned an evaluation of its effectiveness, in this case by a police officer. The findings were not entirely negative, but they did not provide evidence that the strategy was being as effective as publicity claimed it would be. The head of the police service decided that the report should not be published, though it was circulated within the Home Office.

In one division of another large police service, a radical approach to policing was initiated – oriented towards prevention rather than enforcement. In this case, an external evaluation was conducted by a leading academic at one of the country's most prestigious universities. Though isolated examples of achievements were noted in the report, overall no significant effect was detected. The divisional commander felt very strongly that the efforts made had not been understood properly and that the programme had not had time to bite at the time of the evaluation. Again, the report is circulated within the Home Office, but has not been published.

One scheme in the Safer Cities programme had cost £100,000. It had involved eliciting the co-operation of several local agencies. Indeed, it had been an occasion bringing them together and had apparently succeeded in enthusing them for crime prevention partnership work. Unfortunately, according to the local evaluation it did not appear to have had any effect. Whilst the published report provided the data that underpinned this conclusion, the accompanying text continued to maintain that the measure had been an outstanding success.

Each of three crime prevention schemes was accompanied by some welcome reductions in crime. The falls may or may not have been attributable to the measures that had been introduced – there was rather little direct evidence to associate the crime falls with the measures introduced. In one case the authors went on to highlight not only the achievements but their fabulous cost effectiveness. In another the positive crime patterns were stressed and a tale constructed about how they might have been produced by the measures introduced, with muted doubts set alongside it. In the third, the data difficulties in interpreting the crime pattern changes were disregarded and the accomplishments widely championed.

Lest this might seem to paint everyone except the evaluator as scheming, self-interested subverters of both the truth and the lesson-learning that follows from its dissemination, it is worth remembering that evaluators themselves can have agendas that do not always serve the policy and practice purposes of evaluation.

University researchers (archetypal independent evaluators) are primarily interested in developing public knowledge. They want to undertake research in areas that are of personal interest and that are also significant for their academic peers. They are interested in new ideas, and new understanding. Just taking a programme and finding out whether or not it produced its intended effects is often deemed a relatively low-level research activity. Grants for evaluation studies may be welcome, but there will be a strong disposition to turn or use the material in the academic's interests. These interests may not coincide with those of the commissioner of the evaluation. Indeed, Home Office researchers managing research by external academics are apt to complain that university researchers frequently fail to keep to their evaluation briefs. Contrariwise, academics can resent the imposition of an agenda that is of little interest to them.

The academic evaluator may, moreover, not be invulnerable to influence from other stakeholders. There are, of course, very strong mores in science stressing truth telling. Whilst well-publicised examples of scientific fraud certainly exist, the shocked response to them highlights (and reinforces) the seriousness with which the norm is taken. That said, academics also need to publish, and they want to publish material that will be recognised, valued and used by fellow researchers. In Britain, universities now have a research assessment exercise every four or five years in which quality of publications is the leading indicator of strength, and whose results determine a substantial slice of university income. There is, thus, an external imperative to publish, and this may mean that, rather than risk suppression of a publication, some evaluators may try to accommodate those with interests in giving them a particular spin, without exactly falsifying findings.

Though they might all use the same rhetoric about the need for proper evaluation, the various stakeholders in the evaluation jungle tend to start at different points. They have different resources, face different problems, obstacles and difficulties and often try to reach rather different destinations. The academic's publication and truth telling imperatives, the scheme success imperatives and the power differentials amongst various stakeholders provides a potent mix, where public, usable knowledge can easily be the unintended casualty.

Traps, obstacles and slippery snakes

So far, the discussion has focused on the social context for presenting evaluation findings. It has assumed that the facts for evaluation are unproblematic, and that the problem is one of having them published honestly. Unfortunately, facts are not so easy to come by, and they never speak for themselves. Even without fellow stakeholders to contend with, the evaluator faces a difficult environment.

Though there have been very many evaluations of crime reduction initiatives, their quality has generally been poor. Ekblom and Pease (1995) note that there has been, 'a great deal of self-serving unpublished and semi-published work that does not meet even the most elementary criteria of evaluative probity.' Sherman et al's (1997) review of crime prevention evaluations concurs with this judgement. During Phase 1 of the Safer Cities initiative, I was brought in because of the weakness of individual scheme-level evaluations to try to assemble lessons from sets of them, where there was some reasonable data on outcomes. There was rather little to draw on.

Technical problems

The typical weaknesses in evaluation studies follow in part from failure to deal adequately with technical difficulties. There is much literature on social science methodology. The wary traveller in the evaluation jungle is advised to do a good deal of preparatory work before embarking on the journey, and when on it to consult the literature before making major decisions. In this short guide, the aim is only to persuade the reader to keep their wits about them, for it is easy to be misled.

There are many data difficulties that confront any empirical social research. For surveys, for example, weaknesses include:

- *Inappropriate samples* – for example, if a survey is intended to measure change in fear of crime at night in a town centre, the appropriate survey sample might be actual or real potential users of the town centre at that time, rather than random samples of the population as a whole or daytime town centre users.

- *Unrepresentative samples* – it can be very difficult to elicit random samples of relevant personnel. A frequent error is to concentrate only on sample size, without ensuring representativeness. Beyond a minimum size the latter is more important than numbers. An unrepresentative sample, such as one comprising returns of questionnaires published in a magazine, is of little or no value.

- *Samples of insufficient size* – those conducting surveys often fail to consider how large a sample they will need to make realistic before/after comparisons in differing areas.

- *Not asking the right questions* – many surveys are undertaken only to find out that a crucial question has been omitted, when analysis is undertaken.

- *Inappropriate use of open-ended or closed questions* – questionnaires are often designed without attention to how results will be analysed. Even where this is thought about, the result can be the imposing of fixed choice answers where these are inappropriate to the issues being considered.

- *Asking inadequately and inconsistently understood questions* – the respondent is often left to second guess what the question is getting at. There can be no confidence that the interpretation made corresponds to the meaning intended by the person framing the question.

- *Mis-coding answers or picking unsuitable tick-box options* – the options given when tick-box questions are asked will have a substantial impact on findings. Comparisons of answers to the same questions are undermined where answer options vary.

- *Unsuitable ordering of questions* – the same question will be answered differently according to the context provided by the preceding ones.

- *Respondent memory failure* – victimisation surveys suffer from respondents' fallible memories about when incidents took place.

● *Respondent attempts to please the researcher* – where respondents have agreed to answer questions, they are apt to try to please the researcher by giving answers even where they cannot understand the question. Moreover, there is a risk that they will present what are taken to be socially acceptable replies.

Of course surveys are not the only source of data. For example, non-obtrusive measures – signs of behaviour such as scuffed carpets, syringes and broken glass – can be used. Recorded data of various kinds – police data on crime and calls for service or local authority data on exclusions, vandalism and child abuse – may be available. Direct observation of behaviour may also be possible. The problems in surveys are listed not because these other data sources do not lack difficulties, but because they can stand for data problems in general. The overall issue for social science research is picking the right sort of data, being aware of pitfalls in their collection of it, and making sensible use of the data collected.

Technical problems specifically relating to evaluation include the following:

● *Pseudo-random fluctuations in crime rates* – these make interpreting real effects, as against pseudo random short-term variations, difficult.

● *Changes in background crime rates* – notwithstanding fluctuations in small areas, there are background changes in crime rates against which scheme induced ones need to be compared.

● *Other changes in the area covered by a scheme* – areas seldom remain unchanging over the course of time needed to have robust(ish) before and after data. It is difficult to take account of all the other changes, which might affect crime patterns, in addition to the introduction of some specific crime reduction scheme.

● *Changes in patterns of crime reporting and recording* – not all crimes are reported and of those reported not all are recorded. Schemes may have an effect on crime reporting, in various ways, for example, by facilitating their observation or by increasing victim confidence that some benefit will follow from making a report.

● *The use of packages of crime prevention measures* – where a suite of measures is introduced, they may: operate at the sum of their parts; interact to magnify the impact that individual interventions might otherwise have, or there may be diminishing marginal returns with increased crime prevention activity. Measurement of the respective contributions of differing elements clearly raises problems.

● *Floor effects* – where there is a very low crime rate to start with detecting a downwards effect of a crime prevention initiative will be very difficult.

- *Regression to the mean* – where there is an abnormally high initial crime rate, regression to the mean will lead to the appearance of a real impact where there has been none. Evaluating the impact of quickly targeting emerging hot spots produces particular risks of this.

- *Displacement* – if a measure has an effect, the problems may be displaced to another place, time, offence, or crime method. This has to be addressed, remembering though that it can never be shown that there has been no displacement. Moreover, when looking at figures it is necessary to consider not only displacement away from the target scheme but also any displacement into it by other bits of crime prevention.

- *Diffusion of benefits* – schemes may produce what is called diffusion of benefits. That is, the beneficial effects may be felt beyond the immediate limits of the scheme, because offenders are not fully aware of the coverage.

- *Timing* – schemes may take time to bite. They may also have a changing pattern of impact over time. In many cases impact wanes. Difficult decisions over timing have thus to be made.

Conceptual problems

The evaluation jungle presents not only technical traps, but also interpretative obstacles. Where, in any particular case, evaluation findings conclude that the introduction of a scheme was not associated with intended benefits, it is not necessarily because the scheme was a bad idea. Schemes may fail because:

- They are not implemented properly – it is repeatedly found that actually putting measures in place as planned is difficult. It is often the case that they are either not put in place at all, or that they are only there in dilute form, or introduced much later than intended. Here, failure cannot be attributed to the measures planned, but to their partial implementation.

- The provision for measuring success is too insensitive or is ill-directed – here the evaluation simply misses the point at which impact occurred.

- The context for introducing the measure was inappropriate – some measures, for example, mandatory arrest for domestic violence, have been found to 'work' as a way of preventing repeat victimisation in some contexts, but not in others.

Findings of failures have to be interpreted, they do not speak for themselves. They certainly do not mean that the measures to which they relate cannot ever have their intended effects.

Where evaluation research does find that the introduction of a scheme is associated with intended benefits, it does not mean that the measures will always produce that result. Few crime prevention measures comprise direct physical barriers that are impenetrable to prospective offenders, who test them to the limits. Lighting improvements, CCTV, property-marking, after schools clubs, motor projects and so on, do not make crime impossible to commit: they may affect, in some way, the decision making of potential offenders.

Sherman *et al*'s (1997) overview of evaluations of crime prevention initiatives has already been cited. It is magisterial, and was prepared by a team at the University of Maryland for the US Congress. It attempts to summarise findings of a wide range of evaluations, weighted according to the team's judgements of their technical adequacy. They favour experimental studies, involving experimental/control group or site comparisons, and have separated interventions into four categories: 'what works', 'what doesn't work', 'what's promising' and 'what's unknown'. They have, however, recently underlined the importance of caution in interpreting the 'what works' entries:

There are programs that we can be reasonably certain prevent crime or reduce risk factors for crime in the kinds of social context in which they have been evaluated and for which the findings can be generalised to similar settings in other places and times. (Sherman *et al* 1998.)

They also generalise the need for caution for entries under other headings also, conceding that:

The weakest aspect of this classification (into 'what works' and so on) is that there is no standard means of establishing external validity: exactly what variations in program content and setting might affect the generality of findings from evaluations. In the current state of science, that can be accomplished only by the accumulation of many tests in many settings with all major variations on the program theme. None of the programs reviewed in this report have accumulated such a body of knowledge so far. The conclusions drawn in the report about what works and what doesn't should be read, therefore, as more certain to the extent that all conditions of the programs that were evaluated (for example, population demographics, program elements, social context) are replicated in other settings. The greater the difference on such dimensions between evaluated programs and other programs using the same name, the less certain the application of this report's conclusions must be. (*ibid*)

It is impossible, of course, to replicate all the conditions in terms of place, time, personnel and so on. The examples of the conditions for programme-effectiveness listed (population demographics, program elements and social context) could be extended indefinitely, and those relevant will depend on the nature of the intervention. As stressed above, context is relevant to failure as well as success. The depressing conclusion follows from Sherman *et al*'s concessions, that we can learn little for the future from the findings he summarises until there is detailed specification of salient conditions for success (and failure). We know nothing of this yet from the suites of studies using Sherman *et al*'s preferred experimental methods. It is a great pity that the bold headings, 'What works', 'What doesn't work', 'What's promising' and 'What's unknown' are used in the report to Congress. They are (as Sherman *et al* now concede) highly misleading. Less snappily but more accurately, they should read, 'What has been found to work somewhere', 'What has been found not to work somewhere', 'What seems to have worked somewhere', and 'What may work somewhere'.

Sherman *et al*'s report concentrates mainly, though not exclusively, on research in the US. The qualifications about the meaning of findings summarised are clearly of particular importance for readers from other countries, where there may be salient differences in context for some interventions.

Open systems

Sadly, the contexts for the effectiveness of individual crime prevention initiatives are not stable. Crime and crime prevention are not closed systems. Rather, there are exogenous and endogenous sources of change, which undermine the predictability of future effectiveness on the basis of past effectiveness. Paul Ekblom's important work about evolution and crime prevention helps us to understand this (Ekblom, 1997). Ekblom highlights the active roles of preventers and offenders, who are in strategic opposition to one another, well motivated to innovate to stymie the other's efforts. Ekblom suggests that there may be some local end-points (for example, the unbreachable safe), but overall there is a continuous change process, where what works is always evolving. Innovations mean that what works in situational crime prevention, either as a crime prevention method or a secure modus operandi for the criminal, is intrinsically unstable because of endogenous dyadic preventer/offender processes of adaptation and innovation. Furthermore, exogenous developments – for example, in technology, routine activities in social life, commercial practices, social administration or social policy – feed into this dyadic process, furnishing intrinsically new opportunities and obstacles both to the offender and preventer.

The coupled internal and external sources of emergent development mean that evaluations of crime prevention methods will be limited to, 'for now', or 'in these (precarious) contexts'.

Costs and benefits

There is often an interest in calculating the costs and benefits of crime prevention measures, and even in comparing alternative costs and benefits from differing methods. Where these accrue to the same agency and where interest lies only in financial costs and benefits, calculations may be made relatively easily. There are, however, serious problems in other circumstances. Clearly the difficulties already mentioned in measuring and predicting intended (and unintended) effects form part of the difficulty. In addition, the following need to be considered:

- Non-monetary benefits – for example, reductions in fear of crime, in domestic violence or in racial harassment.

- Non-monetary unwanted side effects – for example, increases in fear of crime, harassment of suspicious-looking but innocent people, or aesthetic damage to the physical environment.

- The crime-prevention component of expenditure with multiple aims – for example, that on lighting improvements.

- Long- as well as short-term costs and benefits.

- Benefits allocation where initiatives are conducted by partnerships.

- Longer-term benefits from co-operation, where agencies 'lose' in individual initiatives.

There are currently no established conventions, much less well worked out means of dealing with these difficulties.

Some pointers to a way forward

The discussion so far may seem deeply depressing. It is certainly the case that the evaluation jungle is so replete with dangers and difficulties that the prospects of knowledge-driven policy and practice, informed by evaluation studies, are much more problematic than they seem at first sight.

The following suggestions are for ways of orchestrating evaluation to contribute to improvements in crime reduction policy and practice. These are directed at the various stakeholders travelling in the evaluation jungle.

1. Evaluate selectively

It should be clear by now that valid and reliable evaluation is technically and conceptually tricky. It will be expensive to do it well. Equally, misleading, highly publicised findings from doing it badly risk generating costly mistaken inferences about policy and practice. Proper, professional evaluations of publishable quality are probably only warranted where there is significant uncertainty about likely effects and where findings can be expected to build understanding in ways which can properly help inform decision making.

Less consequential evaluations, designed to inform only local or practitioner decision-making, of course need to attend less rigorously (and less expensively) to addressing technical evaluation problems. Provided that users bear in mind ways in which feedback on outcomes may be partial and potentially misleading, this can help build local evidence-informed practice. Indeed, there is much to be said for practicable, systematic self-evaluation in which practitioners are helped to assess their own practice and its outcomes routinely.

2. Monitor everything

Because there have been so many implementation problems in crime reduction initiatives, it makes sense to make provision for monitoring their inputs, activities, processes and outputs. This will be crucial where evaluations are to be conducted to keep track of what is actually put in place, and at what cost. Even where full evaluations are not planned, monitoring will enable feedback on the project workings, on the basis of which adjustments can be made to improve project efficiency.

3. Ask the right questions

Because nothing works unconditionally in all circumstances, the realistic evaluation question to ask is, 'what works for whom in what circumstances?' It does not make sense to ask the unqualified question, 'what works?' There may be sense in asking 'what has worked?' of particular initiatives, as a prelude to 'what works for whom in what circumstances?' since positive results show that this question is worth asking of a particular measure.

Interventions aimed at crime reduction can often produce policy-relevant side-effects, such as crime displacement and diffusion of benefits. Evaluation studies need to ask broader questions about what produces which unintended outcomes as well as intended ones, and in which circumstances.

4. Don't take the results of experimental studies at face value

Sherman *et al*'s reservations about the inferences that can be drawn from experimental studies need to be taken seriously. These are treated (mistakenly) as a gold standard. At their best, experimental studies have historical internal validity. That is, they show whether interventions were plausibly associated with those outcomes which were measured. They are not designed, and cannot provide, robust guidance to future effectiveness or future outcomes of the interventions evaluated.

5. Use theory

We cannot measure everything. We do not know what to measure unless we have some expectations about what might be significant in an intervention. We know that individual measures may have multiple outcomes according to context What is needed, therefore, is theory which states what it is an intervention is expected to do to bring about its outcomes in the specific and specified contexts in which it is being introduced. This may sound alien to people who stress that they are practical folk, interested in doing things that are effective and not in airy-fairy theorising, yet it is crucial.

Where schemes have not been thought through in advance in terms of how they are expected to affect the actions of those whose behaviour is being targeted, they are liable to be ill-directed and to fail unnecessarily. Moreover, without some theory, the evaluator cannot beam measurements where effectiveness can most be expected.

6. Focus on sub-groups

Programmes rarely, if ever, work in the same way for all subjects in all circumstances. There is intra-contexual variation within programmes. At the design stage of programmes, expectations about how they will work are likely to be pitched at a level of generality that flattens salient variations in the conditions in which they will be introduced. For example, CCTV is introduced into differing types of town centre, neighbourhood watch into differing types of community and family group conferences into differing family set-ups.

It is only during the course of a programme that some of the variations will become manifest. Evaluations need to be attentive to ways in which programmes work variously to generate diverse outcome patterns within a range of targeted subgroups.

If useful lesson-learning is to take place within programmes, to improve their targeting, attention to variations in sub-group experience is clearly needed. Moreover, it is by comparing the way the programme functions amongst its target sub-groups that its theory can be tested.

7. Evaluate in partnership

Whilst bias is an ever-present risk where evaluators become too close to the programmes they are studying, other risks accrue in keeping too great a distance.

What the evaluator loses, if simply looking before and after at rates of targeted behaviour (with or without controls for comparison), is much understanding of the thinking behind and within the programme. So, even if theory is used, the working theory of policy and practice workers may be missed. Yet, together with ideas gleaned from criminological literature and findings from previous studies, this is crucial to ensuring that measurements are made fairly where impacts might be expected.

The treatment of policy makers and practitioners as programme dopes, with no understanding of what they are planning or doing, is both offensive and counter-productive. Practitioners at the sharp end of programme delivery, in particular, have at the least a case by case grasp of findings from what they are doing. Of course, there may be unacknowledged conditions and unintended consequences beyond the ken of busy workers, but this should not blind us to the contents of their reflexive awareness.

In order for the evaluator to take advantage of (sometimes embryonic and unformalised) policy and practitioner programme theorising, acknowledgement of a common interest in testing and refining theories about and within programmes is needed.

It is worth adding a side-benefit of the partnership approach which features theory development and testing. Such evaluation studies will appeal more as exercises to able academics, since what can be generated will be of rather more interest and significance to their peers than answers to vulgar works/doesn't work questions.

8. Take the long view

Refining usable crime reduction theories about what works for whom and in what circumstances will take time for the following reasons:

- individual programme implementation is often difficult and theory-testing evaluations can only begin when there is adequate programme presence;

- programmes are sometimes expected to take a significant period to bite, so outcome patterns can take time to surface;

- the nature of programme impact often alters over time, partly because showcase or Hawthorne mechanisms can operate in the short term, whereby it is not the intervention *per se* that produces the effect, but the mere presence of (often well-publicised) action;

- theory refinement requires a series of interconnected cumulating findings.

The learning that took place through the suite of repeat victimisation related studies funded by the late Home Office Crime Prevention Unit and the Police Research Group, from 1996 to 1998, is testament to what can be achieved by taking the long view (see Pease, 1998 and Pawson and Tilley, 1997).

9. Expect change

Unfortunately, even though abstract ideas explaining how measures can work and in what sorts of contexts may be enduring, specific findings about particular measures and how they work to reduce crime, in concrete conditions, risk being undermined by the powerful processes of change Paul Ekblom describes. For the policy maker and practitioner this is crucial. It means that past findings not only have limited predictive potential where they are underdeveloped theoretically, but also that, even where there is adequate theory at the more substantive level, findings may have a limited shelf life. This suggests need for a flexible and adaptive approach to crime reduction within which significant effort is made to scan the crime and non-crime environments for changes relevant to the causal potential of existing programmes, and the possibilities of additional pre-emptive interventions.

10. Be modest

Excessive claims and over-generalisations of findings have blighted crime reduction, with regard both to success and failure. If local and national policy makers, practitioners, politicians and academics showed a proper modesty about what has been accomplished, what can be concluded from individual studies and what we know and do not know about what works for whom in what circumstances, we would be less likely to be misled and more likely to make sensible decisions.

Conclusions

Evaluations looking as objectively as is possible at the outcomes of interventions cannot ever provide the sole grounds for policy or practice. There are values at stake. A series of evaluation studies may help us understand the means of achieving an objective, and may even tell us of possible side effects along the way. In the long term, they may even be able to deduce costs of some of the interventions and outcomes. There are, however, fundamental value questions to which the evaluator as social scientist cannot give a privileged answer. The issues belong ultimately to political or ideological discourse.

At the start of this chapter, various unsympathetic responses to methods of reducing crime were mentioned, and these reflect the value positions of their adherents. Reference was made to a number of ways in which people may feel hostile to differing approaches to crime reduction: for example, because they involve targeted surveillance, or the development of a fortress society, or sympathetic treatment of offenders. Whilst these suspicions often lead to empirical questions, they reflect basic and differing value positions to which the empirical evaluator can provide no authoritative response. Decisions about what to do and where resources are to be allocated, cannot be answered purely through evaluation studies, though they can clearly be informed by them where part of the rhetoric surrounding value positions relates to supposed effects.

What evaluations can offer over a period of time is a way of winnowing 'what works' in producing varying outcomes, at least for a while, for whom and in what circumstances. It is hard enough to do this: empirical evaluation cannot do more. Discussions about crime reduction as one priority amongst others, and about methods in which it might be achieved, would be clearer if the nature of the value questions raised and positions taken were made explicit. It might be, for example, that there are good value grounds for not using effective methods of crime prevention. It is equally likely that there are balances to be made between responses to crime issues, none of which is without ideological difficulty.

References

Ekblom P (1997) 'Gearing up against crime: a dynamic framework to help designers keep up with the adaptive criminal in a changing world' *International Journal of Risk, Security and Crime Prevention* 2

Ekblom P and Pease K (1992) 'Evaluating crime prevention' in Tonry M and Farrington D (eds) *Building a Safer Society. Crime and Justice* 19 Chicago: University of Chicago Press

Goldblatt P and Lewis C (eds) (1998) *Reducing Offending: An Assessment of the Research Evidence on Ways of Dealing with Offending Behaviour* Home Office Research Study 187, London: HMSO

Pawson R and Tilley N (1997) *Realistic Evaluation* London: Sage

Pease K (1998) *Repeat Victimisation: Taking Stock Crime Prevention and Detection* Paper 90, London: Home Office.

Sherman L, Gottfredson D, MacKenzie D, Eck J, Reuter P, and Bushway S (1997) *Preventing Crime: What Works, What Doesn't, What's Promising: A Report to the United States Congress*, available at internet address: www.ncjrs.org/works/index.htm

Sherman L, Gottfredson D, MacKenzie D, Eck J, Reuter P, and Bushway S (1998) *Preventing Crime: What Works, What Doesn't, What's Promising* National Institute of Justice: Research in Brief, Office of Justice Programs, US Department of Justice

7. The 'wicked' issues: displacement and sustainability
Ivan Hill and Ken Pease

Of the two central objections to purposive crime prevention, one is discussed more than it should be (typically in terms which are both ill-informed and misleading) and the other is discussed too little. The first is displacement and the second, sustainability. Someone professionally engaged in crime reduction will have encountered the first topic, probably *ad nauseam*. They are much less likely to have encountered the second, but should be seeking to introduce the issue at every available opportunity. A third 'wicked issue' sometimes mentioned is replicability, the relevant issues having been fully discussed in Chapter 4.

Displacement

In what follows, the focus is on spatial displacement, that is, the alleged tendency of prevented crime to move to other locales. This is for reasons of brevity and clarity, but primarily because it is spatial displacement, which is most often alleged to offset crime prevention gains. For those wanting a typology of displacement, see for example Barr and Pease (1990). Without exception, the position taken in relation to spatial displacement also applies to displacement of other types.

As the clinician's tap evokes the knee jerk, so the crime prevention project evokes the claim from someone that prevented crime has merely been displaced. The claim almost always has two attributes:

● it is made with supreme confidence

● it is made without evidence.

It also always has two other unappetising attributes

● it serves to justify inaction

● it is indifferent to the spectacular inequalities in victimisation rates.

The reader must forgive the bitterness with which this is written. There is an important debate to be had about displacement, but it has not happened yet. During the Kirkholt experiment in the mid-1980s, a local paper in Rochdale splashed across its front page the claim by a local councillor that the project had merely moved the burglary problem down the road. All the evidence gainsaid this, but the damage was done. Since then, the assertion of displacement dogs every step Ken Pease has taken professionally. Displacement is claimed to have happened in every project undertaken, with the evidence for this crumbling whenever the assertion is challenged. Sometimes the anticipation of displacement is transparently self-serving, with the failure to act being justified by reference to the certainty of displacement.

One of the frustrations for those of us committed to crime reduction is that there will always be a place where crime has risen after an intervention elsewhere. If burglary goes down in the area targeted and in those surrounding it, but theft rises in a shopping centre some ten miles distant, that's obviously displacement, isn't it? The irony is that the obvious checks (for example, whether anyone previously convicted for burglary in the target area is later convicted of shop theft in the distant place) are not undertaken. The burden of proof appears always to be upon the crime preventer, not upon the person who claims displacement and the default position appears to be inaction. Applied to other areas of police work, it would mean, for example, that rival supporters should not be prevented from fighting each other in soccer stadia, since they would only find somewhere else to fight on the way home.

Another way of demonstrating that displacement is more often the cloak of laziness and inertia, than a well-founded criticism of crime prevention comes with a recognition that there is no *a priori* reason to assume that crime will rise rather than fall. While spatial displacement implicitly theorises that offenders thwarted in one place will move somewhere else, another possibility is that being thwarted alerts them to a changed world, in which it is now riskier to commit crime at the boundaries of his or 'range', even when nothing has changed there. This effect, the opposite of displacement, is known as diffusion of benefits. The fact that there was an established literature on displacement before anyone coined that phrase tells us more than we want to know about the real roots of displacement claims!

Crude evidence on displacement

Hesseling (1994) reviewed all 55 published articles on crime prevention measures in which researchers specifically looked for evidence of displacement. He noted that:

> critics of situational prevention... often state that the approach is useless because it only displaces crime to other places or times. Yet these critics tend to base their conclusions on ideological grounds rather than on the basis of sound empirical knowledge.

A careful review of the published studies reveals that:

> displacement is a possible, but not inevitable consequence of crime prevention. Further, if displacement does occur, it will be limited in size and scope. This conclusion is supported by other review studies on the topic.

Hesseling also found diffusion of benefits in six of the studies he reviewed.

There are good reasons for supposing that displacement is seldom likely to be anything like complete. The closest one can imagine to complete displacement would be in respect of what has come to be known as perpetrator displacement, whereby a crime opportunity is so compelling that the removal of any number of offenders will not prevent the crime. The obvious example concerns drug importation from a third world country, in which poverty generates an unlimited pool of volunteers to be mules. More typically, offenders have limited ranges (see, for example, Wiles and Costello, 1999). Other rational choice considerations also lead to the conclusion that the extent of displacement will be limited (Cornish and Clarke, 1987 and Bouloukos and Farrell, 1997).

Displacement and fairness

If one had to have the present level of crime in an area, but could choose how it is distributed, the response might be 'Who cares?' Hopefully not, and if not, it means that different types of displacement would be differentially attractive. This is not to say that displacement typically really does take place, simply that different forms of displacement would not be equally attractive. It is through consideration of how displacement might most equitably take place, whether or not it really does take place, that the notion of fairness in distributing crime should be considered. The idea that the burden of crime should be allocated fairly has not been debated much. Yet the notion that distributive justice should apply to crime as much as to other preventable harms is compelling, however seldom considered.

Distributive justice concerns the dispensation of benefits and services to people, and the systems of taxation that make it possible. A person's perspective on distributive justice is at the core of their political values. Most such perspectives are underpinned by either a straightforward moral (or amoral, such as the reverence for market forces) imperative. This will be qualified by recognition of effects which the absence or abundance of provision would have on some people, that it would not have on others (the old and the well off respectively). In contrast *retributive* justice involves the scaling of penalties in proportion to harm inflicted, both by the specification of maximum allowable penalties and by the maintenance of proportionality between crime seriousness and punishment below that maximum.

Inequality resulting from health, education and welfare provision is a core concern of the discipline of social policy. The distribution of crime across people and places has, by contrast, been historically neglected. The annually published criminal statistics are primarily about offences and offenders, scarcely at all about victims and victimised communities. Indeed, a case could be made that the criminal justice system's emphasis on retributive justice by disadvantaging offenders, is the outcome of making an unrecognised choice between helping crime victims and harming perpetrators. That is, of a relative indifference to the justice of how crime is spread amongst victims.

One of the major developments in criminology over the last two decades has been the recognition of the victim, the consequent development of the sub-discipline of victimology, and most recently (because adequate data was not previously available) the human implications of chronic victimisation against the same people and small areas. This transformation has come about by a number of routes, including the recognition of crimes whose rate of repetition is huge. These include domestic violence, bullying and racial harassment.

The apparent indifference to crime concentration can be gauged by the tenor of the debate about displacement (see Barr and Pease, 1990). There was no suggestion in the literature before that time that displacement could be considered more or less malign, in proportion to the existing crime burden borne by a community. Displacement, dealing as it does with distributions of crime suffered, nonetheless seems to have contrived to escape consideration in terms of distributive justice. There is a debate about crime displacement, but no debate about crime *placement.* The extant distribution of crime is taken to be unproblematic in that debate, as traditionally conducted. Crime as it exists is somehow natural and to be interfered with at one's peril.

As it is for displacement, so it is for data on recorded crime. The smallest geographic unit to be found in the standard volumes on crime, the annual Criminal Statistics will be seen to be the police force area. Adding up crimes and expressing them as a total for a command unit or police force area obscures precisely the thing most needed for police resourcing and deployment decisions – namely how crime experience varies street by street, home by home and pub by pub. The oldest joke about statistics is that if you have your head in the oven and your feet in the freezer, you will be comfortable on average. Combining quiet areas like Bramhall and difficult ones like Wythenshawe to produce an overall figure for Greater Manchester police, and expecting the resulting total to be meaningful, makes no more sense for the corporate body of the police than the oven-freezer predicament does for the human body. Furthermore, the fact that the numbers are routinely expressed in this way shows an apparent total indifference to the distribution of suffering which they entail.

Figure 7.1 shows the total number of crimes experienced in each sampling unit of the *British Crime Survey*. This survey reports an enquiry, which now takes place every two years, into both reported and unreported crime, in England and Wales. The data in Figure 7.1 comes from the 1988 survey and refers to property crime, but the picture is much the same in different years and for crime against the person.

The survey employs around 600 sampling points, at each of which some 30 people were interviewed. The 600 areas were then divided into the ten per cent of areas with the most crime, the ten per cent with the next most crime, and so on up to

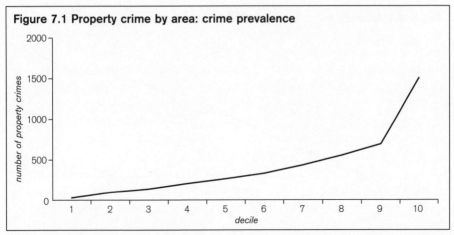

Figure 7.1 Property crime by area: crime prevalence

the ten per cent with least crime. Figure 7.1 simply takes the total number of crimes captured in each decile, and makes evident the ratios between them. This shows *how many times more* crime is suffered by the worst than the best areas.

The shape of the curve shows that the decile with most crime has more than double the amount of crime in the next most crime prone decile. Looking at the worst decile against the best, the worst suffers 43 times as much crime as the least victimised decile. Another way of saying this is that some 40 per cent of all crime experienced happens in the ten per cent of areas most prone to crime. Well over half occurs in the 20 per cent most crime prone areas. Calls logged from the public will also show a massive range of crime densities. The data in the figures is taken from the work of Tim Hope (Hope, 1996).

How should policing be allocated in the light of Figure 7.1? If policing resources were deployed according to the extent of crime suffered, 80 per cent of the country would be getting few police resources. This would be prudent, given how crime is spread, although it may not go down too well with the citizens of Virginia Water and Solihull!

The ten per cent of areas with most crime can get to be that way via one or both of two different routes. First, increasing proportions of people living in the area may become victims, so that perhaps 80 or 90 per cent of people in the worst areas suffer some crime. Alternatively, the same proportion of people could become victims of crime in the worst and best areas, but those victimised in the worst areas would suffer crime more often. The old and unfunny joke is that in England and Wales somebody is getting robbed every 30 minutes – and she's getting sick of it. Unfunny as it is, it shows that more people do not necessarily have to fall victim to crime for the crime rate to rise.

Figure 7.2 shows the proportion of people victimised in each area decile. Thus in decile 10 (the 10 per cent of areas with most crime) some 28 per cent of people are

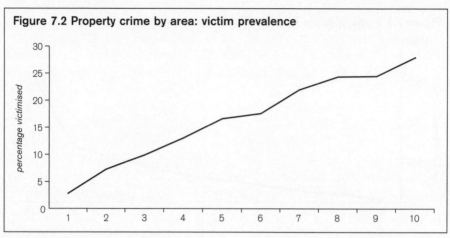

Figure 7.2 Property crime by area: victim prevalence

victims of crime over the year. The proportion increases steadily to that figure from 3 per cent in the least crime-ridden areas. The point to stress, however, is that even if you live in one of 10 per cent most crime prone areas, you have a 72 per cent chance of not being a victim over a one-year period. However, Figure 7.3 shows the number of crimes which people who are victims each suffer. It will be seen that in the worst areas, each victim of property crime suffers an average of nearly five.

The same pattern is even more marked for crimes of violence, where 15 per cent of people in the worst areas suffer crimes against the person, but those who do, suffer an average of six such crimes. In short, most people in the worst areas do not suffer crime over the course of a year. However, those who do, suffer it several times each. Since areas which suffer much property crime are by and large also those which suffer most personal crime, looking at all crime combined yields an even more marked difference between areas in levels of chronic victimisation.

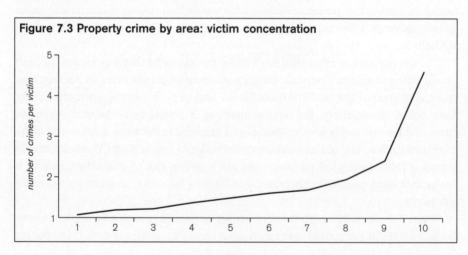

Figure 7.3 Property crime by area: victim concentration

The reason for developing the point at such length is that how it is locally distributed is the single fact about crime that needs to be known if notions of fairness of that distribution were regarded as a salient feature of crime. Yet such statistics are not to be found in Criminal Statistics, and have in the past had to be dragged out of British Crime Survey data after much effort.

A just measure of harm?

Looking for support for the inclusion of risk of harms suffered through criminal actions, as a factor to which distributive justice is relevant, yields statements that are tantalisingly close, but never direct. For instance Giddens (1998) contends:

A renewed emphasis upon crime prevention rather than law enforcement can go hand in hand with the reintegration of policing with the community... These approaches can in fact contribute directly and indirectly to furthering social justice. Where civil order has decayed along with public services and building stock, other opportunities decline also. Improving the quality of life in a neighbourhood can revive them.

Tim Hope (for example, Hope, 1995) identifies the interplay between urban markets and community crime careers, pointing out the ways in which the former shapes the latter, and the variation of forms of individual self-protection within crime-ridden areas.

Social exclusion is one route through which crime victimisation could be introduced into a world in which distributive justice notions prevail. The hope that this might be so was raised by Jon Bright's secondment from Crime Concern to the Government's Social Exclusion Unit. However, a lengthy overview of the definition of and solutions to social exclusion (Oppenheim, 1998) does not incorporate crime and disorder as an element in either.

The discussion of distributive justice in relation to health, education and the like is organised around the classic issues of need, merit and seniority criteria, for the allocation of care and selection for work or training. Such allotment is worth discussing because it lies within the power of those who allocate. Only recently has it been felt that power over rates of crime and other harms is such that it becomes feasible even to consider the manipulation of crime or the dispensing of crime reduction, in the same way as health care or education opportunity. Once that hurdle is crossed, the same difficult questions of rationing and prioritisation present themselves.

To which dimension should the allocation of harm reduction effort and resources be geared? The obvious one is need, indexed by the intensity and severity of prior victimisation. In short, crime and other harms should be added to the lexicon of distributive justice, and resources should be deployed on the basis of need, judged by the history of harms suffered.

In practice, what this means is that distributive justice (the avoidance of the chronic suffering of harm) should be afforded directly to victims, not mediated through the person of the perpetrator, with the uncertainty of success which attends it.

This position would have a number of implications for the funding of measures purporting to afford the reduction of crime and other harms:

- The separation of crime and disorder as a kind of harm should be avoided. This would require the repeal of the Crime and Disorder Act 1998 and its replacement by an act that did not distinguish between harms resulting from human malice and other harms. Current arrangements will lead to (for example) intensive action to reduce pub assaults while more people are being killed on the roads. We have developed this argument elsewhere. Just as Leslie Wilkins' crashes were not subdivided into those where blame could be allocated and those where it could not, neither should harms be divided into criminal and other for the purposes of prevention. The elevation of crime to a privileged position among harms risks the criminalisation of social policy, and the cynical justification of programmes which may be progressive in other ways by reference to their supposed crime prevention potential.

- Measures of harm reduction should be sufferer-centred. The change in the balance of effort and advantage between victim and perpetrator, which a crime represents, acts to the disadvantage of the victim. Therefore distributive justice in relation to crime must focus on the victim. Harm reduction first makes a declaration that the victim has been disadvantaged, and that effort must be made to ensure that the disadvantage does not become chronic. The aspect of preventing repeat victimisation which appeals most is, as the now clichéd phrase has it, it gets the grease to the squeak, not to the unharmed home or club which shouts loudest about its vulnerability.

- Measures to reduce crime must not rely on the remedy of prior distributive injustice against the offender. There are a number of reasons for this, none of them individually compelling. First, the crime suffered by the victim is a real harm. The distributive injustice against the offender is a presumption, both in substance and in its implications for the cause of the crime. Second, the victim risks harm by those beyond the perpetrator. Processing the offender is irrelevant insofar as there are other potential perpetrators against the same victim. Third, in practice, crime prevention programmes are not linked to individual crimes. For example, if young people are deemed to be perpetrators of much local crime, and if it is believed that boredom drives this, then an outreach youth worker may be appointed. Error about the dynamics of crimes against individuals will lead to no protection being afforded to particular victims.

• Fundamentally, harm prevention and blame allocation must be separated. The notion of crime being solved when blame is successfully allocated rather than when its repetition is made less likely is pernicious, and leads back to the monopoly that offenders hold on matters of distributive justice within the crime processing industry.

Limits to harm reduction

Probably all human action has an ethical range of convenience. When a society is grossly unfair, the removal of temptations is not defensible. 'Give us this day our daily bread' comes before 'lead us not into temptation' in the Lord's Prayer. Target hardening the baker's shop is not acceptable in a city of starving people. This is not an argument for omitting temptations and delivery from evil from the list of variables to which distributive justice is relevant, rather it is a balancing of the harms inflicted upon the starving and the bakers. This is no different from organ transplantation, where insensitive harvesting of the organs from the dead causes their loved ones suffering which has to be set against the suffering involved in repeated dialysis or slow death.

Sustainability as a wicked issue

Is crime prevention sustainable, or are we doomed to a sequence in which success breeds complacency, which in turn breeds failure? This is too little discussed. The saddest words in crime prevention are 'That was something we used to do'. Since complaint and distress understandably come from those areas suffering the highest rates of crime, those from whom the burden has been (at least temporarily) withdrawn will tend not to have the continuation of their present happiness given the highest priority. It is argued that the problem is the absence of a financial dynamic towards continued improvement.

There is currently a perverse incentive system whereby high crime rates attract central government money. Decreasing crime rates yield transitory praise followed by conviction that there is no longer a problem, all too often followed by a resurgence of crime. Credit in local authority is too often given to those who attract outside money, not those who use it to sustain improvements. Put most cynically, career development in local authority requires the continued existence of crime hot spots, if only to have areas on the back of whose temporary improvement one can advance one's career.

The writers have been exposed to many forward-looking proposals for burglary reduction. This makes one omission all the more conspicuous. Nowhere have we witnessed any attempt to generate a self-sustaining process, whereby savings from burglary reduction fed further reduction, creating a benign dynamic. One instance of this might be that a portion of savings made by a council in reduced burglary costs be explicitly devoted to further burglary reduction. Another might be the use of some of the reduced costs in police time to purchase equipment to facilitate further burglary reduction. Burglary reduction seems to be locked into a sequence of one-off (albeit worthy) projects to address specific problems, with no attempt to generate a benign dynamic of reduction.

The typical cast of mind appears not to incorporate this perspective. Indeed, factors like the restrictions on expenditure of rent revenue, in areas of mixed housing, operates as a statutory brake on crime reduction. In one sense, the Home Office has colluded in this by funding places where the problem is worst. What is in it, in terms of external money and kudos, for areas that have successfully controlled their burglary problem, beyond the substantial but typically uncosted savings? (The absence of awareness of the sophisticated Milton Keynes crime audit and similar initiatives suggests that authorities remain unmindful and certainly ill informed about burglary costs.)

The next step should surely be the incorporation in proposals of a financial dynamic whereby success in crime reduction is built upon. Until this happens, sustainability of crime reduction may remain elusive. Sustainability should be a matter of policy, not an example of the triumph of hope over experience.

Conclusions

- Crime displacement, where it occurs, is seldom if ever total.

- Sometimes the opposite: crime prevention takes place, when *prevention* spreads to adjacent areas.

- Even if displacement were hypothetically supposed to be total, distributive justice would require action to ensure an equitable distribution of the suffering caused by crime.

- Sustainability is a neglected topic in crime prevention. Attention to the incentive systems operating on those in a position to prevent crime would serve to bring sustainability to the centre of policy concern.

References

Barr R and Pease K (1990) 'Crime Placement, Displacement and Deflection' in Tonry M and Morris N (eds) *Crime and Justice 12*, Chicago: University of Chicago Press

Bouloukos AC and Farrell G (1997) 'On the Displacement of Repeat Victimisation' In Newman G, Clarke RV and Shoham SG (eds) *Rational Choice and Situational Crime* Prevention Aldershot: Dartmouth

Cornish DB and Clarke RV (1987) 'Understanding Crime Displacement: An Application of Rational Choice Theory' Criminology, 25

Giddens A (1998) *The Third Way: The Renewal of Social Democracy* London: Polity

Hesseling R B P (1994) 'Displacement: A Review of the Empirical Literature' in Clarke RV (ed) *Crime Prevention Studies*, 3, Monsey NY: Willow Tree Press

Hope T (1995) 'Community Crime Prevention' in Tonry M and Farrington DP (eds) *Building a Safer Society* Chicago: University of Chicago Press

Hope T (1996) 'Communities, Crime and Inequality in England and Wales' in Bennett T (ed) *Preventing Crime and Disorder: Targeting Strategies and Responsibilities* Cambridge: Institute of Criminology

Oppenheim C (1998) 'An Overview of Poverty and Social Exclusion' in Oppenheim C (ed) *An Inclusive Society: Strategies for Tackling Poverty* London: IPPR

Wiles P, and Costello A (1999) *The 'Road to Nowhere': The Evidence for Travelling Criminals* Police Research Series, London: Home Office

III: Let's do it

III: Let's do it.

8. Making it all happen©
Gloria Laycock and Barry Webb

One of the major issues in the crime prevention field, shared by many others, is ensuring the implementation of what works. Good practice abounds, and there is no shortage of pressure on statutory agencies and others to deliver more effective and efficient services, but somehow the good ideas, if they are shared at all, are not copied, developed or evaluated. In this chapter, some of the reasons for this are explored from a crime prevention perspective, but the concepts discussed are just as relevant to other areas of public policy. Much of the chapter is based upon experience gained from working in the Home Office Crime Prevention Unit (1983-1992) and thereafter in the Home Office Police Research Group. Both organisations had some degree of responsibility for commissioning research and ensuring its later implementation. We learned a lot!

First, a discussion of two key concepts, responsibility and competency (Engstad and Evans, 1980). Then a brief mention of the preventive process of collecting and analysing data, developing measures, implementation and evaluation or monitoring. This discussion will bring out the problems of implementation failure, which emerged in some of the many crime prevention partnerships around the UK. The experience of trying to encourage effective implementation from a central government department has led to the identification of a number of preconditions for its delivery – in particular, a range of levers which can be applied to facilitate action and which are discussed. In a final section, a framework is outlined setting out the requirement, at local and national level, through which emerging crime problems can be identified and remedial action, at the appropriate level, taken.

The two concepts

Responsibility

Who has the responsibility to prevent crime? The traditional assumption is that it is the police, but in reality everyone has a part to play, perhaps none more so than as individuals – parents, teachers, employees and employers – and as citizens. Of course central and local government have a role, but it is worth exploring the nature of their responsibility in contrast to that of the individual. In doing so it is useful to draw a comparison with preventive medicine. As individuals, we all wash our hands in the bathroom and teach our children to do the same; we have children inoculated against a variety of illnesses and we make full use of all the preventive medicine options available to us. This is what responsible citizens do in their own interests and in the interests of those they care for.

We can only do these things, however, if central and local government create a context within which they are possible. A plumbing system, local medical schemes and an option on vaccination clearly have to be made available to us if we are to make use of them. They have to be provided initially and thereafter maintained and developed in an organised and cost-effective manner. This calls for action on the part of central and local government in organising the relevant services and, beyond that, encouraging their use.

To return to crime, while as individuals we have a responsibility to support the crime prevention effort, we rely on local and central government, and the services they support, to create the right context. This context creation includes the provision of the criminal justice system which is clearly important in registering disapproval of proscribed behaviours, in responding to offending when it occurs and in defending the victim as well as, in some cases, incapacitating offenders and deterring crime. But in preventing crime, rather than responding to it, the role of government can be much wider. Under the provisions of the Crime and Disorder Act 1998 in the UK, for example, local groups, including the police, local government and other statutory and voluntary agencies, working in partnership, are required first to produce a local audit of crime and disorder and then a plan of how to tackle it.

The recently announced Crime Reduction Programme covering England and Wales goes wider in, amongst many other things, outlining a role for central government in designing out crime. This means addressing the way in which goods and services are designed, particularly within the private sector, and ensuring that the extent to which they may facilitate criminal activity is addressed at the early design stage (see, for example, Felson and Clarke, 1999 and Clarke, forthcoming). The programme also considers the role of central government in attempting to reduce the motivation for crime at the individual level by specifically addressing the risk factors known to be associated with its development (Goldblatt and Lewis, 1998).

So the notion of responsibility in preventing crime is not as simple as it might at first appear. The responsibility of central and local government, and that of many other agencies, whilst very real, is different in nature from that of the individual in his or her capacity as a citizen, parent, employer or employee. Both roles are equally relevant and necessary.

Competency

While we all have a responsibility to prevent crime in various senses, we do not all have the competency to do so. Competency refers to the individual agency, group, or even individual, with the power or authority to change the situation in some way to reduce the chances of a crime occurring (Felson and Clarke, 1999). Some examples are: motor manufacturers, shopkeepers, head teachers, local authority departments, fuel companies, and credit card designers.

If we feel that car security is poor and this contributes to an increased rate of offending, then it is not the police, the local authority or even central government that needs to act but the car manufacturers. Similarly, if the store layout is felt to encourage crime then the shopkeeper or owner may have to take some action to prevent it – and many now do. Head teachers in schools, staff in local authority departments – generally the suppliers of goods and services across the board – have a responsibility to contribute to the prevention of crime as discussed in the previous section but some also have the competency to do something about it in that they control the context within which crime may occur.

Identifying those with the competency to act is, therefore, a first step in tackling crime. These individuals or agencies will be the key to the implementation of change. Some will both accept their responsibility in this respect and take action on the basis of their competency, but not all. The more reluctant players may need to be persuaded that they should do something, and there are various examples of ways in which action has been levered out of competent but reluctant commercial companies and even statutory agencies.

The car manufacturers, for example, did not see security as a priority for their design teams until the publication of the Home Office Car Theft Index (Houghton, 1992). This listed cars in rank order according to their attractiveness to the thief, taking account of the number of vehicles of each type on the road. It concentrated the manufacturers' minds on the possibility of a competitive edge to be gained by improved security in an otherwise rather static market (Laycock and Tilley, 1995). In that respect, it was a success. The more recent version of the Car Theft Index shows that improvements in car security in the newer models have contributed to the reductions in car theft seen over the past five years (Home Office, 1998 and Crime Prevention Agency, 1997).

Decisions about what to implement, in order to achieve a reduction in crime, have usually, or perhaps ideally, resulted from an analysis of the presenting crime problem. This preventive process is discussed in the next section which also considers some of the rather disappointing areas where lack of effective implementation stems from an inadequate consideration of competency and leverage.

The preventive process

This process is now widely known although perhaps rather less widely used. There are a variety of different formulations (Heal and Laycock, 1986; Crime Concern, 1993; Read and Oldfield 1995 and Hough and Tilley, 1998) but essentially they all begin with collecting data or other information relating to crime or disorder; analysing it in some way; identifying preventive measures to be implemented; implementing them and assessing the effect. It was assumed that the difficult task revolved around collecting and analysing data and much of the Home Office's advice on crime prevention from the early 1980s was directed at this part of the process. Typically, researchers would assist the police or other agencies in analysing their data and the story would end with the identification of what needed to be done to reduce the problem (see, for example, Hope and Murphy, 1983). The assumption was that rationality would reign supreme and that the proposals for crime reduction would, of course, be implemented with some enthusiasm by the various partnership groups often involved in these exercises. Sadly it was not so, and a number of lessons emerged from this experience which inform the remainder of this section. Table 8.1 lists some of the proposed solutions to a range of presenting problems. These are then considered in turn.

Table 8.1 Early crime prevention solutions

- we need to rebuild the estate
- 'they' need to do something
- we need more men on the ground
- call it a local objective and expect action
- set up a committee to deal with it

Rebuild the estate

Some proposed solutions were unrealistically ambitious. Whilst rebuilding an estate may, in extreme circumstances, make sense, it cannot be the preferred solution on the majority of high crime estates, if only for practical and financial reasons. Alice Coleman's work provides an interesting example of where major redesign was implemented following the publication of her book (1985), which argued strongly for the view that the physical environment was a major, perhaps the major, cause of crime. Coleman managed to persuade the government of the day that an experiment of environmental redesign on a grand scale should be funded, and evaluated (DoE, 1997). It was an expensive experiment and clearly an unrealistic option for most public housing areas. The lesson from this was that if you are going to make recommendations which you would like to see implemented, keep them realistic.

'They' need to do something

Comments such as this are another way of saying that the competency for tackling the presenting problem lies elsewhere than within the partnership group or agency considering the data.

An example arose in 1990 with the significant rise in credit card fraud. The police were clear in their view that someone needed to do something and in this instance 'they' were the financial institutions (Levi *et al*, 1991). Interestingly, in this case, whilst knowing that there was a problem arising from the fundamental insecurity of the credit cards, the police themselves were unable to quantify it from their own existing data sets, which are generally constrained by the Home Office counting rules. So, for example, credit card frauds may manifest themselves in police recorded crime as car crimes (where credit cards are stolen from the glove compartment), street robbery (where a handbag snatch involves the loss of cards) or domestic burglary (where credit cards are stolen amongst other things). The only way to arrive at an estimate of the true rates of loss in this sector was to ask the financial institutions themselves to provide information on losses reported to them by members of the public.

This was done by Levi in the course of his research, and constituted the first published account of the scale of the problem. He used data supplied collectively by organisations which were in competition with each other under normal circumstances and reluctant to share such information for commercial reasons (Burrows, 1991). As such it was the first time that the scale of the problem across the whole sector was identified and it illustrated not only that losses were significant (in 1990 over £150 million) but that they were rising rapidly and would continue to do so unless urgent action was taken. The financial institutions (unlike the car manufacturers) decided to collaborate in developing solutions and established the Association of Payment Clearing Services (APACS), which was to co-ordinate the action against fraud amongst other things (Webb, 1996).

There are probably two reasons why the financial institutions co-operated in this way; first any solution was likely to be extremely expensive in its development – eye ball recognition techniques were to be considered, as well as sophisticated fingerprint systems – and sharing the costs made such technological solutions more feasible. Secondly, much of the technology in the financial sector is already shared – electronic payment at the point of sale, for example, and calls for common cash machines capable of reading cards from a variety of suppliers. So, there was a measure of self-interest in collaboration between competitors in this sector. The bottom line was, however, that action was provoked because of concerns about just that – the bottom line. The costs of crime were already being carried by the banks to a significant extent and there was a limit to which losses could continue to be allowed to grow as a result of insecure cards.

The lesson of relevance to the present discussion is that identifying those with the competency to act (in this case the banks) is not enough; there is a need to go beyond that and ask how that action is to be provoked.

We need more staff on the ground

A good example of this is the police crackdown or swamp operation, where an area receives a sudden increase in police resources, either through greater presence on the street or more directed operations. There is a good deal of evidence that these can have an immediate and dramatic impact on crime and other problems, such as drunk driving. Sometimes, even the threat of such increased attention, through publicity, can be sufficient to produce these effects (Laycock, 1992 and Stockdale and Gresham, 1995). Such crackdowns, though, are not sufficient by themselves to produce a sustained impact on crime – it is not usually possible to sustain the level and concentration of resources. The evidence is that the problem often returns after a while, as offenders discover more about the real risks of being caught, or find ways of circumventing those risks (such as open drug markets becoming closed markets – see Edmunds, Hough and Urquia, 1996).

On its own, then, an increase in resources will not guarantee a result. A more strategic approach is required, which targets action on several key aspects of the problem. Table 8.2 is an example of such a strategic framework, in relation to the policing of problem housing estates (Morris, 1996). Increased police attention, in the form of crackdowns, clearly has a role to play in such a strategy, but in the knowledge that its impact will likely be short term. Furthermore, there may be possible side effects, such as antagonising the local community, which will need attention if such measures are not to be counter-productive. A strategic approach anticipates these kinds of problem, including the possibility that the problem may change its form, as well as its size, in response to the measures being taken.

Table 8.2 A strategic approach to the policing of problem housing estates		
	Short-term focus	Long-term focus
Police measures	Targeting offenders Pulse policing Intelligence gathering Counter witness intimidation	Proactive patrols Maximising visibility Problem-oriented policing
Civil measures	Assisting injunctions Assisting evictions	Joint targeting of problems Liaison with civil teams
Community measures	Publicising initiatives Rumour control	Leisure diversion schemes Dialogue with the community Generation of positive contacts Youth programmes Monitoring void properties

The lesson here is that short-term wins may be helpful but they need to be set in a broader strategic framework.

Call it an objective and expect action

The managerial solution! But it is not enough. Experience of initiatives such as Policing by Objectives, in the 1980s, and latterly, of problem-oriented policing (Leigh, Read and Tilley, 1995 and 1998), is that very little will happen if such objectives are not backed up with training, organisational arrangements and performance-management regimes, tailored to supporting the achievement of those objectives. That includes the provision of adequate information of the right kind that enables such problems to be identified, strategies developed and impact monitored. The IT implications are clear. The development of repeat victimisation work in police forces is a particularly good example of the need for objectives or performance targets to be backed up in this way. Without the extensive support and guidance provided by the Home Office research and development programme, it is unlikely that repeat victimisation prevention would have developed as far as it has – and there is still a long way to go (see Pease, 1998).

And then there is the problem of perverse incentives. Great care is needed to ensure that appropriate targets and objectives are set, and that they don't have unwanted side effects. An example in education might be where pressure to improve the quality of exam results leads schools into introducing more stringent entry criteria, thereby excluding pupils deemed unlikely to produce the kind of results expected by the objective. Another example in the complex field of asset investigation and seizure, is where police performance is measured on the size of confiscation orders made, not on the amounts collected – collection is the responsibility of the courts. Thus, the incentive for the police is to maximise their assessment of the value of the defendant's assets. This, though, can create real problems for the magistrates courts who may inherit a situation where the defendant cannot satisfy the requirements of the order, and are thus encouraged to seek ways other than recovery of the assets to clear the debt (Levi and Osotsky, 1995).

Set up a committee to deal with it

In 1984, the Home Office and a number of other government departments issued a joint circular to the police, local, education and health authorities and others commending the establishment of inter-agency working groups (partnerships) as a means of tackling crime (Home Office et al, 1984). The circular was widely welcomed as a step in the right direction but it fell short of identifying which of the many agencies and local groups addressed were to take the lead. In this respect it was criticised by a later report on crime prevention at the local level, generally known as the Morgan report (Home Office, 1991), which suggested that statutory responsibility for the convening of local partnerships should rest with local government, although specifically involving the police.

The Morgan report was slightly ahead of its time. One of the difficulties in being so specific was that there was relatively little knowledge in local government, or even within the police service, for that matter, about precisely how crime prevention should be approached. The fieldwork associated with the Morgan report illustrated the fact that the best schemes were dependent upon the inspiration of individuals from a variety of organisations including local government, the police and voluntary and statutory groups. No one group had a monopoly on good ideas and there was not enough widespread knowledge in any one agency to commend it as capable of leading the field. Indeed, although the police were probably ahead of the game, there was still room for improvement as the most recent inspection of police forces' performance in the community safety field illustrates (Her Majesty's Inspectorate of Constabulary, 1998).

The circular was fairly widely taken up, however, and for over a decade inter-agency and other partnership groups have formed, disbanded and reformed, addressing various components of the crime and disorder problem with varying degrees of success. Some early partnership pitfalls are listed in Table 8.3 and discussed below.

Table 8.3 Early partnership pitfalls
• who's in charge here?
• it's not our job it's yours
• your priorities are not mine
• we'd like to help but it would reduce our profits
• we've got no money, can we have some of yours?
• I'm in from the local voluntary group – what can I do?

In light-hearted manner, the list of comments in Table 8.3 illustrates some of the problems which emerged in the early days of inter-agency working. They are rehearsed in more serious vein in a series of three research reports published in 1994 (Liddle and Gelsthorpe, 1994a, b and c). The first question – who's in charge here? – reflects back on the observations arising from the Morgan report of a lack of an identifiable lead agency. By failing to endorse the Morgan report's recommendations in this respect, the Home Office advice left something of a leadership vacuum, which was often filled by the police and led to criticism of their traditional can do approach to life as a consequence.

'It's not our job it's yours' interestingly illustrates the importance of being clear, within the partnership framework, of where the competency for action lies. There was a trenchant belief in the early 1980s, that the police were both responsible and competent through the criminal justice system, to reduce crime. The partnerships of today know better, and statements of this kind now have legitimacy only insofar as they may be pointing to the agency or individual with real competency to act – the local government agent, manufacturer, or commercial entrepreneur, for example.

The various, and legitimately different priorities held by members of partnership groups need to be acknowledged and dealt with – 'your priorities are not mine' is an aggressive statement of the obvious, but may call for the development of levers to change priorities within different sectors. For example, thefts from prepayment coin meters accounted for about 40 per cent of domestic burglaries on high-crime estates (Hill, 1986), but payment of fuel bills through the use of prepayment coin meters accounted for a very small proportion of fuel company customers, mainly those with debt problems. As Hill showed, since any losses through the theft of cash in these meters was carried by the householder rather than the fuel company, there was relatively little incentive on the part of the companies to reduce their rate of use.

The priority for the police and, for that matter, the customer, to ensure that prepayment meters were less prone to attack, was not the priority of the fuel company. The balance of interest was changed when the fuel companies were told by the government regulators that the meters could be deregulated immediately under existing legislation, if development of alternative and less vulnerable collection methods was not speeded up. Deregulation in this way would have meant that over a million fuel meters would have become illegal with immediate effect. This did indeed have the desired effect of speeding up the development, to the extent that the replacement of cash meters with credit card machines played a significant part in the achievement of burglary reductions on a number of estates (Cooper, 1989 and Forrester *et al*, 1988).

Early partnership groups, like their later counterparts, were also particularly conscious of the need to finance initiatives. They also learned fairly quickly that inaction on the part of some agencies was caused by the threat to their profits. Generally speaking crime prevention measures cost money and a balance has to be drawn between investment and risk. There are now a variety of excellent examples of sensible and proper investment in crime prevention being shown to have a longer-term pay-off in cost benefit terms.

Bridgeman (1996) has some particularly good examples of the way in which crime risk can be managed and be made to work in a cost-effective way. She evaluated the risk-management strategy developed by the police and local authority in Wigan. Convinced that money which they were currently spending on insurance premiums could be better spent on preventing crime and damage, the local authority agreed with their insurers to bear a higher level of loss in exchange for lower premiums. The money saved from paying lower premiums was invested in crime prevention measures such as improving security in council vehicle depots and installing new fire detection systems in schools. The result has been a net saving of £1.9 million in four years.

Further examples of the way in which businesses can invest in controlling crime, to their own advantage, are discussed across a range of sectors by Burrows (1991).

Although companies may still claim that investment in crime prevention leads to reductions in their profits, with adequate data they can be persuaded that it is in their interest to invest.

Of course some of the early partnerships felt the need to develop crime prevention initiatives, some on a fairly small-scale basis, but failed to identify funding to support it. There was a slight tendency, perhaps cynically, to invite what was seen as local sources of funding on to the partnership in the hope that they might be persuaded to provide sponsorship for various worthy schemes. The involvement of local Chambers of Commerce in local partnership groups is a good example of this kind of activity and they did indeed meet with some success.

Finally, in their attempt to be inclusive, the lonely partnerships would invite local voluntary groups and agencies with an apparently marginal relationship to crime prevention on to the group, without any clear and obvious idea what role they might play in reducing crime. To some extent the probation service fell into this category with an assumption that any agency with a criminal justice interest would have an obvious crime prevention function. The role of the probation service in primary crime prevention has never been very clear, but the issues were discussed by Geraghty (1991) who identified a range of possible activities for the probation service in this field.

The lesson here is that simply setting up a committee, partnership or inter-agency group is not enough in itself. The way in which action can be levered from those competent to act needs attention, and the role of the individuals on the partnerships needs to be very clearly specified at the outset.

Having worked through the roles of inter-agency members and considered what might be done, either on the basis of experience or an analysis of the problem, the early partnerships would then announce that the initiative was to be launched – Let's do it! It is at this point that the implementation problems really did become highlighted. Typical comments arising from this exercise are shown in Table 8.4 and are good examples of the need to see initiatives in context.

Table 8.4 'Let's do it'

- I need more support from the top (… or bottom … or middle)
- we need some money/staff advice
- it is now force/ACPO/government policy so it must be happening
- I told them it was their responsibility and they ignored me!

They first point to the necessity for supportive management. Initiatives are not launched in a policy or managerial vacuum; they need senior management support, commitment, sympathy, understanding and follow-up if they are to be implemented and developed further. There have been, for example, a range of locally-based inter-agency groups which have floundered because those attending meetings did not have a remit from their own management hierarchy to commit resources (Sampson and Farrell, 1990). Multiply this across what may be five to ten agencies at any one meeting and it is perhaps not surprising that agreements may be made, but implementation fails.

Supportive management is not, of course, enough if the staff have not been properly trained and are not working within a performance regime that is outcome-oriented and which reinforces initiative and change. There are few organisations in the public sector (and not that many in the private sector), which do this successfully. It is not a feature of the large bureaucracies within which many of us work.

All that notwithstanding, there are examples of individuals who are remarkable in their ability to generate good ideas and to implement them, based locally on not much more than their own enthusiasm and dedication. The development of Vehicle Watch (Honess *et al*, 1994), Alley Gaiter, Safer Shopping (Poole, 1991) and rapid response alarms are all examples where individuals (in these cases, police officers) have made a difference. This has often been with minimal support from their managerial hierarchy and in some cases despite what can be interpreted as outright hostility from immediate line managers. Initiatives which are heavily reliant on the personality of their inventor are, however, at risk of collapse when the individual concerned moves on to other activities. There are also many examples where local community members and activists have taken up the challenge of dealing with crime and anti-social behaviour, often at some personal risk to themselves, and achieved remarkable results as a consequence.

Individual entrepreneurship within bureaucracies or within the communities themselves, needs to be nurtured alongside the more mechanistic approaches to crime control driven by the application of the preventive process model. But neither will happen without an alert and responsive management structure which challenges outmoded and ineffectual practice and which emphatically does not assume that force or Home Office or government (or anyone else's) policy statements will, of themselves, generate changes in local priorities or behaviour. Changes in local service delivery, if that is what is called for, will not happen by magic; levers need to be identified, developed and pulled.

Before moving on to consider how this can be done there are some preconditions which need at least to be considered if crime prevention partnerships are really to deliver change in outcome. These are listed in Table 8.5.

Table 8.5 Preconditions for effective action

- a clear idea of what is to be implemented
- a statement of how it will work
- who will take responsibility for implementation?
- who has the competency to act?

First there needs to be clear and unambiguous statements of: the problems to be addressed; what it is that is to be implemented to reduce the scale or nature of that problem and, particularly, how it is expected to achieve its effect. There are numerous examples where failure in these areas have led to waste. For example, although not without its critics (Safe Neighbourhoods Unit, 1993), the Kirkholt burglary project was probably the most successful crime reduction project ever run on a high crime estate in England. It achieved a reduction in domestic burglary of over 70 per cent in a three year period (Forrester *et al*, 1988 and 1990). The research was published and widely disseminated across police forces and the Safer City schemes operating at the time.

There were numerous attempts to replicate Kirkholt but none met with the same success as the original (Tilley and Webb, 1994). One of the reasons for this replication failure was the lack of appreciation on the part of would-be replicators of precisely what it was about the original project that led to its success. Tilley and Webb point to the need to be clear on the mechanism through which any crime reduction initiative is expected to exert its effect (see also, Pawson and Tilley, 1997).

There also needs to be a sense of who has the responsibility to ensure that implementation occurs. This may be a local partnership group, an agency or even an individual acting alone, but unless they also have the competency to act, not much will happen. Identifying the agency, organisation or individual with the competency to do something to reduce the opportunities for crime, to increase the risk, or to increase the costs is a key step in the process of achieving successful implementation. The next step for the responsible agents is to think through just how that action is going to be provoked – what are the levers?

Identifying levers

One of the most powerful levers is self-interest. The examples discussed above – from financial institutions to car manufacturers – show that action was taken because it was shown to be in their interest to do so. Relying on the social conscience of the retail or commercial sector is optimism indeed.

Another useful lever is data. Figure 8.1 illustrates losses from domestic burglary in successive sweeps of the British Crime Survey. Cash has been an attractive target for theft since the first survey and is increasing its market share, as are cheques and credit cards (which suggests that further action on the part of APACS is now required). Television thefts have reached a peak and now appear to be dropping, although with the arrival of the new, portable and expensive digital machines on the market the television may take off again as an attractive target for theft. Videos have also, apparently, reached a plateau (albeit a high one), although this too may be temporary with the arrival of new, portable, and expensive machines in the near future. An interesting speculative point associated with Figure 8.1 is to ask what might have happened to the rate at which these goods are

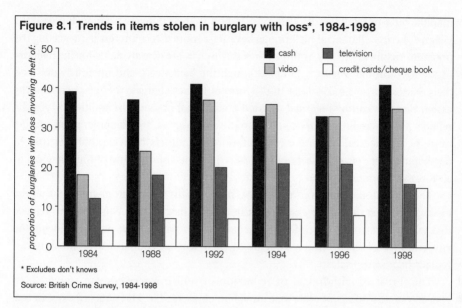

Figure 8.1 Trends in items stolen in burglary with loss*, 1984-1998

* Excludes don't knows

Source: British Crime Survey, 1984-1998

stolen if the manufacturers had been more alert to their vulnerability to theft when they were first being designed, and had taken action at the design stage to deal with it (see Chapter 13 this volume, and Clarke, forthcoming).

If electrical goods such as these are to be better protected from theft and burglary then it is for central government to take responsibility to press for improvements in design. Neither the police nor local government can do this; they do not have the necessary authority at national level, and it is certainly beyond the power of the individual consumer. While, therefore, it may be for central government to take responsibility, it is clearly the manufacturers who have the competency to ensure that the goods are designed in a more thief proof fashion. Built-in security through the greater use of personalised pin numbers, or some other technological approach, such as high security tracking devices incorporated at the design stage, might increase the risk to potential thieves sufficiently for the goods to lose some of their attraction as targets of theft.

Careful analysis of crime data can point to the goods at risk, but it is clearly more sensible to pre-empt the crime boom and design the goods properly in the first place. This requires manufacturers to be far more alert to the risk of crime towards their goods than they have so far shown themselves to be. Felson (1998) outlines the characteristics of highly attractive targets of theft and Ekblom (1997 and this volume) suggests that manufacturers need to 'think thief' more often and with greater design success. But even assuming that the manufacturers were to be alerted to these issues the question still remains, 'why should they bother to build in security?'

With this in mind there is an important difference between, for example, the financial institutions' experience of credit card fraud and that of the general manufacturer of retail goods. This owes in part to their different relationship with the victims of crime. Financial institutions have a far more direct interest in protecting the potential victim where, for example, they themselves are directly liable for the majority of the loss through theft or fraud. Although the banks can, and obviously do, pass these losses on to the customer in the form of higher charges, there is a limit to the extent that this can be regarded as good commercial practice. In addition, given the reliance of the credit industry upon shared technology at, for example, point of sale, there is a powerful incentive for collaborative efforts between competitors in developing more effective technologies to reduce the vulnerability of their services to all forms of criminal abuse.

The general manufacturer in contrast, may actually benefit from crime in that the losses from theft or burglary may result in the purchase of new equipment to replace that which was stolen. One of the consequences for Vauxhall Motors in reducing the vulnerability of in-car stereo systems to theft was a reduction in the volume of replacement stereo sales.

The threat of withdrawal or reduction of policing services can also help to concentrate the minds of otherwise unwilling partners. The HMV record store in one of London's main shopping areas, changed its marketing style, and particularly its approach to the control of shop theft, from detection to prevention, following a threat from the local police to handle shop thieves in the store more leniently.

The use of the law as a lever for action is the exercise of real power and despite the number of law breakers there are still significant gains to be made through regulation in this way. Perhaps the most recent example of this is the Crime and Disorder Act itself, which requires the police and local authorities to produce a crime audit of their areas and an associated plan to reduce the incidence of crime and disorder. The law is being used in this context as a lever for action. There were, of course, a number of local partnerships around the country where, in effect, plans were already available and were being acted upon. The effect of the Act is to bring others into line with the best.

Civil law might also play a part at the individual level in dealing with potential offenders who feel themselves to be beyond the criminal law. There are an increasing number of examples where the police and local authority are working together to tackle local problems of racial abuse or intractable neighbour disputes, using the threat of eviction from public housing stock as a lever for improved behaviour (Morris, 1996).

Finally, the media. It is not only the commercial sector that has an eye on public reaction to new reports. In a democracy, the media plays an important role in influencing public opinion and through that, political will across a range of issues at both local and national level. It is important that the power of the media in this respect is not abused, but it can be used to considerable positive effect as a lever. The publicity associated with the publication of the car theft index illustrates this. A list of levers is given in Table 8.6.

Table 8.6 Levers
• data
• withdrawal of service
• financial
• criminal law
• civil law
• media

A framework for action

There are some structural requirements if crime reduction is to be delivered at the local level. These are certainly facilitated by the Crime and Disorder Act with its statutory requirement for the police and local authorities to work together to carry out a crime audit and to formulate an action plan. To expand on that, the requirements locally are set out in Table 8.7.

Table 8.7 Local structure requirements
• inter-agency co-operation
• to identify good practice
• to identify those with the competency to act
• a communication channel to the centre
• levers to encourage action

Clearly there is a need for inter-agency co-operation at the local level. This can be in the form of partnerships as outlined in the Crime and Disorder Act, but could go beyond them, certainly extending more deeply into communities to the level of schools, neighbourhoods and hospitals.

Good practice also needs to be identified, disseminated and, particularly, replicated. There is a variety of sources for the identification of good practice, including: a regular digest published by the Home Office Crime Prevention Training Organisation, based at Easingwold in York; regular Home Office research reports which are widely disseminated to the police and other agencies, and of course Audit Commission and various Inspectorate publications. Sources are set out quite fully in the guidance for local partnerships associated with the Crime and Disorder Act, which is now available on the internet and from the Home Office in the form of a research report (Hough and Tilley, 1998).

A key requirement locally is the identification of those with a competency to act. In many cases, this will be local partners themselves, particularly the local authority or the police, but it may extend beyond them. Again, a good example is car crime where the design of the vehicle itself has to depend on action by the manufacturers. It is important, therefore, that there is a communication channel from the local level to central government in order to alert the centre to rising targets of crime. This is particularly the case where action is required at national level in terms of the design of goods or services.

Levers then need to be developed to ensure that action is taken at the right level. In an ideal world, this would be no more onerous than perhaps pointing out to agencies, whether statutory or otherwise, the need for appropriate action. Unfortunately, we do not live in an ideal world. In some cases, it may be necessary to generate more aggressive levers, including the threat of withdrawal of service, or the development of a particularly challenging performance regime.

Action at local level needs to be supported within a national framework. Three key points are listed in Table 8.8. There is no point in the local partnerships providing information centrally, in relation to the need to redesign goods and services, or to press for national action, if there is no structure at national level to hear the problems. The Home Office or other national agencies, including many other government departments, needs to be pulling in the same direction and needs to be prepared to take action to address aspects of their own policies and practices which may be facilitating crime at the local level. It also needs to be alert to the notion of identifying levers nationally over commercial industrial or other sectors that might help in reducing the opportunities for crime.

Table 8.8 National requirements

- a structure to hear problems
- to identify levers at national level
- an environmental scanning facility to respond to problems before they happen

---

Finally, it would also help to get ahead of the game, and instead of perpetually reacting to emerging crime problems, set in hand appropriate measures to pre-empt their development. A national environmental scanning facility could deliver this as is currently being developed under the auspices of the Crime Reduction Programme in England and Wales.

References

Burrows J (1991) *Making Crime Prevention Pay: initiatives from business* Crime Prevention Unit Paper 27, London: Home Office

Bridgeman C (1996) *Crime Risk Management: making it work* Crime Detection and Prevention Series 70, London: Home Office

Clarke RV and Felson M (forthcoming) *Hot products: understanding, anticipating and reducing the demand for stolen goods* Police Research Paper, London: Home Office

Coleman A (1985) *Utopia on Trial* London: Hilary Shipman

Cooper B (1989) 'Preventing Break-ins to Pre-payment Fuel Meters' in *Research Bulletin* Home Office Research and Planning Unit, London: Home Office

Crime Concern (1993) *A Practical Guide to Crime Prevention for Local Partnerships* London: Home Office

Crime Prevention Agency (1997) *Car Theft Index* London: Home Office Communications Directorate

Edmunds M, Hough, M and Urquia N (1996) *Tackling local drugs markets* Crime Detection and Prevention Series 81, London: Home Office

Ekblom P (1997) 'Gearing up against Crime: a dynamic framework to help designers keep up with the adaptive criminal in a changing world' *International Journal of Risk, Security and Crime Prevention* 214

Engstad P and Evans JL (1980) 'Responsibility, Competence and Police Effectiveness in Crime Control' in Clarke RV and Hough JM *The Effectiveness of Policing* Farnborough, Hants: Gower

Felson M (1998) *Crime and Everyday Life*, 2nd Ed, London: Pine Forge Press

Felson M and Clarke RV (1999) *Opportunity Makes the Thief: practical theory for crime prevention* Police Research Series 98, London: Home Office

Forrester D, Chatterton M, and Pease K (1988) *The Kirkholt Burglary Prevention Project, Rochdale* Crime Prevention Unit Paper 13, London: Home Office

Forrester D, Frenz S, O'Connell M and Pease K (1990) *The Kirkholt Burglary Prevention Project: Phase II* Crime Prevention Unit Paper 23, London: Home Office

Geraghty J (1991) *Probation Practice in Crime Prevention* Crime Prevention Unit Paper 24, London: Home Office

Goldblatt P and Lewis C (1998) (eds) *Reducing Offending: an assessment of research evidence on ways of dealing with offending behaviour* Home Office Research Study 187, London: The Stationery Office

Heal K and Laycock G (1986) (Eds) *Situational Crime Prevention: from theory into practice* London: HMSO

Her Majesty's Inspectorate of Constabulary (1998) *Beating Crime* HMIC Thematic Inspection Report London: Home Office

Hill N (1986) *Pre-payment Coin Meters: A Target for Burglary* Crime Prevention Unit Paper 6, London: Home Office

Home Office (1991) *Safer Communities: The Local Delivery of Crime Prevention through the Partnership Approach* London: Home Office

Home Office (1998) *Criminal Statistics England and Wales* London: HMSO

Home Office, Department of Education and Science, Department of Environment, Department of Health and Social Security, and Welsh Office (1984) *Crime Prevention* (Home Office Circular 8/1984) London: Home Office

Honess T, Maguire M and Charman E (1994) *Vehicle Watch and Car Theft: An Evaluation* Crime Prevention Unit Series 50, London: Home Office

Hope T and Murphy D (1983) 'Problems of Implementing Crime Prevention: the Experience of a Demonstration Project' *The Howard Journal* 22

Hough M and Tilley N (1998) *Auditing Crime and Disorder: guidance for local partnerships* Crime Detection and Prevention Series Paper 91, London: Home Office

Houghton, G (1992) *Car Theft in England and Wales: The Home Office Car Theft Index* Crime Prevention Unit Paper 33, London: Home Office

Laycock G (1992) 'Operation Identification or the Power of Publicity?' In Clarke RV (ed) *Crime Prevention: Successful Case Studies* New York: Harrow and Heston

Laycock G and Tilley N (1995) 'Implementing Crime Prevention' in Tonry M and Farrington D (eds) *Building a Safer Society: strategic approaches to crime prevention* Chicago: University of Chicago Press

Leigh A, Read T and Tilley N (1996) *Problem-Oriented Policing: Brit Pop* Crime Detection and Prevention Series 5, London: Home Office

Leigh A, Read T and Tilley N (1998) *Brit Pop II: Problem-oriented policing in practice* Crime Detection and Prevention Series 93, London: Home Office

Levi M, Bissell P and Richardson T (1991) *The Prevention of Cheque and Credit Card Fraud* Crime Prevention Unit Paper 26, London: Home Office

Levi M and Osotsky L (1995) *Investigating, Seizing and confiscating the proceeds of crime* Crime Detection and Prevention Series 61, London: Home Office

Liddle M and Gelsthorpe L (1994a) *Inter-agency Crime Prevention: Organising Local Delivery* Crime Prevention Unit Paper 52, London: Home Office

Liddle M and Gelsthorpe L (1994b) *Crime Prevention and Inter-agency Co-operation* Crime Prevention Unit Paper 53, London: Home Office

Liddle M and Gelsthorpe L (1994c) *Inter-Agency Crime Prevention: Further Issues* (Supplementary paper to Crime Prevention Unit Papers 52 & 53 above)

Morris S (1996) *Policing Problem Housing Estates* Crime Detection and Prevention Series 74, London: Home Office

Pawson R and Tilley N (1997) *Realistic Evaluation* London: Sage

Pease K (1998) *Repeat victimisation: Taking stock* Crime Detection and Prevention Series 90, London: Home Office

Poole R (1991) *Safer Shopping: the identification of opportunities for crime in covered Shopping Centres* Police Research Award Scheme, London: Home Office

Read T and Oldfield R (1995) *Local Crime Analysis* Crime Detection and Prevention Series 65, London: Home Office

Safe Neighbourhoods Unit (1993) *Crime Prevention on Council Estates* London: Department of the Environment

Sampson A and Farrell G (1990) *Victim Support in an Inner City Setting* Crime Prevention Unit Paper 21, London: Home Office

Stockdale J and Gresham P (1995) *Combating Burglary: An Evaluation of Three Strategies* Crime Detection and Prevention Series 59, London: Home Office

Tilley N and Webb J (1994) *Burglary Reduction: Findings from Safer Cities Schemes* Crime Prevention Unit Paper 51, London: Home Office

Webb B (1996) 'Preventing plastic card fraud in the UK' *Security Journal*, 7, 23-25

9.   It's good to talk, but it's not good enough
Active consultation as a key to safer communities
Scott Ballintyne and Penny Fraser

Crime and the fear of crime are complex. The search for causation and understanding is long and well documented. Yet one aspect appears to be generally accepted. Crime and fear of crime are higher where there is uncertainty, fragmentation and exclusion. We do not need to adopt the theory of risk society espoused by Giddens and Beck to recognise that these may be unsettling times for many people and communities, or that widespread uncertainty, from whatever source, can undermine any community's ability to work together to tackle crime and reduce fear of it.

The relationship between risk society and community safety is explored in more detail elsewhere in this book. How community uncertainty is addressed, and pressures towards greater social fragmentation combated and social exclusion reduced, remains central to making communities safer. From current evidence, it can be said with a degree of reliability that crime affects some communities disproportionately; some individuals suffer repeatedly from crime; fear of crime is more widespread than crime itself; and, the most vulnerable groups are most affected by fear of crime. Building safer communities requires us to successfully disconnect the flow between crime, fear of crime and instability within communities.

This chapter argues that active, involved community consultation is the essential ingredient for successful, sustained community safety. It is key to reducing crime and addressing fear of crime. It is key to developing a local consensus on community safety which goes beyond crime reduction and to breaking the connection between crime, fear of crime and community instability. If community instability undermines community safety, then consultation is part of the glue that can help rebuild community confidence and involvement.

Tackling crime is an area of social policy fraught with problems at both local and national level. The new Crime and Disorder Act 1998 provides an opportunity to get things more right than has been the case over the last twenty years. This is why partnerships are urged to get consultation right, get community involvement right and to start to make meaningful connections between crime prevention and creating the kinds of safer communities in which people want to live and work.

Consultation alone is unlikely to be sufficient, but is a necessary starting point. It is the means by which local communities can start to be engaged in making their own communities safer. The Audit Commission review (1999) highlights current shortcomings within community safety consultation, particularly the widespread failure of partnerships to consult local people on priorities. This is disappointing but not surprising. Public services and multi-agency partnerships do not have a strong track record in consulting and engaging local communities.

The field of urban regeneration demonstrates the structural, organisational and internal political difficulties public agencies have with community consultation and involvement. Few people will not have heard repeated complaints from poorer communities that local regeneration is passing them by. A recent Joseph Rowntree Foundation study on urban regeneration (1996) found that while there is wide agreement that effective and lasting community regeneration can only be achieved in partnership with the people who live there, the actual nature of the community contribution is contested by different partners. Most community involvement in regeneration programmes was concentrated in the implementation stage of initiatives and not at the stage where the strategic direction of regeneration activity is concerned.

Yet, we may be in danger of making similar errors in community safety. The Crime and Disorder Act 1998 places a duty upon local authorities and police forces to:

- form a statutory community safety partnership;

- conduct an audit of crime and disorder;

- consult the public at key stages, notably on priorities and targets;

- draw up a three year strategy and monitor and evaluate their work.

It represents a radical shift in planning and co-ordination for community safety and is a major step forward. However, there are few moves to involve communities directly in partnerships. The path being followed by community safety partnerships is much narrower and is agency driven.

The Act recognises the benefits to be gained by improving how public agencies tackle community safety but it sets out the community role mainly in terms of setting local priorities and targets for crime reduction. This could give rise to two significant problems for community safety. First, it could result in some local authorities and police forces pigeon-holing community consultation. Being consulted on local priorities and targets, however imperfectly, may be an improvement on previous experience but it falls far short of active community involvement. There is much to be gained through better working relationships between public agencies, but not at a price which restricts the involvement of local communities.

Later in the chapter, a brief history of community consultation on policing and community safety is looked at. A recurring feature is the extent to which it has been consultation, as defined by police forces and public agencies, rather than by local communities. This needs to end if we are to be successful in building safer communities.

Second, the emphasis on priorities and targets for crime reduction may re-inforce the social exclusion of certain groups in the community – or indeed encourage entire communities to continue to pass off responsibility for community safety on to local authorities, police forces and other agencies. If communities are afforded only a restricted, consultative role in community safety, the communities which will suffer most are those which are at greatest risk and are experiencing the highest levels of crime.

A broader community safety agenda, which starts from a community's own experiences is needed. This should recognise that priorities for safety may be as much about safe play areas for children or safety from speeding traffic, as crime and disorder, and should build those into a genuinely multi-agency strategy for improving community safety and reducing crime. This would be more likely to produce greater community ownership of local problems and solutions. Exclusion from the social and economic mainstream is accompanied by political exclusion – an exclusion from decision-making.

Communities under pressure will be only too pleased to take a limited role in setting community safety priorities and targets and to hand responsibility over to others. If consultation is restricted – either through design because it suits the agencies or through a failure to grasp its importance – then the very process which takes power away from local communities and encourages reliance upon others who appear to be better placed to intervene on their behalf, may be reinforced. To build safer communities exclusion needs to be removed from local decision-making.

Both outcomes are counter-productive if active involvement in making their communities safer is sought for local communities. Both place glass ceilings upon community safety and undermine partnership. Agencies can take comfort in limiting their exposure to community involvement, particularly if the alternative is working in partnership with hard to reach or critical communities. Similarly, communities can take comfort in limiting their involvement to commenting upon priorities and setting targets, because it fits the prevailing perspective that others have responsibility for solving community problems, while offering the palliative of having been asked. It allows people to pass the buck, sometimes for the actions of their own children.

In practice, many projects shown to have the greatest, sustained impact upon community safety have been those which have successfully engaged local communities. If community consultation and involvement is essential for success at a project level, then it is also a prerequisite at the strategic, partnership level.

Two major changes are needed to underpin community safety – a culture shift within public agencies to embrace partnership working and the placing of community consultation and involvement centre-stage in community safety development, planning and implementation. The former requires every partnership to build its capacity for partnership, working across senior, middle management and operational levels. It is not sufficient to talk partnership speak, it needs to be carried across agencies and may require specific inter-agency training programmes. The latter requires partnership to engage local communities as active partners in community safety. To do this they need to build capacity within local communities so they can take part in partnership decisions and lead local programmes. This needs to be addressed as a primary strategic theme for the partnership.

The following sections look at the history and development of consultation on policing and community safety. The notion of consultation as community capacity building and ongoing dialogue with local people is revisited. It is argued that the idea of policing by consent, specifically active consent, is a useful benchmark for guiding local community safety partnerships. Thereafter the move is to more practical issues, identifying barriers and setting out ways of making community consultation an inclusive and sustainable process. The importance of inclusive community safety, which seeks to bring communities together and to shift away from the blame culture that can surround some initiatives, is considered. In conclusion, the challenges facing community consultation are addressed, with recommendations for improving partners' work and putting active community consultation and involvement at the centre of the community safety agenda.

Active community consultation and involvement

The present Government has placed community empowerment at the heart of its thinking on crime and regeneration. The Crime and Disorder Act 1998 provides the opportunity to develop inclusive, active consultation practices. But what does active consultation mean? What does it involve? What makes it different from current community consultation?

As seen here, active community consultation has three components – a strategic partnership involvement for local people, an ongoing dialogue with local communities as an equal partner in making their area safer and a direct engagement in implementing local strategies. The main objectives are to help build communities' capacity for participating in making their own communities safer and ensuring local accountability throughout the community safety process.

Active consultation means that communities should be represented at all levels and stages of the community safety process, including strategic involvement in crime and disorder partnerships. Communities, however diverse, need to be afforded the capacity to take part and have the independent support to enable their voices to be heard and listened to.

Community consultation must not be restricted to identifying initial priorities and targets. This could lead, *inter alia*, to crime reduction dominating the community safety agenda even where this may not be the community's safety priority. It could also lead to the community being marginalised or dismissed once priorities and targets are set. Partnerships owe it to local communities to ensure that consultation becomes dialogue and that community involvement is guaranteed at all stages of decision-making and implementation.

There are compelling reasons why active consultation and involvement is a desired goal and why it can lead to safer communities. In this section, a number of those reasons are highlighted.

● *communities understand their problems better than service professionals*

Recent research into Police Community Consultative Groups, which emerged through the Police and Criminal Evidence Act 1984, shows that although such groups were set up with the aim of consulting local communities about crime and policing priorities and concerns, in practice they have frequently taken the form of the police educating communities about policing and the limitations of the police service.

This modus operandi by public agencies is not uncommon. Local authorities have been subject to the same criticism in urban regeneration, where consultation is often seen as a means of conveying bad news about the limits of available funding rather than actively engaging local people. Despite their proximity to their own problems, communities are seen to be less knowledgeable than professional service deliverers. An active approach to consultation and involvement would go some way towards overthrowing one-way, passive, rubber-stamping consulting with local people.

● *communities are often more flexible and creative than large service bureaucracies*

The experience in some areas of consulting around the crime and disorder audit has produced some examples of how – if consultation is approached in the right way – the process can yield creative ideas from residents about how to tackle crime and disorder and develop community safety in their neighbourhoods. There are many examples up and down the country where residents' initiatives have been successful in achieving participation and support from local people where formal agencies could not.

Formal agencies do, however, have a role in supporting bottom-up creativity. Decentralising services can make a significant difference, as can ongoing support by officers and elected officials for existing groups in the community. On occasion all that may be needed to promote a community's involvement in delivering community safety is a more formal recognition of the contribution which is already being informally undertaken by local people. Single Regeneration Budget (SRB) guidance now gives explicit recognition of the untapped or unrecognised talent in the community and advises that up to ten per cent of a programme's funding be dedicated to community capacity building. Research has shown how important it is that regeneration initiatives do not sweep aside existing informal groups and projects run by members of the community in the process. Instead they must work with these groups to build their capacity and influence, whilst respecting their independent status and not seeking to co-opt them into the dominant partners.

- *communities can be cheaper than service professionals*

    This may be harder for some agencies to handle, particularly if it is taken at face value. There may be occasions where local community organisations are able to deliver a better, wider-ranging service at a lower cost than their public agency counterpart. In the main, overheads and staff costs are lower in the not for profit sector. Yet, there can be wider benefits and cost savings to be made if communities are able to deliver services directly. There is direct benefit to the local economy – resources earned locally are spent locally. This is significant for poorer communities where the interplay between financial exclusion and community deprivation is particularly strong. A creative combination of training funds, the re-alignment of public expenditure and community enterprise has potential benefits for making communities safer.

    Contracting communities to deliver community safety may be one significant way of engaging local people and generating sustained involvement in the process. At the very least it is an option which should be considered at all stages of the partnership, if for no other reason than that there are few new public funds available to support the Crime and Disorder Act 1998 and the emerging Best Value regime requires services to be subjected to competitive evaluation. Local communities could well be the competitive provider for some community safety programmes.

This does not imply inattention to the problems that some critics have identified with the involvement of communities in crime reduction. Communities are, of course, contested, diverse and often fragmented. Crime can introduce rifts between sections of the community and attempts to tackle crime – if handled badly – can cement such rifts. There may also be struggles within the community as to who should be represented on partnership bodies.

However, if handled well, community consultation can confront and overcome such obstacles and lead to an involvement which enriches both partnership and community. Consultation, if given a consistent, central priority can help re-establish the social capital which is less evident in excluded, higher crime communities.

Before looking at what needs to be done, and in order to offer some practical guidance a brief exploration should be made of two elements which provide a broader backdrop for the development of community safety in the UK. These have a bearing upon how partnerships might pursue active consultation and involvement. They are:

- the current context for consulting communities about crime (which looks at how the public sector and its partners traditionally consult on crime and community safety)

- the importance of a wider view of consultation and involvement (which explores the importance of community dialogue and policing by consent for community safety).

The context for consulting communities about crime

To understand why crime and disorder partnerships are urged to develop inclusive consultation mechanisms and engage local communities as an integral approach to everything they do, this section outlines the prevailing context for community consultation on crime. This highlights the shortcomings with current arrangements and shows why partnerships need to take a wider view of consultation and involvement – a view which is able to respond positively to increasingly diverse communities and a view which strengthens policing by consent.

Local government and police: existing consultation mechanisms

Effective active consultation with the public has become ever more crucial as communities themselves undergo often rapid change in physical appearance, composition and reputation. There are some obvious connections between such communities which undergo rapid social and physical change, or which experience a high population turnover, and the levels of crime and disorder in those areas. A transient and vulnerable population is less likely than a stable, confident community to engage in informal social control such as Neighbourhood Watch or collective supervision of young people in public areas. For these reasons, it becomes even more essential that police and local authority and other agencies have ways of involving those communities in defining and addressing their changing community safety needs and priorities.

Until the introduction of the Crime and Disorder Act 1998, there was no statutory requirement for local authorities to consult the electorate about the local management of crime. The main way in which this was achieved was indirect, via the representation of locally elected councillors on police authorities informing the preparation of the annual local policing plan. A 1998 Audit Commission survey found that only 44 per cent of local authorities had carried out consultation exercises with the public about their community safety work. Local authority consultation has tended to be at level of wider service surveys and has occasionally been practised in a more focused manner in certain neighbourhoods or estates as part of a specific community safety or regeneration project.

Community consultation was not a significant feature of the work of the Safer Cities projects. Where consultation was carried out, it tended to be: around a specific theme (fear of crime surveys for example); one-off (open days or public meetings) or indirect (via elected councillor representation on Safer Cities project steering committees). Although there were some examples of good practice in sustained and structured consultation, (Safer Cities in Sheffield had a specific strategy for involving young people and Manchester Safer Cities carried out an extensive survey on race and used this to influence the development of the project's priorities) seldom did any of these processes actually influence the project's strategic development.

Crime, and fear of crime may have featured highly in community priorities for many years but until recently they have not featured highly in regular, planned local dialogue.

In the wake of the riots in a number of Britain's inner cities in 1981 and the publication of the report by Lord Scarman, which criticised heavily the lack of dialogue between the police and the communities they policed, the Police and Criminal Evidence Act 1984 made it a legal requirement for the police to consult with communities about local policing matters. However research on the consultative arrangements (the usual model being police-community consultative committees) suggests that they have not, in the main, been effective as forums for public debate about crime and policing, nor have they made the police more locally responsive. Agendas have tended be constructed and dominated by the police. Such forums are least likely to be attended by those with whom the police come into contact during the course of their routine work in communities (particularly young people or people from areas with the highest crime rates).

The Police Act 1996 sought to address some of these shortcomings by requiring the police to consult with the public about the annual local policing plan drawn up by the Police Authority. However, this consultation has remained patchy and has afforded local communities only a limited say in setting local policing priorities. It has not yielded an effective, participatory voice in local policing. At the same time the introduction of key national policing objectives has produced a tension between meeting the views of local people and those of the Home Secretary. The outcome has been an impoverished statutory consultation, which has not actively engaged local communities.

From the mid-1980s however, a number of developments outside these formal statutory processes have encouraged greater levels of activity in seeking the views of the public on crime. The Home Office's biennial British Crime Surveys (first carried out in 1982) revealed the true picture of crime to be up to three times greater than that known to the police. Later sweeps in the 1980s and 1990s also confirmed that there were significant national differences in reporting rates. The implications of these finding for policy were that crime could never adequately be tackled if the official picture alone formed the basis for decision-making.

In 1991, the Home Office Standing Conference on Crime Prevention produced the Morgan Report. The conference accepted the recommendations from the Association of Metropolitan Authorities that the present arrangements for responding to crime were unsatisfactory. They were largely outside the local democratic structure and the recommendation was that they should be changed to enable local authorities to take a lead on community safety, in partnership with police and other agencies. As is well known, the advice of the working party was not followed until, in 1998, the Labour Government incorporated it into the Crime and Disorder Act.

Community consultation and involvement: dialogue, policing by consent and safer communities

Community consultation and involvement have attained buzzword status for policing and community safety. They are used frequently in wide-ranging settings. On one level they evoke images not dissimilar in policing from those raised by beat or neighbourhood policing, and in local government by user involvement or customer care. They are images of a time gone by which appeared safer and more stable, or of a way of working which somehow captures public involvement. On another level they invoke images of public service and a recognition, however imperfect, of some degree of public accountability.

Yet, it can be seen from agencies' patchy engagement in community consultation and involvement that there is little shared understanding beyond a general belief that consulting and involving local communities has some merit and benefit, often for the individual agency or partnership. This appears to apply equally to formal consultation arrangements, for example, the police community consultative groups set up under the auspices of the Police and Criminal Evidence Act 1984, and to less formal consultation where individual police officers discuss problems with local community organisations.

Most agencies which are increasingly engaged in community safety partnerships place varying emphases upon community consultation and involvement and have evolved different ways of consulting. Few, if any, see consultation and involvement as the touchstone that governs and directs their actions and services. In fact, few partnerships would appear to be meeting the minimal requirements of the Crime and Disorder Act 1998 on consultation, that is, those of consulting on priorities and targets. Public consulting, as part of a local community safety audit, was reported by 57 per cent of police forces and 44 per cent of local authorities taking part in a national survey in March 1998. This may rise as partnerships come under the scrutiny of local audits but it highlights two problems. First, it suggests that many partnerships may be missing the central importance of consultation and involvement for successful community safety. Second, it suggests a fairly minimalist approach to the requirements of the legislation. The focus is on what needs to be done to avoid external criticism, rather than how to ensure that the partnership is fit for the purpose it is meant to serve.

In the absence of a clear primacy for community consultation and involvement in community safety activity, it is unsurprising that we have a diversity across agencies and partnerships about what is required, how it might be applied and even how best to go about it. The first task ought therefore to be establishing a shared understanding, across partners, of the importance of community consultation and involvement for making communities safer.

There are three compelling reasons for adopting community consultation and involvement as the touchstone for community safety.

1. Public service and accountability

The ongoing legitimacy of public services rests upon how well they discharge their responsibilities to the public they serve. Community safety is of particular importance for public service in two respects. The Crime and Disorder Act 1998 formally places a duty on local government and police to act as 'responsible authorities' in partnership with others to make communities safer. Secondly, community safety repeatedly features amongst the top three public concerns. Community safety brings together public priority with formal public service responsibility.

It is also important in a more pragmatic way. Community safety cuts to the core of people's daily lives. How safe or unsafe a person feels affects their decisions, their relationship to the wider community and their quality of life. It can increase the cost and reduce the effectiveness of other public services. It adds financial and human burdens on to communities and businesses. Responding to those fundamental public concerns would appear to be adequate reason for public services to be engaged in community safety.

Local authorities gain public legitimacy and accountability through directly elected local representation. That is not to say that this is sufficient for engaging local communities in community safety activity. Current proposals for 'better government' demonstrate the shortcomings with present levels of local accountability and set out wide-ranging ways of improving consultation and involvement with local people.

Policing, however, gains its legitimacy in different ways. The debate about police accountability is long and unfinished, but, in the main, policing draws its legitimacy from two sources – through indirect accountability to elected government, and through broad public consent. It is this latter form of accountability that is critical for community safety. It is this latter form of accountability that requires the adoption of community consultation and involvement as the touchstone for local policing.

Just as partnership needs to be an active process, so too does policing by consent. To be relevant and to legitimise local policing, policing by consent needs to arise from active community consultation and involvement in all aspects of policing. This lays the ground for active community involvement in community safety where communities take a stake in local developments and are able to function in full partnership with public agencies. The alternative is a passive community, uninvolved in partnership, giving consent by its absence and increasingly unable to bring its own resources to bear on the problems it faces.

The message is clear. Public service obligations and the need for accountability suggest that community consultation and involvement must be more than an optional extra if we are to make communities safer. They suggest that communities may not be wholly satisfied with improved actions by agencies, although these are a good start.

2. Improving the quality of services

The changing context for the delivery of local services provides a further imperative for public bodies to consult widely, regularly and consistently. The 1990s have seen significant changes in the management and delivery of public services. The increasing application of performance management to public services accompanied by a broader growth in consumerism amongst the public has shifted the axis from which public services are perceived and evaluated. At the minimalist end of the spectrum, communities are seen as receivers of service who have a right to be consulted, however imperfectly, on priorities and delivery. At the maximalist end communities have acquired much greater powers over local decision-making, including direct budgetary control in some instances.

The combination of compulsory competitive tendering, continuing public budget restrictions and the emergence of Best Value have provided a broad drive towards consulting local people in a more systematic fashion and opened the door to engaging communities in developing and delivering services themselves. The twin components of performance management and public consultation are integral to the recent Crime and Disorder Act 1998 which has a strong managerial ethos underpinning its provisions on partnership, setting local priorities and evaluating local strategies.

Two particular emerging areas have a potentially powerful impact for the development of community safety – the Best Value regime for the development of public services and local regeneration programmes. Best Value sits at the heart of government plans to modernise local government and reinvigorate local democracy. Enhancing direct citizen control over service delivery sits at the heart of Best Value. Government is placing a Best Value duty upon public authorities which includes requirements to consult and competitively evaluate service delivery. Users, taxpayers and the business community are to be consulted at various stages of service delivery from planning through to evaluation. At the same time services are to be subjected to competitive evaluation to determine whether they could be delivered more effectively or efficiently in other ways. This opens up two major avenues for community safety:

- to tap into emerging public consultation programmes across a range of service provision

- to open up discussion on whether local communities might be better placed to deliver safer services either directly, through some form of community enterprise, or in partnership with other public, private or voluntary agencies

It is difficult to see how a public service can achieve Best Value status if it cannot demonstrate how it is contributing to making a local community safer, particularly if community safety is a recurring local priority. Best Value provides a wedge for community safety to enter mainstream public service delivery and tap into mainstream budgets.

The second area of potentially powerful impact is regeneration. Local regeneration, particularly in impoverished areas, has been learning a number of difficult lessons over the past twenty years. They are lessons of partnership and community involvement. A number of studies have highlighted the importance of actively engaging local people if community regeneration is to be successful and sustained.

Steps have been taken more recently to apply these lessons across regeneration programmes such as the SRB and the New Deal for Communities (NDC). Bids are unlikely to be funded unless they clearly demonstrate the way in which communities have been consulted on the proposals and how they will be represented at all stages of the delivery process. Partnership Boards are increasingly appointing local residents as community directors and setting up standing consultative fora. The latest guidance for SRB Round 5 encourages local partnerships to allocate up to 10 per cent of the available budget to building community capacity.

Community safety partnerships could usefully learn from the shortcomings of regeneration programmes and apply those lessons in support of their own development. The first lesson is that community engagement needs to start as early as possible. Agencies may be disposed towards getting their own act together, before involving local communities or voluntary agencies in community safety work. However, the lessons from regeneration show that this exacerbates the gap between agencies and local people and makes it more difficult to gain credible community involvement at any later stage.

3. Problem-solving policing and widening community safety options for partnerships

Actively involving local communities in all aspects of community safety partnerships can widen the options available to partnerships for tackling crime, and more importantly for addressing community problems which are often the source of much local fear of crime. Three major benefits can be seen. It opens up ways of intervening locally in the cycle between crime, fear of crime and response driven policing. It provides the means whereby a partnership can develop alternative, community delivered responses to local community safety problems. More importantly, it can buy community safety partnerships much needed space to facilitate the shift from responding to crime to preventing crime.

Recent work on problem-solving or intelligence-led policing highlights two recurring aspects of current policing. Firstly, police forces are driven in the main by responding to crime rather than crime prevention or reduction. Secondly, a significant proportion of police time is taken up with recurring community problems that rarely result in a crime being recorded. At the same time, police forces, while they are changing, find it fairly difficult to tackle repeat victimisation and there are shortcomings in identifying and then responding effectively to repeat incidents.

It is not an uncommon picture for local policing to be dominated by calls to repeated community problems. For example, young people hanging around local shops or causing noise nuisance, which rarely give rise to recorded offences and which are contained on each occasion rather than resolved. Many police forces have therefore approached community safety partnerships as a vehicle for reducing or managing local demand – a means whereby other agencies, particularly local authorities, can be brought to bear upon issues which are not essentially crime and might better be tackled by others. This has two outcomes. It broadens responsibility across more than one agency and it can reinforce a policing perspective that sees the primary policing function as being tackling crime not community problems.

In this process community consultation and involvement is secondary to partnership with other agencies who are seen to have the resources to intervene. Where consultation takes place it is likely to follow the pattern for much formal police community consultation where police seek to explain the limit to which they believe they can intervene when no criminal offence has been committed.

The preoccupation with responding to rather than solving crime, combined with the attractiveness of partnership with the local authority rather than local communities, is a contributory factor to local frustration with policing, particularly the policing of those quality of life issues which agencies find hardest to tackle. Communities rarely make these distinctions when confronted with community safety problems. Excluding local communities from equal partnership in community safety is self defeating. Not only does it limit what local communities can contribute themselves, it limits partnership potential and it may well help to reinforce the existing dominance of response driven policing.

From a policing perspective, integrating community consultation and involvement into all aspects of community safety partnership offers a valuable route away from response driven policing and an opportunity to redefine working relations with local communities. The outcome is a policing perspective which focuses upon preventing both crime and community problems and widens policing options beyond enforcement. The challenge is to marry this re-focusing of the police role with the demands of the local policing plan and the national key performance indicators, as well as with the cultural resistance to this sort of change within sections of the police.

From a local authority perspective, the same integration of community consultation and involvement into community safety partnerships meets the emerging requirements of Best Value and modernising government, as well as potentially reducing demands upon some services as local communities take responsibility themselves.

What needs to be done?

So, how do we move communities to centre stage in community safety? How do we integrate community consultation and involvement into partnerships, strategies and projects? There are few shortcuts and no single answer. There are, however, better ways of proceeding.

To be successful these issues need to be tackled in three ways:

- Building strategic involvement – which requires us to engage local communities as fully-fledged partners in community safety and, if necessary, to help everyone build the capacity to take part.

- Engaging in community consultation as an ongoing, high-quality dialogue between all partners – which requires us to plan partnership communications as an inclusive process and to prepare a package of continuous discussion, not just an occasional audit or survey of views).

- Building consultation and involvement into implementation – which requires us to establish consultation and involvement targets and outcome measures for all aspects of the community safety strategy.

1. Building strategic involvement – communities as fully-fledged partners

Working with local communities, particularly fragmented and diverse communities, is neither easy nor comfortable. The combined pressures of meeting the requirements of the Crime and Disorder Act 1998, the predisposition of agencies towards working with other agencies rather than local people, and the difficulty in identifying who to talk to within local communities might marginalise local people rather than involve them in partnerships. The main threat, as demonstrated by the Joseph Rowntree Foundation, is that communities are afforded a role only at the implementation stage of any partnership programme. By this time, local people have effectively been excluded from decisions on the overall direction for community safety in their area. This may be partially alleviated by limited consultation on community safety priorities and targets, but it does not build local ownership.

Local ownership, however hard to achieve, is fundamental to community safety. It underpins accountability and reflects a community's right to be involved in decisions affecting it. To build local ownership, community safety partnerships need to go beyond the consultation provisions of the Crime and Disorder Act 1998 and apply the principles of Best Value and the lessons of regeneration partnerships to community safety. Joining up a partnership's approach involves a number of actions:

- *Appointing local residents as community directors to the community safety partnership board.*

  Possibly the single, most effective way of ensuring local communities have the opportunity to become fully fledged partners in community safety alongside the main statutory agencies. It signals the importance the partnership attaches to local communities and it sets the tone for involving all sections of local people in the community safety process. It offers the possibility of an inside seat to counter the established power and influence of agencies which otherwise threaten to distort or filter decision making on community safety.

- *Setting up a consultative forum of local residents to act as a point of accountability for community directors and to contribute to the overall consultative, monitoring and evaluation process.*

  This is key to the practice of inclusive community consultation and for spreading involvement to all sections of a local community. It may well require financial and staff support from the partnership to enable it to get started. The aim is to generate a representative forum, which in due course can be self-sustaining, possibly even delivering community safety programmes directly. It enables local communities to enter into partnership as relative equals and to evolve their relationship and participation in the partnership. In the initial stages it demonstrates an understanding of, and commitment to, partnership which is missing in most community safety initiatives. Partnerships are not simply an extension of existing agencies. To be more successful they need to develop as separate entities with a clear local identification as vehicles in their own right.

  There are two broad routes that can be followed in setting up a community safety forum. Allow everyone within the partnership area to be eligible for membership of the forum, and conduct open elections for an executive body.

It may take time to make sure every section of the community is willing or able to take part but it has a general credibility arising from its transparency and accessibility. Its shortcoming is that it is not always the most practical approach if the partnership area is wide or heavily populated. In this instance, it may be better to establish the forum through inviting representation from the widest possible range of community organisations. Accountability and credibility arise from individuals being asked to represent their organisation. Again, it may take time and effort to ensure all sections of the community are involved.

One route is not advisable. Partner agencies should not select community representatives for the Board or community forum. This has little local credibility and portrays the partnership as an extension of the main agencies. Figure 9.1 sets out the potential functions and responsibilities which can be met through an independent community forum.

Figure 9.1: The functions and responsibilities of an independent community forum

An independent community forum can perform a range of functions and meet a number of partnership responsibilities, including:

- acting as an accountable vehicle for appointing community directors to the partnership board
- ensuring the widest possible representation of local views to the board
- building and delivering significant elements of a community capacity building programme (helping others to take part and to play their part)
- providing direct input to community safety priorities and programmes
- building regular consultation programmes across the community
- helping evaluate and monitor performance on community safety and on consultation and involvement in particular
- assisting in implementing community safety strategies and initiatives and, in some instances, having contractual responsibility for delivering programmes and projects

---

● *Adopting a transparent partnership commitment to consult and involve local communities as part of the contract between partners ·(this should include the steps the partnership is taking to consult and involve local communities).*

By adopting a simple public commitment to community consultation and involvement, a partnership can fulfil a number of obligations as well as laying out a platform upon which it can build. It can indicate openly to community and other partners that it places the role of the community at the heart of its community safety work. It can outline how it intends to consult and engage local communities. It can openly indicate its commitment to including all sections of diverse, local communities and it can start the process it needs to follow to ensure all partners have a shared, common perspective on community safety that involves local people. By signing up to this commitment, a community safety partnership sets out its stall and intimates to communities and staff alike how it intends to proceed. This may appear self-evident but it is frequently overlooked. Establishing the ground for long-term, sustained improvements in community safety takes time and common effort.

- *Preparing a community consultation and involvement programme as a primary partnership task.*

How this might be approached is dealt with in greater detail in a following section. The need for a planned, consistent approach to consultation is highlighted by the Audit Commission. It is an essential step, which needs to go beyond the minimal limits set out in the Crime and Disorder Act 1998.

- *Assigning resources, both staff and financial, to support and facilitate community consultation and involvement.*

The aim is to broaden the current axis on community safety beyond a narrow, agency-driven focus upon crime reduction, into a process which makes communities safer by engaging the energies of the community itself and where a primary responsibility of agency partners is to help create that resilient self-policing community. This takes resources, both financial and staffing. Community safety partnerships should consider how they can kick-start community consultation and involvement. Not only does it require a sea change in their own internal workings and capacities, it also requires an investment in local communities. Partnerships might consider seconding or recruiting development staff to work with local organisations in establishing the community forum and to help it fulfil its roles and responsibilities. Likewise, partnerships might consider providing project funding direct to community organisations to enable them to develop and deliver consultation and involvement.

- *Undertaking a programme of community capacity building as part of the community safety strategy.*

Not all sections of a community are either willing or able to take part in community safety. In this respect community safety is no different from regeneration or a range of other issues that would benefit from community participation, but where it is proving difficult to achieve. It may be, in poorer communities in particular, that the social exclusion of the entire community (or sections thereof) make it difficult for local people to take part and assert themselves on issues which affect their lives. An essential first stage is for partners to identify the barriers that are inhibiting participation and to enlist community organisations in overcoming them. Again, it is a process that takes time, but the potential benefits are significant.

Such developments are rare in community safety. Where they do exist they tend to be project-based, for example the Kingsmead Initiative in Hackney. They are, however, more widespread in urban regeneration. For example, the Community Empowerment Programme in the US has shown a number of promising developments in engaging excluded communities in local economic activity, setting up local enterprises and gaining access to the wider economy. A commitment to community consultation and involvement in making an area safer needs to be accompanied by a commitment to helping communities develop the willingness and ability to take part as equals.

- *Internally and externally auditing partnership arrangements and performance on consulting and involving local communities.*

  Just as saying that a partnership intends to reduce or prevent crime is no longer sufficient justification for releasing public funds, so a public commitment to community consultation and involvement in community safety should no longer be sufficient, in itself, to discharge this responsibility. Partnerships need to set standards and targets for consulting and involving local people at all stages of the partnership process. This is a more fundamental undertaking than that required by the Crime and Disorder Act 1998, but it serves to embed consultation and involvement into all community safety work. Figure 9.2 sets out a checklist of the steps which need to be taken and against which performance can be measured. It also sets out the questions that need to be addressed when partnerships are engaging local communities and moving through to implementing programmes and projects.

Thus, excluding local communities from strategic decision making on community safety is self-defeating. It might appear to be an easily avoided partnership task, since the legislation does not require it, but it is an omission which reduces the long-term effectiveness of the partnership and makes it more difficult to sustain crime reduction.

2. Consultation as ongoing, quality dialogue

In terms of the roles and responsibilities of different partners in community safety, that of the community has perhaps been least clearly defined or there has been least agreement in this area of partnership work. There is no single consultation technique that will meet the aim of quality dialogue with communities. Moreover, careful consultation will produce a complex picture of crime, risk and its effects.

Although most people tend to place burglary reduction at the top of their list of

Figure 9.2 Checklist – building community consultation and involvement into community safety

I. Building a strategic role for local communities

- appoint community directors to the partnership board
- establish local community consultative forum
- adopt consultation and involvement as partnership contract
- prepare a community consultation and involvement programme as a primary partnership task
- assign resources to support consultation and involvement
- undertake an ongoing community capacity building programme
- internally and externally audit partnership arrangements for consulting and involving local communities

II. Consultation as an ongoing, quality dialogue

The key is planned, regular consultation, agreed by all partners, which should include most of the following:

- establish a planned, continuous consultation programme with existing, formal groups and organisations (police community liaison groups, tenants and residents associations, churches and faiths, youth and elderly groups, ethnic minority organisations)
- set up a series of regular focus groups (including hard-to-reach groups)
- consider a wider standing consultation exercise across the district (possibly run by the consultative forum)
- maximise the consultation opportunities afforded by the planning cycles of complementary strategies and plans, particularly in relation to hard to reach groups
- hold regular feedback and informal discussion sessions with local groups and organisations
- consult on priorities, performance and participation at strategic and programme levels
- link with local media to promote participation in surveys and focused, local dialogue
- plan consistent community safety consultation as part of partners' regular communications with local people
- hold specific consultation exercises with hard-to-reach groups, particularly young people and ethnic minorities
- run participation and 'make yourself heard' programmes with schools, colleges, retail outlets and local businesses

III. Implementing community safety programmes, projects and initiatives

- ensure the partnership's commitment to community involvement is supported by a partner's own practices for user or client consultation and feedback
- require all programmes, projects and initiatives to have measurable community consultation and involvement components which show:
  1. how local people have already been consulted
  2. what steps have been taken to consult hard-to-reach groups
  3. how local communities can be engaged in delivering the programme (including whether it is appropriate to transfer delivery to loca people)
  4. what ongoing consultation is planned
  5. how consultation and involvement will be measured
  6. how local people will be involved in defining outcomes, undertaking evaluation and analysing and presenting evaluation findings
  7. how this will promote inclusive community safety
- share good practice across projects and strategies and abandon but learn from failures

crime priorities, opinion is likely to be divided about many other common crimes and incivilities. For example, people may well attach differing importance to dogs roaming around, litter, young people hanging around and racial victimisation. Many people may agree that all these elements are undesirable, but the priority attached to each may well differ according to a range of factors such as direct experience or age. Such differences are not irreconcilable. Nor do they indicate wildly differing visions of community safety. However, their identification reminds us of the need for caution when referring to a community's crime reduction priorities. Care must be taken to consult as widely as possible before deciding a list of priorities for action to be taken in the name of the community.

Similarly, people have different views about what would make their area safer, depending upon such factors as age, ethnicity, length of time lived in the area, personal experience of crime and beliefs about who is offending. No single crime reduction or community safety technique will work for everyone. Community safety strategies have a responsibility to recognise this diversity. Inclusive, ongoing consultation will go some way to ensuring that the needs of different groups in the community are taken into account in the initiatives developed from any action plan.

In the rest of this section, some of the consultation techniques that can enhance the quality of the dialogue are set out. This is followed by three case studies that show how some areas are moving towards more meaningful community consultation. These case studies demonstrate the benefits to be gained from repeat and varied consultation techniques, from consultation which reaches diverse groups in the community, and from a very localised consultation strategy which leads to partnerships with local police and other agencies.

Establishing an ongoing, quality dialogue involves a number of actions:

- *Establish a planned, continuous consultation programme with existing formal groups and organisations.*

  The way in which this is achieved will vary in different areas. Some neighbourhoods, for example, will have established local multi-agency community safety forums or committees (set up with funding from SRB, National Lotteries or other charitable funding) which provide a platform for consulting representatives on local priorities and concerns. In other areas a multi-agency forum may need to be brought together if the partnership is to be able to consult widely and regularly. This process should also incorporate feedback sessions and discussions with all local organisations that have contributed.

- *Set up a series of regular focus groups and other consultation exercises with residents, including young people and other hard-to-reach sections of the community.*

CASE STUDY 1: NORTH EAST LINCOLNSHIRE CRIME AND DISORDER AUDIT
(A repeat package)

The community safety partnership in North East Lincolnshire carried out 60 consultation events with local people to prepare the audit and balance the picture about crime revealed from the official statistics. The methods employed included:
- surveys
- focused discussion with existing groups
- police-community liaison committees
- special events such as 'planning for real'

The focus for all of these events was on what could be achieved by local effort. The emphasis was on realistic solutions rather than on unrealistic demands, such as vast increases in resources or changes to sentencing guidelines.

This set of exercises was not a one-off. The strategy continues to be informed and updated in the light of:
- an ongoing programme of two focused discussion groups per month
- public survey once a year
- youth forum or network twice a year
- North East Lincolnshire Safety Network days
- Partnership Group seminars four times a year
- Regular consultation with elected members

This ambitious programme plan has revealed the need for consultation around crime and disorder – particularly with hard-to-reach groups, to dovetail with planning and consultation cycles of other corporate initiatives to avoid duplication and consultation fatigue among some groups in the community.

CASE STUDY 2: BRADFORD
(Reaching diverse communities)

Bradford City Council has overcome some of the problems for consultation that are inherent in a lack of co-ordination between planning cycles. Bradford carried out a review of its consultation mechanisms in preparation for its community plan and its Best Value on community safety. This led to the establishment of the Area Panels Initiative and 77 neighbourhood forums across the authority. These have been used to provide feedback on community safety concerns. In addition, Bradford City Council has a 'speak out' panel of 2,500 demographically representative residents which regularly surveys on various hot topics including community safety. Outreach programmes were used to include young people and other hard-to-reach groups in consultation for the crime and disorder audit.

CASE STUDY 3: NORTH BENWELL ESTATE IN NEWCASTLE
(Connecting consultation with participation)

North Benwell Community Safety Strategy – 1996 /1998

1. A community safety networker was appointed. This person had been involved in community development work in the area – working with street committees – six months prior to taking on responsibility for community safety. There was already considerable trust extended to this person from many local people.

2. A series of personal and community effectiveness days were run, as part of the process of empowering local people to contribute to what happens in their area. Local people were invited to attend these training days by the Community Safety Networker. As well as inviting people who were already active in the community through the Street Committees, people were accessed through other neighbourhood routes. These included people who were clients of the WorkFinder Project for local unemployed people.

3. The community effectiveness day comprised people who had attended the smaller effectiveness training days. A good mix of ages and experiences was represented, with the common element that everyone in the room knew that they could implicitly trust each other and therefore could speak freely about their crime and community safety concerns.

4. Two community safety days were held. People who were invited were also asked to bring along one other person from the area that they could trust. At the first of these days key issues were identified and debated and representatives from police and other agencies gave talks and voiced support for the community action. People were also given an opportunity to get to know others in their street to form fledgling support networks – for example, for providing witness statements to police. At the second, action groups were formed around specific issues such as housing, environment and crime and policing. These subgroups now meet regularly with senior local representatives from the relevant agencies and preventive measures are being devised in partnership with local people. A total of 40 people from an area comprising approximately 2,500 became regularly involved through this process. A committee was formed and a constitution drawn up.

5. One significant outcome of the strategy was the establishments of a local CAPE (Community and Police Enforcement) initiative. This is a scheme unique to Newcastle's West End, and in the North Benwell neighbourhood is a partnership between the community safety group, the police and individual members of the community. The CAPE member undertakes to provide witness statements to the police and to give evidence in court if required. The community safety group provides immediate and ongoing support to the individual member; and the police will support the individual with personal alarms, direct link telephones and other equipment and personal protection if the case comes to court. Police will also liaise with the community safety group about crime in the area.

6. Another outcome was a joint community and environmental health department of the council initiative to tackle rubbish and litter in the area. There have also been considerable efforts through North Benwell Housing Organisation and the Landlords' Association to improve communication between different housing sectors and to attempt to reduce levels of anti-social behaviour committed by residents.

7. A community safety day was set up for the wider inner-West area of Newcastle. This event enabled members of the community safety group from North Benwell, members of South Benwell Community Association and representatives from other localities in the West End to move towards a combined strategy.

- *Consider a wider standing consultation exercise across the district.*

  Models for consideration are citizens' juries or 'speak out' panels. These juries or panels can be surveyed on a range of topics including crime and community safety.

- *Maximise the consultation opportunities afforded by the planning cycles of complementary strategies and partners' regular communications with the public.*

  This should include consideration of the planning cycles of local authority services – for example, around behaviour support plans, youth justice plans or policing plans. It should also include contributions from the local voluntary sector, perhaps via an umbrella voluntary sector body.

- *Link with local media to promote participation in surveys and focused local dialogue.*

- *Consult on priorities, performance and participation at strategic and performance levels.*

  Ongoing consultation exercises should be structured to gain communities' views on:

  1. how best to consult people in this area

  2. local priorities (being particularly attentive to shifts in priorities over time and why this is happening)

  3. partners' performance in meeting those priorities (and again what might be helping or hindering performance)

  On a wider level, partnerships should determine the extent of local participation in any measures to tackle crime and improve community safety and consult local people on how this might be improved.

3. Consultation and involvement as part of implementing community safety

Community consultation and involvement needs to be fully integrated into programmes, projects or initiatives developed or supported by the partnership. There are two main strands to these proposals:

- *Ensure the partnership's commitment to community involvement is supported by partner agencies' own practices on user and client consultation and feedback.*

  To underpin a partnership's commitment to community consultation, partner agencies should be encouraged to review their own arrangements for user consultation and feedback, ensuring they meet basic minimum standards and that outcomes are fed into any community safety strategy. Members of the partnership should be encouraged to undertake community involvement training alongside community representatives.

- *Require all programmes, projects and initiatives to have measurable community consultation and involvement components.*

All programmes, projects and initiatives need to demonstrate how they incorporate the views of local people at all stages from design to delivery. Particular attention needs to be paid to the steps which have been taken to consult hard-to-reach groups; what ongoing consultation is planned; how consultation has influenced the direction taken by the initiative; how local communities can be engaged in delivering the programme; how consultation and involvement are to be measured and how the social capital of the community will be strengthened through this initiative.

Moving forward

Crime prevention has long been the Cinderella service within police forces. At the same time, with a few exceptions, it has barely caused a ripple in the local authority pond. Few public agencies have spent energy or resources tackling crime, except where it has hurt them directly. Even then it has tended to be containment rather than curative action. Yet throughout the past two decades local communities have consistently placed safety, crime and the fear of crime at the top of their concerns.

A statutory framework for consulting local people on the policing of their area has existed since the mid-1980s in the provisions of the Police and Criminal Evidence Act 1984. However, this has fallen seriously short of expectations. The Crime and Disorder Act 1998 seeks to remedy this by requiring local authorities, in partnership with police forces, to consult local communities on community safety priorities and targets, as part of setting local community safety partnership strategies. It is a framework with potential.

Yet, it would be ironic if the one set of people who have consistently raised the importance of making communities safer – communities themselves – are excluded from, or are afforded a minimal, passive role in, the emerging framework.

That is not to deny that progress has been made nor to argue that recent developments are not improving the way partnerships promote community safety. The next period may well demonstrate the benefits which can accrue from better co-ordination within and between agencies. Similarly, many communities might be expected to become safer places, particularly where resources are applied to environmental improvements in a more consistent fashion. Increasing involvement might also be expected from local authorities, police forces and other partners driven forward by a combination of some visible success, audit requirements, the growth of Best Value regimes and the increasing attachment of regeneration and other public funds to making communities safer.

What is contended, is that improvements in community safety will hit a self-imposed ceiling if partnerships do not go beyond the minimal requirements for community consultation in the Crime and Disorder Act 1998, and afford local communities an active role as equal partners in community safety. Partnerships need to embrace the spirit of Best Value, seeing communities as potential partners in service delivery, and learn the lessons of community involvement from the field of regeneration.

This means seeing local communities, in their diversity, as equal, strategic partners in community safety. It means helping communities build their own capacity to take part in and take responsibility for managing and delivering community safety programmes. It means setting up an ongoing, high quality dialogue with local people, and it means ensuring that all decisions, programmes and projects are subjected to community consultation and involvement at all stages.

It is a large and demanding agenda for partnerships but it is achievable. It might require a culture shift in the way public agencies see local communities and it goes beyond what currently passes for community consultation. It is, however, a legitimate aspiration and it may just hold the key to disconnecting exclusion, crime and fear of crime within communities.

Selected references

Audit Commission (1999) *Safety in Numbers: Promoting Community Safety* London: Audit Commission

Morgan Report (1991) *Safer Communities: The Local Delivery of Crime Prevention through the Partnership Approach* London: Home Office

Robinson D, Dunn K and Ballintyne S (1998) *Social Enterprise Zones – Building Innovation into Regeneration* York: Joseph Rowntree Foundation

Rowntree Foundation (1996) *Community Involvement in Estate Regeneration Partnerships* York: Joseph Rowntree Foundation

Social Exclusion Unit (1998) *Bringing Britain Together: a National Strategy for Neighbourhood Renewal* London: The Stationery Office

10. From audit to strategy: a practice view
Andy Mills and Sarah Pearson

This chapter examines how to produce a community safety strategy. It starts by examining what such a strategy actually is, then looks at the issues involved in creating one: conducting a crime audit, using the information from the audit to write the strategy, and then ensuring that the latter remains a living document.

Written for community safety officers, the approach is from the point of view of practitioners, who have to do most, if not all, of this themselves and who have ultimately to live with the consequences. Therefore, the problems that may well be encountered are highlighted throughout.

What is a community safety strategy?

It is important to be clear about the meaning and purpose of a community safety strategy before embarking upon developing one. Strategy can be defined at very different levels. Is a community safety strategy concerned with the practical measures or means by which crime, disorder and the fear of crime and victimisation is tackled (an emphasis on the actions which will take place)? Or is it just concerned with desired outcomes of the aims and objectives set (an emphasis on the results anticipated by the strategy) – for instance, a reduction in crime across the district? Is it, perhaps, concerned with both?

To define community safety, the Local Government Association definition is a useful starting point (with the caveat that not all community safety measures have to be community-based). It states that community safety is: .

> [the] concept of community-based action to inhibit and remedy the causes and consequences of criminal, intimidatory and other related anti-social behaviour. Its purpose is to secure sustainable reductions in crime and the fear of crime in local communities. Its approach is based on the formation of multi-agency partnerships between the public, private and voluntary sectors to formulate and introduce community-based measures against crime.

The crucial difference between community safety and crime prevention is that the former is broader. It is concerned with improving people's quality of life and thus encompasses measures not specifically aimed at reducing crime – for instance, improving the aesthetics of the physical environment and tackling youth unemployment. Mostly the difference in the definitions is moot, but on occasion there will be conflict. An example is the introduction of intrusive situational measures – high galvanised steel fences and CCTV installation. These may cut crime but other options may achieve the same results in the long term, but without the people-unfriendly impact.

Nevertheless, a community safety strategy should maintain a focus on crime, disorder and fear of crime, in order that it does not become too diffuse. (Everything is mutable, however. Perhaps in the future community safety will metamorphose to include/be included in wider safety/security considerations, incorporating home, fire and public safety.)

A community safety strategy must manage community safety and crime prevention/reduction activity and all the impacts that may develop in the short, medium and long term. To encompass this, and to adequately measure the effects of short- and medium-term interventions, a community safety strategy should therefore be a long-term systematic approach to address all elements of community safety which affect a given geographic area. It should also be concerned with: the desired outcomes, by setting aims and objectives to be achieved; the practical ways and means the outcomes can be achieved and monitored, by demonstrating how the aims and objectives are to be monitored, implemented, managed and evaluated. This should be done by:

- addressing single community safety issues such as reducing car crime, harassment or nuisance

- linking issues together and ensuring no internal policy contradictions take place

- demonstrating the links with wider regeneration and policy issues

- ensuring single- and multi-agency action.

A community safety strategy should, therefore, inform, regulate, manage and evaluate community safety activity and be a living document subject to change. It should also be set within the area's broader economic and social context, linking with other strategies which contribute towards improving the quality of life for people in the area.

Who is the strategy for?

At the outset of developing a strategy it must be clear that there are advantages and benefits in having a strategy. Who will benefit from a community safety strategy? In the long term, all parties – the victim, the offender, the Government, the general public and the private and public sectors – should benefit because it should improve quality of life, by: reducing victimisation and offending (and hence improve the life-chances of people at risk of becoming involved in crime); helping economic activity, and reducing costs to individuals and agencies.

Strategy development

A number of steps need to be carried out before a community safety strategy is created. In essence these steps are to:

- establish a community safety partnership

- conduct a crime audit

- consult with the public.

A partnership body

A multi-agency partnership will need to be created. At a district level the Government has enumerated the bodies which should be involved or invited. It is however inevitable that different implementation structures and frameworks will be established to reflect local dynamics. On one level there will always need to be an umbrella strategic body, but it is likely that the work of the partnership will be broken down into other groups – for example, working parties, task groups and public consultation groups. In this way the largest number of agencies and organisations will be involved in the partnership's work, thus making it an inclusive process, whilst ensuring that the umbrella group does not become too large and cumbersome.

As all places are different, so each locality will have slightly different partnerships in place: what is felt to be appropriate in one area may not be suitable for somewhere else. For instance, the leading players in one area may wish to ensure all voluntary groups are represented within the partnership. In another area this may be felt to be impracticable and some form of representation for the voluntary sector might be sought instead: local dynamics will prevail. In one area there may be an existing partnership which fits the bill (or indeed, the Act!) and which works perfectly well; in another an entirely fresh start will be more appropriate.

There is no blueprint for a marvellous community safety partnership – not yet, anyway! – so the aim should be towards what suits a particular area. In reality, of course, the community safety officer will have little control. One of the wondrous elements of working in partnership is that not everybody shares the community safety officer's (expert and correct) views, and will insist on their own flawed visions being followed instead. Senior officials in all organisations will, or will not, participate to different degrees, and whilst participating will contribute (or not) in ways over which the community safety practitioner has no control. Partnerships are constantly in states of compromise and engaged in conflict and resolution.

The crime audit

When embarking on a crime audit, the first question to ask is 'why is this being done?' (if not asked now, it will almost certainly be asked during the process – many times). The answer, of course, is that the audit is a means to end, an assessment of the prevailing situation to facilitate effective forward movement. Therefore, what the audit looks at will depend on what it is to inform. Is it the district strategy, one which has far-reaching and long-term implications? Is it for a funding bid? Or is it to address a very localised crime problem? It's horses for courses, but, for the purposes of this chapter, it is assumed that the full monty is required.

Auditing can be broken down into four aspects: data collection, consultation, policy review and expert input. There is an especial danger of getting hung up over the first two of these, and paying insufficient attention to the latter two.

Data collection is, it has to be said, becoming easier, in that the tools for data collection and analysis are becoming increasingly sophisticated. Those people with access to a geographical information system (GIS) will know that its use eliminates the problem of pulling information from different agencies with different boundaries (providing of course, that the base information can be transferred or loaded into the system). Once the information is in such a system it can be manipulated to order, and can produce information in a clear and accessible visual form.

Having a GIS does not solve all the problems, though. First, the source agency has to provide the data in the right format, covering the appropriate time period, information and geographical area. It is at this stage that the first obstacles are encountered. Strange as it may seem, provision if such data does not appear to be the life's ambition of many people, indeed, the opposite applies. In the quest for data, numerous blocks will be encountered. Apathy, bloody-mindedness, incompetence, defensiveness and inability to meet deadlines are all there. To be fair, much of this is due to people being irritated by the huge amounts of information demanded by different people for a myriad of obscure purposes, or because they are suffering from initiative overload. So what can be done about it?

Here are one or two practical suggestions. As with the consultation process, all parties must recognise that time is limited – community safety officers have a wide range of duties and few have the luxury of time dedicated to audit and strategy development and nothing else. If possible, arrange through senior channels that each significant agency dealt with appoints a liaison officer who can chase around their own organisation. It must be accepted from the beginning that getting what you want on time (if at all) is unlikely, so deadlines which allow scope for latecomers and follow-up should be set.

As in other areas of community safety, easy wins should be aimed for initially. Those agencies which can be worked with and who can deliver the goods should be used as examples for those who are not pulling their weight. (At district level, the auditing of community safety activity will help, as agencies will be scrutinised for their contributions to community safety.) Mutual benefits should be demonstrated – so, if in possession of a GIS, show how data can be combined with that from other agencies and mapped to inform individual priorities. Offer this facility to them.

Most importantly, negatives should be turned into positives. Obtaining information on a regular basis in an acceptable form from a reluctant agency can become an action point in the strategy. Remember that the audit process should not be a one-off event, but rather the first stage in an on-going development. Thus information exchange and communication structures need to be an essential part of any strategy.

As to what information to request, probably the best rule of thumb is to ask for it, take it if it's offered and don't be alarmed if you can't get it. Initially, exploratory meetings with organisations to explain what is being done and to engage the agency in the process should help to focus the minds of all parties on what is needed. A practitioner should take especial care in ensuring that they do not have to go round personally extracting source data. If they find themselves checking the contents and location of rubbish bins for discarded bottles, in order to determine the nature of the alcohol problem in an area, they should stop. Therein lies madness!

The amount of consultation that can profitably be engaged in is directly linked to time and resources, so the first rule is to be selective. If embarking on a fresh crime audit, then an equally fresh, area-wide public survey is desirable – it certainly gives credibility to audit analysis if people's recent and relevant experiences and concerns can be pointed to. It may be that such a survey cannot be had. In this case, pieces should be taken from wherever possible – other surveys or consultations held which impinge on the same focus, feedback from groups (such as tenant associations) or elected members' surgeries or records of written complaints to agencies. Again, where possible the pertinent agencies should trawl through the detail and provide a summary. Thinking long term, recommending a programme of area-based consultation (perhaps covering a range of service areas), or asking local agencies to add questions to their existing customer care surveys may be helpful. It should be borne in mind that public surveys never paint a full picture of crime and disorder concerns. Domestic violence, or intimidation, to give two examples, are rarely raised as specific issues.

In terms of input from or focus groups or individual members of the public, why not put a request for information or draft strategy into local libraries or, if facilities are available, on to the authority's or partnership's web-site? The feedback may be illuminating and will certainly provide good quotes to bring the dry text of a strategy document alive. It is very difficult to weigh such opinion against that of organised groups or agencies, so be wary. Any questions asked should be specific – three to four is better than fifteen to twenty. Moreover, questions asked of the public need to be carefully framed in order to get a meaningful response. Bear in mind Nick Tilley's caveat, that people are utopian, believing that there should be both improved public services and less taxation simultaneously.

The same applies to consultation with organisations. With the key agencies and individuals it is of course important to make face-to-face contact in order to maintain or progress a productive relationship. For others, seek out ways in which a number of organisations can be accessed at once – such as voluntary sector meetings. Attempt, where possible, to have that group feed back on the issues affecting their sector, instead of trying to contact a myriad number of individual agencies. Hard-to-reach groups are best accessed through utilising the services of agencies which have direct contact with them. Their staff are more skilled in communicating appropriately and will therefore provide better quality feedback.

The problem with consultation is that it operates in a similar fashion to a chain-letter. Talk to one person and they will cheerily suggest another two or three people or groups you simply must speak to. They may well be right, and such contacts are vital. Equally, tail chasing can result, the worst situation being repeated referral to someone else in the agency. Periodically, the practitioner should sit down, look at who they have consulted and ask where further investment can profitably be made. They should avoid spending a lot of time and energy with people who may be able to contribute very little to the accumulated store of wisdom within the timescale of the audit. It might, however, be worth considering whether or not these potential contacts could be sought out at a later stage.

In terms of policy review, if a district strategy, as opposed to a small local audit, is being developed, the whole range of policies, strategies, action plans, performance indicators, service boundaries and organisational structures that impinge on community safety must be considered.

Look at what could be classed as community safety, or that which has an actual or potential impact. This might involve enormous activity, ranging from that which specifically addresses an immediate crime or disorder problem (such as anti-social behaviour action) to that which may have a long-term affect (such as child care provision). Somehow the auditor has to embrace all of this – not just one aspect. And whilst community safety practitioners come from a wide range of backgrounds, not one of us has the range of experience necessary to feel comfortable with it all.

If an authority is large enough, it has a team of policy specialists who need to become involved. In smaller areas, expertise will have to be brought in to help interpret the inter-connections of strategy and structure. This is important. The whole reason behind the audit is, in the end, to effect change. Things need changing because, currently, they are not impacting effectively on crime and disorder: if they were, there would be no need for the audit or a new strategy. It's not just a case of people doing more, it's a case of them doing it better. To do that, the service delivery and focus of a wide range of organisations needs to be understood and then, if necessary, changed, involving communities in different ways. To grasp this, the context and priorities of those organisations must also be understood.

It is also fair to say that practitioners must never get trapped in thinking community safety is the be all and end all. It isn't. It is merely one element, which can affect people's lives. In terms of service delivery, it can contribute to improving people's quality of life – but only if it's part of a package, if it fits in with other strategies that impact on people (there's more on this a little later). As far as the delivery of services to communities is concerned, a new ball game is about to be entered and nothing will be more affected by this than community safety.

Linked to the preceding element of an audit is the need for expert input. If the audit is large enough to justify it, or funds are available, bringing in external consultants is recommended, to help guide the process, providing they are good of course. (One of the offshoots of the Crime and Disorder Act has been to kick-start a huge number of consultants into offering their services. Doubtless these are of variable quality.) Part of the benefit of external consultants, is that they should bring with them a strong knowledge of how other areas approach similar problems. That knowledge will include awareness of structures, policies and initiatives other than community safety, of which the average practitioners, locked as they are in their own cupboard, may be unaware (even if fully up-to-date on their own subject area).

Having said that, it's important to state here and now that the person with the most expertise in community safety in an area is probably the community safety practitioner. Community safety personnel may be drawn from different disciplines and only have a general understanding of a lot of subjects, but that's a wider perspective and a deeper knowledge than virtually anybody else. Bear in mind, there is absolutely no need to reinvent the wheel. There's a great deal of literature out there, and plenty of examples of good, or at least promising, practice on which to draw. Don't be afraid to introduce some of these into the audit pot; indeed, it would be strange not to. (To reiterate: what's gone before obviously hasn't worked as well as it could, therefore something new is needed).

It should be borne in mind that there is a duty to ensure that partnerships incorporate a long-term preventive approach in their strategy. It is too easy to be lulled into a position which takes current crime data as its starting point and seeks to address only those crimes being committed now. Community safety practitioners understand that their discipline involves addressing causes as well as symptoms and that there thus has to be an emphasis on social crime prevention and criminality reduction within the strategy. Focusing only on obvious crimes may lead to an undue stress on situational crime prevention: 'how can we stop this from happening here and now?' as opposed to preventing offending behaviour.

The bonus for the broad-brush approach is that it draws in, and gives importance to, the work of many partners, which may otherwise be overlooked or devalued, by understanding and acknowledging the impact of services/strategies on community safety. The policy analysis that flows from an audit should make the connections between preventive approaches and long-term reductions in crime and criminality clear. Part of the expert input is an educative one, focusing minds on what works rather than what is popular. There is no worse field than that of community safety for the amount of rubbish carried out in its name, doubtless due in large part to so much of this work being funded through short-term programmes, with little quality evaluation taking place.

The community safety strategy's relationship to other strategic processes

This is concerned with identity and ownership. Given the varied causes of crime and criminality, community safety should be seen as inclusive, but it should also be seen as existing within the wider context of social and economic regeneration. A community safety strategy can lead to improvements in health, education, economic development, the labour market, the local economy, social inclusion and community participation. A thorough community safety strategy should be able to stipulate how it can have an impact in these areas. This does not mean that all community safety is a regeneration issue, only that, if it is to be effective, a strategy must recognise the links with other similar community- and area-based and regeneration strategies in existence. For example, those concerned with anti-poverty, economic regeneration, Local Agenda 21, Best Value and the drug action and youth justice plans.

If a community safety strategy is exclusive, the linkage within the wider field of social policy will not be made and this could lead to regeneration disintegrating in local areas. Figure 10.1 indicates how the strategic structure might look. Any number of complementary strategies can be added, and it applies whichever of these strategies is located at the centre of the structure. The circles are shown here as separate – in reality they may overlap and in the ideal world they would never clash!

Strategies need to demonstrate partnership working, linking the practice and policy of different organisations. The importance of working in partnership is illustrated by a process of collaboration. To create a partnership strategy, it must be recognised that different agencies have different objectives and are able or are willing to undertake certain actions only. To be successful, a strategy must manage the diverse agendas brought to the table by partnership members in such a way that the pre-defined aims of the partnership can be fulfilled. This involves initial acknowledgement from all parties that each has their own implicit and explicit aims as to what they hope to achieve from the strategy. Without this acknowledgement strategies become utopian and ineffective.

The community safety strategy will have clear aims for all to buy into. Focusing on these common aims and inviting the active contribution of all partners, especially within multi-agency initiatives, will (hopefully!) contribute to the breaking down of any cultural barriers that may exist within the partnership.

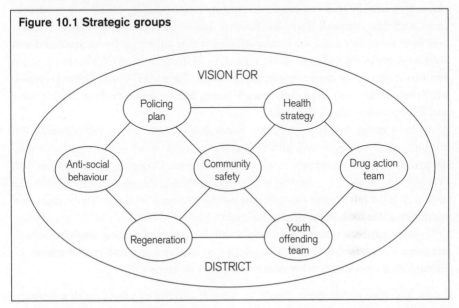

Figure 10.1 Strategic groups

The format of the strategy

The strategy document produced should be aimed at a variety of audiences – fellow public service officers, local organisations, senior staff, the general public, the funding regimes and the Government. Whoever these are, the document is likely to have more than a single sector audience, so a crucial point is: make it clear. As far as possible, it should be a comprehensible read, lucid and jargon free. Some aspects of community safety work – the criminal justice element, for example – seem to be more prone to jargon than others. As a rule, try to take jargon out of your strategy, or else explain terms when they must be included.

The strategy should be broken down into clearly stated aims (the overall intent of that particular portion of the strategy) and hence into objectives, which should be measurable. In order to translate the objectives into something manageable, they then need to be split down into action plans. Attached to every action will be specified agencies or officers, which have responsibility for delivery, targets (in terms of outputs and outcomes), the time-scale for action to be started and completed and the dates for monitoring and evaluation. All of this is vital to establish accountability.

The strategy should obviously be created largely on the basis of the audit findings, though not necessarily. Funding regimes such as the Home Office Crime Reduction Programme will skew your strategy, should you be successful in bidding for funds (and it is likely to be politically unacceptable locally not to apply to such regimes). For example, it may be that you have concerns about introducing CCTV into residential areas, and this approach does not therefore appear in your strategy. However, you may have to submit a bid for such a scheme, which must then be incorporated into your strategy. In the example given, regardless of the success of CCTV, by its nature you can expect to be stuck with it, and its costs, for several years. Other priorities, which may be determined not by the audit but by factors, such as ministerial initiatives and force policing plans, may exist.

In most cases, however, the main issues and content will be self-selecting. For instance, most strategies will address burglary, youth crime and the fear of crime, because these concerns appear to be almost universal. However, some elements will be specific to localities (smuggling in a port, trespass and damage on railway lines, for instance). If for any reason an audit was not comprehensive, there may be gaps, and subjective judgements may have to be made.

Enough has been written elsewhere about this aspect of strategy implementation, but there are two points to be made, which may appear to contradict advice from the Home Office (and which other practitioners may disagree with).

1.   The notion that there should be a small number of objectives in a strategy. Whilst this may be necessary if the whole process of strategy development is rushed, it is likely that an area (even if it is a small, low crime area) will have a large number of community safety problems. The wider the definition of community safety, or indeed the greater the lack of definition, the more problems could be classed as such. These cannot be addressed by a limited number of objectives. Furthermore, limiting the objectives also limits the number of partners who could profitably be included in meeting strategic aims. There is little point in having a broad consultation process, for instance, if potential contributions are then ignored. This is not to say that a certain small number of objectives should not be prioritised – those which have the greatest potential to address the crime problem, or meet the chief concerns, and hence justify resource allocation.

2.   Whilst there is a need for targets, it is important not to get too hung up on them. The body of community safety knowledge is too imprecise as to state which level of intervention will lead to which level of outcome (partially this has been because evaluation has been so weak – more about this later). Crime is a complex issue and, as is well known, often demands, sophisticated solutions. This sophistication means that the precise contribution of any

particular element is usually uncertain. For example, one cannot state with conviction that improving security in 80 per cent of targeted properties will result in a 50 per cent reduction in repeat burglaries: there are too may factors involved. It is, of course, possible to achieve targets of any type if resources are flexible enough to increase input into the objectives, but for most areas this is not feasible. The advice is, 'suck it and see'. Set targets, by all means, make sure everyone delivers as they ought – and then adjust them in the light of reality.

A word of warning: don't be driven by outputs. They may be easy to measure but they will not necessarily either reflect quality of input or lead to a desired outcome. To take our last example: what does improving security mean? A door-chain fitted to a house, or new doors and windows with alarm systems and security lighting? If you want to look at an output-driven bureaucratic process of measuring success or failure, look no further than that developed for the Single Regeneration Budget. Do not let your strategy fall into such a trap.

Finally, it should be stated that the quality of a partnership will be tested throughout on this issue. It will be tested by what is accepted as being a reasonable contribution in the first case, and it will be tested when (inevitably) agencies fail to deliver. Too much shouldn't be expected, perhaps, in the initial year of any partnership. The longer time goes on, however, the more one should expect the partnership to be strong enough to insist that its owners deliver what they say they will, and that it pushes for the changes in both culture and service delivery necessary for the strategy's aims to be met.

Servicing the strategy

Thus, a multi-agency partnership, to own and oversee the strategy development process and to ensure that targets are met, has been established. It is important that responsibility for servicing a strategy does not fall solely on one individual, nor should the partnership body merely engage in a rubber-stamping exercise, endorsing the proposals of whosoever is servicing it. Partnerships must be actively involved in the delivery, monitoring and evaluation of the strategy. Establishing task groups is one way of actively engaging a wide number of partners in the strategy. These will be determined by the outcome of the audit, the priorities identified by the partnership, or by the demands of the process. So, for example, you might decide to have an on-going crime audit task group or a monitoring and evaluation group. These task groups, and their members, will take responsibility for resourcing, target-setting, monitoring and evaluation.

In a multi-agency strategy, it is important that agencies report on their contributions and performance. A systematic approach is required and a standard reporting format for all agencies needs to be established. In trying to determine what works for a particular district, it is essential that a culture of honesty in reporting back is instituted and that partners become comfortable with the principle of accountability. Not everything tried will work, and sometimes different, unintended outcomes will result from actions taken. It is important that these are recorded.

Monitoring and evaluation

Monitoring is relatively straightforward (it just needs commitment) and this process should be made so by the way in which targets are written. Evaluation is a different kettle of fish and is both far more sophisticated and costly. Not every action within the strategy can be evaluated, nor the strategy as a whole. So what can be done?

Time should not be spent evaluating actions that are either likely to work because they are already proven successful measures (unless the monitoring process indicates problems), or are minor and low-cost. Instead, only those measures, which are felt to be crucial to the strategy, resource-intensive and innovative (for a particular area), should be evaluated. If possible, *bona fide* external evaluators should be used to give credibility and an impartial assessment. Again, an honest report on the value of the measures you are undertaking is desirable.

It does need emphasising that the success imperative referred to by Nick Tilley, in Chapter 6, is prevalent. At present there is too much vested interest in securing good news stories. To be sure, no one wants bad practice continued, but no one is keen to stand up and admit that money (usually public) has not been spent entirely wisely – principally because to do so would lead to both political and public criticism locally. There is no reason to believe that this state of affairs will improve, though the involvement of independent auditors in accessing partnership work does give cause for some cautious optimism.

If evaluating single measures is difficult, trying to evaluate the strategy as a whole is more problematic. First, crime and community safety interlink with so many other social processes. Second, the strategy was developed in relation to these processes, often incorporating and interacting with other strategies. The result, in theory, is that if the success of the community safety strategy were measured, the success of all the other related strategies and actions which are interconnect with community safety would also have to be measured. This is plainly an impossible task using community safety perspective and resources alone.

For meaningful evaluation to take place, then, the strategy as a whole should be monitored and certain parts of it evaluated. If the success of the whole strategy is to be judged, one measure would be a quality of life survey on the people living in the area. The results should be treated with caution: a range of factors may influence them, including some which are extraneous to the strategy and the particular area. For instance, fear of crime may be exacerbated by a high-profile crime reported recently in the national press.

To enhance the servicing of the strategy, it is important that all members of the partnership, and all staff involved in cross-agency policy work, have a common, broad level of understanding of community safety. This indicates the need for generic, multi-agency training. Such training will not only serve as a means of developing expertise and knowledge, it will also help to break down barriers between professionals. Although, in the first instance, it may be useful to bring in external trainers to establish the programmes, they should ideally be delivered by staff from the local partnership agencies working together.

A living document

If all the above takes place, the strategy will have an in-built mechanism for accommodating change. The partnership must acknowledge the results of monitoring and evaluation and be prepared to alter its strategy accordingly. For example, if a detached youth work programme on housing estates, due to run for two years, is shown after the first year to be failing or merely to have been an inappropriate response, immediate action should be taken. The programme should be altered and that aspect of the strategy reconfigured. Another example is the flow of information, which will have been established following the audit process. This will especially help accommodate the impact of other strategies and inform necessary alterations.

The strategy becomes a living document when it takes account of:

● the successes and failures of its component parts

● the development of partnership working

● the impact of other strategic processes.

By ensuring the strategy is subject to change, it will remain meaningful throughout its life and not be consigned to the back of a dusty office shelf.

Conclusion

A few simple points to finish with:

1. The audit and strategy are each merely a means to an end, which is the creation of safer communities.

2. The strategy needs to be delivered, and accountability for this needs to be built in.

3. Community safety does not exist in isolation from other policy areas, and the audit and strategy need to acknowledge and reflect this.

4. A strategy is a living document that should change over time.

Selected references

Audit Commission (1999) *Safety in Numbers: Promoting Community Safety* London: Audit Commission

Home Office (1991) *Safer Communities: The Local Delivery of Crime Prevention through the Partnership Approach* London: Home Office

Hough M and Tilley N (1998) *Auditing Crime and Disorder: guidance for local partnerships* Crime detection and Prevention Series Paper 91, London: Home Office

Liddle M and Gelsthorpe L (1994a) *Inter-Agency Crime Prevention: Organising Local Delivery* Crime Prevention Unit Paper 52, London: Home Office

Liddle M and Gelsthorpe L (1994b) *Crime Prevention and Inter-Agency Co-operation* Crime Prevention Unit Paper 53, London: Home Office

Liddle M and Gelsthorpe L (1994c) *Inter-Agency Crime Prevention; Further Issues* (Supplementary paper to Crime Prevention Unit Papers 52 and 53 above)

Social Exclusion Unit (1998) *Bringing Britain Together: a National Strategy for Neighbourhood Renewal* London: The Stationery Office

11. Targeting resources for crime prevention
Alex Hirschfield and Kate Bowers

One of the crucial issues in crime prevention is the prioritisation of different areas, individuals and properties. Given inevitable resource constraints, it is unrealistic to assume that it will ever be possible to assist everyone who might benefit from crime prevention measures. This raises the question of how best to target crime prevention initiatives in order to maximise their effectiveness and impact, given the limited resources available. On closer examination, targeting is rather a complex term. What is understood by targeting will vary according to the objectives of a particular policy or initiative, the activities or strategies which are being adopted to meet those objectives and the recipients or potential beneficiaries of the measures which are being taken.

The intended outcomes of a targeting exercise will, in turn, be heavily influenced by the philosophical and political stance that underpins the policy. This stance might include:

- a desire to reduce crimes experienced by particular vulnerable groups within the community (elderly people, single parents, ethnic groups and so on);

- to give extra resources to deprived areas;

- to concentrate on reducing levels of victimisation affecting particular types of property (small businesses and vulnerable public buildings such as schools);

- to focus on apprehending and detaining offenders or to change attitudes and divert those at risk from anti-social and criminal behaviour.

A crime prevention programme may be driven by any one, or a combination of, these priorities. In short, there are a number of variables that need to be considered to uncover the meaning of targeting and to understand its role.

Information on the geographical location of neighbourhoods, properties and individuals that suffer from excessive levels of crime, is a good starting point for identifying where efforts might be concentrated. In order to do this effectively, appropriate information needs to be available, as do the knowledge, skills and tools for processing that information to generate the right type of intelligence for resource allocation.

What, on the surface, might appear to be perfectly straightforward tasks are, on closer examination, far from straightforward. For example, the criteria used to define high-crime areas are by no means clear and reliable methods for identifying repeat crimes affecting individuals and different types of property (small businesses and vulnerable public buildings, for example). Even when such analyses are possible and baselines can be established, without the necessary procedures for tracking how the beneficiaries of crime prevention measures fare over time there will be little prospect of being able to assess their effectiveness.

The powerful combination of geographical information systems (GIS), geographically-coded property, and crime data and address matching software, can go some way towards resolving some of these difficulties. However, much remains to be done on assembling data on vulnerable individuals, households and properties. Yet information about these issues is increasingly going to be needed in England and Wales as the crime and disorder auditing process gets under way, crime and disorder strategies are formulated and their impact evaluated.

This chapter begins by exploring the philosophy and concept of targeting and moves on to discuss the methods by which information from the police and other sources can be brought together to help target resources for crime prevention and to evaluate the impact of crime prevention initiatives. Particular attention is paid to experiences on Merseyside. For several years, the University of Liverpool, in collaboration with the Safer Merseyside Partnership and the Merseyside Information Service, has been developing information systems to inform the targeting of initiatives to reduce repeat domestic burglary, business crime, arsons and hoax calls to the fire brigade, assaults and criminal damage on public transport, and juvenile disturbances.

The concept and meaning of targeting

Targeting has been a central feature in a number of policy regimes. Most often the practice has been driven by the desire to ensure that scarce resources reach those in greatest need. Perhaps the best examples of this approach are policies and programmes aimed at reducing poverty and deprivation. Two main thrusts of policy have been used to achieve this; social policies aimed at individuals, families, social and client groups (such as pensioners, elderly people and disabled people) and urban regeneration programmes aimed at turning round the fortunes of deprived areas.

In the UK, the former comprise, mainly, welfare benefits and income maintenance programmes such as Income Support, Family Credit and Housing Benefit. These are means-tested benefits targeted at individuals and families whose incomes fall below a defined threshold. Other programmes use income levels in conjunction with data on the health and social circumstances of individuals to target resources. Examples of these policies include benefits for single parents, extra payments to those suffering sickness and ill health and benefits for disabled people. The resources released through each of these programmes go directly to individuals wherever they may live.

Regeneration programmes, which are also driven by the need to ameliorate or even to reverse poverty and deprivation, operate in a very different way. In the UK, examples of such programmes include economic regeneration initiatives such as the

Urban Development Corporations and Enterprise Zones, housing programmes such as Housing Action Areas and General Improvement Areas, and schemes with a social emphasis such as City Challenge and, more recently, the Single Regeneration Budget (SRB) Challenge Fund. Resources provided through these initiatives tend to be targeted at discrete areas or neighbourhoods identified as having high levels of deprivation.

Unlike social welfare policies, the actual recipients or beneficiaries of geographically-targeted regeneration programmes are often difficult to identify. Part of the problem lies in ensuring that benefits go to appropriate individuals within the target areas. This is somewhat less of a problem with means-tested social benefits, but even here there are substantial difficulties with under-claiming by those entitled to do so and with benefit fraud.

Programmes seemingly aimed at regenerating deprived areas, have often benefited, not those in greatest need, but rather relatively highly-skilled and previously-employed workers often living outside of the designated areas, who commute in to take up new employment opportunities on offer. Evaluations of employment generated through a range on inner-city initiatives found that, on average, only 17 per cent of jobs went to previously unemployed inner-city residents (Haughton, 1990)

Another fundamental problem with spatial targeting is that small areas, however they are delineated, are only ever likely to contain a minority of deprived people. Even in an age which has seen a widening gap between the richest and poorest groups in society, increasing social polarisation and the marginalisation of municipal housing estates, the spatial concentration of individual aspects of deprivation (unemployment, overcrowding, absence of housing amenities) is still relatively low. Unless priority areas are large enough to contain a sizeable proportion of the population (that is, covering one third or more of all residents) more deprived people are going to live outside them than are contained within them (Deakin and Edwards, 1993).

A further criticism is that some of the areas being targeted for regeneration initiatives have been areas of opportunity rather than the areas of need. The argument here is that the driving force underpinning the choice of targets has been to pick areas that will flourish and do well rather than to focus attention on communities which face more difficult and intractable problems.

A third strand of targeting is the provision of resources directly to organisations set up to provide services – for example, targeting schools without adequate equipment or books and with large class sizes and hospitals without proper facilities. The beneficiaries in these cases are the under-resourced institutions and service outlets.

Finally, a fourth type of targeting can be identified in terms of policies aimed at countering and compensating people for discriminatory practices in the operation of key resource allocation markets (such as housing, employment and education). The policy instruments include training in equal opportunities for resource managers and 'gatekeepers', action to tackle racial and sex discrimination through tribunals and the courts and special programmes to ensure that groups who experience discrimination (ethnic minorities, women, disabled people) are given equal access to opportunities.

A range of concepts have been used to describe this form of targeting, including positive discrimination, affirmative action, positive action and reverse discrimination. The more assertive forms of positive discrimination, especially the adoption of employment quotas for women and racial groups, have been particularly controversial (Edwards, 1987 and Mitra, 1990).

It is possible for the various strands of targeting to be combined in order to tackle a particular problem. Clearly, a policy aimed at reducing educational disadvantage might conceivably target resources at deprived pupils, deprived areas or deprived schools. Each of these priorities would require not only data from different sources in order to identify the targets, but also fundamentally different strategies to achieve their objectives. These would include measures to make the home environment more conducive to learning (a focus on deprived pupils), measures to redress the under-resourcing within schools (deprived schools) and an attempt to improve the residential environment from which children are drawn (deprived areas).

Targeting and crime prevention

Although there may not be direct parallels, all of the issues discussed above do have relevance for the targeting of crime prevention and community safety programmes. The choice of the scale or entities prioritised to receive resources is just as important in targeting crime prevention as it is in anti- poverty or regeneration programmes. The different entities or scales involved are set out in Figure 11.1 (overleaf).

Targets of crime and disorder that need protecting may be:

- individuals (actual victims of, or those vulnerable to, assault, rape or robbery)

- households and family units (victims of, or those vulnerable to, domestic violence)

- social, ethnic or client groups (victims of racial violence, and offences committed by bogus officials)

- properties (arson, car crime, burglary)

- organisations and institutions (fraud, white-collar crime and theft)

- public places (affected by disorder or juvenile disturbances).

Similarly, crime prevention measures aimed at reducing the vulnerability of potential targets may be directed at any one of these targets. Personal attack alarms, for

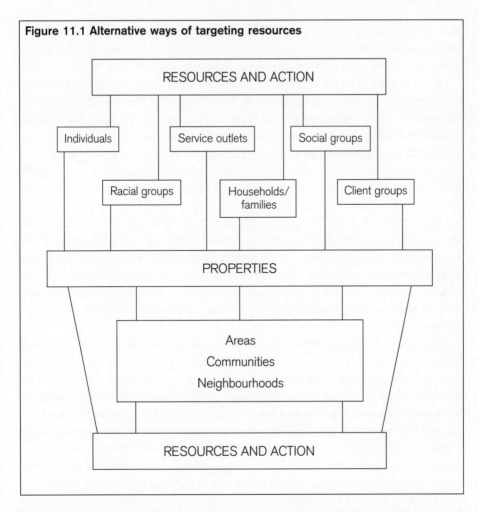

Figure 11.1 Alternative ways of targeting resources

individuals, mediation programmes for households and family units, racial harassment units for social and ethnic groups, target hardening for properties and CCTV or Town Centre Wardens for institutions and organisations or 'dangerous places'.

Two additional factors which affect the logistics of targeting are the temporal dimension (when to target or intervene) and the spatial dynamics of targeting (whether to stick to the same area, the same properties and the same individuals over time, or switch to new targets).

The decision of when to target depends on the objectives of the policy. In proactive crime prevention strategies, there will be a need to reach vulnerable targets before they become victimised. In this case, targeting would be a key element in an early warning system and the targeting decision will be influenced by intelligence on likely risk factors. Alternatively, the programme might seek to protect victims of crime from further victimisation. The targeting decision will be influenced by data on recorded crime and the location of past hot spots. Identifying potential targets from risk factors is technically a more complex exercise than reaching out to existing victims of crime.

The flexibility of a crime prevention programme to re-target resources in response to information about changing needs, is dependent upon the availability of good intelligence on emerging crime and disorder problems, but might also reflect a programme's objectives. For example, a social crime prevention initiative, focusing on a particular area (perhaps a patch used for detached youth work), might be unable to shift to new areas in response to the changing distribution of the problem (juvenile disturbances, for example), because of a rigid policy commitment to operate only within the demarcated area.

The entities that are being targeted are not always static or stationary. For example, diversion programmes targeting young people at risk might operate in a defined patch, but would need to shift location if juvenile disturbances displace to new areas. Several of the detached youth work projects on Merseyside recognise this and target young people wherever they congregate. Similarly, burglary programmes might need to target a new group of properties if they have been successful in reducing victimisation in the original target area.

This choice of targets for crime prevention is also intrinsically linked to the type of intervention sought. The form of targeting in Figure 11.1 relates to measures which make people, buildings, organisations and places less vulnerable. However, the emphasis might be placed on reducing crime by targeting the offenders. This might involve diversion and rehabilitation programmes aimed at changing the motivation or behaviour of actual and potential offenders, or focused action by the police on target criminals to improve the detection rate and apprehend prolific offenders.

The targeting of crime prevention measures might include developing screening criteria for resource allocation, which utilise several scales or entities. For example, an anti-burglary initiative, designed to impact upon repeat victimisation, might offer assistance only to those properties which have been burgled at least once and which are located in the most disadvantaged areas. Clearly, this would eliminate dwellings that fall outside the boundary. If the available resources are particularly scarce, the targeting could be refined further by aiding only those properties which are in the most deprived areas and which also contain either an elderly person living alone or a lone parent with dependent children. Thus three scales or levels of targeting would be applied simultaneously; the property (whether it had been previously burgled), the area (whether or not it is deprived) and the social characteristics of the occupant(s) (whether or not they are in a vulnerable client group).

The extent to which the number of previous burglaries is taken into account in the targeting decision, will depend upon the programme's objectives. Are they to prevent a repeat burglary, by protecting vulnerable properties before they are victimised, or do they offer protection and reassurance to those who have already become repeat victims (That is, proactive versus reactive strategy)?

Targeting dilemmas

Dilemmas confront all efforts to target resources whether this be done socially, spatially, to organisations and institutions, or using various combinations of all three. They usually revolve around questions of fairness, equity and territorial justice. As a form of rationing, targeting inevitably focuses minds on who or what is excluded, as well as included, in the resource allocation. If priority areas are used as a means of rationing, there will inevitably be debate about the ability of the boundaries to differentiate fairly between high and low levels of need and entitlement. Victimised households with equal entitlement to crime prevention measures would be identifiable both within and outside priority areas. The question for the practitioner is often one of how to present a spatially-targeted crime prevention strategy to the community.

Reasons for concentrating crime prevention initiatives in particular geographical areas are likely to be based primarily on the increased risk of victimisation in those areas. Previous research has shown, for example, that the *per capita* risk of victimisation is higher within deprived areas (Hirschfield *et al*, 1995). This type of information will be particularly effective for proactive schemes aiming to prevent victimisation – in this case deprivation is a risk factor.

However, area-based targeting is also used in reactive crime prevention strategies. Its use here appears to be more associated with the concept of rationing, since there will be definite incidents of victimisation falling outside these areas as well as within them. So what is the justification for using such area approaches in these situations?

It is often the case that crime prevention schemes can benefit more than just the direct victim. For instance, improved street lighting outside a victimised retail establishment is likely to improve lighting to the whole row of shops. Likewise, encouraging victims to become more active in crime prevention (through the likes of Homewatch Schemes for example) will be of benefit to neighbours as well as to victims. This will be of greater effect in areas that are generally high risk, such as deprived areas.

There are also likely to be secondary benefits of crime prevention schemes. For instance, protecting a retail establishment from further victimisation might just keep it in business, which in turn has an impact on the economic activity of the area. In turn this will have an impact on the community as a whole, since areas with thriving business activity will be seen as more desirable places to live. Hence, a crime prevention scheme may have wider implications for the regeneration of areas. Areas such as deprived areas are once again likely to have the most to gain from these processes. So, in well thought-through crime prevention initiatives, there should be reasons as to why particular priority areas are chosen.

A further way to ease the dilemma of spatially-targeted schemes may be the adoption of a more flexible system whereby the levels of support on offer to households or businesses taper off as levels of deprivation decline. This might be handled by defining a series of buffer zones, forming a cordon surrounding the boundary of the main priority area. The availability of GIS and geographically referenced crime and disorder data now makes this a much more feasible task than in the past. It is certainly one of the issues that local authorities and the police service will need to confront when producing their crime and disorder strategies.

Whether a scheme is to be based on priority areas or not, it is important to weigh up the advantages and disadvantages of such an approach to the targeting of crime prevention resources. In summary, the perceived strengths of this practice include the belief that:

● resources are more likely to make a measurable impact if targeted than if spread thinly

● objectives become more achievable (spatial rationing)

● synergy with other programmes is maximised (for example, with SRB, Pathway programmes and anti-poverty strategies) it assists disadvantaged communities and is therefore fair.

The Home Office evaluation of anti-burglary schemes implemented through the Safer Cities programme suggests that targeting resources on burglary hot spots can and does impact significantly upon crime in such areas (Ekblom *et al*, 1996). Resource inputs can also be maximised through the synergy that is generated with other programmes targeted at the same areas. The opportunities for a more holistic approach to tackling the problems of deprived areas in the UK are likely to increase given the Government's current emphasis on inter-departmental approaches to combating social exclusion and the establishment of a number of thematic policy zones in deprived areas (Health, Employment and Education Action Zones).

Inevitably, there are also drawbacks of spatial targeting which include the fact that:

● many victims of crime will live outside the priority areas

● it is territorially unjust

● it directs attention away from wider underlying causes of crime which impinge upon society as a whole and cannot wholly be tackled locally.

The extent to which it is possible to tackle the causes of crime by targeting areas of high crime is a more fundamental point. The extent to which problems *in* high-crime areas are problems *of* high-crime areas will vary according to the nature of the offence. Clearly, there are situations where the characteristics of an area render it highly criminogenic, for example, where different land uses converge or where surveillance and guardianship are poor. However, the area and its characteristics cannot be held responsible for generating criminal and anti-social behaviour within the population or for changes in lifestyle and routine activities that make people more vulnerable to victimisation. These factors are influenced by broader social, demographic, economic and cultural changes operating at societal level rather than at that of the neighbourhood. In this sense:

> there is a futility in drawing lines around areas on maps on the assumption that by so doing the forces leading to decline could be cornered, countered and even reversed. (Atkinson and Moon, 1994.)

However, in practical terms, action needs to be taken and decisions need to be made about how to deliver crime prevention programmes which benefit local communities.

Identifying the targets

There are numerous sources of data that report levels of risk against individuals, properties and areas in relation to incidents of crime and disorder. The most widely used of these are recorded crime records and command and control data (that is, calls for service to the police from the public).

However, there is also information from crime surveys such as the nation-wide British Crime Survey (1996) and the Commercial Victimisation Survey (1995). Furthermore, there are sources of information relating to the costs of crime (such as insurance claims) and the fear of crime (such as public perception surveys). Each of these data sources generates information that measures different concepts.

For instance, an analyst cannot claim that he or she has a measure of the actual level of crime in a particular area using recorded crime information, since a large amount of crime goes unreported to the police. A survey design can address this issue by asking individuals directly about their experiences of crime, but has the drawback that its accuracy often relies on the memory of respondents. Command and control data will capture information on anti-social behaviour and disorder as well as alleged criminal activity and can be seen as a measure of the public's demand for police services. Unlike information on recorded crime, command and control data suffers both from under-reporting (especially on incidents of anti-social behaviour and crimes on public transport) and over-reporting (where the same incident is reported by several members of the public and repeatedly logged).

Data relating to the cost of crime from insurance claims is an incomplete picture of the actual level of loss, since many less serious losses, through incidents of crime, are never claimed by the victims. It is therefore important to consider both the limitations and the possible interpretations of data sets relating to risk of crime or disorder before processing them for use in resource targeting.

Another issue that it is important to consider at the stage of data collation, is the level at which targeting information is processed. It is possible to produce meaningful data relating to the level of risk to individuals, properties, groups of individuals or properties, and geographical areas. Some examples of this are:

● disaggregate victimisation data – such as a list of repeatedly burgled properties

● aggregate victimisation data for groups of people – such as the total number or the percentage of adults aged between 16 and 24 who have experienced an incident of assault

● aggregate victimisation data for geographical areas – such as the number of sexual assaults per 1,000 residents in each electoral ward or for specific residential housing estates.

In the last of these examples, information relating to the population at risk is required for the production of rates. This highlights the need for data other than that indicating crime risk. The Population Census is an obvious source of contextual information. However, this has the limitation that it only provides extensive data on the characteristics of an area's residential population. Comprehensive information on the number and type of non-residential properties in an area and the people who utilise them, is not available.

It is often useful to have access to figures specifying the visiting population in certain areas at different times of the day – this will obviously be very different from the residential population in areas such as town and city centres. The use of such information to construct crime rates will give a more accurate estimate of crime risks by reflecting the variations in risks to individuals at different times of the day. This will be crucial information to area-based schemes aimed at decreasing the risk to properties such as schools, retail establishments or healthcare facilities.

Sources of reliable data on visiting populations and non-residential properties are very difficult to identify. City centre visitor surveys, in conjunction with residential population figures from the Census, can be used to estimate daytime, evening and night-time populations in such areas. Statistics on non-residential properties might be available from local authority databases of small firms and commercial rates registers.

A further issue in relation to data used for targeting is that of data cleaning. There is inevitably a certain percentage of geographically referenced data that does not pinpoint precisely the location of an incident. For example, an incomplete address from a police recorded crime information system, which specifies the street name but not the house number, may still be geographically referenced. However, the Eastings and Northings (or the x and y co-ordinates) are likely to relate to the midpoint of the street and not to an individual property. This lack of precision is of less consequence when aggregate statistics for large areas are being processed, but is of more concern when identifying victimisations against individual properties. This is especially true in attempts to quantify levels of repeat victimisation against particular properties.

There is little that can be done with incidents containing incomplete addresses, but those with addresses that are misspelled, or recorded slightly differently (such as 'The Green Cafe, High Street' instead of '131, High Street') can be cleaned to produce more accurate data using fuzzy matching procedures and relational databases. Such cleaning will invariably increase the number of cases of repeat victimisation.

The role of geographical information systems (GIS)

As well as having data at appropriate levels of resolution, the identification of targets can be facilitated considerably by being able to display the geographical location of vulnerable and victimised individuals, properties and areas. A GIS is particularly well suited to these tasks. In addition to the straightforward mapping of crime incidents, a GIS enables crime information to be cross-referenced with other geographically referenced data, to produce value-added data sets.

A simple example of this may be the cross-referencing of individual residential burglary locations with census Enumeration Districts (EDs). This would add an ED code to each individual record relating to a burglary. This information could then be aggregated by ED to give an overall count of the number of residential burglaries within each ED. This count would be used to produce a rate using information from the census (for example, the number of residential burglaries per 1,000 households for each ED).

This kind of aggregate level analysis does not need to be confined to ED areas, although they are often used since population statistics are produced directly for these areas. Crime analysts might be interested in rates for areas such as 100 metre grid squares (this is the basic level at which command and control data is provided) or crime hot spots produced by crime pattern analysis applications. It is possible to program GIS applications such as Map Info to produce crime rates for areas of any size. Such programmes apportion ED populations to specified units (such as 100 metre grid squares) on the basis of the percentage of the ED's overall land area contained within that unit. A similar procedure can be used to produce populations for hotspot areas (see Hirschfield and Bowers, 1997).

A further use of GIS in processing targeting information is in the identification of characteristics of the priority areas of potential crime prevention schemes. In some cases, the priority areas for schemes will have been decided before data processing commences. An example of this might be where a crime prevention project is being implemented within an existing urban regeneration initiative that has a well-defined boundary. In these cases a GIS can be used to identify the concentration of the problem within these defined priority areas (for instance, the number of juvenile disturbances and the rate of repeat burglary to households). Such information can be used as a baseline for future evaluation of the effectiveness of a scheme devised to combat the problem.

In other cases, priority areas may be less rigidly defined and may be used as a means of concentrating limited resources into high crime hot spots in order to maximise the impact of the given scheme. Here a GIS can be used to help define crime hot spots and identify possible priority areas.

Recently, there has been an increase in the availability of crime pattern analysis packages that operate within or interface with a GIS. (Some examples are STAC, SCAS and Harlequin. A good web site with details of these packages is www.geo.nottinham.ac.uk/~jerry/cpa/index). However, the types of hot spot which they define are dependant upon the purposes for which they are used (for example, meeting the targeting requirements of a specific crime prevention scheme) and the types of data that they utilise.

For example, a hot spot showing the location of acts of assault might well be in a city centre area. A hot spot concentrating on the location of the victims or perpetrators of assault is more likely to be located in a residential area (such as a deprived housing estate). Furthermore, such priority areas are likely to be dynamic and move over time, which could mean redefinition of the scheme's area of operation at fairly regular intervals.

An alternative method of defining priority areas is on the basis of risk factors of crime or on issues of importance to a particular crime prevention initiative. Some examples are initiatives focusing on deprived areas, residential areas, non-residential areas, areas that lack social cohesion, areas containing a particular type of housing, areas with low levels of night-time guardianship or a combination of these areas. The primary concern of these initiatives might be focusing on issues that are known to have a significant impact on particular types of crime, or on areas that have been predicted as being potentially high-crime in the future, on the basis of their risk factors. A GIS can be used to flag up areas that exceed a certain threshold on such characteristics and produce priority areas from them.

Matching targets with appropriate crime prevention measures

The sections above have indicated that some thinking needs to be done in relation to the aims and objectives of a crime prevention initiative, even before the data processing stage for target identification. It is far from realistic to expect that by processing all the data available a ready-made set of targets for a viable new initiative will be created. For instance, it is important to know before data processing whether a potential initiative will be aimed at individual properties or people, or groups of individuals or properties. A scheme aimed at specific individual properties will require disaggregate data, whereas a scheme that intends to target groups of properties or people will benefit from aggregate information specifying the rate of victimisation against these groups in different areas of interest.

In most cases therefore, initiative aims and objectives will be known before targets are identified. This will often make the process of implementing appropriate crime prevention measures fairly straightforward. For example, a scheme aimed at decreasing the risk to individual residential households suffering from high levels of victimisation needs a crime prevention measure that is directly associated with a given property, such as target hardening. Likewise, decreasing the risk to rows of shops may involve external measures such as CCTV systems or a Business Watch scheme to encourage the businesses to take an interest in each other's security.

There are other situations in which knowledge of the aims and objectives of an initiative will not necessarily lead to clear crime prevention measures. For example, a scheme might aim to discourage young people from anti-social behaviour by altering their attitudes and lifestyles. Analysis of command and control information might have identified areas with high concentrations of calls to the police reporting alleged juvenile disturbances. Having a high police presence alone in such areas is unlikely to discourage anti-social behaviour, although it might well shift it to other areas. In order for a social crime prevention project to impact upon the target groups, a process of behavioural change needs to take place through labour-intensive, one-to-one work with vulnerable individuals in outreach schemes, providing them with support and alternative activities.

Merseyside Case Studies

This section describes the process of identifying targets for three different crime and fire prevention initiatives. The initiatives are all part of an SRB-funded partnership operating on Merseyside, the Safer Merseyside Partnership (SMP). The Partnership has its own priority areas which are the Pathway Areas, or deprived areas, of Merseyside defined for the allocation of EU regeneration grants under the Objective 1 programme. Hence the common theme of the initiatives is that they operate within these areas. The three case studies include a target hardening scheme for small businesses, a fire safety initiative and a Youth Action programme that aims to meet the needs of young people and to divert them from disruptive and/or criminal behaviour.

Target hardening small businesses

The SMP created a scheme primarily aimed at local businesses that offered financial assistance towards target hardening vulnerable, non-residential properties. In its initial stages the scheme was operated on an open application system which invited businesses to approach the Partnership with their case for assistance. This resulted in an overwhelming number of applications and the virtually impossible task of identifying those that were genuinely high-risk establishments.

A second phase of the strategy, therefore, aimed to use crime risk information to identify vulnerable properties within the Partnership's priority areas, which could then be offered crime prevention assistance and financial aid towards target hardening. Recorded crime information from Merseyside Police was used to identify non-residential properties that had been repeatedly burgled within a one-year period. This was a far from straightforward task, since non-residential addresses are recorded by the police in many different formats, making it difficult to produce accurate counts of the number of victimisations against each property. Furthermore, there is no simple way of identifying the type of establishment the non-residential property is, since non-residential burglary records cover schools, churches, sports facilities, businesses and even garden sheds, and do not have a separate sub-category specifying type of property.

The extensive manual processing that was involved in creating information on repeatedly burgled businesses falling within Merseyside's priority areas, effectively meant that it was unfeasible to use police recorded crime data as a means of identification. The strategy also aimed to assist businesses experiencing robbery, shop theft, fraud, assault and criminal damage in addition to non-residential burglary. Many incidents of these crimes (especially shop theft) go unreported to the police, so trying to produce a victimisation history for each property by linking all incidents for each property together, is likely to be very difficult. Hence the second phase of the strategy was based on a victimisation survey that assessed the vulnerability of each property, on the basis of its experience of all these crime types and the level of security that was already in place.

The first stage of this process was to identify potential targets for the strategy that could then be assessed by survey. Business databases were obtained from each of Merseyside's five metropolitan districts, which contained information on the size, type and location of each business in the given district. The scheme's overall objectives were to help small businesses in priority areas that had an impact on local communities. These objectives were used to produce criteria for potential targets of the scheme. These were that the business:

- had less than 25 employees and was not part of a larger business

- was located in a Partnership priority area

- was of a particular type (this included manufacturing, retail, entertainment, wholesaling and some healthcare establishments)

- was in a residential area and hence served a local community.

Using the district business databases and a GIS it was possible to identify the properties that met these criteria. This reduced the number of potential targets from the 30,000 businesses across Merseyside to approximately 2,500 that met the criteria, and left a manageable number of properties to survey. The victimisation survey asked the managers of these businesses about their experiences of crime in the past year. The business premises were then categorised in to high-, medium- and low-risk properties using a scoring system that had been devised in a pilot phase of the survey. This allocated approximately 400 of the 2,500 businesses into the high- and medium-risk categories. These businesses became the identified targets for the scheme, which offered crime prevention advice and part-funding towards a target hardening measure such as a burglar alarm or a CCTV system.

Fire safety

Targeting does not necessarily have to involve allocating resources or focusing action directly on the intended beneficiaries. Indirect targeting can also occur. The Merseyside Fire Brigade's Fire Safety campaign provides an example of indirect targeting in action. One of the objectives of the Campaign has been to introduce fire education materials into schools in areas where there are a disproportionately high number of hoax calls made to the fire brigade. To assist the Merseyside Fire Brigade in this endeavour, the University of Liverpool collected information on every hoax call made to the brigade over a fourteen-month period. Items recorded for each included:

- time and date of the call

- the caller's telephone number which was logged automatically

- the address of the alleged incident.

The type of property or site which it was alleged was on fire was derived, by the evaluation team, from the address or location of the incident. Thus a classification distinguishing domestic dwellings, commercial premises, public buildings, vehicles and wasteland was derived. Although the addresses given by the hoaxers were not actual fire sites, their locations were significant because they were the places to which fire engines were falsely diverted. This abuse of the service could have dire consequences for those in genuine distress. Where possible, postcodes were identified for the alleged addresses to enable the mapping of this pseudo geography to be carried out.

The telephone number denoted the origin point of the call. Calls made from telephone kiosks were identified by comparing the hoaxer's telephone number against a correspondence table containing the numbers of each public call box. Where the two corresponded there was a match and because the information obtained about each kiosk included a grid reference pinpointing its location, it was possible to determine from where calls were being made.

The targeting was indirect because the kiosks repeatedly used to make hoax calls were identified first and these locations used to select the schools into which fire education materials were to be introduced. The choice of schools was informed by their close proximity to high call volume kiosks. However, the kiosks themselves were also targeted as part of covert surveillance and a poster campaign aimed at deterring offenders at the point of the offence.

A number of telephone kiosks were being used repeatedly to make hoax calls. One was used to make 94 calls and nine kiosks were identified, each of which was used to make over 50 hoax calls during the period in question. This gives an indication of how concentrated the hoax calls were. GIS analysis also revealed that a large majority of the multiply-used telephone kiosks fell within the Partnership's priority areas, showing that these areas are a useful way of rationing fire safety resources.

A resource-targeting table was produced to present the hoax call data in a more digestible form. This sorted the kiosks on the basis of the number of hoax calls that had been made from them. The table revealed that 20 per cent of all the hoax calls were made from under 3 per cent of the kiosks on Merseyside, which translated into just 33 kiosks. Thus by targeting these 33 kiosks, the Fire Brigade could effectively deal with a fifth of the problem.

The results from this and subsequent analyses, which also take into consideration the peak times of the day and days of the week used to make hoax calls (time hot spots), are currently being examined by the Fire Brigade. These will be used to pinpoint future covert surveillance operations aimed at apprehending the perpetrators temporally as well as spatially. Maps are also being produced identifying schools in close proximity to the multiply used kiosks. An example of these maps, used in the targeting of educational programmes in schools, is shown in Figure 11.2 (overleaf).

Youth Action programme

The Partnership's Youth Action programme is an example of a social crime prevention initiative in which targeting information is employed at several different levels and in several different forms. The programme comprises twelve detached youth work projects, which operate in some of the most disadvantaged areas of Merseyside. A common aim of all twelve projects, which are funded for a fixed period, has been to provide alternative programmes of activities that divert young people away from anti-social and criminal behaviour. The schemes operate by approaching young people using small teams of outreach workers who encourage them to become involved in purposeful activities.

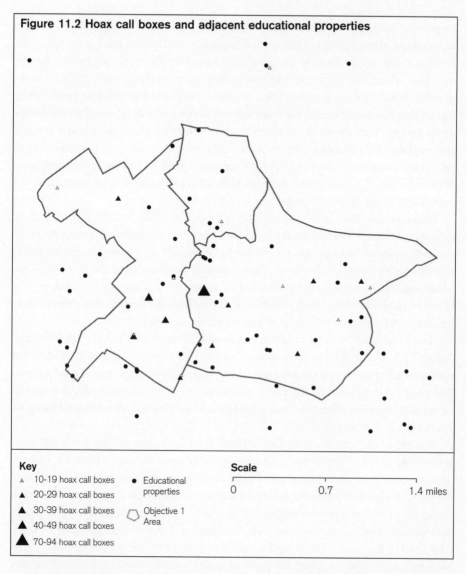

Figure 11.2 Hoax call boxes and adjacent educational properties

Key

▵ 10-19 hoax call boxes	● Educational
▲ 20-29 hoax call boxes	properties
▲ 30-39 hoax call boxes	⬠ Objective 1
▲ 40-49 hoax call boxes	Area
▲ 70-94 hoax call boxes	

Scale

0   0.7   1.4 miles

The first level of targeting involved the definition of the areas of operation of the schemes. The operational areas or patches for the youth work projects fall within the Partnership's priority areas, but do not cover them entirely. The youth action areas are often fairly small, tightly defined patches covering several streets or parts of housing estates. This helps to ensure that the work that is done in the areas impacts upon the community of young people who live and/or congregate in the area.

The areas were originally defined by youth workers who had much experience and grass roots knowledge of the areas frequented by vulnerable young people. Once the areas were defined, a second level of targeting was required – identification of where within these areas young people tended to gather, and where there were particular problems with youths causing annoyance. These two geographies are not necessarily the same. The detached teams undertook their own reconnaissance of the areas to establish where young people tended to gather and socialise prior to approaching them. Reconnaissance counts are essentially estimates of the numbers of young people on the streets. They are made by youth workers observing young people at a distance and without establishing any contact. This provides the youth workers with information relating to the potential need for youth work within the operational areas of the schemes. It has identified the vulnerable groups that need to be targeted, or the population of young people at risk.

However, this information alone does not give the youth workers a picture of the locations at which juvenile disturbances and incidents of minor disorder repeatedly occur. In order to identify these, command and control data from Merseyside Police was processed using a GIS system. This produced maps showing the frequency with which specific locations have been identified as the site of a juvenile disturbance. The locations in question are small parcels of land that have been repeatedly referenced by the command and control system in respect of the incidents.

Some examples of these maps for the Arundel Project in Liverpool are shown in Figure 11.3 (overleaf). The map shows that there is a certain clustering of incidents within specific parts of the project area. These clusters identify the vulnerable locations that need to be targeted by the youth action schemes. Where vulnerable groups and vulnerable locations coincide, there are particular problems that can be addressed by youth diversion schemes.

It is likely that the intervention of youth workers in the project areas will have some effect on the distribution of juvenile disturbances over time. Figure 11.3 shows how the command and control calls in the target area, and two peripheral buffers of the area, change in the months following implementation of the scheme. In this case, the level of command and control calls within the target area have decreased considerably over time – in fact there has been a 5.7 per cent decrease in calls, compared to the year prior to implementation. However, the peripheral buffer areas have seen a 25.5 per cent and 4.5 per cent increase in the number of calls. This may indicate some displacement from the scheme area.

Not only do the maps in Figure 11.3 give some indication of how juvenile disturbances might be changing in response to targeted youth work, they also provide some clues as to how the operational area might best be redefined to capture more of the problem. They are the first step in the development of a more dynamic targeting system.

The last element of targeting in relation to the Youth Action programme is the targeting of vulnerable individuals over time. A self-assessment questionnaire has been

Figure 11.3 Arundel Youth Action Area

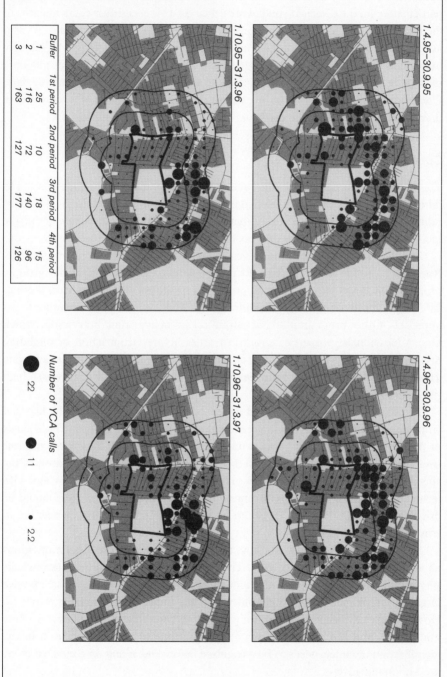

Buffer	1st period	2nd period	3rd period	4th period
1	25	10	18	15
2	116	72	140	96
3	163	127	177	126

1.4.95–30.9.95

1.10.95–31.3.96

1.4.96–30.9.96

1.10.96–31.3.97

Number of YCA calls

22   11   2.2

designed for the young people who have been engaged by, and who are actively participating in, the detached youth work schemes. This elicits their views in terms of their lifestyles, attitudes, behaviour and aspirations. The same individuals are then asked to fill in the questionnaire on subsequent occasions. This will identify individuals upon whom the schemes have had a positive impact. It will also identify those that have gained, to a lesser degree, from the Youth Action schemes to date. Once more, this information can be used for the dynamic targeting of resources over time, by concentrating on the needs of individuals whose problems remain.

Conclusion

This chapter has set out some of the issues relating to the targeting of crime prevention initiatives. Limited resources makes some form of rationing inevitable. As a form of rationing, targeting helps to ensure that the resources that are available get to the individuals, properties, groups or areas that need them most.

Programmes that target crime prevention resources may be reactive or proactive. Reactive targeting assists victims of crime, be they individuals, social groups, properties or businesses, in order to protect them against subsequent victimisation. The target hardening of small businesses on Merseyside is an example of this approach. Other programmes concentrate on proactive crime prevention, which targets individuals, properties, groups or areas before victimisation or offending occurs. The proactive identification of targets relies on the identification of risk factors. This may point to areas with particular social problems or to individuals with a high risk of becoming victims of crime.

The scale at which targets should be identified is a complex issue. The fact that crime prevention initiatives can target individuals or properties, groups of individuals or properties, organisations, areas or indeed, a combination of these elements, has been demonstrated above. The key to this issue lies in the aims and objectives of the specific crime prevention initiative. The application of data analysis and GIS techniques, to identify appropriate targets for crime prevention measures, should be driven not by what data sets happen to be available, but by the priorities set out in crime and disorder strategies.

Lastly, and possibly most crucially, targeting procedures raise general questions about territorial justice and fairness. The mechanism of targeting will, through its very nature, exclude some vulnerable individuals, properties, groups or areas. Effective targeting will minimise such exclusion within the limits of the available resources. However, the advantages and disadvantages of all types of targeting need to be fully understood and the interpretations and limitations of information used in the identification of targets needs to be recognised before embarking on a targeted crime prevention initiative.

References

Atkinson R and Moon G (1994) *Urban policy in Britain: the city, the state and the market* Basingstoke: Macmillan

Deakin N and Edwards J (1993) *The Enterprise Culture and the Inner City* London: Routledge

Edwards J (1987) *Positive discrimination, social justice, and social policy Moral scrutiny of a policy practice* London: Tavistock

Ekblom P, Law H and Sutton M with Crisp P and Wiggins R (1996) *Domestic Burglary Schemes in the Safer Cities Programme* Home Office Research Findings

Haughton G (1990) 'Targeting jobs to local people: the British Urban Policy Experience' *Urban Studies* 27

Hirschfield A, Bowers K and Brown P (1995) 'Exploring Relations Between Crime and Disadvantage on Merseyside' *European Journal on Criminal Policy and Research* 3

Hirschfield A and Bowers K (1997) 'The Development of a Social, Demographic and Land Use Profiler for Areas of High Crime' *British Journal of Criminology* 37

Mitra S (ed) (1990) *Politics of positive discrimination: A cross national perspective* London: Sangam

Mirrlees-Black C, Mayhew P and Percy A (1996) The 1996 British Crime Survey: England and Wales *Home Office Statistical Bulletin 1996*, London: Home Office

Mirrlees-Black C and Ross A (1995) *Crime Against Retail and Manufacturing Premises: Findings from the 1994 Commercial Victimisation Survey* Home Office Research Study 146, London: HMSO

12. Crime and urban layout: the need for evidence
Bill Hillier and Simon CF Shu

The debate on urban layout and crime over the past two decades has been long on ideology – defensible space, territoriality, and so on (Newman, 1972) – but short on evidence. This chapter aims to begin to provide a new level of evidence. Using point of entry data for burglary, and space syntax analysis of the urban layout, the relation between the two is explored on a case by case basis in three areas in UK. These are towns selected to be socially and spatially very different from each other, so that any relationships between crime and space across the areas are unlikely to be due to social factors. The results suggest that the built-in security advantage that many have argued belongs to the cul-de-sac, in fact belongs to the street, with its greater potential for movement, its greater mutual visibility for higher numbers of neighbours, and greater protection from the rear. The results confirm earlier findings from the Space Syntax Laboratory (Hillier, 1988) and challenge the many aspects of the current defensible space orthodoxy. Further studies are required to see how far the patterns brought to light in these studies are general.

The need for evidence

This study seeks to answer the following: what features of urban layouts increase vulnerability to burglary and car crime, and what features reduce it? Are cul-de-sacs really safer than through roads? Does it help to separate vehicles from pedestrians? Do you really benefit from having small groups of neighbours, or are you safer with more? Should we group houses into territorial units? Or is it better to be on a more anonymous street?

The only way to answer these questions is through a body of evidence created with them in mind. It appears that there is no such body of evidence; recent debate on urban layout and crime over the past twenty years has focused on ideology rather than on precise evidence. Ideology is congenial because it persuades us we know more than we do. It leads us to believe that we know the principles, even if they lack evidential support. Evidence is more worrying because it may tell us that we don't know. The essence of a scientific approach is that evidence undermines our preconceptions, and makes us think new thoughts. This chapter is about evidence, considered, hopefully, without the filter of ideology.

Overcoming area differences

Why after all this time is there so little systematic evidence? One reason is that it is very difficult to study the relation of urban layout to crime in such a way as to isolate built environment effects from social effects. To show that more crimes occur in one type of location than another, data must be aggregated in some way. In the past, most studies have aggregated data by area or by estate, and posed questions about layout in terms of general descriptions of areas: how high the buildings are, how big the blocks, how many entrances, how many walkways, and so on (Newman, 1972 and Coleman, 1985).

Unfortunately, as soon as you aggregate by area you hit trouble. Whether through markets or bureaucracies, our societies send different people to different areas. The rich go this way, the poor go that way, the good families go to this estate, the problem ones to that. So, even if it is shown that the crime rate in an area is higher than in another, or even that more criminals come from one area than another, it still isn't known whether the high rate has been produced by the area itself, or by the social process that put its population there. In principle, it ought to be possible to resolve this statistically by using multivariate analysis to isolate the influence of different factors. In practice, the large number of variables involved, and the wide differences found within the same area, make this a hazardous procedure.

One way out of this impasse would be to learn to study the location of crime in the urban layout at the much finer scale of the individual crime and the spatial circumstances of its exact location. It needs to be understood, in spatial terms, why this crime occurred in this location and that one in that – where criminals have the full range of choices available (so that they can choose between individual locations in the same area, rather than between areas). Locations can then be compared across socially and spatially different areas, and area differences turned to advantage if it is shown that, regardless of social differences, certain crimes tend to occur in certain types of location, rather than in others. Consistencies found at this level could not then be explained away as the products of social differences.

That said, how can it actually be done? The key is to learn to describe spatial layouts in a way that is precise and consistent enough to show how they might facilitate crime in some locations and deter it in others. In technical terms, more effort to 'control the layout variable' needs to be made. The aim of this chapter is to show how this can be done and how such studies can therefore be carried out. It also presents results from a set of initial studies, which both show consistencies across very different areas, and are also in some ways quite surprising, suggesting clear, if provisional, answers to most of the questions noted above. If these results were to be reproduced in other studies, then revision of some of our current assumptions about designing out crime would have to be made.

To put it briefly, the results from these studies suggest that traditional urban common sense – lining up buildings to face both sides of linear streets and linking the streets into integrated and well structured networks – is the best way to make life more difficult for the burglar or car criminal. The corollary is that many currently (or recently) fashionable theories about housing area layout, based on the notions of defensible space and territoriality, are very likely to be wrong and may even produce effects contrary to those intended (Hillier and Hanson, 1984, Hanson and Hillier, 1987 and Hillier, 1988).

The studies presented here are of three areas in different towns: a middle of the road estate in a new town; a suburban area in an affluent town; and an edge of town area in a less affluent town. It sounds like a sensible sample, but in fact the towns selected themselves by the fact that there were highly-committed crime prevention police associated with them who didn't think that all the answers were there, and wanted to understand more. Gratitude goes to them for providing this long sought opportunity to study the relation of urban layout and crime, in the detail that it requires.

Using points of access from public space rather than addresses

What, then, is meant by the exact location of, say, a burglary? Simply to note the address of a crime could be misleading if the crime was committed from a rear alley, for example, since it would be clear that the rear alley was the point of vulnerability. To burglarise a house, a burglar must gain access to the interior of a house from some part of public space. The key question is: which part? The focus will always be, then, on the point of entry to the dwelling and the part of the public space from which it was accessed. If a dwelling's front entrance faces on to a cul-de-sac but is burgled from a footpath, then the burglary is assigned to the footpath, not the cul-de-sac. In this way a clear picture of the real vulnerability factors in layouts can be built.

Using points of entry rather than addresses as the basic unit does of course mean that dwellings will differ in the number of points of access from public space that they have. Corner houses are likely to have more than those in the middle of a street or cul-de-sac. A house facing on to the street but with a rear footpath will have more than one without a rear footpath, and so on. Also, where spaces are clearly accessible from the public realm – for example, spaces for groups of garages, or ungated driveways – then they are treated as parts of public space, in effect, since they may well provide the spatial means by which access is gained to the house.

One reason for using point of entry rather than address data is that recent results from the British Crime Survey (BCS) (Budd, 1999) suggest that this may be a key factor in vulnerability. For example, it shows that when the influence of social and other factors are weeded out detached houses are the most vulnerable house type, and flats the least. These differences are small, but they are very unlikely to be produced by social factors, since detached houses are normally inhabited by better off people, and many 'high crime estates' will have a higher proportion of flats than other types of area. The survey also shows that end of terrace houses are more vulnerable than mid-terrace houses. Again, this is very unlikely to reflect social differences.

Types and attributes of public space

The public spaces from which entry may be gained need to be categorised, taking into account all the layout factors that might be involved. This is not as simple as it might seem. If, for example, a distinction is made between cul-de-sacs and through roads, it quickly becomes apparent that many spaces are cul-de-sacs for vehicles but allow through movement for pedestrians. Also, many spaces seem, at one level, to be through movement spaces, but turn out to be parts of larger cul-de-sac complexes, which eventually lead back the way they came. The overall layout configuration, of which a space is part, may be as important as its more obvious properties.

An adequate means of telling the key differences between one type of space and another is needed, therefore, taking their full contexts into account. Where should this begin? The simplest and historically the commonest kind of urban space is probably the best starting point. This is the linear through space, lined continuously on both sides with building entrances, with movement in and out of the buildings using the same space as movement through the space. In some guises this is called a street, in others a road, an avenue, or a boulevard. The important properties of this basic spatial form are linearity, 'throughness' and continuity of facing entrances on both sides. The majority of spaces in most cities traditionally had these properties

The difference between spaces can be tracked by thinking of them as variations on this basic theme. For example, through space can be converted to non-through space for vehicles, but the continuous relation to two lines of entrances kept. This can also be done in more than one way. A single, non-through space can be created, that links only to a through space, but is kept linear and continuously lined with building entrances. Or a whole complex of spaces can be created, which requires coming back the way you came. Or, as is often the case, a cul-de-sac complex for vehicles can be made, which allows through movement for pedestrians.

First, a set of basic categories of space needs to be defined, on the basis of different kinds of line of movement elements. Attributes can then be added to these elements. The basic categories are:

- through carriageways – spaces through which vehicles move and which are part of a through movement system

- through footpaths – the same, but for pedestrians

- cul-de-sac carriageways – spaces down which vehicles can move but which, for vehicles, lead to a dead end demanding return along the same way

- cul-de-sac driveways – dead-end driveways to small numbers of dwellings, a single block or even a single dwelling

- cul-de-sac front footpaths – dead-end paths accessible only to pedestrians, which lead to houses with front doors on the footpath

- rear dead-end footpaths – situated at the back of a number of dwellings.

The attributes then added are:

- distinction between distributed and non-distributed – a distributed space is part of a through movement system, while non-distributed space is part of a cul-de-sac complex. For cul-de-sac carriageways, for example, with the non-distributed attribute added, it is known that that space is part of an overall cul-de-sac complex, not one with through movement for pedestrians

- distinction between constituted and unconstituted spaces – if a space has more than 75 per cent of its adjacent dwellings facing front on to the space, then it is called constituted (the space has more or less continuous front entrances on both sides). If not, it is unconstituted. About one in three through streets in the sample are constituted in this sense, one in four are cul-de-sac carriageways, but only one in 98 is a footpath

- the number of line neighbours on a line – the number of other potential points of entry to dwellings along a particular line element. If combined with constituted, then most of these will be front entrances.

Space syntax measures

There are also, however, other properties of spaces which are less obvious to the naked eye but which can be brought to light by computer analysis. These have to do not with the immediate characteristics of each space, but with how each fits into the overall configuration of the layout. This turns out to be critical in studying crime patterns, because of the importance of movement and visibility, both of which are affected by the layout configuration as a whole.

Figure 12.1 (see colour section between pages 246 and 247) for example is an axial map of the street system of a large part of London, analysed by computer. An axial map is where the lines represent not named streets but the longest and fewest lines of sight and movement that pass through all the space of the street network. In effect it describes all the routes. As so often with organically grown cities, there appears at first to be no obvious order or pattern. In fact, there is a powerful interior logic. This is brought to light by analysing the system, on a basis different to the normal one. Instead of treating street intersections as elements and the street sections between them as links (as traffic engineers do), the lines are taken as elements, and simple questions asked about how they might be used in moving about the system.

In syntactic analysis of route systems, each line in the axial map is picked up in turn. The minimum number of intervening lines that must be used, in whole or in part, to go from one line to all other lines in the system, up to a certain radius, is calculated. The smaller the total, the more integrated the line: the larger the more segregated. Radius means the number of lines, away from the chosen line, which is taken into account. If it is the whole system, the result is called global integration. If, as in Figure 12.1, the radius is set at three, it is called local integration.

The map is then shaded red to blue according to the integration of each line: the more integrated, the redder the line; the more segregated, the bluer the line. An integrated, or red, line has relatively simple routes to everywhere else. A segregated or blue line has more complex routes. The reddest (most integrated) line in London is Oxford Street, which is of course also the main shopping street. The next reddest are the lines that link Oxford Street to the City of London, with the next few linking these towards the edges of the system in several directions. The patterns shown in Figure 12.1 seem to correlate strongly with intuitive ideas about London, and how it is put together, even though the layout has only been analysed mathematically.

The measures of spatial integration give a quantitative meaning to the intuitive sense that some bits of the urban grid are more accessible than others, and more likely to feature in ordinary movement around, and visual experience of, the city. They can also be used as powerful predictors of movement: redder means more potential movement, bluer means less. The pattern of colours (or, in fact, the mathematical values the colours represent) has also been shown to relate to many other aspects of how cities function: how local centres build up, how housing estates go wrong, how local areas are formed, and so on (Hillier, 1996). Here, the interest is in whether anything can be learned about crime patterns. Are different kinds of crime more or less likely in integrated or segregated locations, for example? Current ideas tend to emphasise segregation as a general insurance against burglary. The opposite will be seen to be the case.

The method for the studies, then, is to link points of entry to the dwelling with the lines of sight and movement available in the different types of public space. It is then to ask in what types of space, with what kinds of attributes and what kind of locations in the layout, rates of crime are higher or lower. An important advantage of this method is that it allows movement beyond the identification of clusters or hot spots, to identify spatial patterns where crimes occur in similar locations, even when these are diffused throughout the layout.

Previous studies

The technique of using space syntax in the study of urban crime patterns was originally pioneered over a decade ago through the work of Dr Lena Tsoskounoglou (Hillier, 1988). Her results suggested that layout factors might play a significant role in the location of burglary, but not in the direction expected. Figure 12.2 shows an analysed axial map of one of her study areas, the gentrifying inner London area of Barnsbury. Burglaries within a 12-month period are shown as black dots. Without the axial map it would be hard to make much sense of the pattern. With it we can see that there seems to be less burglary on the longer, more integrated red and yellow lines connecting edge to centre, and more in some of the more segregated, green and blue areas. More spatial integration (and more potential movement and better visibility along the lines) seems to mean less burglary.

This proposition was tested statistically in a very simple way. Every house has an integration value of the line on which it opens assigned to it, and the simple question 'is there a statistically significant difference with regard to the integration value between burgled and unburgled dwellings?' is asked. The answer is yes. More-integrated dwellings are indeed less likely to be burgled.

This finding was repeated across two housing estates with a similar result. For over 2,800 dwellings over a twelve-month period, it was shown that more-integrated lines, with more movement potential and visual connection along the line, had less burglary than more-segregated lines. One housing estate showed another interesting result: that one factor protecting a place from burglary was whether or not the lines connecting its line to the outside were themselves constituted, that is, had entrances opening on to them. Burglars sought segregated locations, but preferred them to be where escape routes to the outside went only down lines with blank walls.

The results of these studies were published in 1988 (Hillier, 1988), and clearly cast doubt on the then prevailing ideology of defensible space. In spite of previous criticism of her work, Alice Coleman declared herself to be completely in accord with the published article. Unfortunately, attempts to obtain funding for the further studies that were needed were unsuccessful. Progress had to wait until inward investment from the Far East made its appearance in the form Taiwanese PhD student, Simon Shu.

The Shu studies

To comply with the Data Protection Act, the three residential areas studied by Shu have been anonymised. They have been labelled as Town A (a middle-of-the-road area in a new town), Town B (a largely up-market area, though with down-market pockets, in a fairly affluent town) and Town C (a mixed area in a generally less-affluent town). The three areas combined have 213 burglaries and 306 car crimes over a one year period, distributed amongst 3,548 dwellings with 5,704 points of entry adjacent to public spaces. On average, for all three areas combined, one dwelling has 1.61 points of entry adjacent to public spaces, with houses on through streets having slightly fewer (1.55) than cul-de-sacs (1.66). These 5,704 points of entry are distributed on 854 lines, of which 78 (or nine per cent) are through roads,

41 per cent are cul-de-sac carriageways, 12 per cent are cul-de-sac footpaths, and 23 per cent are through footpaths. The remainder constitutes various combinations and special cases.

Work proceeded with the original crime records, which recorded the point of entry to the house (through a code), and often the point of entry from public space through the method of operation description (over the rear fence). Each burglary was plotted on the map in its exact location, including the point of access to the house, by a red dot. A short line was then added linking this to the point of entry from public space. In a few cases, where the records are not clear, a most probable reconstruction is used based on the point of entry to the dwelling. Where, for example, the point of entry to a detached or semi-detached dwelling is at the rear (69 per cent of burglaries in the sample have rear points of entry to the dwelling), but there is no back access, and where the method of operation does not mention access through other gardens, the burglary is assigned to the front.

The average rate of burglary for the three areas is 1 in 27 for points of entry, and 1 in 17 for dwellings. The latter is broken down by area in Table 12.1.

Table 12.1

	Burglary	Car crime	Vandalism
Town A	1 in 17	1 in 12	1 in 59
Town B	1 in 29	1 in 16	1 in 49
Town C	1 in 11	1 in 9	1 in 55

As we would expect from the BCS, Town B (the more affluent town) is best for both burglary and car crime, and Town C (the least affluent) the worst, with rates of burglary being three times as bad as Town B, and car crime twice as bad. As will be seen, the patterns of burglary and car crime reflect similar spatial patterns, though the pattern of vandalism (also recorded) is far less clear.

Three sketches

These begin with a visual inspection of different ways of representing the spatial layout of the three areas, with burglary and car crime plotted, to see if any obvious patterns or trends suggest themselves. In each case, four figures (a to d) are shown, with burglary plotted as red dots (with tails showing the point of access from public space in plans a and b), and car crime as blue dots:

a   the layout plan of buildings and streets

b   the public space plan with footpaths marked in green

c   the axial map with integration from redder to bluer colours (more potential movement and better visual connection to less potential movement and visual connection)

d   an (unanalysed) axial map with the constituted lines (those with more than 75 per cent of dwelling front entrances on both sides) marked in light blue.

In what follows, the prime focus will be on burglary, although car crimes are also plotted. Statistically, the differences for car crime rates follow those for burglary closely, but the differences by space type and attributes are generally smaller. All rates given below, unless otherwise stated, are for points of entry off public space.

Town A (new town) – Figures 12.3a, b, c and d

This area has main roads to the top, bottom and left (relatively separated from the interior) but to the right there is open parkland and, at some distance, a railway line with a footbridge. There is a striking tendency for burglary to be concentrated in the area to the right, which is also spatially and visually more broken up (therefore lines tending to the blue, see Figure 12.3c).

A spatially segregated cul-de-sac near the right-hand edge has a particularly strong concentration of burglary, with some rear and some front points of entry, as does a footpath-access line of houses (with cul-de-sac carriageways serving as rear parking) in the same area (see Figure 12.3b). In the rest of the plan, it is very clear that the relatively linear through routes (which are also constituted, for the most part – see Figure 12.3d) are entirely lacking in burglary.

Where burglary occurs, it is usually in the more broken-up spaces away from these linear routes. Statistically, through carriageways are by far the safest spaces in this area (1 in 63 points of entry burgled) with cul-de-sac carriageways comparatively unsafe (1 in 29). Through footpaths, however, offer even greater vulnerability to points of entry (1 in 17). Cul-de-sac drives are the most vulnerable (1 in 13). Car crime shows a similar, though more diffuse pattern, again with very little on the linear routes and much more in the broken-up spaces, though also with concentration where there is rear access car parking. Strikingly, there is no case of burglary on a constituted through road, and very few on constituted, non-through spaces.

Town B (generally affluent) – Figures 12.4a, b, c and d

The area chosen is a largely affluent area, with a small industrial complex in the centre, very large houses to the bottom and left, good but more modest housing in the central area and a much less affluent complex to the top right. About 29 per cent of its points of entry are on through roads, which make up ten per cent of its spaces.

There is a footpath complex in the less affluent top right area, linking a tree-like vehicular layout (see Figure 12.4b). Otherwise there are few footpaths apart from a narrow top-bottom footpath in the centre. The overall rate of burglary in this area is much lower than in the other areas.

There is a concentration of burglary in the less affluent top right sub-area, which is also the most spatially segregated area (see Figure 12.4c). This area is partly flatted, but no burglary was recorded in off-the-ground flats in the period of study. In the more spatially integrated affluent sub-areas, there are relatively few burglaries, but those that are there tend to occur either at the end of short cul-de-sacs, or from off the road spaces such as small cul-de-sac drives, and long driveways to individual houses or small groups.

There is a marked tendency for burglaries not to occur on the longer linear spaces, including long linear cul-de-sacs, provided they are constituted, though dwellings on corners of both through and non-through lines are sometimes vulnerable. Particularly striking is the absence of burglary on the spatially integrated (Figure 12.4c) and constituted (Figure 12.4d) through route from bottom right to top left, which has exceptionally good linear intervisibility and front entrances on both sides. In contrast, the parallel through road to the bottom, where dwellings are for the most part separated from the road by long driveways and high hedges, and which consequently has virtually no intervisibility of house entrances, has a good deal of burglary.

Statistically the constituted linear through-carriageway spaces (1 in 196 burgled) are seven times as safe as the average for the three areas. In contrast, points of entry off dead-end footpaths (1 in 14) and cul-de-sac driveways (1 in 12) are particularly vulnerable. Car crime is also concentrated in the spatially broken up top right sub-area, and elsewhere, is more dispersed than burglary, though low rates are still apparent on the linear integrated routes, and higher rates on more spatially segregated parts of the through movement system.

Town C (less affluent) – Figures 12.5a, b, c and d

This town has the highest rates of burglary and car crime for all three areas. Apart from the peripheral through streets, the layout is characterised by a tree like vehicular cul-de-sac system, linked by a complex system of footpaths. There is a very strong concentration of burglary in the bottom left. This is focused, for the most part, on two cul-de-sacs with very low-grade housing, but with access in most cases from rear footpaths (see Figure 12.5b), so most burglaries in these cul-de-sacs are assigned to the footpaths, not the cul-de-sacs themselves. There is also a school adjacent to this area.

There are two other concentrations in the top right and top left areas. Both of these are better-off residential areas, but have visually broken-up and spatially relatively segregated space (see Figure 12.5c). Little burglary occurs on the carriageways with continuous front facing entrances in these sub-areas, and there is relatively little on the constituted first lines from the through roads into the cul-de-sac system (see Figure 12.5d). There is a marked tendency for burglary to migrate to the deep parts of the cul-de-sacs, and for the point of entry to be at the front in these cases. Again the tendency for linear through carriageways (1 in 37) to be lower on burglary than cul-de-sac carriageways (1 in 24) is repeated here, although the through carriageways are less constituted.

Statistically, points of entry from footpaths (particularly dead-end footpaths) offer greatest vulnerability with more than 1 in 6 points of entry from dead end footpaths, and 1 in 14 from through footpaths, being burgled. Car crime shows a similar pattern, with very little on main linear through routes, and concentration in segregated parts accessible through footpaths. The studied crime record of these three areas was a one year period between 1994 and 1995. Interestingly, when the police were later revisited, the distribution patterns of burglary and car crime in Town B and Town C, for the year 1997, were found to be strikingly similar to the patterns for 1994-1995.

Outline of the analysis

How can what has been seen be pinned down with numbers? First, it should be borne in mind that the analysis below is not based on the dwelling. It is based on the point of entry and how it relates to the lines of sight and movement in the area as shown in our line (or axial) maps of the longest and fewest lines of sight in the public space system. This seems the most accurate procedure and the one that eliminates most ambiguity. It properly models the effective choices that burglars have in looking for points of entry to dwelling, and in actively seeking out (not simply by walking down streets) the parts of the public space system which most facilitate a break-in point to a targeted house.

The units of analysis in the data table, on which the analysis below is based, are therefore the lines of the axial maps to each of which the appropriate type and attribute characteristics and the appropriate number of points of entry are assigned. Simple rates per line cannot be used, because long lines will tend to have more dwellings and more points of entry. So, the sporadic nature of crime will tend to mean that the longer the line, the more the numbers of crimes will simply be divided by a larger number of dwellings, thus creating a potentially misleading statistical artefact.

The method used instead is to take each type of line, with whatever set of added properties is appropriate (including syntactic values), and total the number of points of entry for such lines. These are compared to the total numbers of say, burglaries, on those lines, by dividing the latter into the former. This gives a rate – one out of how many – for that type of line across all three areas. Using this simple technique, all of these variables and their interrelationships across all three areas, or within any of them where this would be illuminating, can be explored.

The rates for point of entry could, of course, then be converted to rates per dwelling to give an overall picture. However, there is a danger that this might be misleading. For example, saying that the burglary rate for dwelling on through roads was such and such, might give the impression that this was the case regardless of how many potential points of entry the dwelling had. The vulnerability of an individual dwelling requires the combination of all potential points of entry. In time it will be possible to make these calculations from known averages, but for present purposes it is more accurate, as well as clearer, to present the data in its most precise form for the understanding of real vulnerability: that is, in terms of points of entry.

Data analysis

The basic data is presented in Tables 12.2, 12.3, and 12.4. Table 12.2 tabulates the numbers (in bold) of lines of each type and with each attribute. The figures in parentheses after the number are the percentage of total lines, and the pair of figures in parentheses below refer to the total points of entry on such lines, and their percentage of the total for the three areas as a whole. It can be seen that about half the lines are carriageways, and half not, but that 73 per cent of the points of entry are on carriageways, and only 27 per cent are not.

These differences become more marked when through carriageways are distinguished from cul-de-sac carriageways. Through carriageways have 24 per cent of all points of entry, but have only nine per cent of the lines, while cul-de-sac carriageways have 48 per cent of the points of entry and 41 per cent of the lines. Non-carriageways have 50 per cent of the lines but only 27 per cent of the points of entry. For cul-de-sac driveways, 16 per cent of lines carry only four per cent of points of entry. Through footpaths with 23 per cent of lines take up 17 per cent of points of entry. Cul-de-sac front footpaths share 2.8 per cent of points of entry on 4.6 per cent of the lines and, finally, rear dead-end footpaths have four per cent of points of entry on seven per cent of lines.

The differences become more pronounced if the distinction between constituted (>75 per cent lined with visible front entrances on both sides) and unconstituted is taken into account. Constituted through lines (the most common type of urban space in traditional cities) account for only three per cent of the lines but nearly 11 per cent of the points of entry (nearly all front entrances). Constituted cul-de-sac carriageways account for ten per cent of the lines and 21 per cent of the total points of entry. Overall, the cul-de-sac complexes of layouts account for 91 per cent of lines but only 76 per cent of points of entry.

This data indicates very deep differences between the traditional street parts of the urban layouts and the parts that are essentially cul-de-sac complexes of one kind or another. In streets, the lines of sight are longer and potential movement is stronger. There

Table 12.2 Number of lines of each type and number of points of entry for each type: spatial types

	Constitutedness		Distributedness		Line neighbours		Total
	con	uncon	dis	non-dis	more	fewer	
all carriageways	105 (12%) (1799, 32%)	323 (38%) (2342, 41%)	228 (27%) (3029, 53%)	200 (23%) (1112, 19%)	152 (18%) (2981, 52%)	276 (32%) (1160, 20%)	428 (50%) (4141, 73%)
through carriageways	22 (3%) (608, 11%)	56 (7%) (768, 13%)	78 (9%) (1376, 24%)	0 (0%) (0, 0%)	33 (4%) (1060, 19%)	45 (5%) (316, 6%)	78 (9%) (1376, 24%)
cul-de-sac carriageways	83 (10%) (1191, 21%)	267 (31%) (1574, 28%)	150 (18%) (1653, 29%)	200 (23%) (1112, 19%)	139 (16%) (2020, 35%)	211 (25%) (745, 13%)	350 (41%) (2765, 48%)
all non-carriageways	3 (0.4%) (28, 0.5%)	423 (50%) (1535, 27%)	196 (23%) (947, 17%)	230 (27%) (616, 11%)	157 (18%) (1164, 20%)	269 (32%) (399, 7%)	426 (50%) (1563, 27%)
cul-de-sac driveways	0 (0%) (0, 0%)	132 (16%) (209, 3.7%)	0 (0%) (0, 0%)	132 (16%) (209, 3.7%)	57 (7%) (142, 2.5%)	75 (9%) (67, 1.2%)	132 (16%) (209, 3.7%)
through footpaths	0 (0%) (0, 0%)	196 (23%) (947, 17%)	196 (23%) (947, 17%)	0 (0%) (0, 0%)	87 (10%) (751, 13%)	109 (13%) (196, 4%)	196 (23%) (947, 17%)
cul-de-sac front footpaths	3 (0.35%) (28, 0.5%)	37 (4.3%) (134, 2.3%)	0 (0%) (0, 0%)	40 (4.6%) (162, 2.8%)	17 (2%) (125, 2.1%)	23 (2.6%) (37, 0.7%)	40 (4.6%) (162, 2.8%)
rear dead-end footpaths	0 (0%) (0, 0%)	58 (7%) (245, 4%)	0 (0%) (0, 0%)	58 (7%) (245, 4%)	31 (3.6%) (195, 3.4%)	27 (3.2%) (50, 0.9%)	58 (7%) (245, 4%)
all lines	108 (13%) (1827, 32%)	746 (87%) (3877, 68%)	424 (50%) (3976, 70%)	430 (50%) (1728, 30%)	290 (34%) (4242, 74%)	564 (66%) (1462, 26%)	854 (100%) (5704, 100%)

are more points of entry along the line and more of these are likely to be front entrances. All these factors are helpful in deterring crime, as can be seen from Table 12.3, which is the same as Table 12.2, but with the rates of burglary per point of entry inserted. Table 12.4 tabulates the burglary rates against syntactic measures of integration, indicating the strength of lines of sight and potential movement for each line in each area.

Table 12.3 Rate of burglary for each combination of spatial type and attributes: spatial types

	Constitutedness		Distributedness		Line neighbours		Total
	con	uncon	dis	non-dis	more	fewer	
all carriageways	1/51	1/33	1/47	1/27	1/52	1/24	1/39
through carriageways	1/304	1/48	1/76	–	1/88	1/53	1/76
cul-de-sac carriageways	1/36	1/29	1/35	1/27	1/38	1/21	1/31
all non-carriageways	0	1/14*	1/21	1/10	1/15	1/13	1/15
cul-de-sac driveways	–	1/11	–	1/11	1/16	1/7	1/11
through footpaths	–	1/21	1/21	–	1/20	1/22	1/21
cul-de-sac front footpaths	0	1/13*	–	1/16	1/21	1/9	1/16
rear dead-end footpaths	–	1/8	–	1/8	1/7	1/13	1/8
all lines	1/52	1/22	1/36	1/17	1/37	1/15	1/27

* There was no burglary on constituted cul-de-sac front footpaths, where there are only 28 points of entry in total.

Table 12.4 Rate of burglary for each combination of spatial type and syntactic property: spatial types

	Constitutedness		Distributedness		Line neighbours		Total
	con	uncon	dis	non-dis	more	fewer	
all carriageways	1/53	1/29	1/55	1/25	1/51	1/29	1/39
through carriageways	1/94	1/63	1/102	1/45	1/118	1/43	1/76
cul-de-sac carriageways	1/37	1/28	1/42	1/23	1/37	1/26	1/31
all non-carriageways	1/20	1/11	1/20	1/10	1/23	1/7	1/15
cul-de-sac driveways	1/13	1/9	1/13	1/10	1/30	1/9	1/11
through footpaths	1/27	1/17	1/20	1/22	1/22	1/17	1/21
cul-de-sac front footpaths	1/24	1/13	1/35	1/8	1/85	1/9	1/16
rear dead-end footpaths	1/16	1/5	1/20	1/5	0/46	1/6	1/8
all lines	1/41	1/18	1/39	1/17	1/39	1/16	1/27

The effects of individual factors

It is useful to review the tables by first considering the effects of one variable at a time, then looking at them in combination. Against a background average of burglary of 1 in 27 for points of entry for the three areas as a whole (which averages to about 1 in 17 for dwellings), following points can be made:

Differences by type of space

- dwellings are safer from burglary from points of entry on carriageways (1 in 39), whether through or cul-de-sac, than from points of entry on non-carriageways (1 in 15). Since these rates can be very simply multiplied, it can be said that points of entry from carriageways are nearly three time as safe as others

- dwellings are safer on through carriageways (1 in 76) than cul-de-sac carriageways (1 in 31). If cul-de-sac carriageways are limited to the pure type, those without connecting footpaths, the rate worsens slightly to 1 in 27

- points of entry on non-carriageways break down as: cul-de-sac drives (usually serving a small number of dwellings) 1 in 11; through footpaths 1 in 21; cul-de-sac front footpaths 1 in 16, and rear dead-end footpaths 1 in 8. All types of non-carriageways are therefore considerably more vulnerable than all types of carriageways.

Differences by attributes of space

Making the same analysis by attributes we find:

- constituted (more than 75 per cent continuous front entrances on both sides) spaces of all kinds (1 in 52) are safer than unconstituted spaces (1 in 22)

- distributed spaces (part of the pedestrian through movement system) at (1 in 36) are safer than those that are part of an overall pedestrian cul-de-sac complex (1 in 17)

- spaces with more than the average number of line neighbours (7), that is more than the average number of points of entry on your line (1 in 37), are safer than those with fewer (1 in 15).

Differences by syntactic measures of layout configuration

- more globally integrated spaces, that is those with better visual fields and movement potentials with respect to the area as a whole (1 in 41) are safer than those that are less globally integrated (1 in 18)

- more locally integrated spaces, that is those with better visual fields and potential movement with respect to their immediate surroundings (1 in 39), are safer than those that are less locally integrated (1 in 17)

- lines with more connections to other lines (1 in 39) are safer than lines with fewer connections (1 in 16).

Combinations of properties: through carriageways

However, when the types, attributes and syntactic measures are considered together, an even clearer picture emerges. If a start is made from through-carriageway lines (1 in 76), restricting them to the more integrated (the top 50 per cent), the rate improves significantly to 1 in 94. If the less integrated lines are taken (the lower 50 per cent), the rate is 1 in 63. If, however the least integrated quartile (lowest 25 per cent) is taken – the small number of through roads (18 lines in the whole sample) that are relatively segregated – then the rate is a good deal worse at 1 in 30. This is slightly worse than the rate for all cul-de-sac carriageways, which is 1 in 31. Thus, to get the benefit of through streets properties must be spatially integrated.

If the numbers of line neighbours is taken as the attribute, the rate improves to 1 in 88 for those with more than the average number of through carriageways (18), and worsens to 1 in 53 for those with fewer. With both more integration and more line neighbours, the rate improves to 1 in 98. Constitutedness is more difficult to combine with other variables, because there are only 22 constituted through lines in the three areas, with 608 points of entry at an average of 28 per line (against the overall average of seven per line) and all are relatively integrated. There are only two burglaries from these 608 points of entry, a rate of 1 in 304, in contrast with 1 in 48 for unconstituted lines.

There are too few cases to break this data down further. However, if more integrated and less integrated through carriageways are taken, then unconstitutedness is bad for both, with 1 in 58 for integrated unconstituted lines, and 1 in 42 for segregated unconstituted lines.

Combinations of properties: cul-de-sac carriageways

If cul-de-sac carriageways (1 in 31) are then taken and the attributes varied in the same way, the rate improves to 1 in 37 for the more integrated, while for more segregated it deteriorates to 1 in 28. This is a much smaller difference than for through carriageways, but is in the same direction. Similarly, if those with more than the average line neighbours for cul-de-sac carriageways (8) are taken, the rate improves to 1 in 38, decreasing to 1 in 21 for those with fewer. More integration and more line neighbours together take the rate to 1 in 43, worsening to 1 in 18 with less integration and fewer line neighbours.

Constituted cul-de-sac carriageways also improve to 1 in 36, while unconstituted ones worsen to 1 in 29. The rate for all three attributes taken together is 1 in 41. The effect of the attributes on cul-de-sac carriageways thus follows the direction of their effects on through carriageways, though with smaller differences.

This is not yet comparing like with like, of course, because the average integration and line neighbours for through carriageways is greater than for cul-de-sac carriageways. A more direct comparison can be made by setting the bands for the two variables between the same values. This means setting the through carriageways to the values of cul-de-sac carriageways, because if done the other way, there are not enough cases. The rate for through carriageways, which are more integrated and have more line neighbours than the average for cul-de-sac carriageways, is 1 in 84, compared to 1 in 43 for cul-de-sac carriageways. If constitutedness is added in, the rate improves to 1 in 300. If the influence of these variables is equalised, therefore, through carriageways are seen to be much safer than cul-de-sac carriageways.

Combinations of properties: pure cul-de-sac carriageways

If pure cul-de-sac carriageways are considered, that is, those without connecting footpaths, the rate is 1 in 27, compared with 1 in 35 for the impure ones. In other words, the expectation that pure cul-de-sacs will be safer than impure ones is not fulfilled. However, when the attributes are taken into account, pure cul-de-sacs become a great deal better than impure ones. More integration improves pure cul-de-sacs to 1 in 43, compared to 1 in 34 for impure. More line neighbours improves them to 1 in 46, compared to 1 in 35 for impure and constitutedness improves them to 1 in 51, against 1 in 31 for impure ones. If all three are taken into account there is only one burglary among 134 pure cases, in contrast to 1 in 33 for impure ones.

In other words, pure cul-de-sacs are in general not safer than those with through footpaths, but they do become so when they have greater integration, more line neighbours and are constituted. Even so, they are less good than through carriageways that also have these properties – though they are a good deal better than through carriageways that lack them.

What, then, produces the higher overall vulnerability of pure cul-de-sacs compared with impure ones? The answer is the lack of these vital attributes of good integration, good number of line neighbours and constitutedness. When pure cul-de-sacs are segregated, their rate worsens to 1 in 21, compared to 1 in 37 for impure. With fewer line neighbours the rate is even worse at 1 in 17, compared to 1 in 34 for impure.

Unconstituted pure cul-de-sacs have a rate of 1 in 22, compared with 1 in 40 for impure. Taking all three attributes together, the rate plummets to 1 in 17 for the pure cul-de-sacs, compared to 1 in 27 for the impure ones.

These are vital findings in two senses. First, it means that pure cul-de-sacs without connecting footpaths are not safe in themselves, but become safe when they have the attributes that also make through carriageways even safer. Conversely, they become highly vulnerable when they lack these attributes. Secondly, it means that impure cul-de-sacs, with connecting footpaths, are less badly affected by the lack of these attributes. This can be related to a further important detail in the data. If the most integrated quartile of through footpaths is taken, (those that are likely to have most visibility and most potential movement), then the burglary rate for points of entry off these is 1 in 49, in contrast to 1 in 18 for all other footpaths. This indicates that for a footpath to be relatively safe, it must be very integrated, presumably so that pedestrian movement can compensate for the lack of surveillance from vehicle related activity.

Car crime

Table 12.5 shows the effects of the main spatial types and attributes on car crime, confining the data to carriageways for obvious reasons. The figures show that rates of car crime respond to the main type and attribute variables in the same way as burglary, but that the differences are much more modest. However, there is an exception for the case of cul-de-sac carriageways where the relation between through and non-through shows a result contrary to that for burglary: there is less car crime on carriageways where there are no linking footpaths. This supports the idea that it is the easier targets from the linking footpaths that take burglary away from the carriageway parts of the cul-de-sac complex. In general, however, the fact that car crime varies with space in the same way as burglary, is striking, especially the positive joint effects of the combination of constitutedness and more integration. This suggests that, as with burglary, those committing car crime prefer to do so in spaces with poor visibility and little movement.

Table 12.5 Rate of car crime for each combination of spatial type, spatial attributes and syntactic property: spatial types

| | Constitutedness | | Distributedness | | Integration Rn | | Constituted | Total |
	con	uncon	dis	non-dis	more	less	+integrated	
through carriageways	1/30	1/17	1/21	---	1/23	1/20	1/34	1/21
cul-de-sac carriageways	1/17	1/12	1/12	1/19	1/14	1/14	1/17	1/14
cul-de-sac driveways	---	1/13	---	1/13	1/15	1/11	---	1/13

Note: There are a few car crimes which occured in non-carriageways, but they are too few to be statistically significant.

Relation to the British Crime Survey: effects of types of dwelling

The 1999 Home Office Statistical Bulletin, based on the BCS, shows that if you ignore social, locational and other ambient factors, flats seem to be the most vulnerable type of dwelling, followed by terraced houses (Budd, 1999). However, both are more likely to be in inner-city areas where crime rates are higher and people are poorer. When these factors are taken out, and the data analysed so that households are identical in all respects, apart from living in a different dwelling type, then the results are the opposite. Flats are safest, followed by mid-terraces, then corner terraces, then semi-detached houses and, finally, detached houses (ibid).

How does this square with the data here? If each point of entry is assigned to the category of house type to which it belongs, the crime rates for types are strikingly similar to the Home Office figures. Points of entry on detached houses are the most vulnerable at 1 in 22. Then come semi-detached at 1 in 25, then corner terraces at 1 in 31, mid-terraces at 1 in 40 and flats at ground level at 1 in 34. In the data here, only ground level flats were taken into account as only they have points of entry at ground level, and there were no recorded burglaries above ground level in the period of the sample. Evidently, when all flats are taken into account, they will be the safest category by a good margin.

Are these variables then more important than the ones discussed above? There is a simple way to test this. The house types must be considered separately to see how far the patterns found for all types taken together are reproduced for each type on its own. In all key cases the results are reproduced.

For example, points of entry in detached houses have a 1 in 22 chance of being burgled, but if they are in a more integrated location it becomes 1 in 45. If they are on a through road it is 1 in 56 and if they are on integrated through roads, the rate improves even further to 1 in 104. If they are on through carriageways, with more line neighbours, the rate is 1 in 101 and for constituted through carriageways it is 1 in 115, so their positive influence can be noticed on the house type.

For semi-detached houses the base rate is 1 in 25. When semi-detached houses are located on more integrated roads, the rate improves to 1 in 32, for a through road it improves further to 1 in 72 and for integrated through roads the rate is 1 in 120. The effect of more line neighbours is noticeable in the rate of 1 in 111 and constituted through roads also do better with 1 in 87.

For terraced houses the base rate is 1 in 37 (1 in 40 for non-corner), for integrated locations it is 1 in 94, for through roads it is 1 in 81 and for integrated through roads it is 1 in 80 (1 in 84 for non-corner). Terrace houses on through carriageways with more line neighbours have a rate of 1 in 77, whereas for constituted through roads the rate is 0 in 399 (that is, no burglary).

Flats have a base rate of 1 in 34, more integrated roads improve this rate to 1 in 60 and through roads have no burglary at all with a rate of 0 in 77. Again integrated through roads have a rate of 0 in 73, through roads with more line neighbours stand at 0 in 68 and for constituted through roads the rate is 0 in 7. Obviously the last figures are based on small numbers and should therefore be treated carefully.

The worst case scenario is for detached houses on corners (1 in 18), worsening to 1 in 10 if they are spatially segregated (and 1 in 3 on a cul-de-sac drives). This improves to 1 in 31 on more integrated lines, 1 in 33 on through roads and 1 in 103 for integrated through roads. Detached, non-corner houses have a base rate of 1 in 27, which improves to 1 in 151 for through roads (only one case). On integrated roads the rate is 1 in 82 and 0 in 103 for integrated through roads. Some of the figures in these statistics are very small, but they do consistently repeat the same pattern for each house type as for the sample as a whole.

The fact that the main results of the survey presented here are preserved for each different house type, while at the same time being similar to the BCS figures where they are comparable, shows that the spatial types, spatial attributes and syntactic variables do exercise an influence on burglary, which is independent of house type.

Relation to British Crime Survey: road types

The Home Office Statistical Bulletin also has data from the BCS on road types suggesting that cul-de-sacs (4.3 per cent) are safer from burglary than either main roads (6.6 per cent) or side roads (6.2 per cent). This data is raw in the sense that, as with the raw data on houses types, social, locational and other ambient factors have not been taken into account. As was seen when these factors were taken into account through multivariate analysis of house type, the results were reversed: flats and terraced houses, which in the raw data had appeared the most at risk, were in fact the safest.

Unfortunately, the Home Office team were unable to carry out the same multivariate analysis on road types as on house types, because they had only one year of data rather than two, and because the data itself is drawn from a complex question in the BCS with many possible ambiguities. It is intended that more accurate data will be sought in the next survey.

Would the cul-de-sac finding in the raw data of the BCS then be weakened, or even reversed, under the multivariate analysis that took out the influence of economic, locational and social factors? On the face of it, it seems possible and even likely. The overall burglary rate for inner-city areas is 10.3 per cent, as against 6.3 for urban areas and 3.9 for rural. Similarly, owner-occupiers (5.3 per cent) with good incomes (5.6 per cent) are much less likely to be burgled than social renters (8.9 per cent) on low incomes (8 per cent). Since cul-de-sacs with well-off owner-occupiers are more common in outer areas, and through streets with tenants on lower incomes are more often found in inner-city areas, it seems likely that multivariate analysis would at least considerably diminish the apparent advantage of cul-de-sacs. It might possibly go so far as to bring the findings into line with those outlined in this chapter.

However, the difference in the raw data in favour of cul-de-sacs is quite substantial, and on present evidence, it is not possible to be confident of the result either way. On present evidence it would be as much an error to assume the findings would be reversed, as it would be to assume that it would survive. Pending further evidence, the result of the present study is the best data to hand, although it is of course possible that the areas studied are uncharacteristic and that further studies would show different results.

What is persuasive about the present data is the consistency with which type and attribute variables behave across very heterogeneous groups of study areas. Also, it should not be forgotten that the data in the present study is based on an accurate reconstruction of points of access from public space. Data based on addresses will not be sensitive to this critical aspect, and may tell a somewhat different story.

Discussion

To sum up the results of the studies, the public spaces from which burglary is least likely to occur are those on through carriageways, with good movement potential and visual links, and with a good number of line neighbours opening on to both sides of the carriageway. Those from which you are most likely to be burgled are rear dead-end footpaths with little movement and visibility and few line neighbours. All other types of space lie in between these extremes, with their vulnerability determined largely by their score on these variables. House types are important, but more so in association with these other variables, on which road types are also highly dependent.

More generally, positive features of layouts are linear spaces forming parts of integrated through networks, with good numbers of continuous (and contiguous) line neighbours on both sides giving high intervisibility. Negative features are visually and permeably broken-up spaces, poor movement, few line neighbours, poor intervisibility and spaces without front entrances.

The news is not all bad for cul-de-sacs. Where they are linear carriageways, attached to and visible from linear streets with continuous front entrances, and have enough line neighbours, they can do quite well. However, burglars tend to avoid dwellings on the first line into the cul-de-sac off the through street, and seek out those in the deeper, more segregated parts.

It cannot simply be concluded that through streets are better than cul-de-sacs. They can be, but it depends on all the other properties being present. In Town B, for example, there are two parallel through roads adjacent to each other, one with very high intervisibility of dwelling entrances, the other with entrance intervisibility broken up by long driveways with high hedges, concealed entrances, and cul-de-sac drives giving secluded access to a few dwellings. The former has virtually no crime, while the latter is a veritable crime hot line. It should be expected, then, that there are areas where linear, well-constituted, shallow cul-de-sacs will be safer than poorly constituted, visually broken up and spatially segregated through spaces. It all depends on how the local menu of layout targets is put together. Criminals will always select the most vulnerable locations on offer.

These results do, however, clearly suggest that the built-in security advantage that many have argued belongs to the cul-de-sac, in fact belongs to the street. A street has greater potential for movement, greater intervisibility for higher numbers of line neighbours, and the natural protection from the rear that a street layout more easily provides. It would be interesting to compare the results with the findings of Poyner and Webb on crime distribution in north-east Northampton (Poyner and Webb, 1991). They may well be compatible, for the most part, although these authors did not have access to exact break-in point data or deal with the detailed level of spatial layout.

Most strikingly, the results, preliminary as they are, suggest that the most common type of space in historic cities, ever since we began to build them, scores best on security from crime, provided it has all the right attributes. These are, of course, the linear spaces with continuous entrances on both sides, forming part of a network in which all spaces have some degree of movement, and in which through movement mingles with movement to and from the buildings. In other words, it is the common or garden street.

Other recent evidence (Hillier, 1996) also suggests that street networks may work well socially, in ways that did not come to light before computers allowed analysis of street networks in order to understand their structure and function. It would therefore seem to be time to rethink some of our most basic ideas about layout. However, about eight to ten further studies would be needed to be sure that the patterns found here are general.

One reason further studies are needed is that the present results show that spatial factors seem to affect each other in layouts, in that burglars select the most vulnerable spaces from the menu on offer in an area. For example, in one of the areas, linear cul-de-sacs seem to be safer because short cul-de-sac drives with good concealment offer preferred targets. How different types of space interact in different types of layout should be a key theme in future studies, and an important aspect of this would be a more detailed understanding of the factors that can make through streets vulnerable.

Design guidance

Much of current design guidance is based on solid police experience and gives correct emphasis to the central role of natural visibility and surveillance. But from this sound foundation, it then tends to underestimate the advantages of the street from this point of view and, at the same time, overestimate the potential surveillance from the dwelling of small groups of neighbours grouped around a vehicular turning circle. The evidence suggests that these deep, non-linear spaces at the ends of cul-de-sacs can be more vulnerable than others, including the linear spaces in cul-de-sacs which lead to them.

In preferring small numbers of neighbours and non-linear spaces, current design guidance seems to be less influenced by direct police experience than by the architectural ideology of territoriality and defensible space. This endorses the break-up of space into small inward looking fragments with few dwellings, virtually no movement and a tendency to generate vulnerability from the rear as well as from the front. Neither of these concepts has a credible scientific foundation and their social benefits seems largely conjectural. If, one might ask, the hierarchical cul-de-sac organisation of space advocated as defensible space (Newman, 1972) is basic to human kind, then why are most historic cities based on an entirely different form of spatial organisation: the street network.

In the present state of knowledge, design guidance should seek to combine hard research results with the excellent fund of police experience that now exists, and avoid universal nostrums based on social and spatial ideologies that are rapidly losing scientific credibility. It is clear that those who endorse the idea of defensible space perceive the local residents in an identified small territory as being the key factor for crime prevention. The evidence here suggests that this is at best ineffectual, at worst counterproductive. It would be more sensible and effective to try to understand which spatial features the offenders look for in selecting their targets for committing crimes, and to base design guidance on these factors, rather than the more nebulous communitarian hopes of defensible space and territoriality.

On current layout practice, the view here is that the highway engineer's cul-de-sac complex, usually requiring footpath interconnections to create reasonable pedestrian accessibility, leads to exactly the kind of break-up of space, lack of everyday movement and limited intervisibility of dwellings, that tends to increase vulnerability. Layouts should in general be based on networks of interconnected streets or avenues, formed by outward facing blocks (to protect the rear of as many dwellings as possible), with key alignments continuing into and from neighbouring areas to ensure exchange of movement. Within this overall discipline, a smaller number of linear cul-de-sacs with direct visibility from the street could be included where this would add desirable variety to the available spaces. Work is underway with a number of designers, developers and local authorities to design and evaluate possible layouts using space syntax software and, where appropriate, observation techniques.

Figures 12.1-12.5

for Chapter 12
Crime and urban layout: the need for evidence
by Bill Hillier and Simon Shu

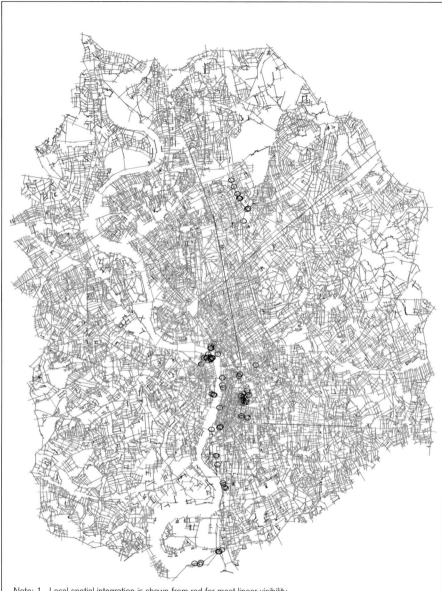

Note: 1   Local spatial integration is shown from red for most linear visibility
            and potential movement through to blue for least.

        2   ○ marks an unlinked junction

Figure 12.1 London local integration – axial map, radius 3

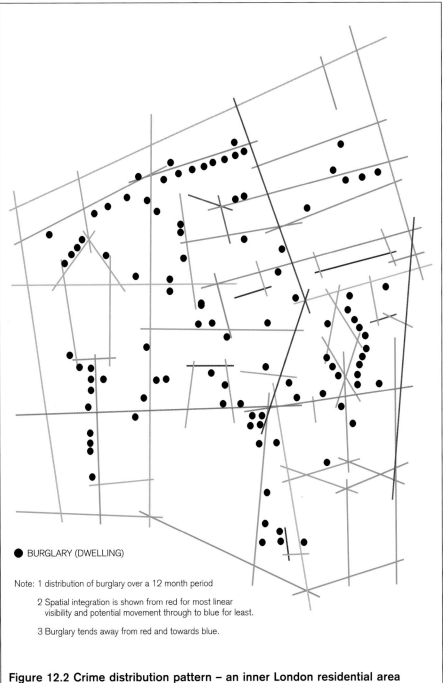

● BURGLARY (DWELLING)

Note: 1 distribution of burglary over a 12 month period

2 Spatial integration is shown from red for most linear
visibility and potential movement through to blue for least.

3 Burglary tends away from red and towards blue.

Figure 12.2 Crime distribution pattern – an inner London residential area

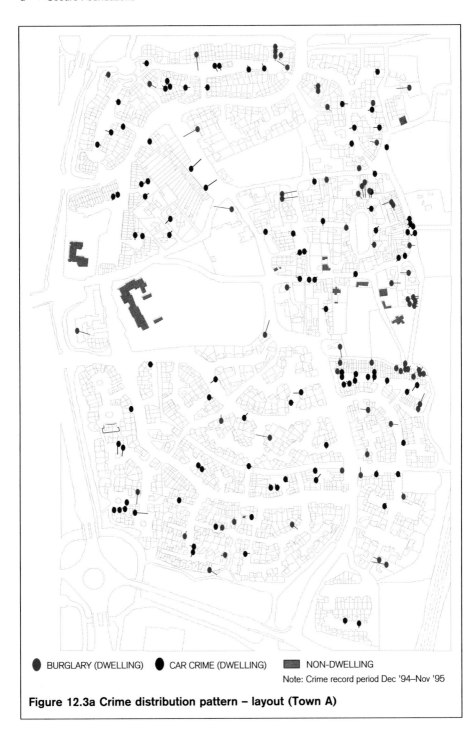

BURGLARY (DWELLING)   CAR CRIME (DWELLING)   NON-DWELLING

Note: Crime record period Dec '94–Nov '95

Figure 12.3a Crime distribution pattern – layout (Town A)

FOOTPATH

GREEN AREA

BURGLARY (DWELLING)

CAR CRIME (DWELLING)

Note: Crime period Dec '94–Nov '95

Figure 12.3b Crime distribution pattern – layout and footpaths (Town A)

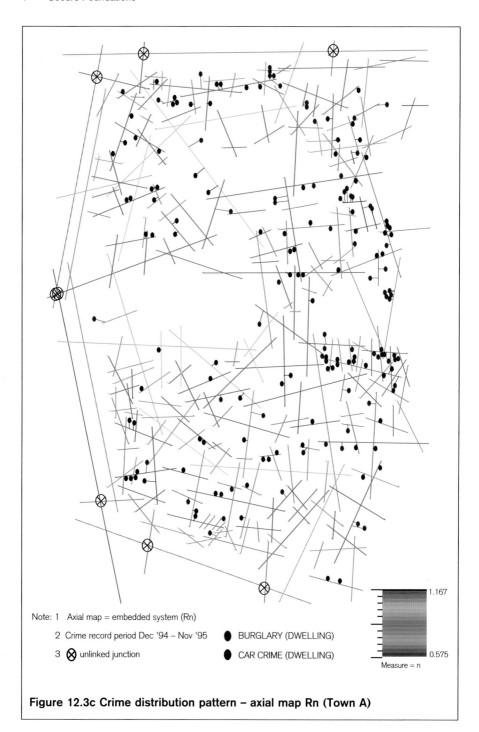

Note: 1 Axial map = embedded system (Rn)

2 Crime record period Dec '94 – Nov '95   ● BURGLARY (DWELLING)

3 ⊗ unlinked junction   ● CAR CRIME (DWELLING)

1.167

0.575

Measure = n

Figure 12.3c Crime distribution pattern – axial map Rn (Town A)

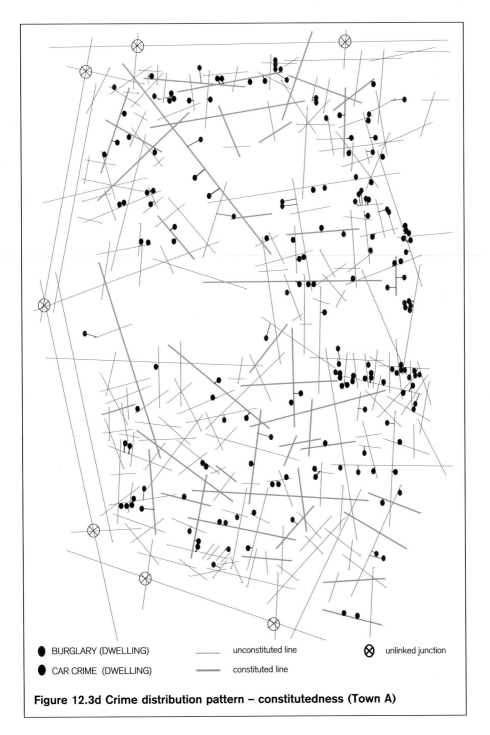

BURGLARY (DWELLING)   unconstituted line   ⊗ unlinked junction

CAR CRIME (DWELLING)   constituted line

Figure 12.3d Crime distribution pattern – constitutedness (Town A)

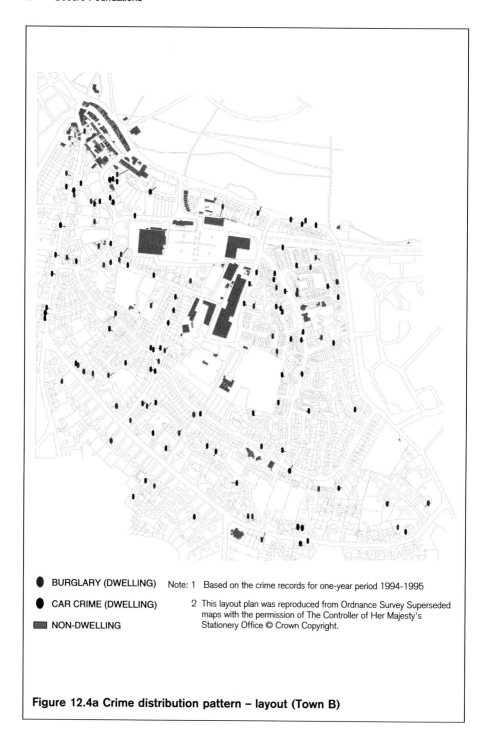

BURGLARY (DWELLING)   Note: 1 Based on the crime records for one-year period 1994-1995

CAR CRIME (DWELLING)   2 This layout plan was reproduced from Ordnance Survey Superseded
                                 maps with the permission of The Controller of Her Majesty's
NON-DWELLING   Stationery Office © Crown Copyright.

Figure 12.4a Crime distribution pattern – layout (Town B)

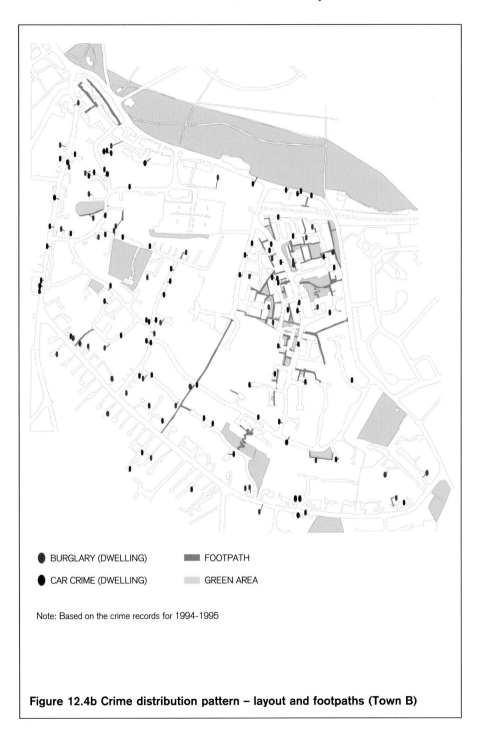

BURGLARY (DWELLING)   FOOTPATH

CAR CRIME (DWELLING)   GREEN AREA

Note: Based on the crime records for 1994-1995

Figure 12.4b Crime distribution pattern – layout and footpaths (Town B)

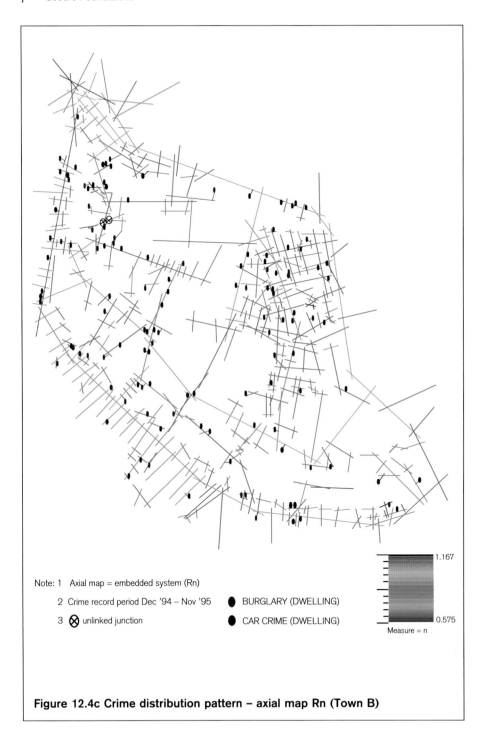

Note: 1 Axial map = embedded system (Rn)

2 Crime record period Dec '94 – Nov '95   ● BURGLARY (DWELLING)

3 ⊗ unlinked junction   ● CAR CRIME (DWELLING)

1.167

0.575

Measure = n

Figure 12.4c Crime distribution pattern – axial map Rn (Town B)

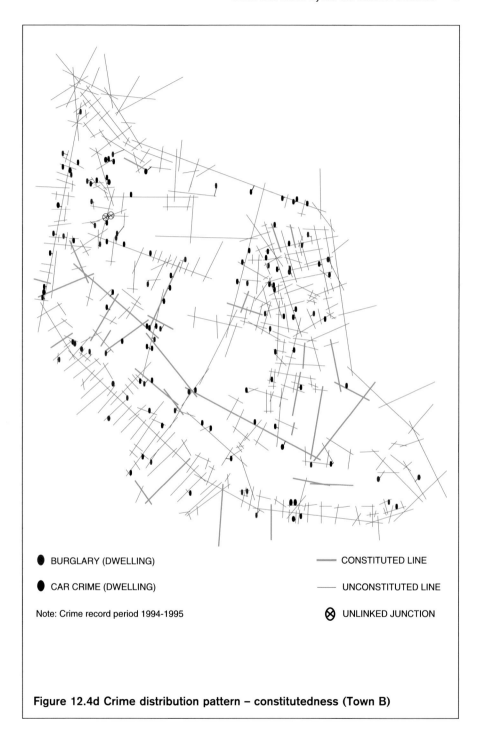

BURGLARY (DWELLING)

CAR CRIME (DWELLING)

Note: Crime record period 1994-1995

CONSTITUTED LINE

UNCONSTITUTED LINE

UNLINKED JUNCTION

Figure 12.4d Crime distribution pattern – constitutedness (Town B)

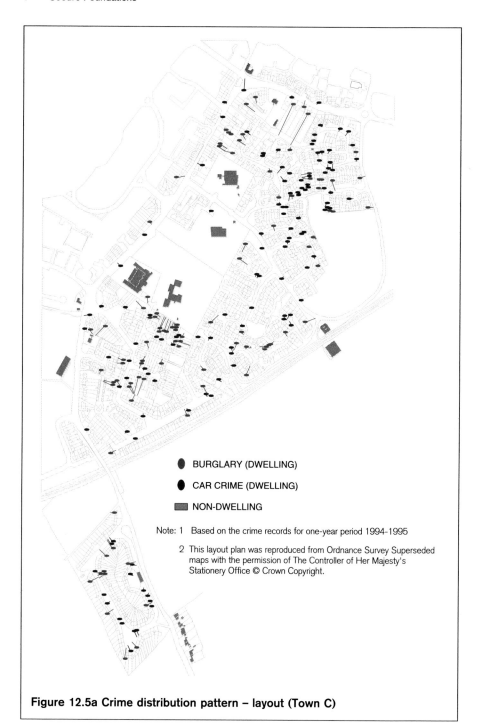

BURGLARY (DWELLING)

CAR CRIME (DWELLING)

NON-DWELLING

Note: 1   Based on the crime records for one-year period 1994-1995

2   This layout plan was reproduced from Ordnance Survey Superseded maps with the permission of The Controller of Her Majesty's Stationery Office © Crown Copyright.

Figure 12.5a Crime distribution pattern – layout (Town C)

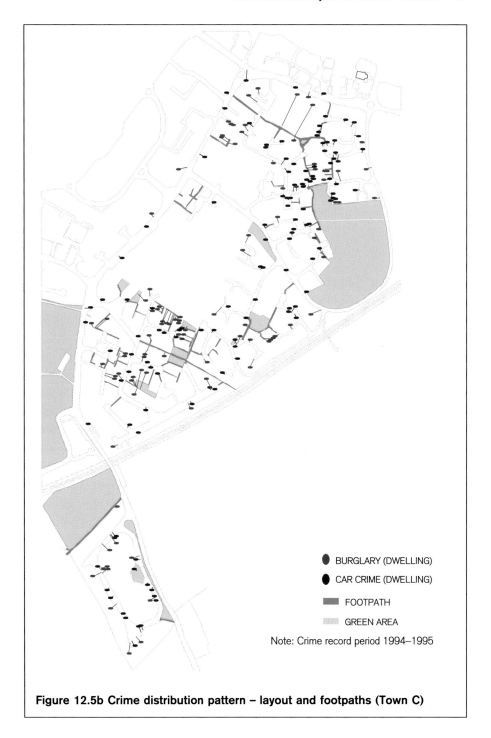

BURGLARY (DWELLING)

CAR CRIME (DWELLING)

FOOTPATH

GREEN AREA

Note: Crime record period 1994–1995

Figure 12.5b Crime distribution pattern – layout and footpaths (Town C)

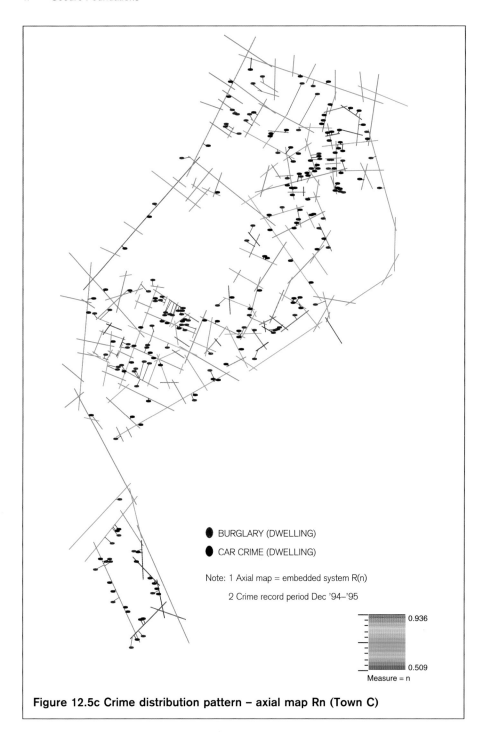

Figure 12.5c Crime distribution pattern – axial map Rn (Town C)

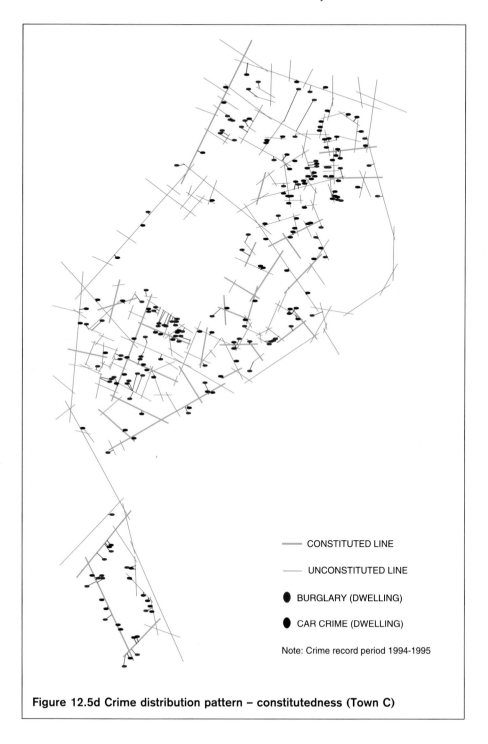

CONSTITUTED LINE

UNCONSTITUTED LINE

BURGLARY (DWELLING)

CAR CRIME (DWELLING)

Note: Crime record period 1994-1995

Figure 12.5d Crime distribution pattern – constitutedness (Town C)

this page intentionally left blank

Finally

Two points need to be reinforced. First, more research is needed. Although existing data is sufficient to give a plausible model of layout principles for minimising vulnerability, this model must be regarded as provisional, and treated with caution. Spatial properties interact with each other, and not enough is known about these interactions yet to be sure how each aspect of an overall design will work in different spatial circumstances. For example, although overall cul-de-sacs are in general less good than through roads, and in some circumstances much less good, there do seem to be circumstances – internal linearity, protection by a constituted linear through road – when certain kinds of cul-de-sacs can perform well. This will not be a certainty until more is known about the interaction of factors. It is vital that these interactions be tested on a wider range of studies. In particular, how far one vulnerable layout feature affects others by providing preferred targets within an area, must be looked at.

Second, how vulnerability factors interact with all the other consequences of residential layout (formation of communities) must be studied. In the past, the preference for cul-de-sac design against crime has been supported by the idea that cul-de-sacs are socially preferable because they lead to the creation of small, self-identifying communities. The fear is that by moving to more street-oriented design, these local pockets of social cohesion would be put at risk. This is an unreal fear, and a broader social morality for residential layout could be suggested: the problem with cul-de-sac design as a general principle is that it implies – and in fact directly leads to – the impoverishment of the public realm (which is essentially the system of through streets). If too few people occupy the public realm, then it becomes less secure. It has already been seen that, from the point of view of crime, the ideas that through roads are less safe than cul-de-sacs is for the most part false. There are no such benefits.

A new moral model for residential design is thus proposed: each of us has a right to privacy, but also an obligation to the public realm, just as each of us has the right to resources for one's own needs, and the obligation to pay taxes for the public good. In a street form, privacy comes with the dwelling, and the responsibility for the public realm comes from the relation of the dwelling to the street. By simply living on public streets, we help to make them safe. To the extent that greater collective privacy is sought for small groups of neighbours, by distancing them from the public realm through cul-de-sacs, then the narrower the community on behalf of whom public spatial responsibility is exercised. By encouraging street-based residential design, the contribution of individuals to the safety and animation of the public realm will be maximised, without, as has been shown, any penalty at all, either for security or, it is conjectured, privacy.

References

Budd T (1999) *Burglary of Domestic Dwellings Findings from the British Crime Survey* Home Office Statistical Bulletin, 1999:4, London: Home Office

Coleman A (1985) *Utopia on Trial* London: Hilary Shipman

Hillier B and Hanson J (1984) *The Social Logic of Space* Cambridge: Cambridge University Press

Hanson J and Hillier B (1987) 'The architecture of community' in *Architecture and Behaviour* Special Issue on the work of the Unit for Architectural Studies, Bartlett School of Architecture and Planning, University College London

Hillier B (1988) 'Against Enclosure' in Teymour N, Markus T and Wooley T (eds) *Rehumanizing Housing* London: Butterworths

Hillier B (1996) *Space is the Machine* Cambridge: Cambridge University Press

Newman O (1972) *Defensible Space* London: Architectural Press

Poyner B and Webb B (1991) *Crime Free Housing* Oxford: Butterworth Architecture

IV: Beyond the year 2000

13. Hot products: a new focus for crime prevention
Ronald V Clarke

Focusing resources where they are most needed – 'Getting the grease to the squeak' – is a widely accepted goal of crime prevention policy (Hough and Tilley, 1998). To assist this goal, criminologists have coined two important concepts: hot spots and repeat victimisation. The former refers to the concentration of crime at particular places (Sherman *et al*, 1989) and the latter to its concentration on particular victims, whether individuals, businesses or organisations (Farrell and Pease, 1993). These concepts have stimulated new research into the situational conditions giving rise to crime concentrations. They have also helped to shape interventions designed to reduce these concentrations and, ultimately, the overall level of crime.

A recent Home Office publication (Clarke, 1999) argued that crime is concentrated in a third important way, on hot products, the consumer items preferred by thieves. It is well known, for example, that residential burglars are likely to steal cash, jewellery and electronic goods, such as TVs and videos (or VCRs), while leaving behind a host of other items. The reasons for this seem obvious – the items stolen are portable and valuable – but rather little is known about how the burglar disposes of this property, the prices obtained and the goods or services acquired with the proceeds, all of which may hold lessons for prevention. Little is also known about what is stolen in many other kinds of theft, including commercial burglaries, shoplifting from various stores, truck hijackings, theft of livestock, art theft, construction site theft, and so forth.

More information about hot products would help businesses protect themselves from theft and would help the police in advising them how to do this. It would help governments in persuading industry to find ways to avoid the crime waves sometimes generated by new products. It would help consumers avoid purchasing items (such as particular models of car) that put them at risk of theft, and it may lead them to demand greater built-in security. Finally, improved understanding of hot products would assist police in thinking about ways to intervene effectively in markets for stolen goods.

Besides reviewing what is known about hot products, this chapter will discuss some questions arising from the review that have implications for criminological understanding and for preventive policy.

What we know about hot products

The review of hot products for the Home Office (Clarke, 1999) concentrated on five principal categories of theft for which good data existed. These were shoplifting, residential burglary, theft from cars, theft of cars and theft of commercial vehicles. Though few in number, these categories are important and varied enough to provide a basis for generalising about products attractive to thieves. The review resulted in the following conclusions:

1.   Cash is the ultimate hot product. Marcus Felson has called it 'the mother's milk of crime' (Felson, 1998). It helps determine the distribution of many kinds of theft, including commercial robberies, muggings, burglaries and thefts from ticket machines and public phone boxes. The British Crime Survey shows that in thefts involving personal possessions (including household burglary, theft of/from private motor vehicles, bicycle theft, theft from the person and street robbery) cash is taken more frequently than anything else (see Table 13.1). It is easy to see why this should be so. Unless bank notes are marked, or their serial numbers recorded, cash is anonymous and almost impossible to identify as stolen. It is light and easy to conceal and, unless in large notes or low-value coins, it can be immediately used by the thief.

Table 13.1 Items stolen in all incidents involving theft of personal property, British Crime Survey 1996 and 1998

	Percentage of incidents*	
	1996	1998
Cash	18.8	20.4
Vehicle parts (not radio)	11.3	13.7
Clothes	9.7	10.6
Tools	9.5	9.8
Purse/wallet	9.4	11.4
Bicycle	7.3	7.0
Car radio	6.2	6.2
Credit card	6.1	7.3
Stereo/hi-fi	5.8	5.4
Jewellery	4.7	4.2
Car/van	4.5	3.6
Briefcase or bag	4.2	3.8
Documents	3.5	3.0
Video/camcorder	3.0	3.1
Television	2.2	1.5
Cheque book	2.0	2.2
Camera	1.9	1.6
Computer equipment	1.5	1.3
Mobile phone	1.0	2.1
Motorbike/moped/scooter	0.7	0.6
Other	36.3	31.7
Number of thefts (unweighted)	5291	4191

*Multiple responses permitted. Excludes 'don't knows'

Source: Clarke (1999)

2.   Apart from cash, the goods targeted for theft depend upon the nature of the offence. Those targeted in residential burglaries – jewellery, videos, cash, stereos and televisions – have already been mentioned (Budd, 1999). In

Table 13.2 Items most often stolen by apprehended shoplifters, US 1995

	Chains	Stores	Apprehended shoplifters	Most stolen items
Book shops	1	111	678	Cassette tapes; magazines
Department stores	12	641	10,995	Clothing; shirts; jeans Hilfiger and Polo items
Discount stores	12	5,677	120,415	Clothing; undergarments; CDs
Drug Stores/pharmacies	16	1,517	3,060	Non-prescription medicines cosmetics; cigarettes; batteries birth control
Fashion merchandise stores	13	2,216	3,120	Sneakers
General merchandise stores	8	2,447	300	'Costume' earrings
Groceries/supermarkets/ convenience stores	49	4,990	25,532	Non-prescription medicines cosmetics; cigarettes video cassettes
Hardware/DIY stores	15	755	1,402	Hand tools
Recorded music shops	3	284	433	CDs
Sporting goods stores	4	241	4,047	Nike shoes
Theme park shops	8	152	1,881	Jewellery; key chains
Toy shops	3	408	603	Action figures; children's apparel

Source: 1995 National Retail Security Survey (Hayes, 1997)

shoplifting, the items at risk depend on the store. Thus, book shops are most likely to lose magazines and cassette tapes while groceries, supermarkets and convenience stores are likely to lose cigarettes, video tapes, cosmetics and non-prescription medicines (see Table 13.2).

3.   Despite this dependence on the setting, there is some cross-setting consistency. For example, both residential and commercial burglars often target electronic goods such as videos. Data from the US shows that certain items are shoplifted wherever these are sold. These include cassettes, cigarettes, liquor, and fashion items such as Hilfiger jeans and Nike sneakers (see Hayes, 1997). In many cases, these items are pleasurable to own or use.

4.   Which cars are most likely to be stolen depends on the purposes of theft. A US study found, for example, that joyriders prefer sporty models, that thieves looking for cars to sell prefer expensive luxury models, and that those seeking components to sell prefer models with easily removable, good-quality radios (Clarke and Harris, 1992).

5.   Body-type helps determine which lorries and commercial vehicles are stolen (Brown, 1995 and Brown and Saliba, 1998). Vehicles used by the construction industry, such as tippers and drop-side lorries, seem particularly at risk (Table 13.3 overleaf). Among heavy goods vehicles (HGVs), the highest risk was for livestock carriers, many of which are private horseboxes. Certain makes of vehicle, particularly Bedfords, were also at high risk of theft. The facts about

Table 13.3 Heavy Goods Vehicles stolen, England and Wales, 1994

Body type	Number stolen	% of incidents	Theft rate per 1,000 registered
Tipper	920	30.2	16
Drop-side lorry	582	19.1	27
Flat-bed lorry	565	18.5	14
Goods lorry	349	11.5	9
Livestock carrier	156	5.1	56
Insulated van	88	2.9	7
Skip loader	86	2.8	13
Tanker	29	1.0	2
Bottle float	12	0.4	3
Refuse disposal	10	0.3	1
Other	248	8.1	1
Total	**3047**	**99.9**	**6**

Source: Brown (1995)

goods vehicles most at risk may be related to their marketability. For instance, there may be a thriving second-hand market in vehicles used by the construction industry because many small firms, operating with low profit margins, compete in that industry. This legitimate market would make it easier for thieves to sell vehicles they had stolen. Similar explanations can be provided for the high risk of theft for horseboxes (which may often be bought and sold second-hand) and Bedfords (which are older vehicles frequently dismantled for spare parts).

6.   In general, there is a strong, interdependent relationship between hot products and stolen goods markets.

Why hot products are craved by thieves

Few criminologists have attempted to develop theoretical understanding of the preferences of thieves. The best known effort is that of Cohen and Felson (1979) made twenty years ago in the course of their initial statement of routine activity theory. This theory holds that the occurrence of a predatory crime depends on the convergence of a likely offender with a suitable target in the absence of a capable guardian. Cohen and Felson defined suitable targets in terms of their value, inertia, visibility and accessibility, which they encapsulated in the acronym VIVA.

VIVA was described in a single paragraph and was never intended to be a definitive model of hot products. Rather, it was a first attempt to summarise the attributes of the broader class of targets of predatory crime. Had the authors focused on targets of theft, they might have produced a somewhat different model. Their determination to avoid motivational concepts also resulted in their neglect of more subjective elements of target choice, which would be given a greater role today, particularly in the more recently developed rational choice perspective on crime. Finally, they seem to have paid more attention to the actual commission of crime than to the equally important stages of (i) contemplating crime and, (ii) concealing or disposing of goods afterwards.

These theoretical limitations, together with the fact that VIVA was formulated before much research on hot products was available, suggest that a more adequate model of target suitability could be developed. In the Home Office review, CRAVED was offered as the model that identifies six key attributes of hot products. Goods falling into this category are generally: concealable, removable, available, valuable, enjoyable and disposable.

Available

Availability is a necessary condition of being hot. This relationship can appear at the macro (or societal) level in mini theft waves resulting from the introduction of some new attractive product, such as the mobile phone, which quickly establishes its own illegal market. At the meso (or neighborhood) level, availability can show up in terms of the accessibility of hot products to thieves. For example, the fact that cars become at greater risk of theft as they age, may be due to the fact that they become increasingly likely to be owned by people living in poorer neighborhoods with less off-street parking and more offenders living nearby. At the micro (or situational) level, availability may show up in terms of the visibility of objects at the point of theft. This is why householders often conceal jewellery and cash in the hope that they will not be found by burglars. This definition of availability therefore encompasses two of the four components of VIVA (accessibility and visibility), but is broader than both.

Valuable

As VIVA recognises, thieves will generally choose the more expensive goods, particularly when they are stealing to sell. When stealing for their own use, other components of value become important. Thus, juvenile shoplifters may select goods that confer status among their peers, but which may not be expensive. Similarly, joyriders are more interested in a car's performance than its financial value. Two components of value, apart from monetary worth, merit separate treatment: the enjoyment of owning and using particular goods, and the ease or difficulty of selling them.

Enjoyable

Hot products tend to be enjoyable things to own or consume, such as liquor, tobacco and cassettes. Thus, residential burglars are more likely to take videos and televisions than equally valuable electronic goods, such as microwave ovens or food processors. This may reflect the pleasure-loving lifestyle of many thieves (and their customers). Burney's (1990) interview study with street robbers in Lambeth (cited in Barker *et al*, 1993) reported that the majority of the offenders interviewed said they robbed for money. 'By their accounts they spent the money on expensive clothes, particularly the expensive "Nike" trainers, luxuries and cannabis' (Barker *et al*, 1993).

Disposable

It may be obvious that the thief will tend to select things that will be easy to sell, but its importance for explaining crime has been neglected. Only recently, has systematic research begun on the intimate relationship between hot products and theft markets (Sutton, 1998). Research by Langworthy and LeBeau (1992) has shown that the creation of a fencing market can stimulate theft. They showed that when police set up a sting operation to buy stolen cars, this increased the rate of car theft in the immediate locality.

Removable

As VIVA recognised, products that are easily moved are more likely to be stolen, a fact well understood in security practice. How easily security can be defeated depends on the circumstances of theft. This point is substantiated by US data from the Food Marketing Institute (1997) showing differences in what is stolen from supermarkets by shoplifters and burglars. Both groups target cigarettes, liquor, medicines and beauty aids, but these are taken in much larger quantities by the burglars.

Concealable

Items are less likely to be stolen, if they (1) cannot be concealed on the person, (2) are difficult to hide afterwards, or (3) are easy to identify. This explains why we write our names in books and why cars must be registered and licensed. It also helps explain why car thieves do not generally steal Rolls Royces for their own use, but steal instead less valuable cars that merge into the surroundings. The same principle helps explain why cars stolen in the US, for export to Mexico, are mainly models that are also sold there legitimately (Field *et al*, 1991) – stolen cars do not then stick out like sore thumbs. In some cases, thefts may even be concealed from the owners of goods, as in the case of thefts of unmeasurable material like bricks and coal (Mars, 1983).

Some burning questions

By identifying what makes products hot, the CRAVED model helps us understand why opportunity-reducing measures do not inevitably lead to displacement (Clarke, 1997). Thieves have very particular reasons for their choices of goods to steal. Few products meet the necessary criteria, and those that do not are relatively safe from theft. The motivation for theft is not independent of the opportunities and incentives to steal. Rather, the existence of many attractive and relatively unprotected goods is likely to stimulate and encourage theft.

Displacement is just one of the questions relevant to preventive policy that is raised by the concept of hot products. Others will be addressed below.

Might hot products only be luke-warm?

Various studies have suggested that about five per cent of offenders may account for 50 per cent or more of crimes. Repeat victims (Farrell and Pease, 1993) and hot spots (Weisburd, 1997) have also been shown to account for very significant proportions of the total volume of crime. These statistics about crime concentrations reinforce the policy value of these concepts.

Because so many goods exist, it would be impossible to obtain similar measures of crime concentrations for the whole population of hot products. The best that might be done would be to compare BCS data on goods stolen in burglaries with detailed inventories of all household possessions, which would have to be developed specifically for this purpose. A particular advantage of this approach is that households probably contain a large proportion of the products available in modern societies.

More realistic, and possibly more useful, would be to measure theft concentrations for particular categories of goods. In doing so, it is not enough to show that theft risks are much higher for some items than for others. One must also know what proportion of the total volume of goods in the category being examined is represented by the hot products. For example, among HGVs, livestock carriers have by far the highest risk of theft at 56 per 1000 (see Table 13.3). However, because there are relatively few livestock carriers on the road, they only account for 5.1 per cent of total thefts. This means that, even if thefts of livestock carriers were entirely eliminated (which is unlikely), there would be only a small reduction in the overall numbers of HGVs stolen.

The data for HGVs may not provide a basis for generalising about theft concentrations, but it illustrates the kind of calculations that are needed for many other categories of goods. New opportunities to make these calculations will be provided by the electronic stock control and sales records systems being introduced in the retail industry. These will enable the contribution of each item of stock to a store's overall shoplifting problem to be calculated. In turn, this will permit estimates to be made of the concentration of theft on particular products. Until these estimates have been made, a question mark is likely to remain over the extent to which theft can be reduced by focusing interventions on hot products.

Does hotness wax and wane?

Gould (1969) and Felson (1997) have argued that the vulnerability of products to theft changes with their novelty and availability. For example, when products are newly introduced, they have fewer customers and are more awkward to use and to fence. They are therefore less likely to get stolen. Products in their growth periods are especially attractive for consumers and for thieves alike. When products have been sold for a long time, they are widely owned and the market for fencing is therefore restricted.

Further studies of these relationships are required, building on earlier studies by Gould and his colleagues of how the availability of motor vehicles influences car theft rates. Gloria Laycock (personal communication) has suggested that regular monitoring by the BCS of changes in the theft risk of particular products could be an avenue for such research. For example, the BCS data in Table 13.1 suggests (differences in numbers of thefts in the years concerned make this uncertain) that videos and hi-fi equipment were stolen at similar rates in 1996 and 1998, whereas thefts of TVs declined in 1998. Contrary to Felson's (1998) speculations about the consequences of an increasingly cashless society, thefts of money seem to have increased in 1998.

Research is also needed into the further possibility that theft risks change considerably as each hot product moves from factory to consumer. The steps include manufacture, shipping, warehousing, retailing, ownership and re-sale. Knowing the point of maximum vulnerability will help to focus prevention where it is most needed. For example, higher risks may make it more cost effective to protect videos in shops than in people's homes.

Is CRAVED too good to be true?

By being relevant to its subject matter, CRAVED is more than an acronym; in fact, it was deliberately contrived to be a mnemonic. This may have resulted either in the neglect of properties that did not assist the mnemonic, or in their mis-specification.

In fact, no simple acronym could capture all the properties of hot products. For example, library data suggests that thieves frequently steal books on sex, not just because these are enjoyable to read, but perhaps also because they are embarrassing to check out in the normal way. Similarly, data from US drug stores show that some products that may be embarrassing to purchase, such as remedies for piles, have high theft rates (Hayes, 1997 and Clarke, 1999). There are so few embarrassing products that the inclusion of this element in the acronym would not be warranted.

The only missing element with a strong claim to inclusion might be whether a product is fashionable. This is because juvenile thieves frequently steal fashionable items of clothing that confer status in their peer group. On the other hand, fashionable items are enjoyable to wear and seem to be adequately covered by this element.

Is disposability all that really matters?

CRAVED is a general model, intended to cover all hot products, though particular elements will sometimes be of special importance. In shoplifting, for example, goods must be concealable on the person, whereas this is not necessary for commercial burglary.

Could it be, however, that certain elements are more important overall than others? This question may be misconceived because the elements of CRAVED are interdependent, but it is tempting to argue that disposability may be the vital element of hot products. This is because thieves can steal only a certain number of goods for their own use. Just how many videos does anybody want? Keeping stolen property around the home is also risky and may lead to arrest. On the other hand, there are fewer limits to theft if the stolen property is sold.

Disposability may therefore be merely one of several factors in explaining which products are stolen, but it may be the principal factor in accounting for the volume of thefts.

Is fencing really the weak link?

Because disposability seems to be so important, researchers are now beginning to pay more attention to the markets for stolen goods (Sutton, 1998). According to a recent Australian study, burglars dispose of stolen goods quite quickly – usually within an hour – to support drug habits (Stevenson and Forsythe, 1998). These findings are consistent with those of other studies in suggesting that disrupting the market for stolen goods could yield substantial dividends. The trouble is that there are many kinds of markets and these often seem unorganised and fluid. Burglars often seem to fence or exchange goods with drug dealers. Some of them have relationships with particular neighbourhood fences, while others may sell goods in clubs and pubs or door-to-door. Occasionally they make use of jewellers, pawnbrokers, second-hand shops and even small ads in newspapers. Many burglars use all these methods.

It is therefore difficult to see how these various markets could be disrupted and, if they were, how this would achieve more than temporary or local reductions in crime. Sutton (1998) and Stevenson and Forsythe (1998) have suggested that efforts should be made to persuade people who buy stolen goods that they might be driving up their own risk of victimisation because they are encouraging burglary, but this is a complex message to deliver. In any case, most people will not forgo an immediate benefit in the hope of securing a less tangible one in the future.

This does not mean that attempts to intervene in stolen goods markets should be abandoned since these markets play a vital role in theft. Rather, it means that unwarranted optimism about the likely effects of these interventions should not result in the neglect of other ways to prevent theft of hot products.

Can manufacturers be held responsible for theft?

The most efficient way of reducing theft might be to build-in better protection of hot products at manufacture by such means as benefit denial (for example, security coding for all electronic goods) and enhanced property identification (such as parts marking for new vehicles). This suggestion has been resisted by manufacturers because, according to some commentators, they profit from the need of victims to replace stolen goods (see Karmen, 1981, for example). Instead, manufacturers have blamed the police and society for high levels of theft.

Governments have been reluctant to introduce legislation in this field and have generally relied on behind-the-scenes persuasion of manufacturers (Laycock and Tilley, 1995 and Laycock and Webb, this volume). Frustrated by continuing high levels of car theft, Home Office ministers have recently resorted to another tactic – publishing the Car Theft Index (Houghton, 1992 and Crime Prevention Agency, 1997), which shows the relative standing of all popular models. This has the dual function of informing car owners about their risks, and of shaming the manufacturers with the worst records.

This could be taken a step further by sending the manufacturers of the most stolen cars a notional bill for the costs of car theft (with copies to the news media). This would estimate how many thefts beyond the average were experienced by their models and would calculate the costs of dealing with these additional thefts in terms of police and court time. This might not be altogether fair since poor security is not the only reason for a high theft rate – some cars are also stolen because they are enjoyable to drive. On the other hand, perhaps these are the very cars that should be given additional protection.

Fair or not, these bills for car theft might grab the attention of manufacturers who have been too ready to deny responsibility for the problem. If they were to undergo a change of heart, they would need help in predicting which products needed additional protection (Ekblom, 1997 and Pease, 1998). This would require researchers to think thief, to learn more about *modus operandi*, and to undertake attack testing of new products. These are some of the objectives of 'From Crime to Design', a project currently being undertaken by the Home Office and Huddersfield University (see Rogerson *et al* Chapter 14 this volume).

Do retailers suffer knock-on costs from theft of hot products?

Theft of hot products may hurt retailers in three important ways, beyond the loss of the goods themselves. First, by reducing the stock of popular items, it might serve to divert customers who would have purchased other items during their visit to the shop. Second, it might give the shop an unsavoury reputation among ordinary customers who would begin to avoid it. Third, it might result in additional thefts of other goods by thieves who were attracted by the hot products. If any of these suggestions were borne out by research, retailers would have additional incentives to prevent the theft of hot products, beyond the obvious existing ones.

Some evidence in support of the last of these three suggestions already exists in the findings of a study undertaken in New Jersey. This showed that when a large electronics retailer provided additional protection in its storerooms for hot products (principally videos and video cameras), not only was theft of these items reduced, but also theft of all other goods (Masuda, 1992). Thus, the general result of protecting hot products may not usually be to displace the attention of thieves to some other product (which they probably know about already). Rather, it may be to discourage them from theft altogether.

Does an aversion to used goods protect Japan from theft?

Most used cars in Japan are sold overseas to Australia and other countries in Asia and the Pacific. This is because the Japanese do not generally buy second-hand goods. One reason for this, suggested by Marcus Felson (personal communication), is that their homes are small and they must limit the numbers of their personal possessions. There are no corresponding limits, however, on the quality of their possessions because Japan is (still) an affluent society. This helps to explain why the Japanese do not generally purchase used goods. In turn, it helps to explain Japan's low theft rates since much of the motivation for theft is removed. In other affluent societies, people have much more space in their homes to be filled by possessions. This encourages a market in used goods and perhaps also provides the cover for one in stolen goods.

Do hot products fuel drug use?

It is widely believed that much theft by shoplifters, burglars and robbers is undertaken to support drug habits. Indeed, the study mentioned above of the stolen goods market in New South Wales provides strong corroborative evidence of this fact (Stevenson and Forsythe, 1998). It showed that 83 per cent of the 256 burglars interviewed regularly spent money on drugs, with a median weekly expenditure of AUS$900. This was much higher than their income from legitimate sources (median of AUS$140 per week), but was easily covered by their weekly income of AUS$2000 from burglary.

The conclusion usually drawn from facts such as these is that reducing illegal drug use would prevent crime. However, the demand for drugs is not independent of price, and high levels of drug use may only be sustainable because thieves can easily get the money for drugs. Under this view, drug use is crucially dependent on the market for stolen goods – and the market thrives on hot products. Thus, by failing to protect their goods from theft, manufacturers of hot products may be contributing to drug addiction. Maybe this message would help get their attention!

Conclusions

Many of the speculations above go beyond the available evidence and may not be supported by further research. Yet, if they arouse interest in hot products they will have served my wider purpose, which is to bring criminological analysis to bear on preventive policy. Beyond that, the concept of hot products might have another value in helping to redress an imbalance of contemporary criminology. Despite recent changes, this still lavishes far more attention on the criminal than on the circumstances of the crime (Felson and Clarke, 1998). There is now greater understanding of the ways in which the opportunity structure for crime gives shape to crime, but still too little knowledge of its role in determining the volume of crime (to which hot products make a particular contribution).

Given that there are dozens, perhaps hundreds of different theories explaining the roots of delinquency, it is quite remarkable that until now VIVA has been the only attempt to provide a theory of target choice. Further academic work on this topic may assist criminology in becoming both more relevant to policy and more complete in its science.

References

Barker M, Geraghty J, Webb B and Key T (1993) *The Prevention of Street Robbery* Crime Prevention Unit Paper 44, London: Home Office

Brown R (1995) *The Nature and Extent of Heavy Goods Vehicle Theft* Crime Detection and Prevention Paper 66, London: Home Office

Brown R and Saliba J (1998) *The Nature and Extent of Light Commercial Vehicle Theft* Crime Detection and Prevention Paper 88, London: Home Office

Budd T (1999) *Burglary of Domestic Dwellings. Findings from the British Crime Survey* Home Office Statistical Bulletin 1999:4, London: Home Office

Clarke RV (ed)(1997) *Situational Crime Prevention: Successful Case Studies*, 2nd ed. Albany NY: Harrow and Heston

Clarke RV (1999) *Hot Products. Understanding, Anticipating and Reducing the Demand for Stolen Goods* Police Research Series Paper ??, London: Home Office

Clarke RV and Harris PM (1992) 'A rational choice perspective on the targets of autotheft' *Criminal Behaviour and Mental Health* 2

Cohen LE and Felson M (1979) 'Social change and crime rate trends: a routine activity approach' *American Sociological Review* 44

Crime Prevention Agency (1997) *Car Theft Index 1997* Communications Directorate, London: Home Office

Ekblom P (1997) 'Gearing up against crime: a dynamic framework to help designers keep up with the adaptive criminal in a changing world' *International Journal of Risk, Security and Crime Prevention* 2

Farrell G and Pease K (1993) *Once Bitten, Twice Bitten: Repeat Victimisation and its Implications for Crime Prevention* Crime Prevention Unit Paper 46, London: Home Office

Felson M (1997) 'Technology, business, and crime' In Felson M and Clarke RV (eds), *Business and Crime Prevention* Monsey, NY: Criminal Justice Press

Felson M (1998) *Crime and Everyday Life*, 2nd ed, Thousand Oaks, CA: Pine Forge Press

Felson M and Clarke RV (1998) *Opportunity Makes the Thief* Police Research Paper 98, London: Home Office

Field S, Clarke RV and Harris P (1992) 'The Mexican vehicle market and auto theft in border areas of the United States' *Security Journal* 2

Field S (1993) 'Crime prevention and the costs of auto theft: an economic analysis' in Clarke RV (ed) *Crime Prevention Studies 1* Monsey, NY: Criminal Justice Press

Food Marketing Institute (1997) *Security and Loss Prevention Issues Survey* Washington DC: Food Marketing Institute

Gould LC (1969) 'The changing structure of property crime in an affluent society' *Social Forces* 48

Hayes R (1997) 'Retail theft: an analysis of apprehended shoplifters' *Security Journal* 8

Hough M and Tilley N (1998) *Getting the Grease to the Squeak: Research Lessons for Crime Prevention* Crime Detection and Prevention Paper 85, London: Home Office

Houghton G (1992) *Car Theft in England and Wales: The Home Office Car Theft Index* Crime Prevention Unit Paper 33, London: Home Office

Karmen AA (1981) 'Auto theft and corporate irresponsibility' *Contemporary Crises* 5

Kock E, Kemp T and Rix B (1996) *Disrupting the Distribution of Stolen Electrical Goods* Crime Detection and Prevention Paper 69, London: Home Office

Langworthy R and LeBeau J (1992) 'The spatial evolution of a sting clientele' *Journal of Criminal Justice* 20

Laycock G and Tilley N (1995) 'Implementing Crime Prevention' in Tonry M and Farrington DP (eds) *Building a Safer Society Crime and Justice 19* Chicago: University of Chicago Press

Mars G (1983) *Cheats at Work* London: Unwin Paperbacks

Masuda B (1992) 'Displacement vs. diffusion of benefits and the reduction of losses in a retail environment' *Security Journal* 3

Pease, K (1998) 'Changing the context of crime prevention' in Goldblatt P and Lewis C (eds), *Reducing Offending: An Assessment of Research Evidence on Ways of Dealing with Offending Behaviour* Home Office Research Study 187, London: Home Office

Sherman L, Gartin P and Buerger M (1989) 'Hot spots of predatory crime: Routine activities and the criminology of place' *Criminology* 27

Stevenson RJ and Forsythe LMV (1998) *The Stolen Goods Market in New South Wales An Interview Study with Imprisoned Burglars* Sydney: NSW Bureau of Crime Statistics and Research

Sutton M (1998) *Handling stolen goods and theft: a market reduction approach* Home Office Research Study 178, London: Home Office

Weisburd D (1997) *Reorienting Crime Prevention Research and Policy: From the Causes of Criminality to the Context of Crime* National Institute of Justice Research Report, Washington, DC: US Department of Justice

14. Crime reduction and the benefit of foresight©
Michelle Rogerson, Paul Ekblom and Ken Pease

The Government Technology Foresight programme aims to harness development within industry and commerce, to promote wealth creation and quality of life in the UK. The objective of the programme is to identify the opportunities and threats facing the UK in the future. It seems suspicious that to date this programme has largely ignored crime and crime reduction, both as a threat and an opportunity. A review of the Foresight reports concluded three things:

- that although not one sector covered by the programme escapes the consequence of crime, the reports lacked any real discussion of the problem.

- that this represented a weakness in the programme's findings and recommendations

- that the second round of Foresight should not ignore crime reduction.

Manipulating the world to produce a more desirable future

So why should a programme concerned with the future of UK industry and commerce be concerned with crime and crime reduction? This depends largely on how crime is viewed. The most fundamental fact about crime is that it is largely determined by factors outside of the criminal justice process (Pease, 1998). Crime is the consequence of the products we design and use, and the business and social arrangements to which we subscribe. In Felson's (1994) terms, crime is a routine activity that builds on other routine activities. Viewing crime in this way recognises that the manipulation of these products and arrangements can positively or negatively change the crime we experience.

It was suicide (no longer a crime) which did most to demonstrate this point. Total suicides declined in England and Wales as the carbon monoxide content of domestic gas declined. A similar story can be told about the link between suicide and the introduction of catalytic converters in vehicles in the US (Clarke and Mayhew, 1988). If the supply of opportunities influenced a decision as momentous as killing oneself, *a fortiori* it should influence the decision to commit crime.

It is difficult to know if it is preaching to the converted to make the point that opportunities drive rates of crime. It chimes with the way in which the prudent among us act in our everyday lives, by locking our cars and changing the passwords on our computers. Perhaps the astonishing thing is how criminal justice has come to occupy the heartland of criminology. For those hypnotised by passé criminology and by media depiction of crime, a few instances may suffice.

Obscene and threatening phone calls have been reduced by call tracing (Clarke, 1990 and Buck *et al*, 1996). Shop theft can be reduced by electronic or other tagging (DiLonardo, 1996). Car security has resulted in a decline of vehicle thefts particularly when compared with attempts (Webb, 1997). Plastic card fraud seems controllable by simple checks on card acquisition and use (Levi, 1992). Restrictions on the availability of poisons has changed poisoning from being the most common method of murder to a very rare one (Walsh, 1994). Rates of TV theft are predictable by the weight of sets (Felson, 1994).

Innovation and crime

Victims, tax payers, the police and practitioners in the crime reduction community are regularly required to respond to crime problems generated by misguided technologies and innovations. Unfortunately the link between innovation and opportunities for crime displays a recurrent pattern. Typically, all innovations go through three phases (Pease, 1997):

1. *design with indifference to crime consequences* – innovation is introduced, for example, a new technology, financial package, or policy. The crime consequences are not considered during the design stage

2. *reaping a crime harvest* – criminals, on the other hand, are quick to recognise these opportunities. They readily exploit new vulnerabilities reaping a crime harvest. Products may become targets to be mistreated or misappropriated (mobile phones for example), or tools misused in the commission of crime (as cordless drills were used to target telephone boxes and safes). New or modified environments can also help crime or hinder those who would prevent it

3. *the criminal consequences are recognised in retrospect* – resulting in the reversal of change or the retrofitting a partial solution.

This can be simply illustrated by the case of ram-raiding. Old-style shop windows stopped at thigh height, being supported on a substantial wall. This precluded ram-raiding. When shopfitters supplied floor-to-ceiling windows to increase display space and attractiveness, ram-raiding became possible. Suffering the crime harvest led to counter-measures such as security posts in front of the windows. The example is chosen for simplicity, but there are many others (see Ekblom, 1997 and Pease, 1997).

The number and magnitude of crime harvests can be reduced if steps to block, deter and discourage crime are built into the design and implementation of innovations. Ideally crime consequences should be anticipated and responses built in at the prototype stage. Where this is not possible, adequate feedback loops need to be established to revise the design of later batches once vulnerabilities have appeared in practice.

Victims, tax payers the police and crime prevention practitioners bear the brunt of these crime harvests, but when they are not privy to insider knowledge about the forthcoming innovations, they cannot prepare for them. Meanwhile, designers and manufacturers are not fully addressing the criminal opportunities that their work generates. This is most likely due to a lack of awareness that these side effects exist.

Using foresight (and Foresight), the cycle of innovation and crime can be broken. Rather than pessimistically accepting that technology has negative side effects, we can manipulate innovation to create a context within which crime does not flourish. However, the development of technology is not under the control of state. Legislation and central government levers have been effective in the past, some examples are discussed in Laycock and Webb, Chapter 8 in this volume. However a more desirable option would be for developers to began see genuine benefits in blocking or designing-out crime in the products and services they produce.

For example, predictions are rife that the advent of digital television will generate a burglary bonanza. However if security of these televisions is taken seriously now, this need not happen. Digital televisions have uniquely identifiable microprocessors. It is technically feasible to interrogate these microprocessors from a remote location. This effectively means that stolen sets can be identified and deactivated. A television could look for itself on a list of stolen sets, if it finds its own number it switches itself off and remains unusable until it is returned to the rightful owner.

For this solution and others to be successfully implemented, designers need to be alert to the potential to reduce crime, and have the incentive to develop solutions. Designers need to be trained to think systematically and generically about crime consequences.

For this reason the reduction of crime has a natural place in the Foresight programme and a crime reduction panel is included in the new array of panels in its second round.

The Foresight programme and crime reduction

The Foresight programme aims to identify technological and business opportunities that will emerge during the next ten to twenty years. It provides recommendations on how to harness these opportunities to promote wealth creation and quality of life, and steer UK industry towards a desirable future and away from undesirable outcomes.

The first round of the Office of Science and Technology's Foresight Programme, launched in 1984, gathered the opinions of experts from diverse sectors of industry on the future opportunities and threats to UK industry. However a closer look at the findings of this first round of Foresight reveals that one undesirable outcome, crime, is conspicuous by its absence. This is despite the fact that crime is a key economic and social driver, creating opportunities and generating losses for both quality of life and wealth creation. Not one of the sectors in the first round of Foresight is untouched by crime, and it is safe to assume that the same will be true of round two (see Figure

---

Figure 14.1 Sectors in Round Two

Sectoral panels

Built environment and transport	Chemicals
Defence	Aerospace and systems
Energy and natural environment	Financial services
Food chain and crops for industry	Health care
Information	Communications and media
Materials	Retail and consumer services

Thematic panels

Ageing population	Crime prevention
Manufacturing 2020	

Underpinning themes

Education, skills and training	Sustainable development

14.1, overleaf, for a list of panels). Round one panels that noted crime consequences addressed the 'more of the same' variety of crime. Car crime continues to be a serious concern to the transport panel, and fraud remains a continuing burden to the providers of financial services. Many crime consequences, that would be evident to practitioners immersed in crime reduction, had been missed.

Designing out crime for quality of life and wealth creation

Quality of life

Within a safe community people should be able to pursue the benefits from their lives without fear or hindrance from the criminal or the anti-social behaviour of others. The first round of Foresight largely ignored the impact that innovation will have on quality of life in the UK. This was due to an absence of a clear definition of quality of life to guide the panels. If Foresight is to successfully meet its objective to improve quality of life, it cannot ignore the crime consequences of forecasted developments, or the crime prevention potential of others.

There is substantial, previously unrecognised scope within this programme to explore the means to develop products and systems which are more resistant to crime. This aim is also a major consideration of the Government's crime reduction programme. To contribute to quality of life, technology can help with people's perception of risk: perception of coping and control and knowledge of how to keep safe are other areas where new technology can help.

Wealth creation

The other aspect of the Foresight panels' remit is wealth creation. Crime has significant impact here and crime reduction can certainly contribute to competitiveness.

Crime inhibits progress. Crime and the fear of crime can prevent the successful uptake of products and services. This applies to services as diverse as public transport and internet banking. Businesses suffer losses through theft or interference with products in transit or in store. Shops and other businesses often do not survive in high-crime areas. Areas unable to sustain or attract new businesses then fall further into decline. Crime (or loss) prevention can cut production, distribution and retail costs, freeing funds for additional investment.

There are opportunities for businesses to exploit specific markets for products and services, to enhance security, reduce crime or to provide offenders with resources to avoid crime. Goods and services more resistant to crime will attract more custom and could even achieve product differentiation, gaining a competitive edge over rival output from other companies or countries. Businesses can also promote and withhold a reputation for caring for customers and society, and maintain business confidence. Reducing the burden of crime overheads to society can attract investment in the UK and produce a workforce that is safer and more secure, confident and trusted – and consequently, more productive.

Those with a cynical view of industry and commerce would argue that it benefits from crime and therefore has little incentive to reduce it. For example, replacements for stolen goods lead to increased sales. This may be particularly useful for those industries that want to encourage consumers to regularly upgrade the products they buy, for example, motor and electronic goods industries.

A further difficulty arises from the way in which measures of economic performance can be distorted by criminal activity. In the same way that traffic jams falsely inflate GDP by adding to the country's fuel consumption and wear and tear on vehicles, the money invested in tackling crime may also inflate economic indicators. Revised indicators that discount sums from activities that detract from social progress, such as crime, would help to provide a truer measure of the negative affect that crime has on national well being, and business profits.

Crime in Foresight Round One

Threats to wealth creation

The financial services, retail, and distribution and transport sectors appeared most aware of the problem of crime and the consequent loss of wealth within their sectors. These are sectors that have felt the impact of crimes in the past. Car crime is of 'serious concern' to the Transport Panel (Transport: 20), and fraud is a 'continuing burden' to the providers of financial services (15). These problems are not expected to go away in the future. In the retail sector problems of shrinkage and theft are expected to increase (Retail: 14). It is feared that crime will prevent the successful uptake of new developments. Opportunities to provide a wider range of services over electronic networks like teleshopping and telebanking are tempered by fears that networks will not be secure.

The Foresight panels predict a 'continued growing demand for novel technology in the home' (Communications: 61). Progress in a wide range of industrial sectors is contributing to the development of novel technology that continues to be smaller and more portable. The downside of these developments is that these highly desirable products will be equally desirable to criminals.

Hot products do not have to be a high tech. A problem currently facing retailers is the theft of vouchers for prepaid mobile phones. These vouchers are cardboard, and have no real face value. However they provide access to phone calls and are usually placed in easily accessible store locations.

The best response to crimes that target specific goods is to identify in advance which products will be vulnerable and then to build in crime prevention as an integral feature of the product's design. In this volume, Clarke provides the acronym CRAVED as a useful aid to think about a product's attractiveness to thieves. The difficulty is that the problem of thefts may not be apparent to manufacturers, and factors that render products insecure may not yet have materialised. Theft impacts directly on the owner and his/her insurance company, but to the manufacturer the only indicator of the crimes may be the sale of replacement goods. And when sales are up there appears little need to radically change the product.

While some products may be attractive targets to criminals. Other technologies are useful tools for the commission of crime. It is often the case that the full application of a new product is not anticipated during design. These unanticipated applications may be quite legitimate, but in many cases quite innocuous products are used to criminal ends.

For example, telephone subscribers will be assigned a personal number, which can be accessed to route calls from all over the world. The cloning of this personal number could have implications similar to the problem of cloned mobile phones (IT and Electronics: 93 D65).

The second round of Foresight began in April 1999. It includes a new thematic panel on crime reduction. This panel will guide the other Foresight sectoral panels in the development of new capacities to identify and respond to technological and social trends that foster criminal opportunity and motivation.

Some panels have noted the crime reduction opportunities of the developments they anticipate. 'Individual dwellings make widespread use of easy-to-use security systems, for example, central locking and remote alarm systems' (Construction: 65). More often than not however, such opportunities have been overlooked. The Materials Panel highlighted new methods to make an unconventional glass that does not break, the crime-reducing benefits of this new material, including the curbing of pub violence, were not noted.

Foresight Round Two

Investing in crime reduction at each stage in the development and implementation of innovation can deliver significant commercial benefits. For this task to succeed we need:

●   to foster awareness that design can influence crime risk, for better or for worse

●   to disseminate knowledge of what the risks are and how to tackle them

●   to motivate industry to tackle the risks.

If this process is to gather momentum, it is essential that a partnership be struck between all levels of industry, the police and crime reduction practitioners. The forum of the Foresight programme is an ideal springboard for these activities. Crime prevention practitioners can bring guidance for 'thinking thief' and 'thinking preventer' to the Crime Reduction Panel.

Suggested issues for the thematic Crime Reduction Foresight Panel

At this point, it would be useful to make some suggestions for the more specific tasks in which the Crime Reduction Panel might engage. Before doing so, it is worth making one central point, that the causes and victims of crime do not sit neatly within industrial sectors, and technologies created within one sector have crime and crime reduction implications for the whole range of other sectors.

For example, it has been the combined developments within the IT sector of desk top publishing software and quality copying and printing machines that has led to increases in the number of forged cheques, bringing losses to those working in financial services. Consequently, the anticipation and prevention of new crime trends requires the co-ordinated participation of experts from all of the science and technology sectors represented within the Foresight programme.

Crime also interacts with the other thematic panels, Ageing Population and Manufacturing 2020, and the underpinning themes of education, skills and training, and sustainable development. It is for this reason that the crime panel for the second round of Foresight will be cross cutting, fully interacting with the work of other panels, rather than a minimalist panel isolating crime reduction activities from other panels.

A further criticism of the first round of Foresight is that it did not sufficiently engage commerce and industry at ground level. This is particularly important when we are looking to engage businesses in activities that they currently view as far removed from their work. The new round of Foresight plans to encourage wider participation through a knowledge pool and task forces. There is promise that a number of professional and trade organisations have registered their interest in developing proposals for the link programmes that will stem from the Crime

Reduction Panel, these included the Royal Society of Chemistry. The involvement of these organisations in Foresight will aid the wider dissemination of crime reduction issues throughout industrial sectors. This demonstrates the potential within Foresight to create a snowball effect, generating ever greater awareness and action.

The problem space

In more detail, a crime reduction panel could map out what engineers call the problem space of crime reduction. This includes devising, or encouraging, the development of ways to help designers, product marketing strategists, and those in other panels, to anticipate upcoming crime risks that need addressing. An essential tool for this task is a generic understanding of the causes of crime (in both design, and the wider product environment) in a form relevant to their work. Predicting future crimes and crime targets is all about predicting changes in the precursors of the criminal event and changes in the ways they come together. Ekblom's 'conjunction of criminal opportunity' framework is useful here (see Chapter 2).

The panel could also develop systematic aids to thinking thief and thinking preventer, and how to spot new/upcoming products likely to be inherently vulnerable or attractive to offenders as targets for crime, or useful as resources for offending. This task requires both experience of working with crime and knowledge of how designs take shape. Thinking preventer could be helped by further development of penetration testing approaches, hopefully using hardware, procedures and software rather more sophisticated than the local 'retired' car thief can muster.

Designers are required, often by law, to consider a host of issues including health and safety and environmental considerations, throughout the design process. The Crime Panel needs to study other models used to guide design practice and adapt them to crime where they are relevant. For example, to ensure adherence to electromagnetic compatibility (EMC) directives, manufacturers of electronic goods can assemble a technical construction file (TCF) detailing the product's conformity and providing technical data as evidence to support this claim. Work on the TCF begins at the first stage of design and continues throughout the process, ensuring that EMC is not overlooked at any point in the process.

Manufacturers are likely to encounter conflicts between crime reduction and other priorities including privacy, aesthetics, convenience and cost. So the panel must find strategies for identifying and handling these troublesome trade-offs. Really inventive design allows us to avoid compromise. So, we can have a lightweight laptop that is secure and easy to carry and use legitimately. In other words, simultaneously user-friendly but abuser-unfriendly aspects, and secure engineer's back doors, that allow legitimate access for servicing or repair but keep out knowledgeable offenders. New technologies can often help bypass trade-offs that once placed severe limits on what could be practically achieved. All Foresight participants should be on the alert for these.

The panel must develop a wider capacity to spot when new technological and social trends are fostering criminality and criminal motivation – whether this means they are driving social exclusion processes or encouraging networking and social reinforcement among offender groups; bringing together new targets, offenders, and environments for crime; or removing or hindering preventers (as in substituting machine-based financial transactions for ones involving a suitably suspicious human intermediary).

The solution space

Once the capacity to identify the problem is developed, the corresponding solution space will require attention. This entails setting out the complete array of generic crime reduction methods, their trade-offs and side-effects, which have to be taken into account in good design. It requires setting out some generic ideas to assist those in other panels to spot technologies likely to be useful in crime reduction. The struggle between offenders and preventers closely resembles an arms race. As a result, crime prevention measures are wasting assets in designs, so there is a need for an early warning system to spot design failures and design obsolescence where offenders have beaten a previous solution as soon as they become apparent.

This includes identifying the new tools and modus operandi that offenders use to bring them about. Information on offenders' methods needs to be systematically communicated from crime scenes to designers. Sources of information on new methods are diverse and include the police, SOCO, probation, loss adjusters and repair and maintenance staff. Again good practice can be learned and adapted from other disciplines, perhaps a modification of the procedures used by centres monitoring new mutations of diseases.

To ensure that other Foresight panels are fully alert to the crime consequences of the futures they envisage. The Crime Reduction panel should carry out systematic reviews of any mid-term reports or other products of the other Foresight panels. This would identify potential new causes of crime gleaning from new technologies. The panel should consider whether new technologies or services, which could be used as tools for crime, should in some way be restricted, and how. This might apply to latter-day equivalents of the colour photocopier, encryption or the credit card reader. These reviews should also identify applications, which could be pressed into the service of crime reduction, for example, electronic vehicle transponders, which can provide services such as road charging, collision awareness and stolen vehicle tracking and recovery.

A similar review has been produced by the Health and Safety Executive, who have created a database of technological change and its affect on health and safety at work, including new machinery or chemicals.

Finally, because manufacturers (and marketing strategists) have commercial interests, they will require incentive and motivation to incur the necessary costs for incorporating crime in design. In addition crime prevention practitioners need to be aware of the contribution they can make to industry's attempts to restrict criminal opportunity, and the benefits they have to gain from this partnership. As Laycock and Webb argue in Chapter 8, the participants in Foresight need to feel that they have a responsibility to reduce crime and that they have the competence to act.

Evaluating the Foresight programme's contribution to crime reduction

The success of the crime reduction panel cannot be directly measured by any future changes to crime rates. Not least because it may take some time to integrate new practices and reap the rewards. Foresight can only be evaluated by its ability to improve the capacity to reduce crime through the anticipation of new crimes and responses to them. Measurable deliverables of the Crime Reduction Panel's success might include:

- developing a measure of the level of awareness of crime reduction in other panels

- the number of crime consequences and crime prevention technologies identified by other panels in the programme

- the number of products emerging on to markets advertising crime resistant qualities, and the relative sales of these against comparable non crime-resistant models

- the number of design course incorporating substantial crime reduction course components

- the incorporation of crime reducing procedures, resembling the technical construction file, into design procedures

- the existence and quality of information systems designed to handle and disseminate information on emerging criminal methods to those incorporating it within design.

The Crime Reduction Panel should engage in a mix of tasks. They should address current and emergent crime problems and make steps to anticipate those in the long-term future. Tasks will range from the immediately practical and highly specific application of waiting for an anticipated new technology to arrive, to generic design guidance and to the blue sky analysis of crime threats and crime reduction opportunities. Ultimately, the task will be strategic thinking about how to run arms races, or better still how to avoid them altogether. Success in the anticipation of future crime trends requires the police, and others in the crime reduction community, to collaborate with industry and commerce. The practices of identifying and developing responses to new crime problems need to become a central task in the remit of each of these groups.

References

Buck W, Chatterton M and Pease K (1996) *Obscene, Threatening and Other Troublesome Telephone Calls to Women in England and Wales: 1982-1992* Home Office Research and Planning Unit Paper 92, London: Home Office

Clarke (1990) 'Deterring obscene phone callers: preliminary results of the New Jersey experience' *Security Journal* 1

Clarke RV and Mayhew PM (1988) 'The British gas suicide story and its criminological implications' in Tonry M and Morris N (eds) *Crime and Justice* 10, Chicago: University of Chicago Press

DiLonardo RL (1996) 'Defining and measuring the economic benefit of electronic article surveillance' *Security Journal* 7

Ekblom P (1997) 'Gearing up against Crime: a Dynamic Framework to help Designers keep up with the Adaptive Criminal in a Changing World' *International Journal of Risk, Security and Crime Prevention* 4

Ekblom P (1998) 'Situational crime prevention: effectiveness of local initiatives' in Goldblatt P and Lewis C (eds) *Reducing Offending* Home Office Research Study 187, London: HMSO

Felson M (1998) *Crime and Everyday Life* (2nd ed) Thousands Oaks Ca: Pine Forge Press

Levi M (1992) 'Preventing credit card fraud' *Security Journal* 3

Pease K (1997) 'Predicting the Future: The Roles of Routine Activities and Rational Choice Theory' in Newman G et al (eds) *Rational Choice and Situational Crime Prevention* Aldershot: Ashgate

Pease K (1998) 'Crime, Labour and the Wisdom of Solomon' *Policy Studies* 19

Walsh D(1994) 'The Obsolescence of Crime Forms' in Clarke RV (ed) *Crime Prevention Studies* 2, Monsey NY: Criminal Justice Press

Webb B (1997) 'Steering Column Locks and Motor Vehicle Theft: Evaluations from Three Countries' in Clarke RV (ed) *Situational Crime Prevention: Successful Case Studies* (2nd ed) Guilderland NY: Harrow and Heston

For further information about the UK Foresight programme, contact: Foresight Directorate Office of Science and Technology Albany House, 94-98 Petty France, London SW1H 9ST Fax: 0171 271 2015 or www.foresight.gov.uk

15. Community safety in the age of the risk society
Gordon Hughes

Future trends in crime control and community safety are by no means certain nor easily amenable to technical fixes. Previous chapters in this collection have already alerted us to the importance of the moral dimensions and value positions, as well as the practical and policy issues, associated with the work of community safety practitioners. This is not to deny the laudable concern with trying to answer the question of what works – neatly captured in the title of Mike Hough and Nick Tilley's (1997) paper on research lessons for crime prevention, *Getting the grease to the squeak*. However, it is equally important to foster a critical and reflexive culture around this 'wicked issue' of community safety.

Perhaps this chapter's contribution should therefore be subtitled *Getting sand in the Vaseline* (with due acknowledgement to Talking Heads). Community safety is thus a wicked issue not just for the challenges it raises as non-compartmentalised practice and policy about harm reduction, but also for the theoretical, moral and political challenges associated with its nascent and contested agenda in the new governance of crimes and harms.

In particular, this chapter makes a case for locating and understanding current developments in community safety, and their implications for practitioners, in terms of the wider historical transformations opened up by the sociological thesis of the risk society. In the following discussion, the connections between what are termed here, for heuristic purposes, the macro-transformations of risk, late modernity and globalisation, the meso-level transformations in governance and the micro-transformations around the developments in crime prevention and community safety, are explored.

In terms of the last-mentioned micro dimension, possible scenarios for the present and future imperfect are focused on in a brief picture of the dystopian reading of current trends – the catastrophic side of the possibilities that exist. Then discussion turns to what may be termed some 'reasons to be cheerful'. In this, some earlier attempts to develop an agenda beyond criminology are returned to. These regard the possibilities of progressive, anti law and order politics, and involve the promotion of more inclusive social politics of community safety as well as possibilities of a replacement discourse around social harms and public goods, social justice and inclusion (Hughes, 1996 and 1998a).

Community safety has, until recently, had the unenviable status of being the Cinderella missing from not just one but two academic balls. This new institutional complex and its budding profession (of community safety officers) have been largely ignored in both of the mainstream academic disciplines of criminology and social policy. Such neglect says much for the new challenges associated with the emergent community safety agenda, which may lie beyond the traditional boundaries of both social policy and crime control.

'Fings ain't wot they used to be'! Tales of new dangers and risks

There appears to be no end of media reporting of crime, disorder and violence, all of which builds up a picture of a society increasingly engulfed, uncertain and at risk from the epidemic of social unrest and hazards. To take just two examples recently reported in the broadsheet press. First the 'Profession at risk' story (*Guardian*, 2/12/98) which begins with the following sentence:

> The killing last week of Jennifer Morrison at an appointment with a mentally-ill client in a south London hostel was a stark reminder of the vulnerability of front-line social workers everywhere.

The other news story, 'Urban nightmares disturb the slumber of Metroland' (*Independent on Sunday*, 15.11.98) began as follows:

> The terrified youth was chased from the wine bar by a gang. He managed only to get across the road before he was trapped on a railway bridge. He was kicked and punched before his tormentors lifted him over a wall and dropped him on to the electrified tracks below... Another everyday occurrence in Moss Side perhaps? No: this time it was Northwood, a well-to-do suburb on the borders of north-west London and Hertfordshire... The violence that was part of the lives of less well-off people in dangerous places like Wembley and Kilburn had finally arrived on the doorsteps of the middle classes... Not very long ago, crime in suburbs like Northwood was a relatively harmless affair. But now there is an abiding sense that all is not well. The facts bear out people's misgivings.

So what are we to make of such frightening tales of society seemingly engulfed by a tidal wave of crime and violence and the corollary of heightened risk, fear and uncertainty? We may ask, 'why now?' Are we witnessing a moral crisis or what sociologists term a media-manufactured moral panic? The rise of fears in areas of employment (social work) and residence (suburbia), previously perceived to be safe, complement the rise to prominence of safety, and community (both separately and in tandem as community safety), as emergent key policy concerns and rhetorical political devices across contemporary societies. This is surely no coincidence.

Witness New York's Mayor Giuliani's 1999 policy agenda which prioritised safety and also the obsession with safer communities in Labour's Crime and Disorder Act of

1998. In a similar fashion, David Donnison (1998) has noted a recent survey regarding people's hopes for the future in which the wish for safety for themselves and their families came out as the second highest priority behind only the wish to earn a living in a decent job. The prominence of the idea of new risks versus old certainties is also something which academic social scientists have been proselytising, especially proponents of the Third Way such as Anthony Giddens (1998).

It is not likely that issues of safety and risk will be disappearing from current populist political and academic social science discourses on crime prevention and community safety. This chapter begins to explore why there is an ascendant preoccupation with community safety at this historical juncture although the history of this idea has still to be written. It is of course important to note that the concern with risk, safety and security is not new. For example, note the old Beveridge deal in post-war UK society, which represented a social democratic project of collective risk management (Hughes, 1998b). However, the idea of qualitatively different forms of societal risks and hazards, seemingly both incalculable and global, conjures up images of immanent implosion for the social order of societies like the UK.

'On your guard!' Welcome to the risk society

The analysis of the backdrop of major historical changes has not been a mainstream criminological concern in examining the detailed changes in crime prevention / community safety policies and practices. Indeed any attempt at a sustained exploration of the new politics of community safety still seems a marginal and possibly unwelcome activity for most self-professed criminologists. What are then the key features of the macro thesis regarding the inter-connected processes of globalisation, late modernity and risk? What practice implications do the latter processes raise for community safety practitioners?

Proponents of the risk society thesis such as Beck (1992) and Giddens (1990) have argued that one of the key societal changes brought about by late modernity is the alteration in the environments of both trust and risk, and the growth of what is known as ontological insecurity. (This is even compared to that seen in the era of modernity from the 19th to mid-20th centuries, never mind that of pre-modern traditional societies.)

In brief, it is argued that modernity increasingly undermines the salience of kinship ties, fractures the hold of local community and undermines the authority of appeals to tradition. It is claimed that these effects can be attributed to the disembedding mechanisms associated with globalisation, that detach social relations from local contexts and restructure them across indefinite spans of space and time.

The, by now, well-acknowledged process of globalisation involves an intensification of world-wide social relations which link distant localities in such a manner that local happenings are shaped increasingly by events occurring greater distances away, and vice versa. Put simply, the world is becoming both more interconnected and more uncertain.

It is contended that we now inhabit the late modern world where trust is both embedded in personal and intimate relations and vested in disembedded abstract systems of expert knowledge. Giddens has described living in late modernity as being akin to 'riding a juggernaut'. Late modernity is thus somewhat like a runaway engine of enormous power, which can be steered to some extent, but which also threatens to run out of control. A key consequence of this is the recognition that current and future trends are complex, contingent and uncertain with a puzzling diversity of options and possibilities opened up. It is not a simple matter of there now being greater risks than in past, unlike the mistaken view of critics of the risk society thesis such as Frank Furedi (1997), but rather that there is a greater knowledge of, and attempt to assess, risks than in previous times. Why is this so?

Ulrich Beck has written about the consequences of scientific and industrial development during the twentieth century as unleashing a set of risks, the likes of which humanity has never previously faced. These risks are not just the 'already destructive consequences' of technological developments but also the 'potential element' of risks in the future (Beck, 1992). In accord with this development, our survival is now dependent on modernisation becoming reflexive (for example, being critical of scientific and other expert claims to know best). In Beck's terms, science's monopoly on rationality is broken and yet technical experts are still given the pole position in defining agendas. They impose bounding premises on risk discourses, in whatever field we wish to examine, be it food production, environmental control or the management of crimes and other hazards in the emergent profession of community safety experts.

Beck has defined risks as being the probabilities of physical harm due to given technological or other processes. Unlike the factory-related hazards of the 19th and first half of the 20th centuries, it is argued that risks are no longer limited to certain groups or localities, instead they exhibit the tendency towards globalisation. These are of course very grand and sweeping claims and are controversial in themselves. It is arguable, for example, that we are actually living in the second era of globalisation, following that of 19th century imperialism. Beck thus seems conveniently to forget the global risks of enslavement, opium addiction and colonisation associated with imperialism in the past!

Risk society theorists would contend that there is a clear link between the growing concern with both individual and collective security/safety and heightened awareness, and thus fears, of risks. Risk society is thus characterised by a fundamental uncertainty about the present and, in turn, a nostalgia for a normative horizon of lost security and broken trust. However, the centre of risk consciousness lies not in the present, nor the past, but in the future. It would seem we become active today in order to prevent, alleviate or take precautions against the problems and crises of tomorrow and the day after tomorrow. A troubled consciousness indeed, and a fertile breeding ground for appeals to both community and personal safety.

A clear break is assumed to be occurring between the old industrial society and the emergent risk society. According to Beck, industrial class societies were to be understood in terms of the normative project of the ideal of equality. However, Beck suggests that this is not so for late modern risk society. Instead its normative counter-project is safety, and consequently the utopia of the risk society remains peculiarly negative and defensive.

Its driving force would thus seem to be not about attaining something good, but about preventing the worst. It is seen as a society driven and both held together and torn apart by a commonality of anxiety. In turn, the workings of the major institutions of risk society are viewed as being increasingly dominated by the question of how the risks and hazards, systematically produced as part of late modernisation, can be prevented, minimised, or channelled. Calculable risks are viewed as being to the fore with the provident state, and risk-fighting per se is now increasingly big business across the public/private divide.

What then of the practice implications and the possible futures for community safety according to this self-consciously polemical thesis? It appears to offer us both dystopian and utopian possibilities. According to the negative, dystopian reading of the possibilities, Beck sees the strong chance of a 'scapegoat society' emerging and of 'a tendency to a legitimate totalitarianism of hazard prevention' (Beck, 1992). The dangers of crime, disorder and other threatening epidemics of various guises may become viewed as so great that liberties, freedoms, democratic debate and the like may be sacrificed and replaced by an all-powerful single political authority. In other words a latter-day vision of the Big Brother state, with authoritarian conformity for the normal and exclusion and punitive containment for the demonised risky 'other'.

On a more optimistic front, it is argued that we are, not least, expected to live with the most diverse and contradictory global and personal risks. We all now face, as individuals, risky freedoms, the answer to which seems to lie in a new form of non-nostalgic, self-critical, radical communitarianism (see Nellis, Chapter 3 and Hughes, 1996). Thus alongside the dangers of an authoritarian totalitarianism offering protection at great cost to freedom and diversity, new inclusive politics of community safety, built on a project of solidarity in the context of individualisation and diversity, is hinted at. This is illustrated in the following plea from Beck: 'the question as to the we, that is able to bind and motivate the individualised individuals, becomes urgent' (Beck, 1992).

It is important at this juncture to note that the risk society thesis is not without its critics and flaws. Furedi (1997) in his critique of the current 'worship of safety' has correctly cautioned us about the dangers of making safety the cardinal virtue of our society and thereby eschewing innovation and positive risk-taking. Furthermore, according to Furedi, proponents of the risk society thesis have added intellectual fuel to the moral panic over risk and safety. This is open to dispute given that commentators such as Giddens have emphasised that opportunity and innovation are the positive side of risk.

Similarly, Furedi's claim, that risk society proponents ignore the fact that previous times and societies have been objectively more dangerous environments than our present western societies, is simply wrong. In fact Giddens does not deny this fairly obvious point but suggests that a heightened collective and individual awareness of, and critical knowledge about, risks is now evident. Perhaps more importantly, the risk society theorists' claims of a radical break with the past should be disputed, to point instead to the current period's close links to, and continuities with, neo-liberal capitalism.

Indeed the recognition that the risk society is still one premised on the capitalist market is acknowledged by some of its leading advocates. Thus, Ericson and Haggerty (1997) remark on the inflationary logic which develops with the commodification of risk (and safety) whereby market forces encourage novelty that will create new demand, as opposed to merely adjusting the level of supply to meet existing demand.

Despite these qualifications to the thesis of a risk society, the broad debate remains helpful in exploring the connections between trends in community safety and the wider social transformations of our times. Arising out of these macro developments, the role of the state and nature of public/private agencies – and the practitioners engaged therein – have also undergone significant transformations. This meso-level will be examined next.

'Re-inventing government?' New modes of governance and the crime and safety problem

There has never been total state sovereignty over crime prevention (note, for example, locksmiths, privately employed watchmen and so on), but for much of the last two centuries, the job of crime prevention has largely been that of statutory state agencies (Bottoms and Wiles, 1996). According to some social scientists, we are currently witnessing the decline of both the idea and reality of the sovereign state's monopoly, not just over crime control (Garland, 1996), but over other areas of public concern such as social welfare (Rose, 1996).

This historical shift is captured well by the distinction between government (in the past) and governance (in the present and future). Government has generally been seen as being synonymous with national government or the nation-state involving monopoly powers. Governance, on the other hand, implies that the practice of rule or social ordering is becoming less identified with the Government *per se*, and is more wide-ranging as a result. In Giddens' words:

> 'Governance' becomes a more relevant concept to refer to some forms of administrative or regulatory capacities. Agencies which either are not part of any government-cum-governmental organisations, or are transnational in character, contribute to governance. (1998)

What appears to be the key change, of late, in the governance of crime control and of community safety is that it is increasingly at a distance from the Government and works in complex, dispersed and hybrid forms. The polity is now increasingly differentiated and made up of new networks, and of those policy icons and panaceas of our time, partnerships. What are the features of these new institutional contexts and their characteristic modes of contested expertise? How do such institutions, in the making, relate to the national and supra-national government agendas? These are crucial need-to-know questions for all practitioners in the field of community safety.

It is now clearly impossible to discuss multi-agency crime prevention and community safety, in the UK and beyond, without engaging in a debate about the changing modalities of state power in relationship to civil society and the public. Indeed, notions of local and central state are themselves becoming increasingly problematic with the rise of the dispersed state or new modes of governance. As a result of these, we are witnessing not a diminution of the state's role but rather an extension of particular forms of state power, although through new and unfamiliar means (Clarke and Newman, 1997).

This development is well illustrated by the example of state power being exercised through indirect rather than direct agency, as in the present fashion for partnerships against crime in the UK. Put simply there has been a shift from the central state rowing (or doing things itself) to steering (through policy formation and facilitation) the Good Ship Society. Much of this development is illustrated by the inter-related processes of contracting out, voluntarisation and civilianisation, active citizenship, the expansion of private security and the rise of realms of private governance, across what was once termed the public sphere (Crawford, 1997).

In these changing conditions, responsibility for setting up and running multi-agency crime prevention initiatives at the local level, is increasingly put out to tender. Bids from rival competitors are invited rather, than presuming it to be the natural responsibility of statutory agencies of the criminal justice system. In the UK, these competing bodies are often private companies, or more often charities such as Crime Concern or the National Association for the Care and Rehabilitation of Offenders (NACRO), in which the public/private distinction is hard to draw.

Responsibility for crime prevention and community safety is thus being re-located and re-articulated. In some ways, it is evident that prevention is now a means by which the state is able to absolve itself from hands-on or complete responsibility: indeed the fault is increasingly 'ours' as the new citizen-consumer subjects. The broader context in which to locate this hive of activity is in the new social politics of neo-liberalism with its cultivation of entrepreneurial individuals, who are literally formed in responsible families and then located in active communities. The broad term used to describe this attempted hegemonic project in the late 20th century, is the strategy of responsibilisation (O'Malley, 1996).

There are both dangers and opportunities for community safety practitioners in this brave new world of multi-agency partnerships, as previous contributions to this volume have shown and which Jon Spencer addresses in greater depth in the next chapter. Sheila Stokes-White noted (Chapter 5) that partnerships around social regeneration are able to move beyond a narrowly defined crime prevention paradigm and, in turn, can generate new trust relations across institutional boundaries. Paul Wiles and Ken Pease argue (Chapter 1) that community safety strategies which adopt a genuinely pan-hazard approach may enable us to manage risks in specific localities as a totality for the first time. Such potentialities for innovation are clearly linked to the broad political and organisational shifts associated with the new governance.

However, all is not clear blue skies of optimism in terms of these meso-level transformations. Given the emphasis on responsibility, there is the risk of placing yet more strain on the backs of the most stressed, least affluent and least connected communities in the name of communitarian self-help promoted by moral conservatives such as Etzioni (1996 and see Nellis, in Chapter 3, for a different reading of Etzioni) and arising out of the benign, if often wrong-headed, intentions of community consultation. In the context of Labour's Crime and Disorder Act the emphasis on a potentially authoritarian communitarianism is mixed with an appeal to managerialism. If Blair's pre-election mantra was 'education, education, education', then the new mantra for evaluating what works in the public services seems to be 'count, count, count', by means of the latest technicist silver bullet of the best value for money audit, sponsored not least by the Audit Commission.

There is a related danger. The wider ambitions of some local authorities, in bringing about social regeneration through community safety, may be lost. This is given the statutory requirement of a local crime and disorder audit (rather than a community safety audit), in which the hazards of crime and certain forms of anti-social behaviour are prioritised over other hazards. The possible future career for community safety practitioners may thus be that of technical managers absorbed in the production (or manufacture) of measurable performance indicators of success in the war against crime.

Goodbye cruel world? Visions and realities of community safety discourse

This chapter contends that the future cannot be predicted with any certainty, despite the claims of proponents of technical fixes and both radical and conservative writers pointing to urban dystopia. Instead, some intimations of possible futures, of varying pessimistic and optimistic degree, can be made.

These begin with a brief resume of the well-trodden path to the urban dystopia of risk- and security-obsessed paranoia, involving ultra-safe, gated communities, and the violent, excluded territories of the 'underclass'. This is the community safety scenario where the cult of privatised security (for the affluent) joins forces with the coercive politics of exclusion and containment (for the poor). According to this reading of current developments, new defensive strategies against personal crimes and in support of enhanced personal and familial security have emerged.

The concomitant rise of a culture of anonymity also means that individuals increasingly turn to abstract systems in which they can place trust (for example the reassuring technology of the intercom or mobile phone). In the marketplace there are now new providers of guardianship, particularly in the guise of the private security police. Safety here is thus commodified as a private rather than collective good, to be bought in the market by the consumer. Technological guardianship devices also become a normal part of the urban landscape, such as CCTV. Alongside these technological fixes, we witness the related development of an insurance-based logic of actuarial justice, in which the risk assessment of whole categories of consumers comes to the fore. Such developments appear to be closely associated with the market-driven logic of neo-liberal privatism.

Critical commentators, particularly from North America, have pointed to three main features to this changing face of social control, which are examined below:

The militarisation of city life and the rise of the fortress city

In Mike Davis' influential study City of Quartz (1990), some grim greetings from the metropolis of Los Angeles are given. Davis' depiction largely accords with Beck's fears regarding the negative and defensive utopia of the risk society. Indeed Davis sees trends in LA as a precursor of similar developments in the 'emerging built environment', elsewhere in big cities. He places great emphasis on the tendency to merge urban design, architecture and the police apparatus in 'a single, comprehensive security effort' (Davis, 1990). At the same time there is a growing market in private security alongside the new partnerships of public and private agencies in crime prevention. Clear evidence it would seem for Furedi's concern over the spread of the 'precautionary principle' and 'stranger danger' (Furedi, 1997).

What of the redundant poor in this scenario? According to Davis, the poor and homeless of LA become perceived as 'the other', the underclass who are to be contained and segregated in the new townships and subjected to the militarised policing, or low-intensity warfare, of the LAPD. As a consequence of these trends, Davis argues that we live increasingly in fortress cities, brutally divided between the 'fortified cells' of affluent society and the 'places of terror' where the police battle the criminalised poor. Davis' thesis thus indicates that in LA risk (and community safety) is class-specific and racialised and, thereby, contradicts some of Beck's wilder claims about the break with the past, industrial, class society, and the supposed universalising of risk conditions across class and race.

Perhaps the central message of Davis' portrayal of LA is the danger of the destruction of accessible public space (see Hillier and Shu (Chapter 12) on the importance of the living street for the public realm). Space becomes either privatised for the affluent (in the safe, gated community) and the paranoid, or it is segregated into ghettos made up of ethnically strong, almost tribal, territories. As Nikolas Rose (1996) notes, the gated city is one of the variety of new ways of 'imagining security', by which the collective logic of the community is brought into alliance with the individualised ethos of neo-liberal politics, in what may be termed 'new prudential regimes' of risk-obsessed late modernity.

In many cities of the world then, the erection of real physical barriers is being witnessed, as well as economic and social exclusions between the affluent and the poor (McLaughlin and Muncie, forthcoming). If the distribution of crime prevention and community safety were to left to be the rules and vagaries of the marketplace, certain groups would inevitably be excluded from the market place, since they could not afford to pay and thus participate. In extremis, this situation could lead to the creation of a dualised society of fortress-like, defended locales for the affluent – united by Beck's commonality of anxiety – and undefended badlands of crime and insecurity. In the latter, membership of the gang often offers some hazardous protection and sense of belonging for those who cannot compete in the marketplace. In Davis' chilling expression, the result of all this is 'urban apartheid'.

New, insurance-based and amoral modes of management of risky populations

Feeley and Simon's work (1992) specifically examines the emergence of a new strategy for managing the risks of crime and victimisation, which they term the 'new penology'. This new insurance-based strategy is characterised as follows. It focuses on the probabilistic calculation of risk (actuarialism) and the analysis of statistical distribution as applied to populations. Actuaries are experts in insurance who calculate potential risks and determine insurance premiums accordingly. As a crime prevention and community safety approach, actuarial justice is organised around the principles of social utility and efficient management rather than the principles of responsibility and culpability.

Central to this emergent discourse, is a new policy objective, namely the clear categorisation of risky people to identify and manage. Its techniques for the management of the identified risky people are by means of surveillance and low-key exclusion for the generally potentially risky categories (or the non-affluent, in general), penal incapacitation for high risk offenders and holding pens for middle range risk populations.

The new penology's emphasis is thus on the amoral, probabilistic calculation of risk and the analyses of statistical distributions as applied to populations, focused on managing rather than changing people. In Ericson's expression, the model of 'risk-surveillance-security' displaces the conventional concern with 'deviance-control-order' (Ericson, 1996). It would seem that questions of social utility and efficient management are prioritised over questions of individual responsibility and blame.

Crime and incivility are thus risks to be managed, in a sense to be lived with, rather than eliminated or reformed. The target becomes not the offender nor the criminal justice system but the community of potential offenders. The danger posed by this strategy is that the priorities of risk management may override justice, and the disadvantaged, non-changeable and risky underclass increasingly become subjected to Draconian containment or elimination. Once again community safety here is synonymous with the rise of the exclusionary society.

The growth of subtle forms of prevention and regulation through the seductions of privatised consumerism

Finally, commentators such as Shearing and Stenning (1985) highlight the emergence in the late 20th century of a new managerialism and a privatisation of policing and criminal justice together with the rise of a non-carceral (or, loosely, non-custodial) disciplinary mode of social control. This new mode of control is both instrumental and preventive in character and it fits easily with Beck's characterisation of risk consciousness as being future-oriented. It is based, seemingly, on an amoral profit/loss calculus of the corporation versus legal and moral questions of right and wrong, and involves entire non-criminalised populations being subjected to increasing surveillance and regulation (chiefly via situational techniques and information technology) and drawn into acting as control agents (due to communal/familial responsibilities).

Corporations concerned with the consumption of goods and services stand at the forefront of this development. In shopping malls and theme parks we witness the clearest and most advanced expression of this preventive and seemingly non-coercive disciplining of subject populations. Disneyworld is arguably the apogee of this trend towards pervasive, seductive control. Here community safety is a linguistic slippage for the happy shopper and consumer safety, in which we are likely to see the growth of community safety managers employed by retail company partnerships.

What then are the practice implications associated with this first dystopian scenario? The overall message for the UK, from critical criminologists from North America, is that we are in the throes of a process of the exclusionary privatising of safety and security (as against being a public good). This is resulting in both a demise and residualisation of the civic ideal and an eclipse of the solidarity project of the post-war welfare state. In turn, this exacerbates the tendency for the more affluent to retreat into exclusive club-like safe enclaves from which troublesome and dangerous minorities – criminalised as Bauman's 'flawed consumers' (1997) – are both excluded and subjected to coercive policing and containment elsewhere.

At the risk of generalising, it does appear that late modern societies may be moving beyond a crime prevention paradigm to that of risk management. As David Garland (1996) notes, crime can no longer be seen as an aberration but is viewed rather as an everyday risk to be managed, like air pollution and road traffic, with high rates of crime being viewed as normal. Increasingly, there is declining confidence in the capacity of the state to solve, prevent or fight the problem of crime. The result of all this, according to Garland, is the 'erosion of one of the foundational myths of modern society: that the sovereign state is capable of providing security, law and order and crime control.' Out of this crisis, Garland suggests that a complex mix of new modes of government of crime has developed, namely:

● the increasing involvement of the private sector (especially the selling of policing and security as commodities)

● the model of crime as a risk condition to be calculated, or an accident to be avoided, versus a moral aberration needing special explanation

● the development of a supply-side policy that seeks to modify the routines of everyday life

● a strategy of making citizens responsible for crime

● the managerial ethos of performance indicators that judge criminal justice agencies by self-referential measures that have nothing to do with reducing crime.

Is it, then, the end of crime prevention as we have known it? There is an irony in all this, that Garland notes, namely: alongside the emergence of this responsibilising, calculating risk management strategy, the state simultaneously swings into episodes of hysterical and populist denial of these very limitations (as reflected in the currently exploding prison population and the burgeoning custodial crime control industry in the UK). State sovereignty over crime is thus simultaneously denied and transferred to private security corporations or responsible, active citizens and symbolically reasserted. Despite this contradictory picture, the Australian criminologist, Pat

O'Malley, has noted correctly that the old statist governance of the social democratic state has now been radically refigured. He argues that relations of individual competition, epitomised in the figure of the market (primarily competitive) and the community (primarily co-operative), now offer the preferred models for governing the terrain of crime prevention. However, the extent to which such developments are truly hegemonic in the UK must remain open to some scepticism, sitting as they do alongside a still massive state industry of crime control.

Are community safety practitioners thus increasingly likely to be risk assessors involved in the politics of sanitation rather than being promoters of justice and well-being? There are problems with such a sweeping, if elegant, dystopian scenario as that offered above. We still need to ask ourselves: what of the messy complexities of the global-local mix and the countervailing forces which may resist this seemingly new master pattern of social control? Not least among the countervailing forces, and hidden in the above pessimistic account, is the radical and progressive potential of local community safety strategies.

Reasons to be cheerful?

Most commentators on the links between late modernity, risk society and trends in social control have taken up the above dystopian side to the thesis. However, within the late modern risk society thesis, there is also an alternative reading of possible, progressive trends. Remember Beck's urgent, radical communitarian question as to 'the we, that is able to bind and motivate the individualised individuals'. The less frequently explored possibilities of the new social politics of community safety are now addressed, pointing to the potential of seeing safety as a public good and risk as something needing inclusive, participatory sharing and collective co-ordination. Throughout what follows, it is also crucial to remember that whilst safety is a prerequisite for a vision of a better tomorrow, it is not an end in itself.

A new progressive local governance and civil society

In contrast to the old social democratic faith, shown in the centralised, top-down nation-state, to solve social problems like crime in earlier decades of the century, radical debates on the public sphere and civil society point to the participation of citizens and communities, and to local strategies from cities and regions, as a way forward. This is allied with positive state actions (see also Nellis, Chapter 3 and Ballintyne and Fraser, Chapter 9).

It is now accepted that there is a counter-argument to the claim that globalisation is necessarily equated with the decline of local communities and identities. As Giddens (1998) notes, whilst the process of globalisation pulls powers away from the nation state, it also pulls down powers creating new demands and new possibilities for regenerating local identities. Thus, there is a line of argument that the social and economic changes of the late 20th century are leading people, in some important ways, to become more, rather than less, attached to their locality and immediate community.

It is true that since the 1970s, the UK, more than any other western European country, has witnessed a systematic dismantling of the powers of local authorities by the central state. There now exists a profound democratic deficit in the arena of local democracy in the UK. Furthermore, what now seems certain is that the old paternalistic welfare state, which to a large extent was synonymous with the local delivery of public services, has now had its day. Out of this uncertain scenario, it is both intellectually possible and politically crucial to imagine a more participatory and democratic future, for local governance generally, and community safety in particular, beyond both the old unresponsive public service bureaucracy model and the exclusionary frameworks of neo-liberal marketisation.

Put briefly, the alternative is that of a more expansive democracy in which citizens are not empowered by their ability to exit, as in the consumer's option of going elsewhere to shop. Rather they are empowered by the option of voice: making demands as citizens on, and being heard by, their political representatives, and actively participating in the democratic process of dialogue and conflict resolution.

In turn local government is increasingly a mobiliser and co-ordinator of services, rather than a direct provider. The big tasks of the new networks of local governance appear to lie in answering the question 'how are public purposes to be accomplished?' For radical communitarians, there is the common emphasis on constructing a more expansive conception of local government as enabling, and even constituting, new participatory democracies in specific locales.

A re-awakening is also seen of the concept of civil society as a common space and public good, to be populated by an active citizenry which also retains particularities and recognises difference. Consequently this progressive, pluralist variant of communitarianism is not synonymous with regressive attempts (such as Etzioni's conservative communitarianism), to recapture lost forms of local communal solidarity. This admittedly utopian realist agenda (see Nellis, Chapter 3) is best captured in Walzer's vision of 'critical associationism', in which citizenship mediates other associations that individuals have, and cuts across them in an inclusive yet pluralistic fashion:

It would appear to be an elementary requirement of social democracy that there exists a society of lively, engaged, and effective men and women – where the honour of 'action' belongs to the many and not to the few. (Walzer, 1992).

Here the possibilities of a new etiquette, a new civility, begin to be seen. Carter (1998) has usefully defined civility as the sum of the many sacrifices we are called to make for the sake of living together. These are especially associated with relationships and feeling secure in our encounters in public places, with individuals we may never see again, namely the comfort rather than fear of strangers. It is about living without the enemy and it is predicated on new forms of trust relations, themselves based on the promotion of mutual understanding and co-existence, as against the currently dominant neo-liberal trend of the marketisation of trust. Here we see the possibilities of an inclusive community safety project to be struggled for.

Visions of inclusive safe cities in Europe: squaring the circle of solidarity and difference?

It is important to realise then that there are significant changes in both inter-governmental relations and forms of local autonomy in Europe, as the new millennium begins. Such changes again have clear implications for a programme of progressive governance of crime and community safety. With a fair dash of hyperbole and Eurocentrism, Manuel Castells (1994) has contended that, 'In this troubled world, Western Europe has, in fact, become a fragile island of prosperity, peace, democracy, culture, science, welfare and civil rights'. This said, Castells does recognise the dangers of the selfish reflex of trying to preserve this heaven by erecting walls which would undermine the very fundamentals of European culture (namely the appeal of fortress Europe and the criminalising demonisation of non-EU immigrants).

Castells was confident that the basic prerogatives of the nation state would have been shifted to European institutions by the end of the century. And overall, the expression of specific interests will have shifted to the regional and local levels and away from the national. Castells sees a crucial and difficult role for local (city) governments, both in managing the new urban contradictions and conflicts and in avoiding the danger of the USA-style dual city.

The fostering of citizenship participation is one of the key policies necessary for such new politics of managing cities, alongside the promotion of the interconnection and co-operation between local governments throughout Europe. Finally, Castells holds out the following hope which community safety activists may take comfort in:

> Because European cities have strong civil societies, rooted in an old history and a rich, diversified culture, they could stimulate citizen participation as a fundamental antidote against tribalism and alienation.' (Castells, 1994).

Such a vision appears particularly important in any contemporary debate on community safety and, more broadly, social justice. As the abolitionist criminologist,

Rene van Swaaningen (1997) notes, Europe is characterised by a 'stronger social democratic communitarian tradition' than the USA. However, it is a tradition that is under grave threat given the current importation by politicians across Europe (including New Labour in the UK) of neo-liberal US ideas of de-regulation, privatisation, consumer choice and the criminalisation of those unable to 'choose'.

A specific, albeit tentative, illustration of the new social politics of community safety is evident in Massimo Pavarini's work (1997) on secure cities in Emilia-Romagna in Italy. In accord with risk society theorists, Pavarini recognises that there is an obsession with security and risk in most late modern societies, including Italy. This obsession often results in making security a commodity to be purchased on the private security market. Its most likely effect, in Pavarini's eyes, is a strong tendency towards the 're-feudalisation of social relations'. By this, he means the destruction of any sense of civil society and of universal laws, and their replacement by small, mutually exclusive and hostile micro-societies led by politicians or bosses of any type, offering protection and security to their fiefs.

As an alternative to this scenario, Pavarini argues for the need for new conditions of belonging and safety in the future social state, which must be sought in political, social, cultural and economic strategies. These, more than legal norms, will meet society's demands for security and safety where possible, without involving the criminal justice system. According to Pavarini, the crime question must be confronted in terms of political and economic democracy, in what he admits is a project as ambitious as it is uncertain. In other words, the solution to the problems of insecurity and fear of crime necessarily lie outside the criminal justice system.

For example, situational crime prevention cannot be the answer, since it is only feasible in contained, physical social spaces and for a limited time. Total reliance on technically based prevention is therefore both illusory and politically dangerous, in that it is impossible to turn modern a metropolis into a neo-medieval fortified city. Instead, displacement on to other areas necessarily takes place and technically based prevention is counter-productive, since it may augment collective feelings of insecurity.

As an alternative community safety strategy, Pavarini points to local prevention initiatives that appeal to social participation. Even if such collective campaigns, spaces and networks do not prevent crime, Pavarini sees a positive public and civic pay-off by producing social representations of greater security. Such safety policies based on participatory spaces and dialogic projects are thus to be seen as part of social action in the wider sense of the word.

Of course some healthy scepticism about the prospects for such initiatives may be warranted. These suggestions may look great theoretically. Yet, without guarantees of security (perhaps based in part on high technology security strategies) it is likely that the well-heeled and middle-aged will shun these participatory spaces. Without the political clout of the middle classes, these spaces may have little prospect of getting going or, more crucially, surviving.

Finally the radical project of safety politics, must, in turn, remember to argue for what Rene van Swaaningen has called the re-moralisation of the social, facilitative role of the state, and press for the crucial role of the state as the main protector of the public interest. Indeed the state needs to expand the role of the public sphere. In this way we may recapture community safety as a public good, based on citizenship, solidarity and the recognition of difference rather than the club good of smaller, paying members only exclusive communities of risk sharers, which have been fostered by neo-liberalism.

Beyond the negative discourse of crime prevention

Community and safety, when viewed separately, are quite empty words: they are arguably even emptier when combined. This emptiness may be viewed as a fundamental flaw in current thinking and practices around community safety. Alternatively this very emptiness could offer potential for filling up these spaces with more progressive, humanistic values than the currently hegemonic, neo-liberal notions of privatism.

Once again we face an uncertain, Janus-faced future. As a backlash to the numbing mundanity of managerially driven strategies of crime management, is it fanciful to view the appeal of the idea of community safety to local actors as a means of rekindling concerns over social solidarity and collective concern over the wider social environment? Under the canopy of this new rallying call of community safety, some significant, progressive initiatives have already emerged across Europe. In particular, are developments designed to tackle the problems of domestic violence, racist and homophobic violence and harassment and the schemes to divert offenders from custody, in some local community safety strategies.

Personal research in this area suggests, tentatively, that some local government community safety strategies in the UK at times draw on and create agendas and projects with an anti-despotic potential, that move beyond the dominant reactionary law and order populism and privatised prudentialism of central government (Hughes 1997 and Hughes *et al*, 1998c).

In a similar way, Edwards and Benyon (1999) point to the example of some authorities using community safety as a conduit for the political reconstruction of the issue of crime prevention as one of social regeneration. Again, it is wise to countenance some caution here. Such progressive initiatives may be too ad hoc, too local and too fragmented to make much of a dent in the armoury of the dominant agenda on crime prevention and punishment, not least in shadow of the oppressive features of the Crime and Disorder Act (Ashworth *et al*, 1998).

A positive replacement discourse would take us beyond the negative discourse of prevention, risk, insecurity, fear, and so on, which has trapped us in a criminalising, law and order agenda, though this risks charges of unreconstituted utopianism. There is much potential then in a shift from a discourse around the prevention of crime to that of the promotion of social goods. Indeed the focus on crime as that sanctioned by criminal law, results in a failure to recognise and thus prioritise other harms and hazards, which are at times more serious. Perhaps the positive politics of community safety should prioritise broader notions of goods, social justice, collective trust, human rights and social inclusion. It is time to re-figure the public interest as a positive good that may liberate us from the suffocating appeal of both moral authoritarianism and hyper-individualism.

Few attempts have been made to go beyond the inherently limited boundaries of crime prevention discourse, even by radical critics. Thus, continuing emphasis on crime prevention acts to systematically exclude other readings of the relationship between social problems and social order. In a similar way, van Swaaningen (1997) has argued that the negative politics of law enforcement and exclusion are one of the key political strategies of risk society. This strategy is oriented towards the negative rationale of limiting risk rather than producing positive outcomes and aspirations (such as social justice, trust relations and empowerment).

As a consequence of this logic, solidarity is not based on the positive feeling of connectedness but on the negative communality of fear. Furthermore, the meta-narrative of human rights is crucial to this project, further illustrating the dangerous political naïvety of post-modernists who deny the existence of the old truths of collective struggles against misery and oppression. As Cohen (1990) notes, in support of the discourse of human rights and collective justice: 'For most of the world, the old truths of racism, naked injustice, mass starvation and brutal physical repression still apply.'

These old truths surely lie at the heart of any radical agenda for socially just safety politics. Such an agenda both moves beyond the technicism of administrative criminology and cannot avoid the messy, normative questions of what constitutes the good society and how relations amongst people and between people and major institutions, may be refigured. The discourse of human rights and social justice also raises the key issue of how solidarity in the contemporary world is to be understood. The major task remaining is that of reconciling what has been termed the 'politics of redistribution' with that of the 'politics of recognition' (Fraser, 1997).

It has been widely noted that the last decades of the 20th century, across neo-liberal societies, have seen the criminalisation of social policy, not least through the burgeoning trade in crime prevention techniques. Crime is thus not only an indicator of social ills but more importantly it has become a, and sometimes the, defining factor in the allocation of resources. It is of course crucial that social theorists critique existing crime prevention policies.

However, it is also vital that attempts are made to see beyond the present and imagine other possible futures. It is hoped that this chapter may help further nurture the debate about the possible shift from the criminalisation of social policy and towards the socialisation of criminal justice and crime prevention policies. The subordination of questions of crime control to those of social justice may open up a new discourse of possibilities, beyond the current obsession with prevention, for all involved in the contested politics of community safety.

References

Ashworth A, Gardner J, Morgan R, von Hirsch A and Wasik M (1998) 'Neighbouring on the Oppressive: The Government's 'Anti-Social Proposals' *Criminal Justice* 16

Bauman Z (1997) *Postmodernity and its Discontents* Cambridge: Polity Press

Beck U (1992) *Risk Society* London: Sage

Bottoms A and Wiles P (1996) 'Crime prevention and late modernity' in Bennett T (ed) *Preventing Crime and Disorder* Cambridge: Institute of Criminology

Carter S (1998) *Civility* New York: Basic Books

Castells M (1994) 'European Cities, the Informational Society, and the Global Economy' *New Left Review* 204

Clarke J and Newman J (1997) *The Managerial State* London: Sage

Cohen S (1990) *Intellectual Scepticism and Political Commitment: The Case of Radical Criminology* Amsterdam: Bonger Institute

Davis M (1990) *City of Quartz: Excavating the Future of Los Angeles* London: Verso

Donnison D (1998) *Policies for a Just Society* Basingstoke: Macmillan

Edwards A and Benyon J (forthcoming) 'Networking and crime control at the local level' in Ryan M et al (eds) *Criminal Justice Networks* Buckingham: Open University Press

Ericson R (1996) 'Making Criminology' *Current Issues in Criminal Justice* 8

Ericson R and Haggerty K (1997) *Policing the Risk Society* Toronto: University of Toronto Press

Etzioni A (1995) *The Spirit of Community* London: Fontana

Feeley M and Simon J (1992) 'The new penology: notes on the emerging strategy of corrections and its implications' *Criminology* 30

Fraser, N (1997) *Justice Interrruptus* New York: Routledge

Furedi F (1997) *Culture of Fear* London: Cassell

Garland D (1996) 'The Limits of the Sovereign State: Strategies of Crime Control in Contemporary Society' *British Journal of Criminology* 36

Giddens A (1990) *The Consequences of Modernity* Cambridge: Polity Press

Giddens A (1998) *The Third Way* Cambridge: Polity Press

Hough M and Tilley N (1997) *Getting the Grease to the Squeak* Crime Detection and Prevention Paper 85, London: Home Office

Hughes G (1996a) 'Communitarianism and Law and Order' *Critical Social Policy* 16

Hughes G (1997) 'Policing Late Modernity: Crime Management in Contemporary Britain' in Jewson N and Macgregor S (eds) *Transforming Cities: Contested Governance and New Spatial Divisions* London: Routledge

Hughes, G (1998a) *Understanding Crime Prevention: Social Control, Risk and Late Modernity* Buckingham: Open University Press

Hughes G (1998b) '"Picking over the remains": The welfare state settlements in the post-War UK' in Hughes G and Lewis G (eds) *Unsettling Welfare* London: Routledge

Hughes G, Pilkington A and Leisten R (1998c) 'Diversion in a culture of severity' *Howard Journal of Criminal Justice* 37

McLaughlin E and Muncie J (forthcoming) *Walled Cities*

O'Malley P (1996) 'Post-social Criminologies' *Current Issues in Criminal Justice* 8

Pavarini M (1997) 'Controlling social panic: questions and answers about security in Italy at the end of the millennium' in Bergalli R and Sumner C (eds) *Social Control and Political Order* London: Sage

Rose N (1996) 'The death of the social' Economy and Society 25

van Swaaningen R (1997) *Critical Criminology: Visions from Europe* London: Sage

Walzer M (1992) 'The Civil Society Argument' in Mouffe, C (ed) *Dimensions of Radical Democracy* London: Verso

16. Democratic politics and crime prevention
Jon Spencer

Developing scenarios for the future is a risky business. In undertaking such a task there is a temptation to either develop those doom-laden scenarios which usually include frightening technological applications and the abuse of modern technology to transgress human rights and citizenship. Such scenarios only confirm the view that the future will be concerned with attempting to control both thought and action. An alternative vision is that most things stay the same – there is little change to the rhythms of everyday life. However, this is also an incorrect forecast of the future. Some changes can be predicted, for example, the increase in the number of people working from home, but the effects of such a change to day to day life, in relation to crime, are not easy to predict. Will it result in more family violence? What will the new types of white-collar crime be in such working practices? How will the Internet become a site of everyday crime? The most tantalising thing about the future is generally our failure to predict it.

As the contribution to this volume by Mike Nellis (Chapter 3) argues there are good moral and social reasons for arguing the case for community justice. The debates concerning crime prevention and community safety are perhaps made more complex than they need be and at the cost of being able to see the advantages that a degree of shared aims would bring. This paper is concerned with navigating a passage through the theoretical positions of community safety and crime prevention in order to clarify what those shared aims might be. It pays particular attention to what can be termed primary crime prevention, concerned with finding solutions to defined crime problems, and secondary crime prevention, concerned with understanding how social process contributes to the problem of crime in our society (Pease, 1997).

The debate between primary and secondary crime prevention is an important one. Democratic politics is at a point where its relevance to contemporary life is increasingly brought into question. Issues of crime and punishment are often, sometimes for political capital, placed at the centre of this debate. They are presented as the litmus test of the efficacy of the political system, its ability to protect law abiding and decent citizens. The structure of this contemporary political discourse of crime and punishment is not the language of democratic politics but that of social exclusion. It feigns genuine concern for the rights of citizens.

For example, the registration of certain types of offenders is presented as taking account of the concerns of, and affording protection to, local residents. However, it does neither. It is a cynical attempt to use anxieties about community safety to demonstrate political toughness, and at the same time it suggests that such strategies are crime reductive when there is no evidence to suggest that this is the case. It is, therefore, contended here that the types of crime prevention strategies implemented have an effect on the type of society in which we live.

Crime has been on the increase since the end of the Second World War. There has been much sophisticated analysis by criminologists that details the decreases and increases in relation to particular crime types and the relationship of such patterns with economic patterns (see Field, 1991). So, whilst acknowledging that different crime types have different rates of being reported and recorded over time, it is now generally accepted that crime is on an upward trend. This of course introduces an element of pessimism into the discourse about crime and has resulted in cynical and pragmatic solutions to the crime problem designed to fulfil political ends.

The main flaw in such a strategy, apart from its inherent cynicism, is that politically driven solutions tend to have a considerable momentum at the beginning but run out of stamina very early on. Consequently, such strategies are vulnerable to changes of political will, commitment and direction at the first sign of what is perceived as policy failure or the changing demands of policy focus, which usually results in the reallocation of resources. For example, witness the removal of the unit fine from the 1991 Criminal Justice Act, when the impact of fines hit those who had previously been immune from the punitive element of fines, owing to their cushion of disposable income.

Owing to its politicisation over the past two decades (Downes and Morgan, 1997), criminal justice policy in the UK is constantly battling against the perception that crime is an increasing problem. Crime has not diminished with greater prosperity. Whilst crime surveys do not provide such a bleak picture as that which is commonly painted by media interests, they are at times used to reinforce the perceived threat of victimisation. It sometimes seems that we have become more fearful of this possibility of victimisation regardless of the statistical chances of being a crime victim. This relationship between our increased vulnerability to crime and the increased fear of crime have become part of an accepted wisdom about modern society, but this may be little more than a modern myth (see Walklate, 1998).

Increased chances of victimisation are just one concern. The criminal justice system is perceived as failing. Media presentations of the images of crime are presented in particular forms that enable us to be efficient consumers (see Sparks, 1992). One outcome of this is that the realities of crime, how it is experienced in daily life, and the media construction of crime, become difficult to distinguish. So, some crimes become high profile and the media pays attention to every detail of these. Sentences for these crimes are more often than not considered too lenient, with the haphazard yardstick of punishment being the only measure or expression of society's disapprobation.

Politicians, however, use the concerns about crime, from time to time, to demonstrate their punishment credentials. Consider, for example, the media outcry and the behaviour of Michael Howard, the then Home Secretary, to the sentencing of the two boys found guilty of killing James Bulger. This demonisation of two young children took place without any attempt to debate in the public domain the more disturbing issues of why children kill (see Sereny, 1998).

There is a media presentation of the criminal justice system that views it as being out of touch, evidenced by its leniency and seeming inability to take account of the victim. At the other end of the spectrum the criminal justice system is perceived as being both excessively fallible and open to abuse. The faith in the system, through the principles of due process, that it convicts only the guilty and allows the innocent to go free, has become less secure. This loss of faith has occurred through the number of high profile Irish cases along with an increasing number of other cases where a miscarriage of justice has demonstrably taken place. No longer are people content to believe that the system will ensure fair play. Of course this contradiction of a system prone to leniency and error is rarely highlighted.

Loss of confidence in the criminal justice system has a number of consequences: the increasing privatisation of criminal justice tasks. The process of privatisation fundamentally changes the role of the state in the process of maintaining law and order and incarceration. These privatisation measures are predominantly ideological, the demonstration of a commitment to the market. It is believed that the market will result in a more efficient and effective system of criminal justice. Privatisation has been used as a strategy for the restoration of confidence in a system that it is seriously under stress. The stress factors include increasing numbers of people to process and financial constraints, but most importantly that seepage of confidence itself. This has been created by the punitive discourse of politicians in their endeavour to make crime a political issue. However, the process of privatisation has done little to restore confidence and little to reduce the increasing financial burden of the system on state finances.

What all of this amounts to, Adam Crawford has argued (Crawford 1997), is the perception that the capitalist state has failed in its core function, that of maintaining law and order. One response to this failure has been an emerging discourse that highlights the need for increased public protection and at the same time introduces the concept of safety. This idea of safety becomes articulated through the use of such programmes as Safer Cities, and through the introduction of crime prevention as a core element of a community safety strategy.

The process by which crime prevention became a core strategy in tackling crime is outlined by Felson (1994). Crime prevention, initially that of situational crime prevention, was a strategy that was in direct response to ever-increasing levels of crime. At the same time, because it was perceived as being new, it was viewed as representing a new and different criminal justice strategy to those that had gone before and had been primarily rehabilitative – solely concerned with changing the offender.

For the first time crime prevention appeared to be a strategic response that took victimisation seriously. The approach of crime prevention was to turn the crime problem on its head – that is how to stop an object being vulnerable to crime rather than rehabilitative strategies which were concerned with 'treating' offenders with a view to them stopping offending. Rehabilitative strategies were cast aside as deeply flawed and unresponsive to the problem of crime reduction. The emerging Thatcherite social policy of the 1980s did not include in its moral framework of individual responsibility rehabilitative concerns. It can be argued that current criminal justice strategies which are focused on the offender are not generally concerned with the broader issues of citizenship, community or justice but are part of that cynical pragmatism which relies on a pessimistic view of human nature and community responsibility.

In criminal justice policy terms there has over the past ten years or so been a period of restructuring, spanning a range of strategies. The proportionate approach to sentencing contained in the 1991 Criminal Justice Act was quickly undone. The 'prison works!' rhetoric of Michael Howard, and the concern with both crime and disorder, which has a degree of moral authoritarianism about it, was contained in the 1998 Crime and Disorder Act. In considering these strategic responses there is a considerable debit side on the balance sheet, however on the credit side there can be seen a commitment to crime prevention and the development of the idea of community within this policy approach. However, in such a policy development cynical pragmatism is never far away.

Generally the construction of community by politicians is one where community has both a positive value and is politically neutral. The community is presented as being harmonious, supportive, stable and resourceful. This is an idealised view of community. Many communities are conflictual, unsupportive and unstable due to the transient nature of their population. However, the idealised view ignores the complexity of community, it is seen as a harmonising force, a means of bringing people together and creating strength. So, Tony Blair in his 1998 Labour Party conference speech used, as many politicians did before him, the idea of community as a binding concept: "And if the spirit of the nation is willing, it can make the body of the nation strong. One nation, one community..." (Labour Party, 1998). This is a view that presents community as inclusive and unproblematic, a concept of community as unarguably good.

One element of the politicisation of community is its inclusion within the crime discourse, but this process is particular. It is not concerned with empowering communities in order to allow them to develop responses to crime for that particular community. The process of politicisation relies upon the spirit of community as something special. So, this process of politicisation does not create a definition of community in which there is:

... a more openly accountable, inclusive and socially just framework of local governance in the field of crime control, emphasising the need for negotiation within a framework which mitigates differential power relations. (Crawford, 1998)

The politicisation of community attempts to render it a concept that is acceptable to official definitions of crime and the official understanding of the effects of crime on communities, which are various. Crime has different consequences on different social groups. There can be no doubt that some crimes are extremely harmful to communities and others less so. We know that levels of victimisation are disproportionate and dependent upon such variables as area of residence, age, race gender and social class. Of course the likelihood of being an offender is effected by these variables as well. What is important to understand is that the presentation of community as a means of combating crime can be overly simplistic if it removes these socio-economic and political issues and permits individualised notions of crime causation to be dominant.

There is a need to theorise a range of solutions to the crime problem that takes account of community and the complex dynamic of crime. There is another crucial issue that needs to be addressed: how is the process of crime prevention made relevant to democratic processes? As Crawford (1997) has argued there is a political imperative to develop more accountable and socially just frameworks and in developing these, there is a need to take account of how power is socially distributed. At the same time it is important to balance a future perspective that takes account of the developments and gains made by crime prevention. As Ken Pease has commented:

Witnessing how simple problem solving approaches get drowned in a sea of funding problems, political rhetoric appealing to (particular) communities, defensiveness about community safety priorities among practitioners, played out against changing patterns of social and trust relationships in late modern societies, makes it clear that understanding the technology of crime prevention is less difficult than its organisational context. (Pease, 1998)

This is a key problem in relation to crime prevention and community safety: how the knowledge gained from primary crime prevention is brought together with the concerns of secondary crime prevention, and how programmes of community safety and crime prevention are successfully implemented. A central question that requires an answer is how to apply the technology of crime prevention in an organisational context that promotes the application of relevant technology and, at the same time, does not prevent the empowerment of communities.

Within the crime prevention literature it is clear that there is a demanding and complex series of debates in relation to crime prevention and community, whose depth this volume reflects. At the very least our expectation is that crime prevention theory and practice should result in less crime (measured by using a range of techniques), and a sense that communities are safer (again established by using a range of measurement techniques, both quantitative and qualitative). However, as Crawford and Jones (1996) argue, one of the problems is to know which crime prevention measures are effective. This by necessity requires us to develop more sophisticated and detailed forms of project evaluation and analysis (see, for example, Sherman, 1998).

Pease (1997) supports this view when he argues that a definition of crime prevention is not too difficult to provide: it is concerned with 'disrupting crime events'. The main problem in relation to operationalising this definition is to know what are the most effective means of disruption (Pease, 1997). Furthermore how do we know in which communities intervention is appropriate through crime prevention projects?

The purpose of crime prevention is clear, less crime and a sense of a safer community. But how do we know which are those communities where crime is a significant problem and which have, in addition, feelings of insecurity. Pease suggests that the way of how best to protect communities from crime is achieved by being able to identify those communities where crime is a significant problem. In order to identify such communities he argues that there is a range of statistical data available: official crime statistics, victimisation surveys, repeat victimisation surveys and hotspot mapping, to name but a few.

The use of such statistical data allows us to identify the vulnerable communities, work towards removing the opportunity for crime and, by so doing, remove vulnerability to victimisation. Repeat victimisation studies consider the individual circumstances of a crime, how to protect the most vulnerable, and that the highest incidence of repeat victimisation is in areas where there are the highest rates of most serious crime. Consequently, by analysing the patterns of repeat victimisation and implementing crime prevention strategies based on this analysis, resources are placed into the most needy areas.

> Repeat victimisation thus has profound implications for criminology. In the present context, it is simply argued that probably the most effective way of deploying resources on crime prevention. It also brings the functions of victim support and crime prevention together. Those who need victim support are, it turns out, those in most need of crime prevention help.
> (Pease, 1997)

So the argument runs that if project initiatives take account of research findings then such projects have a greater probability of reducing crime and the community will have a greater sense of security. This perspective subscribes to the view that crime prevention not only requires good research and policy implementation strategies, but that the aims are clear and attainable. This sits comfortably within the primary crime prevention agenda that is concerned with the reduction and removal of crime opportunities.

However, Pease argues that the crime prevention agenda has become complicated and muddled through the introduction of agendas that are not concerned with primary crime prevention but with secondary and tertiary crime prevention. Secondary crime prevention is concerned with changing people who are identified as being high risk and tertiary crime prevention is concerned with stopping criminal careers. It is this move away from primary crime prevention to crime prevention which is focused on the '... complex and the communal' which Pease argues places worthwhile crime prevention projects at risk of political interference and ideological rigidity. So, this is evidence of the workings out of a complex political agenda:

> For all its success, primary crime prevention may fall further out of fashion, to be replaced by secondary and tertiary measures where efficacy is much less impressive and which carry with them the baggage of blame and punishment. Primary prevention will, however, remain the practice of choice in the private sector and among affluent households where the benefits of crime reduction fall to those investing in it. (ibid)

The future is stark here, whilst public policy will succumb to all kinds of political interference, those with the requisite resources will continue to utilise, successfully, the strategies of primary crime prevention. However, the future mapped out by this perspective suggests that it should be remarkably easy to manage. What is required is a concentration on primary crime prevention by the proper utilisation of research findings. This will assist in management of the crime problem by establishing effective crime prevention measures, which prove to be successful. There is a strong case made against doing nothing. The outcome of doing nothing, argues Pease, is that those who are most socially vulnerable experience the highest levels of crime, and the most vulnerable are the poor and live in the most disadvantaged areas. This is no doom-laden image of the future, but rather a truly pragmatic view that argues for the need to implement what is proven to work, and take account of emerging trends in crime commission so as to enable responsive crime prevention programmes.

This pragmatic view could be accused of taking an unproblematic view of crime prevention. It assumes that all communities that are vulnerable to crime are equally able to adopt crime prevention strategies. This is not to say that there is no consideration of the issues that hinder crime prevention projects, but there seems to be less attention to the obstacles to crime prevention projects than is perhaps necessary.

It is in considering these obstacles to crime prevention strategies that we are required to take account of the successful gains made by primary crime prevention and also to recognise its limitations. It is these limitations that may stop crime prevention initiatives being taken up by the people and communities who need them most. Hope (1995) notes that the structure of a community may well be influential in determining the type of crime it is subject to and how it is experienced. So, he sees crime in a community as being more than just 'aggregation of individual propensities for criminality and victimisation.'

In strong communities, those which have developed and stable networks with representative institutions to ensure that tenants' views are taken into account, and where there is little tolerance of crime as socially acceptable behaviour, there is, he argues, more likely to be lower incidence of crime and victimisation. However, in weak communities, where the population is likely to be more transient, the social networks are likely to be much less well developed and robust, due to people being moved on or where people move out for a range of reasons. In such communities there is also more likely to be a sense of alienation and distance from society, with crime being viewed as a more acceptable form of behaviour. Thus the community is '... more likely to experience the problems of powerlessness in resisting crime' (Hope 1995).

Such a community may also have a different set of definitions for what it considers to be significant crime. As Hope comments, there are three characteristics of high-crime areas. These are: high levels of male unemployment, high proportion of children aged between five and fifteen and what he terms a 'composite variable', which includes the proportion of young adults, single-adult households and households not living in self-contained accommodation. It is, therefore, the very structure of the community and how these issues of structure interact, that are core features of the lived experience of crime in those particular areas.

These issues identified by Hope are those which Pease sees as being associated with secondary crime prevention and therefore responsible for muddying the waters of implementing primary crime prevention programmes. Hope argues that the reconstruction of urban areas '... may be producing a sociopolitical exclusion of the "dangerous poor".' These processes of reconstruction are one outcome of a society that is highly consumer-orientated and market-driven. So that, as inequality deepens it may be that the levels of victimisation and its severity change. Rates of victimisation begin to increase and levels of seriousness also increase. The increase in the levels of violence experienced are as an outcome of social alienation and exclusion (Hope, 1995).

In considering the possible outcome of social alienation and exclusion Hope describes, with a sense of bleakness, a future where the consequences of socio-economic policy need to be addressed. These socio-economic processes enhance social exclusion that result in the damaging experiences of crime and victimisation:

> ...the residential concentration of youth poverty seems to be creating communities with concentrations of high risk offending, often young jobless men – and multiple victims – often female heads of households – linked together in a powerless, victimising and – victimised culture of primary relationships. (ibid)

This gets to the rub: how do we instigate primary forms of crime prevention which are responsive to the needs of communities, victims and the wider society, whilst at the same time overcoming the consequences of social policies which are crime generating?

Hope clearly outlines the relationship between victimisation and crime commission. For many communities this relationship is established across a relatively small spatial area. As Foster (1995) has commented, it may not be the problem of crime that is of concern to the community, but the social features of those communities, the levels of social disorganisation and disturbance. It is not the offenders who are the problem but those who cause social unease.

So, is it enough to claim that primary prevention measures are successful without considering or addressing the impact of such measures on the wider community? Is it appropriate to argue that the more complex issues of crime prevention only serve to deflect attention away from the primary purpose, and by doing so damage primary preventative techniques? How are communities consulted and included in the crime prevention process and how should communities be involved if we are to overcome what are the damaging consequences of exclusion and alienation?

It is to these questions which we must now turn. To think about them requires us to consider crime issues by more than a straightforward statistical analysis to define the area with highest crime rate. Importantly, defining high-crime areas in this way leaves out a series of important social processes. As Foster (1995) has noted, analysing communities through comparison of statistical data only serves to mask the social process of how one particular area becomes singled out as being high-crime, whereas another area with similar crime rates is not so defined.

So, one of the first issues is to understand how one particular area becomes defined as an appropriate area for crime prevention attention. There are a range of micro- and macro-policy decisions which effect the outcome in relation to crime on estates, housing allocation policies, the profiles of residents and the general demand for housing (Foster 1995). This means that hard to let estates are more likely to experience high levels of crime, not just because people who live there perceive that they have little choice about their area of residence. The way in which people come to reside in a particular area should be examined, the structure and form of social life within the community, the residents' perceptions of official agencies and those who remain as residents over time, and why they choose not move. It is these factors which Foster argues are crucial in determining appropriate and relevant crime prevention strategies in particular.

There are core elements of social life which are important in assisting us to understand issues of why crime is, or is not, present to significant levels in any community. It also provides us with a form of intelligence in understanding the specificity of crime in a local area and how best to respond to it. This approach, argues Foster, challenges official notions and definitions. Attempting to understand crime in a particular area by analysing the social processes might demonstrate the view that local people have of their community. This view may not coincide with that constructed from official crime data sources and victimisation surveys. A high-crime area, as defined by official statistics and the British Crime Survey, may not be perceived by residents as being a high-crime area. It may be that they are more tolerant of particular types of crime, or they are less likely to be victimised, of that they have definitions of crime which are at variance to official ones. This means that for residents the definition of the crime problem in their area is different to that of the police and other officials. Foster's research suggests that there are:

> ...a number of contradictory factors which emerged... First, housing officials' views of the estate as crime prone were reflected in the levels of crime measured by Home Office surveys. Ethnographic data, however, suggests that tenants did not perceive crime to be a problem and that a diverse range of offending was to some degree tolerated by residents on the estate. (Foster, 1995)

Research by Farrall *et al* (1997), in relation to fear of crime, tends to confirm the findings reported by Foster. They argue that it is very difficult from the data to measure the level of fear in relation to crime and victimisation. They argue that the usual questions contained in fear of crime surveys 'fail to address contexts, spatial, temporal and social'. Again in agreement with Foster, they argue that the over-reliance on qualitative measures creates a range of problems in determining the level of the fear of crime. So, they conclude 'that the results of fear of crime surveys appear be a function of the way in which the topic is *researched*, rather than the way it *is*.'

Crawford and Jones (1996) also argue for an approach to crime prevention that takes account of the social processes. In their view the situationalist perspective is one which leaves out the complicating features of crime prevention and control. They argue that it is, in part, the way in which crime prevention activities are structured which leads to this short-termism: there is always a pressing need to demonstrate outcomes before outcomes can be properly assessed:

> There is a danger, however, that by prioritorising easily quantifiable short-term measures, preference is given to physical or situational type

interventions at the expense of the more social and structural approaches which offer the least tangible short term results. (Crawford and Jones, 1997)

Once again the debate between those in favour of primary and secondary forms of crime prevention is stark. However, this time it those committed to secondary measures that see the crime prevention agenda being dominated by those of primary persuasion. This is evidenced, they argue, by the fact that crime prevention in the UK is project driven (Crawford and Jones, 1997), and that this observation is supported by the manner in which crime prevention is funded:

> In a simplified and caricatured form this approach involves; targeting an area; intervening in that area; getting results; moving on. In part this stems from pressure imposed by both funding bodies and the media for immediate 'success' stories. (Crawford and Jones, 1997).

This approach argues that crime prevention is concerned with something more than just simply preventing crime. It is concerned with leaving viable and sustainable forms of interventions that address the social processes which are crime creating. The argument goes further than those who advocate primary crime prevention in that there is a belief that projects can have more than a marginal impact on social factors. The problem here is that there is a tendency to overlook the gains of primary crime prevention which can also be seen to have a positive affect on people's lives by reducing the amount of crime they experience and their vulnerability to victimisation.

The battleground is established between those scholars who consider that the only ethically viable way forward is to adopt primary crime prevention strategies and those who are concerned with secondary crime prevention strategies, which they view as socially inclusive and democratically accountable. Primary crime prevention strategies are proven to work. They address the problems of crime in particularly disadvantaged areas, take account of repeat victimisation and are ethically sound because they put in place strategies which are proven to work and therefore make a concrete difference to people's day to day lived experience.

The alternative position is put forward by those who argue that primary crime prevention becomes focused on the technology and analysis of statistical data to such an extent that it loses sight of the very real issues which effect people's lives, those central and crucial elements of social process. In this approach crime is but an element of the social process. Crime is caused by a range of other social factors that need to be addressed when implementing crime prevention strategies. The problem is, how is it possible to bring these two traditions together? Is it possible to develop a series of strategies that are from a situational crime prevention perspective, that reduce crime and take account of the broader-based community issues and social processes? Is it possible to make such strategies politically accountable?

In addressing these questions the first part of the process should be how to define the level of problematic crime. This moves away from the idea that all crime is problematic and that crime prevention should address all crimes. The British Crime Surveys assist us in determining which crime is problematic and therefore of significance. However, the British Crime Surveys also inform us that a large number of incidents of victimisation are not reported to the police. There is a range of reasons for not reporting incidents of victimisation, which include perceived levels of seriousness, the value of property lost, the extent and seriousness of injuries received and the anticipated attitude of the police in taking the report and their chances of success in apprehending the offender. So, we should not be surprised that Crime Surveys, which explore issues of victimisation reveal higher levels than are reported to the police.

A critical approach to victimisation and crime prevention requires us to detail how we assess the problem of crime in any given community. Official statistics provide an indication of reported crime rates and will also provide some indication of how serious the level of crimes are that are recorded, for official statistics are indicative of trends and activity (Bottomley and Pease, 1985).

However, this form of intelligence, in relation to crime in a particular community, only provides one means of assessing the level and official determination as to the seriousness of crime. Therefore, it is also important to gain an understanding of what local people define as the problem of crime in their locality. This is of course problematic. If we are asked what crimes we are afraid of, we will provide a truthful answer. If we are then asked how likely we think we are to be victims of crime, our senses are heightened in relation to being a possible victim. So, the focus of the questions on crime may distort the answer. However, if we are asked what we consider to be the problems of living in our locality, we may consider crime as only one problem among many, not necessarily the most acute problem, and we may not even view crime as a significant problem. This may be so even if the official statistics demonstrate an entirely contrary picture.

It may be that the problem of crime does not figure so highly as criminologists might like to imagine. As Foster comments:

Tenants simply did not express a sense of helplessness about dealing with crime, the classic response highlighted by 'broken windows' cycle. There was still a belief they could do something about the glue sniffers on the walkways, loud noises causing a disturbance, and tackling racial harassment on the estate, even though the *generalised* fears about crime made residents reticent to intervene. (Foster, 1995, emphasis added)

What this demonstrates, is that it is important to detail what the issues for residents are in relation to crime, how optimistic they feel about tackling the issues, and which issues they feel they have already tackled. Indeed, Farrall et al (1997) outlined a seven point research agenda to establish the relationship between the issue of crime and a local community. They suggested that researchers need to develop better methods of validating their data in relation to fear of crime questions, that they should recognise that fear of crime has different facets and these need to be included in any research programme.

They also argued that fear of crime is not something that is static, so our ideas and responses change over time and these changes need to be accounted for in any research and in project design. In order to achieve relevant crime prevention strategies it is necessary to develop on-going forms of measurement and to include in this what they call concrete fear of crime questions, rather than formless ones. So, questions concerning the fear of crime should be placed within a geographic context that requires questions concerned with the everyday lives of the respondents (Farrall et al, 1997).

The second problem is that having a detailed understanding of crime in a particular locality is how this information is used in order to provide a form of crime prevention or community safety that is relevant to the community. A significant element of the problem is how to develop 'meaningful forms of participation' (Jones et al, 1996).

Crawford (1997) also addresses this issue of how democratic accountability is achieved and he offers, as one part of the solution, the idea of proper forms of representation and the development of community-based partnerships, structured to ensure the fullest participation of local people (Crawford, 1998). Whilst, theoretically this seems a relatively worthy position, the problem raised by Hope (1995), that the most crime prone communities are those that have the weakest structures, still needs to be addressed. How are those people who feel the most dislocated, disenfranchised and excluded from our society going to develop structures that enhance democratic forms of participation and accountability?

It is at this point that the temptation must be to move back to the primary forms of crime prevention. However, this would be a mistake. For it is here that the analytic forms of crime prevention and community safety can be melded with primary crime prevention. Primary crime prevention measures can be used to tackle those crimes about which residents feel the most strongly. Primary crime prevention strategies can also be used to ensure that structures are put in place through the development of partnership schemes.

However, they will need to draw from secondary prevention strategies to ensure that such partnerships actively share the power across all participating groups, including local residents. Such power-sharing strategies should provide communities with a form of power sharing that takes account of their concerns about crime and other social issues. A form of power sharing such as this should be part of a community empowerment strategy which draws from the good practice of crime prevention. It is empowering not only because it provides communities with a strong voice in the decision making process, but because it devises structures that can be seen as being democratically accountable at the local level, with the potential to be democratically accountable at the regional and national levels (Crawford, 1997).

One method of establishing accountability is through community-based groups. These groups vary in composition, size and aims. However, it is clear that such groups that bring together community justice professionals – police, crime prevention and community safety personnel, social workers, educational workers and probation officers along with residents, business interests and those of the voluntary sector – are the means by which participation and accountability are developed, fostered and encouraged. This is not unproblematic. The research on community-based crime prevention groups (Sutton, 1996) suggests that they are prone to internal turf wars and the furtherance of agency agendas, rather than a genuine attempt at partnership.

In order to overcome these problems, practitioners need to address the following issues. First, how are they going to agree a shared view of what the particular crime problems are in relation to the area in which they are working? How, in coming to this view, are they going to put to one side the priorities of their agency in order to establish a true set of priorities from the community? It is important to include as Hough and Tilley (1998) argue both voluntary and statutory interests, it is also important to ensure that local community interests are represented and have a truly equal voice as official agencies.

This is not uncontentious, because, first, not only are practitioners being asked to put aside their own agendas but also to share power with those who are not defined as professionals.

Second, it is important that a set of goals is established and this needs to be done after the issues of crime have been researched at a local level. It is important to take account of how local people define their lived experience rather than rely on official forms of data to inform strategic initiatives. The imposition of a definition of the problem is the one thing that will result in local people abandoning community safety and crime prevention initiatives. Strategies to address problems also need to be negotiated and refined so as to ensure that the local community accepts the strategic responses as being ones they agreed to during the consultation phase. So, there is a shared sense of what the goals are and how these are to be achieved.

Third, there is a need from all parties involved to know what their level of commitment is going to amount to in relation to the project. Local communities may have few resources and those they do have might be in terms of people rather than funds. Local agencies should be clear as to what they are going to contribute and once the commitment is made it should be kept to, by ensuring that it is reviewed and monitored through local management procedures.

Finally, partnerships should have a focus on specific problems, they should not be concerned with just addressing crime as a broad problem. The local partnership arrangements should be able to identify which of the strategic responses to specific crime issues it has instigated and maintained. This will require some forward planning at the beginning of the project and the following questions are relevant in terms of planning the initial stages of the project.

- What are the aims and objectives of the project and on what data have they been based?

- How will the project be monitored?

- What are the relevant performance criteria by which to measure success?

- How is success defined?

- What are the anticipated outcomes of the project?

- How will the management of the project be established and evaluated?

- How will those responsible for the project be accountable to the local community, the management group and their own agencies?

Conclusions

In order to develop democratically accountable and relevant crime prevention projects, practitioners are required to ensure that the following criteria are met. First, forms of research that take account of the lived experience of people; second, structures that address the issues which they have identified; third, forms of simple intervention that may be most commonly defined as primary crime prevention, but for which local people are responsible. Finally, it is necessary to develop structures that provide information to allow people to make considered decisions.

It should also be central to developing crime prevention strategies that the experience of local communities should inform how structures are established and that community-based groups should be assisted in developing strategies that are meaningful to them. This approach brings together both the primary and secondary forms of crime prevention. It develops strategies that highlight the need to overcome the organisational problems whilst at the same time addressing the problems of democratic accountability and community participation.

This is all well and good. However, one final and difficult problem remains. If, as Gilling (1999) argues, community safety is only an extension of the Thatcherite politics of law and order in the 1990s, then attempts to develop democratically accountable forms of crime prevention are indeed going to be hard fought. Gilling views the move to community safety as being of concern:

> It is alarming how easily the commitment to community safety can sit with support for zero tolerance, but when one sees the positive public and media reaction to 'confident policing' ... and one sees for oneself how the public supports the assault of New York's finest upon squeegee merchants, one is quick to recognise the populist political value of such measures. (Gilling, 1999)

However, the demands of politicians to have their law and order cake and to eat it, do not have to be met by practitioners. They can establish projects that have the underlying values of democratic accountability, social inclusion and empowerment within a framework of tackling the socially harmful consequences of crime. Gilling, with his pessimistic view of community safety which justifies coercion 'for the benefit of the community, not the state' argues that as a consequence:

> ...the idea of a law and order society is not so far fetched now. What this means, in effect, is that there is still an element of the fortress mentality, but it has changed from a defensive 'home as castle' to a fortified citadel from which all the uncontrollable and anti-social elements are to be ejected. (ibid)

This view may in time come to be a justified account of community safety, and with a historical view it will be clear that community safety was nothing other than a strategy to increase state control. However, the approach of practitioners who are concerned with ensuring that those communities that experience high rates of victimisation get a fair deal, will necessitate community involvement, project accountability and the reinforcement of an individual's and community's right not be blighted by crime. If this is to be successful, then democratic politics, which insists upon community justice, will ensure citizenship rights and political accountability.

References

Bowers K, Hirschfield A and Johnson SD (1998) 'Victimisation Revisited' *British Journal of Criminology* 38

Crawford A (1997) *The Local Governance of Crime* Oxford: Clarendon Press

Crawford A and Jones M (1996) 'Kirkholt Re-Visited: Some Reflections on the Transferability of Crime Prevention' *Howard Journal of Criminal Justice* 35

Downes D and Morgan R (1997) 'Dumping The Hostages to Fortune? The Politics of Law and Order in Post-war Britain' in Maguire M et al (eds) *Oxford Handbook of Criminology* 2nd ed Oxford: Clarendon Press

Farrall S, Bannister J, Ditton J and Gilchrist E (1997) 'Questioning The Fear of Crime' *British Journal of Criminology* 37

Foster J (1995) 'Informal Social Control and Community Crime Prevention' *British Journal of Criminology* 35

Gilling D (1999) 'Community Safety: A Critique' in Brogden M *The British Criminology Conference: Selected Proceedings* 2, Papers from the British Criminology Conference, Queens University, Belfast 15-19 July at www.lboro.ac.uk/departments/ss/bsc/bccp/vol102/07GILL.HTM

Hebenton B and Thomas T (1996) 'Tracking Sex Offenders' *Howard Journal of Criminal Justice* 35

Hope T (1995) 'Community Crime Prevention' in Tonry M and Farrington D (eds) *Building a Safer Society* Chicago: Chicago University Press

Hough M and Tilley N (1998) *Getting The Grease to The Squeak* Research Lessons for Crime Prevention Paper 85, Home Office: London

Jones T, Newburn T and Smith DJ (1996) 'Policing The Idea of Democracy' *British Journal of Criminology* 36

Labour Party (1998) Speech of the Rt Hon Tony Blair, Leader of the Labour Party to the Labour Party Annual Conference Blackpool 1998 http:\\www.labourparty.co.uk\CONF.HTML

Master G and Smith D (1998) 'Portia and Persphone Revisited' *Theoretical Criminology* 2

Pease K (1997) 'Crime Prevention' in Maguire M et al (eds) *Oxford Handbook of Criminology* 2nd ed. Oxford: Clarendon Press

Sereny G (1998) *Cries Unheard: The Story of Mary Bell* London: MacMillan

Sparks R (1992) *Television and The Drama of Crime: Moral tales and the place of crime in public life* Milton Keynes: Open University Press

Spencer J and Hebenton B (1999) 'Crime and Insecurity in the New Europe: Some Observations From Poland' in Brogden M *The British Criminology Conference: Selected Proceedings* 2, Papers from the British Criminology Conference Queens University, Belfast 15-19 July at www.lboro.ac.uk/departments/ss/bsc/bccp/vol102

Sutton, Mike (1996) *Implementing Crime Prevention Schemes in a Multi-Agency Setting: Aspects of Process from in the Safer Cities Programme* Home Office Research Study 160, London: HMSO

Walklate Sandra (1998) 'Excavating the Fear of Crime: Fear, Anxiety or Trust?' *Theoretical Criminology* 2